REAL ESTATE FINANCE

FIFTH EDITION

WALT HUBER
GLENDALE COLLEGE

LEVIN P. MESSICK
MT. SAN ANTONIO COLLEGE
PRESIDENT, AC APPRAISALS, INC.

EDUCATIONAL TEXTBOOK COMPANY, INC.
P. O. Box 3597
Covina, California 91722
(626) 339-7733
FAX (626) 332-4744
www.etcbooks.com

EDUCATIONAL TEXTBOOK COMPANY, INC.
P. O. Box 3597
Covina, California 91722
(626) 339-7733
FAX (626) 332-4744
www.etcbooks.com (Constructive suggestions are welcome)
Call Glendale College Bookstore to order all ETC books:
    1-818-240-1000 ext. 3024
    1-818-242-1561 (Direct)

Library of Congress Cataloging-in-Publication Data
Real Estate Finance/ Huber, Walt; Messick, Levin P. - 5th ed.
Includes index

1. Real property—United States—Finance. 2. Mortgage loans—United States.
3. Housing—United States—Finance.

ISBN: 0-916772-43-8

Printed in the United States of America

Preface

We, the authors, have designed *Real Estate Finance* to be a flexible tool for both novice and professional alike. We've highlighted essential finance concepts for particular emphasis, bolded definitions within the material for memory enhancement, and included concise summaries for easy review. Our unique approach clarifies the process of qualifying standards, disclosure requirements, and loan documents, making this the most user-friendly finance book on the market.

The text is divided into three-chapter increments, for a total of six parts. Each section covers a specific area of interest and eliminates the need to wade through all the material to find the desired subject matter. In addition, we've condensed the subjects into fifteen nationally-oriented chapters, including the basics, such as primary and secondary lenders, information on credit scoring, and loan applications. Part six (the last three chapters) covers loan information specific to individual states, as well as escrow procedures. Our unique formatting is just one of the methods we employ to create a textbook that is applicable to everyone, making it both an educational tool and a valuable reference source.

The authors would like to extend a warm thank you to the following individuals and companies for their help, encouragement, and constructive criticism during the writing of this text: Larry Bivins, Michael Layne, Sanford T. Jones, and Lawrence P. Woodard of AC Appraisals, Inc. who took time from their busy schedules to read and comment on the rough manuscript draft. Don Kinnsch, Mike Woods, and Pam Woods of United California Financial and Ron Perrot of All Lenders Mortgage provided information and examples of many of the documents used in the loan process. Steve Costello of FNC very kindly provided information on comparable property data collection. Darlene Messick provided invaluable assistance in helping to format the rough text.

We also received helpful advice and suggestions from the California Department of Real Estate (**www.dre.ca.gov**), and the California Association of Realtors (**www.car.org**).

A special debt of gratitude is owed for the invaluable assistance we received from the designers and editors of this book, including: Rick Lee, layout and pre-press editor; Colleen Taber, chief editor; Philip Dockter, art director; and Melinda Winters, cover design. Further acknowledgement is gratefully given to: Linda Serra, Business Division Chairperson from Glendale College,

Appraiser Edward S. Stahl; Donna Grogan, CPM from El Camino College; Larry Bevins, from Fullerton College; William Nunally from Sacramento City College; Kim Tyler, real estate law specialist, from Shasta College; Jim Michaelsen, from Santa Rosa Junior College; Nick Zoumbos, accounting specialist, from Crafton Hills College; and Joe Newton, fellow author, from Bakersfield College. And as always, thanks to William Pivar, a trusted friend, excellent author, and a heck of a fisherman. Finally, a special thanks to Mary Ann Zamel and Arlette Lyons, from Mount San Antonio College; real estate expert Joe Ribertelli; and financial analyst Walt Zozula, branch manager, from Community Commerce Bank in Woodland Hills, California.

Acknowledgments

David Kemp
Palomar College
San Marcos, California

Gary Goldberg
Santa Barbara City College
Santa Barbara, California

Alfred E. Fabian
Ivy Tech State College
Gary, Indiana

Chris Grover
Victor Valley College
Victorville, California

Ignacio Gonzalez
Mendocino Community College
Ukiah, California

Steve Herndon
Santa Rosa Junior College
Santa Rosa, California

Patricia Moore
Los Medanos College
Pittsburg, California

Dr. Nick Sacrafas
San Diego Mesa College
San Diego, California

Ron Maricich
Los Angeles Harbor College
Wilmington, California

Ed Culbertson
MiraCosta College
Oceanside, California

Nick Faklis
San Joaquin Delta College
Stockton, California

Jerome L. Fox
West Los Angeles College
Culver City, California

Walt Zozula
Glendale College
Glendale, California

Larry Cowart
Morehead State University
Morehead, Kentucky

Sandra Johnson
Shoals School of Business
Florence, Alabama

Preview of Internet Sites

T M

The History of Credit
www.didyouknow.cd/creditcards.htm

Map of 12 Federal Reserve Banks
www.stls.frb.org/publications/pleng/district_map.html

Board of Governors: Federal Reserve
www.federalreserve.gov

National Consumers League: Debit Cards
www.natlconsumersleague.org

U.S. Census Bureau
www.census.gov

Fannie Mae
www.fanniemae.com

Ginnie Mae
www.ginniemae.gov

Freddie Mac
www.freddiemac.com

FIRREA
www.fear.org/fedstat2.html

Credit Unions Online
www.creditunionsonline.com

NAREIT
www.nareit.com/aboutreits/thestorytext.cfm

Farm Service Agency
www.fsa.usda.gov/pas/default.asp

Farmer Mac
www.farmermac.com/plane/frames.htm

Bankratre.com
www.bankrate.com/brm/ratehm.asp

HUD
www.hud.gov/offices/hsg/sfh/buying/buyhm.cfm

Single Family Insurance Programs
www.hud.gov/offices/hsg/sfh/insured.cfm

FHA Mortgage Limits
https://entp.hud.gov/idapp/html/hicostlook.cfm

VA Home Loan Guaranty Services
www.homeloans.va.gov

Marshall & Swift: The Building Cost People
www.marshallswift.com/index.asp

Online Mortgage Calculator
www.countrywide.com

State Housing Agencies
www.trackproservices.com/links/statelnk.html

State and Local Government Information
www.statelocalgov.net

Alaska Home Loan Program
www.ahfc.state.ak.us/Department_Files/Mortgage/loans-main-page.htm

Delaware Home Loan Program
www2.state.de.us/dsha/home_buy_frame.htm

Florida Home Loan Program
www.floridahousing.org

Maryland Home Loan Program
www.dhcd.state.md.us

New Jersey Home Loan Program
www.state.nj.us/dca/hmfa

New York Home Loan Program
www.nyhomes.org/sony/sonyma.html

Oregon Home Loan Program
www.odva.state.or.us

Texas Home Loan Program
www.glo.state.tx.us/vlb/vhap/index.html

Wisconsin Home Loan Program
http://dva.state.wi.us

Table of Contents

Table of Contents

PART III - HOW THE LOAN PROCESS WORKS

CHAPTER 7 - FINANCE INSTRUMENTS   129

CHAPTER 8 - OVERVIEW OF THE LOAN PROCESS   153

Table of Contents

PART IV – OTHER TYPES OF FINANCING

CHAPTER 10 – ALTERNATIVE FINANCING   205

Table of Contents

Table of Contents

— PART I —
(CHAPTERS 1, 2, AND 3)
INTRODUCTION TO REAL ESTATE FINANCE

CHAPTER 1 - THEN AND NOW: A SHORT HISTORY OF FINANCE

The roots of our modern financial system extend back to the Roman Empire. These roots are evident in the language of finance today. The United States bases its system of laws, banking, finance, and real estate ownership on British models.

CHAPTER 2 - REAL ESTATE CYCLE AND THE SECONDARY MARKET

The real estate cycle has four phases, beginning with an expansion of real estate activity that leads to a peak, and then a decline to a bottom or trough. The establishment of a national secondary market to buy and sell mortgages has worked to diminish drastic swings in the real estate cycle by insuring that mortgage money is available at all stages within the cycle.

CHAPTER 3 - SOURCES OF FUNDS: THE PRIMARY MARKET

The primary market is mostly made up of local banks, savings banks, and mortgage companies. Deregulation of banking laws had an adverse effect on the S&Ls and permitted other lenders to take over part of their market share. This same deregulation has allowed other institutions such as credit unions, insurance companies, and pension plans to enter the primary market.

CHAPTER 1

THEN AND NOW: A SHORT HISTORY OF FINANCE

I. Lending in Ancient Times

A. THE ROMAN INFLUENCE

The American financial system has roots that extend back to the ancient Roman Empire. The Roman system of finance is reflected in the language that we use today. The term *FIDUCIARY*, *meaning a relationship of financial trust*, is from the Latin word *fides*, which means faith or trust. The Latin word *moneta* is the origin for the word money. *MONEY is any paper currency or metallic coin authorized by a government to represent value and accepted as a medium of exchange.*

Roman law and customs would not disappear with the empire but would continue on in various forms throughout western civilization.

1

CHAPTER 1 OUTLINE

B. MEDIEVAL INFLUENCES

The medieval period of western civilization saw the rise of feudalism throughout Europe.

In this system, the king owned all the land and would parcel it out to faithful retainers for their loyal services. These retainers, in turn, would further parcel out their holdings to others loyal to them. All such holdings were considered a life estate only, and would revert to the king upon the death of the holder. A **LIFE ESTATE** *is an interest in real estate or real property that is limited to the lifetime of the owner.*

In the middle of society were tradesmen and craftsmen. Most were required to be members of a guild and undergo a lengthy apprenticeship before being able to practice their trades. The lowest classes of citizens, if they could be called that, were serfs. Serfs were considered chattel and were bound to the land, meaning they were transferred with it to each new owner and lord. **CHATTEL** *is personal property.* Today, chattel may or may not be transferred with the real estate.

Serfdom was a form of slavery.

Our understanding of the system is based greatly on the study of the *Domesday Book*. This was a survey and tax roll commissioned by William the Conqueror in 1066 to ensure that the king knew the value and extent of all his new holdings.

As might be imagined, there was little room for upward mobility within society. Further, loans on real estate were virtually non-existent. Such lending, as existed, was for an amount given against a **PLEDGE** *(pawn)* of personal property or real estate if the loan was defaulted. Any such loan generally did not bear interest, as medieval religious authorities interpreted any payment of interest as usury. Today, **USURY** *is defined as an interest payment in excess of the legally permitted rate.*

C. THE END OF FEUDALISM IN ENGLAND

This political, economic, and social life arrangement would be wrenched apart in England by the events of the 14th Century. First

The History of Credit

Credit was first used in Assyria, Babylon, and Egypt 3000 years ago. The bill of exchange—the forerunner of banknotes—was established in the 14th century. Debts were settled by one-third cash and two-thirds bill of exchange. Paper money followed only in the 17th century.

The first advertisement for credit was placed in 1730 by Christopher Thornton, who offered furniture for sale that could be paid off weekly.

From the 18th century until the early part of the 20th, tallymen sold clothes in return for small weekly payments. They were called "tallymen" because they kept a record, or tally, of what people had bought on a wooden stick. One side of the stick was marked with notches to represent the amount of debt and the other side was a record of payments. In the 1920s, a shopper's plate—a "buy now, pay later" system—was introduced in the USA. They could only be used in the shops that issued them.

In 1950, Diners Club and American Express launched their charge cards in the USA, the first "plastic money." In 1951, Diners Club issued the first credit card to 200 customers who could use it at 27 restaurants in New York. But it wasn't until the establishment of standards for the magnetic strip in 1970 that the credit card became part of the information age.

 From "Did You Know?"
www.didyouknow.cd/creditcards.htm

the English would engage in a costly century-long war in France. Then, in 1348, England was struck by a bubonic plague epidemic called the "Black Death." The death toll was so severe that the entire social, political, and economic life of the country was disrupted. Serfdom, in England, ceased to exist as peasants flocked to the cities to take jobs formerly open only to guild members. There were too few lords alive to force them to return to the land. The advances in navigation that would soon bring about the discovery of new colonial lands to the west would also accelerate the opportunities for trade and the need for a stable financial system as well.

II. Banking in the Renaissance

In the rest of Europe, both the forces of the Renaissance and the Reformation would gradually allow the formation of modern banking practices.

The wars of religion and nationalism were expensive for monarchs. They were often forced to borrow from the new wealthy merchant class to finance their wars. Two wealthy merchant families in particular would rise to prominence in this period as lenders. These were the Medici family in Italy and the Fugger family in Germany. These merchant princes would also underwrite commercial expeditions for a share in the merchant's profits. An *UNDERWRITER makes loans based on assessment of risk.*

A. BRITISH INFLUENCES

By the 17th Century, England was an established trading nation with the beginnings of a colonial empire abroad.

The English Civil War, early in the century, had further restricted the power of English kings. The monarch operated in a constitutional role and his power was regulated by a parliament. Individual property rights were considered to be in fee simple estate. A *FEE SIMPLE ESTATE is the highest legal form of property ownership with rights that are assumed to continue forever.*

The country did indeed seem to be a "nation of shopkeepers" as Napoleon would call it a century later. These shopkeepers were becoming increasingly wealthy in cash assets with no safe place to keep their extra cash.

1. Goldsmith Accounts:The Birth of English Banking

While the British treasury might be a perfectly secure place to store money, the suspicion remained that the king and his ministers might conveniently forget whose money it really was. Thus, most merchants preferred to place their extra cash with the London goldsmiths. In return for the cash, the goldsmiths provided receipts that were redeemable on demand. The goldsmiths soon discovered that their clients often left the money in their keeping for very long periods of time and often continued to deposit additional sums of money with them. Many customers, rather than withdrawing their gold to pay a debt, would simply sign over their receipt to whomever they owed the debt. As a convenience to their customers, the goldsmiths created notes that were payable to the owner or to "the bearer on demand." A ***BEARER NOTE*** *is payable to whomever presents it.*

Goldsmiths' bearer notes marked the beginning of the first circulating paper currency.

The fact that the customers did not often withdraw all their money also allowed the goldsmiths to make loans of this additional cash. As an inducement to the depositors to keep their money in the goldsmiths' strongboxes, the goldsmiths shared the profits of the loans with the depositors in the form of an interest payment. For many goldsmiths the lending of money was becoming more profitable than making jewelry.

2. Stocks and Bonds

During this same time period, England was launching great private trading ventures. Among these were the Muscovy Company, the Hudson's Bay Company, and the East India Company. The great size and cost of these enterprises brought about the idea of "stock subscription" to fund their endeavors. ***STOCK*** *is an ownership interest in an institution or company.*

This allowed the cost of funding to be borne by many rather than a few. Additionally, the government also invested in these enterprises. However, the size and scope of these companies often exhausted these sources of initial funding and they were forced to borrow money. They managed this by the issue of "bonds." *BONDS are debt instruments that bear a stated "face value" or principal amount payable to the bearer in a specified time.* They are generally sold at a discount from this amount and the difference between the stated amount and the discount is the rate of interest return. As might be imagined, the London goldsmiths/bankers saw opportunities to make additional money in the bond market.

3. The Bank of England

In 1694, a consortium of bankers, led by William Patterson, established the Bank of England.

The bank made a loan of its entire capital to the British government. From that point forward, the British treasury deposited all its monetary reserves in the bank. In return, the bank received the sole right to issue notes and engage in commercial lending. In effect, it became the banker's banker. With the right of issue, it controlled the circulating currency. It also acted as a lender of last resort to other banks. It was then, and is now, what we call a central bank. *CENTRAL BANKS control the economy of a nation. The Federal Reserve System is a central bank.*

III. The American Colonies

The American Colonies were a mixture of proprietary land grants and direct royal holdings.

In most cases, these large holdings were sold in fee simple estate to individual colonists. A great problem throughout the colonial period was the lack of sufficient currency to support the needs of colonial trade. This was solved, in part, by the establishment of land office banks by the various colonies. The land office banks would make loans to colonists against a mortgage on their land. The mortgage moneys were paid out in the form of bearer notes issued in the name of the colony.

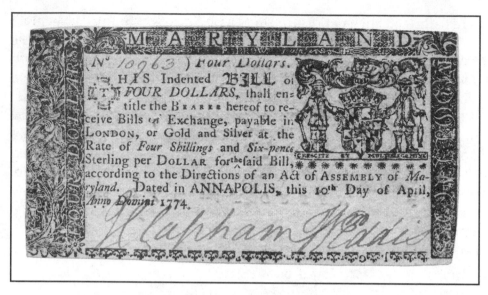

This provided a greatly needed form of circulating currency in the colonial period. The British outlawed this practice in 1741. However, like many British laws of the period, it was conveniently ignored by the colonists.

A. A NEW NATION

The issue of fiat paper money by the colonies and the Continental Congress financed the American Revolution. So much worthless paper money was issued that the phrase "not worth a Continental" was added to the American vocabulary. *FIAT MONEY is issued by decree of the state, often in times of war. It is issued with no regard for economic stability. It is almost always paper money and always inflationary.*

This new distrust of paper money would later be enshrined in the U.S. Constitution by the requirement that the states could make nothing but gold and silver legal tender. *LEGAL TENDER is money that is legally required to be accepted by the public in payment of any debt.* This well-intentioned requirement on the part of our founding fathers would later be circumvented by court interpretations that everyone except state governments could issue paper currency!

B. THE BANK OF THE UNITED STATES

The first Treasurer of the United States was Alexander Hamilton.

Hamilton was a fiscal conservative who was well aware of the stability provided to the British economy by the Bank of England. He persuaded congress to establish a central bank, based on the British model, to ensure that the new nation would commence on a sound financial footing. Congress went along with the plan, but was only willing to allow the new experiment in national finance a twenty-year charter. The charter lapsed in 1811. The result of this bad timing was that the government was forced to issue treasury bills to pay for the War of 1812 at high interest and state chartered banks with dubious capital assets multiplied.

In 1817, Congress re-chartered the bank as the Second Bank of the United States. Once again, it had only a twenty-year charter. Both banks provided the young nation with financial stability and safety while allowing moderate growth. The first experiment with central banking was curtailed by President Andrew Jackson, a westerner who was distrustful of a central monetary authority of any kind. He also had a great distrust of the eastern establishment who, he thought, were choking off western financial expansion. Jackson felt that federal monies would be safer spread around in state banks. He proceeded to veto the re-charter of the Bank of the United States and withdrew all

federal funds from the bank. The end result of this action was a massive loss of federal funds and a severe depression. However, this occurred after Jackson left the presidency and the blame for it was attached to his successor, Martin Van Buren.

C. STATE CHARTERED BANKING

The era that ensued after the demise of the Bank of the United States in 1837 was a period of great territorial and business expansion in the United States. Initially, the nation went through a great depression from 1837-1840. However, in 1841, the establishment of a sub-treasury system for federal funds provided security and safety for the governments monies at least. After 1841, the nation would experience inflationary conditions until another depression in 1857.

1. The Wildcat Era

With no central bank and a lack of federal or, in most cases, state regulation, banks proliferated like rabbits. While many of these institutions were honest and sound, many more were fraudulent. The term "wildcat banking" was coined to describe institutions that shared quarters out with the wildcats. In other words, they were located where it was impossible to find them if someone desired to redeem one of the many beautifully engraved notes that they issued.

In the period from 1837-1863, over 16,000 banks existed, of which at least 5,000 were totally fraudulent.

These banks issued over 36,000 different designs of currency. The average citizen who accepted a bad note could only console himself with the thought that he at least held a nice example of contemporary art.

However, there were positive developments during this period. The first building and loan societies started up during the 1830s. These were the pre-cursors of the modern savings and loans. Mutual savings banks appeared in the 1840s. They provided a safe haven for workers' deposits and functioned in a similar way to today's credit unions. Many states created lending and usury laws in an attempt to regulate predatory banking and real estate lending practices by individuals and institutions.

D. THE NATIONAL BANKING ACT OF 1863

The Civil War (1861-1865) was the most costly war in the nation's history up to that time.

Gold and silver were hoarded by the population, forcing the government to ask the banks for large loans of currency. The banking system was quite happy to loan the government their notes and deluged the Treasury with them. The problem was that these notes were of all different designs, values, and sizes. Those that circulated outside their local areas did so at a heavy discount. Secretary of the Treasury Chase, in an effort to introduce some sort of order into the chaos that ensued, issued U.S. Notes (Greenbacks) that had no backing other than the government's promise to pay. Further, he persuaded the administration to submit a bill to Congress to create a uniform note issue for the entire nation.

The result was the ***NATIONAL BANKING ACT OF 1863***. *The new law set minimum capitalization and reserves for any bank that applied for a National Bank Charter.* The banks could then buy government bonds with their capital. Upon deposit of their bonds with the U.S. Treasury, the banks could then make loans of up to 90% of the value of the bonds they had deposited. The loans would be made using a standardized national banknote provided by the government. This system provided the government with low interest loans. Further, it

provided the banks with interest on the bonds and interest again on the loans that they made. Lastly, it provided the nation with a uniform circulating currency that was backed by government securities and not subject to discount. This system worked so well that in 1865 congress drove out all privately issued bank notes by placing a 10% federal tax on them that had to be paid each time they were exchanged.

While the nation had a secure uniform circulating currency, several problems remained to be addressed. The rapid industrialization and westward farm and ranch expansion of the nation after the Civil War created dramatic swings in the business cycle. The nation went through severe depressions in 1873, 1893, and 1907. Because the banking system was still local in nature, it was unable to respond to these crises and often the response of the local banks worsened the problems. Perhaps the most troubling aspect was that national banks were not allowed to engage in mortgage lending. *MORTGAGE LENDING is the practice of loaning money that is secured by real estate and real property. The loan document is called a MORTGAGE LIEN*.

Mortgage lending during this period was still largely carried out by private individuals or by the building and loans (now more frequently called savings banks). Most mortgages were short term and often had a balloon payment at the end. *A BALLOON PAYMENT is a payment of principle at the end of a mortgage that is much higher than the typical mortgage payments*. A consequence is that the loan generally has to be refinanced. At the end of the 19th Century, it was becoming apparent that the U.S. economy was functioning sluggishly as a result of a lack of cohesiveness and direction in the lending system.

IV. The Federal Reserve Act of 1913

The passage of the Federal Reserve Act of 1913 attempted to solve the existent problems of the banking system.

The original purpose of the system was to discount commercial paper and provide additional bank regulation. A positive aspect of this law was that it allowed the member national banks of the system to engage in

Then and Now: A Short History of Finance

The Federal Reserve System

www.stls.frb.org/publications/pleng/district_map.html
(Interactive Map of 12 Federal Reserve Banks)

mortgage lending. For the first time since the demise of the Bank of the United States in 1837, the nation had a central banking system. The system would slowly begin to assume a centralized control over the economic life of the nation. It would really commence its modern functions during the great depression.

A. THE ROLE OF THE FEDERAL RESERVE

The *FEDERAL RESERVE is a central bank.* For its member banks, it is the "lender of last resort" or "the banker's banker." The Federal Reserve is made up of thousands of member banks.

There are twelve Federal Reserve Districts across the nation. A District Federal Reserve Bank represents each.

Each of these twelve banks has a nine-member board of directors. Each of the twelve banks is actually owned by the member banks in the district—all member banks are required to buy stock in the district bank. The seven-member *BOARD OF GOVERNORS oversees the*

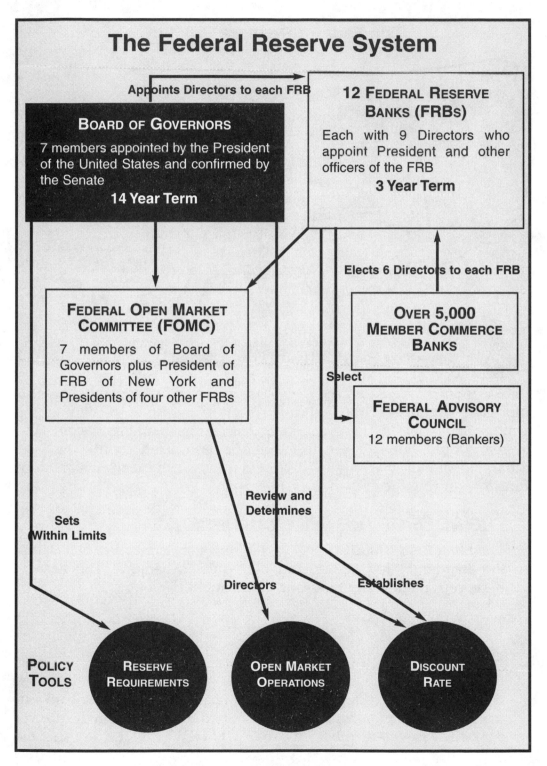

Then and Now: A Short History of Finance

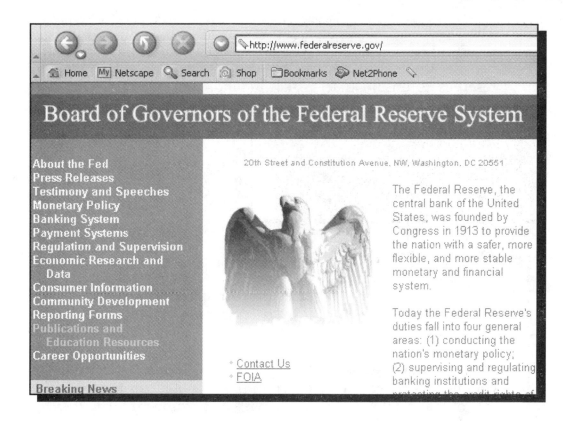

entire system. All seven members are appointed by the President of the United States and confirmed by the U.S. Senate.

The Federal Reserve controls the monetary policy of the United States in a number of ways.

1. The Power of Issue

The *POWER OF ISSUE is the legal authority to print money.* During the 1930s, the Federal Reserve would begin the withdrawal of National Bank notes from circulation. Government gold and silver certificates, as well as U.S. Notes, would also be withdrawn. In their place, a new uniform federal reserve currency was issued. This process is still ongoing.

The Federal Reserve is now the only entity to have the power of currency issue.

The "Fed," as the Federal Reserve is known, also controls the reserve requirements of the member banks. Ostensibly, this permits the Fed to require its member banks to retain enough reserves to ensure that sufficient funds are on hand to satisfy customer withdrawal needs. Actually, this power is also used as a tool to manage the banking system's ability to make loans.

By raising the reserve requirement, the Fed limits the amount of money available for loans. By lowering the reserve requirement, more money becomes available for loans.

2. Control of Interest Rates

The Fed also controls interest rates throughout the nation. This is accomplished by the discount rate. The **DISCOUNT RATE** *is the interest rate that the Federal Reserve charges to member banks to loan them money.*

A bank can borrow money from the Fed by pledging its commercial paper (short-term promissory notes) for the loan. The rate of interest to the bank is known as the prime rate. The **PRIME RATE** *is a bank's lowest rate, generally given only to its best customers.*

Upward or downward changes in this rate will create upward or downward changes in the rate charged by the bank to its customers. The rate to a bank's customers will generally be higher than the prime rate. *The* **FEDERAL FUNDS RATE** *is the interest rate at which depository institutions lend balances at the Federal Reserve to other depository institutions overnight.*

While the Federal Reserve rate is for short-term loans only, it is often used as a benchmark for the rates that banks set to their customers for other loans.

3. Open Market Operations

The Fed also carries out open market operations that have an effect on the nation's economy. **OPEN MARKET OPERATIONS** *consist of the buying and selling of United States Treasury bonds, as well as the securities of federal agencies such as the Federal Home Loan Bank*

System, *Federal Housing Administration (FHA), and the Government National Mortgage Association (GNMA).* Sales of these securities have the effect of tightening the money supply.

Purchases of federal agencies' securities increase the money supply (money available for lending). This is perhaps the most important tool in the Federal Reserve's arsenal.

The *FEDERAL OPEN MARKET COMMITTEE carries out open market operations.* The importance of this committee may be gauged by the fact that seven of the twelve members of the committee are the Board of Governors themselves. The other five members consist of one member from the Federal Reserve Bank of New York and four other members who serve in rotation from the other eleven district banks.

4. Truth in Lending Law (Regulation Z)

The Fed is also responsible for supervising the Truth in Lending Law. The *TRUTH IN LENDING LAW requires lenders to inform borrowers of the total costs of obtaining a loan.* This law, passed by congress in 1968, is also known as **Regulation Z**. Since the Fed regulates the economy, and by extension the lenders, it was made responsible for enforcing the act.

V. The Role of the Federal Government and Government Agencies

The actions of the federal government have a great impact on the economic life of the nation. Increases in government spending beyond the income taken in by the government in the form of taxes require the U.S. Treasury to borrow funds on the open market. This has the effect of making money less available for private borrowers. It also creates higher interest rates for private borrowers who are competing with the government for available funds.

Since the 1930s, the federal government has taken an active role in trying to assure home ownership for all Americans. A number of government

17

agencies have been created to provide loan insurance and to create a market for mortgage securities. The actions of these agencies have an effect on the real estate market and on the national economy as well. We will discuss these agencies and their operations in the chapters that follow.

VI. The Future of Money

Our forefathers could never have anticipated that gold, silver, and finally paper money would one day be replaced by credit and debit cards with magnetic strip coding, let alone wireless banking and computer chip technology. Nor can we, in the twenty-first century, possibly imagine the changes and advances that will be made in our future. Perhaps we will one day become a truly "cashless society." With technology growing in leaps and bounds, it doesn't seem so far-fetched as it would have just a few years ago.

In order to understand some of the advances the future may hold, it is necessary to look at how the banking industry has changed recently. Some of the advances seen just in the past few decades include the advent of credit cards, automated teller machines (ATMs), debit cards, and online banking, bill paying, and check writing.

A. ATM MACHINES

ATM machines, introduced in the 1970s, were seen by banks as a way of saving money by reducing the need for tellers. Initially, they were only installed inside or immediately outside their banks' branch offices.

In the early years, the cost of training and employing tellers proved to be more expensive than processing deposits and withdrawals via ATMs, even with the relatively expensive computer technology of the late '70s and early '80s.

To encourage customers to embrace the new technology and overcome their fears about putting checks into an ATM rather than a teller's hands, banks did not initially charge customers any fees for ATM use. Banks that embraced the ATM prospered, growing far faster than those who did not. Soon banks began imposing fees. First, they began charging their own customer's "off-use" fees when they used another bank's machine. As is often the case, this "nickel-and-dime 'em" strategy irritated consumers, but didn't enrage them. Also, the banks had the political wisdom to spend millions of dollars on campaign contributions and top lobbyists—and to not impose fees on ATMs located in or near government offices. A 1998 study found that the only Wells Fargo ATM that did not charge fees in the entire state of California was the one that sat in the basement of the state capitol in Sacramento. The new fees supplemented the banks' profit turn-around, which started at about the same time.

By the mid-90s, a number of large banks decided they needed to charge a second fee for the exact same operation, but with a different justification; banks should be allowed to charge non-customers for using their machines. In other words, banks should be compensated for installing ATMs and for their wear and tear.

Legislation was introduced in the U. S. Senate to ban the surcharge. Also, from 1996-98 at least two dozen states attempted to ban surcharges legislatively. All these efforts failed. However, in the wake of the ordinances banning the ATM surcharge in Santa Monica and San Francisco, California, surcharge legislation is not a dead issue.

What will happen to ATM fees is not clear, but it is clear that ATMs are larger profit machines than their promoters could have ever imagined 25 years ago.

B. DEBIT CARDS

Debit cards, also known as "check cards," look like credit cards or ATM (automated teller machine) cards, but operate like cash or a personal check. Debit cards differ from credit cards in that credit cards are a way to "pay later," whereas a debit cards are a way to "pay now." When you use a debit card, your money is quickly deducted from your checking or savings account.

More shoppers are using debit cards instead of cash, according to a survey by the American Bankers Association. Shoppers used debit cards in 26 percent of retail purchases in 2001, up from 21 percent in

1999. In contrast, buyers relied on cash for 33 percent of purchases in 2001, compared with 39 percent in 1999. Credit card use remained almost the same, at 21 percent.

You may not realize that you have a debit card. Many banks are replacing their standard ATM cards with upgraded ATM cards with a debit feature. You may also receive in the mail what looks like a credit card, when in fact it is a debit card. Debit cards allow you to spend only what is in your bank account. It is a quick transaction between the merchant and your personal bank account.

Obtaining a debit card is often easier than obtaining a credit card.

Advantages to a Debit Card:

1. Using a debit card, instead of writing checks, saves you from showing identification or giving out personal information at the time of the transaction.

2. Using a debit card frees you from carrying cash or a checkbook.

3. Using a debit card means you no longer have to stock up on traveler's checks or cash when you travel.

4. Debit cards may be more readily accepted by merchants than checks, even when you travel.

 From the National Consumers League
www.natlconsumersleague.org

VII. SUMMARY

The roots of our modern financial system extend back to the Roman Empire. These roots may be seen in the language of finance today. The United States based its system of laws, banking, finance, and real estate ownership on British models. After the failure of the first central bank, neither the federal government nor the states did much to regulate financial activity before the Civil War, and chaos was often the result. In the aftermath of the Civil War, and throughout the 20th Century, the federal government assumed an increasing role in the national economy. With the establishment of the Federal Reserve as the nation's central banking system, and the creation of federal agencies to foster home ownership, the nation finally had a financial system that was capable of moderating severe swings in the business cycle. This system, while not foolproof, is a role model for the world.

VIII. CHAPTER TERMS

Balloon Payment	Legal Tender
Bearer Note	Life Estate
Bonds	Money
Chattel	Open Market Operations
Central Bank	Prime Rate
Discount Rate	Power of Issue
Federal Funds Rate	Stock
Federal Open Market Committee	Truth in Lending Law
Fee Simple Estate	Underwriter
Fiat Money	Usury
Fiduciary	

IX. CHAPTER 1 QUIZ

1. Personal property that is often included with real estate is called:

    a. fee estate.
    b. chattel.
    c. serfs.
    d. pawn.

2. A fiduciary is:

    a. a person who is a lawyer.
    b. a person who lends money.
    c. a person who has a relationship of financial trust.
    d. a person who invests in real estate.

3. The highest form of property ownership is a:

    a. life estate.
    b. fee simple estate.
    c. fiduciary estate.
    d. mortgaged estate.

4. The first central bank in the world was:

    a. the Bank of the United States.
    b. the Federal Reserve System.
    c. the Bank of England.
    d. the National Banking System.

5. A central bank:

    a. has the power of issue.
    b. is a depository for a nation's treasury.
    c. regulates the economy of a nation.
    d. is all the above.

6. The Federal Reserve System controls interest rates with all of the following, except:

    a. the discount rate.
    b. the federal funds rate.
    c. open market operations.
    d. Regulation Z.

7. Usury is defined as:

   a. a legal tender.
   b. an excessive interest rate.
   c. a mortgage lien.
   d. none of the above.

8. The London goldsmiths:

   a. developed deposit banking.
   b. developed bearer notes.
   c. made loans from their clients' money.
   d. all the above.

9. The first federal legislation concerning banking was:

   a. the National Banking Act of 1863.
   b. the establishment of the Federal Reserve System.
   c. the establishment of the Sub-Treasury System.
   d. the establishment of the Bank of the United States.

10. Open Market Operations are:

   a. carried out by the U.S. Treasury Department.
   b. sales and purchases of U.S. Treasury Bonds by the Federal Reserve.
   c. government loans to homeowners carried out by the GNMA and the FHA.
   d. sales of mortgages to the Federal Reserve.

ANSWERS: 1. b; 2. c; 3. b; 4. c; 5. d; 6. d; 7. b; 8. d; 9. a; 10. b

CHAPTER 2

REAL ESTATE CYCLE AND THE SECONDARY MARKET

I. The Real Estate Cycle

Activity in the real estate market fluctuates according to the real estate cycle.

The **REAL ESTATE CYCLE,** *like the business cycle, refers to the activity of the real estate market as it reacts to the forces of supply and demand.* A cycle is characterized by a general expansion of real estate activity which peaks and then begins to contract leading to a bottoming out of activity. At this point activity again turns up leading to a new peak of activity. This cycle has four phases, which are shown in **Figure 2-1**. A widely accepted rule of economics is that all business activity, including the real estate market, reacts to the forces of supply and demand. It is also an accepted principle that supply and demand will always seek to balance each other.

A. SUPPLY AND DEMAND

When demand for a product (such as housing) exceeds the supply, the price for the product tends to increase. In real estate this period is often called a ***SELLER'S MARKET***. Higher prices encourage the suppliers, in this

25

CHAPTER 2 OUTLINE

Figure 2-1

Real Estate and Business Cycles
Four Phases of all Business-Type Cycles

The real estate cycle described here is a generalization of the business cycles we actually experience. No two cycles are quite the same, yet they all have much in common. In real life, actual business cycles will vary, but the characteristic patterns described here (peaks, recession, bottom and recovery) can always be observed. You should learn to identify the distinctive aspects of each phase of peaks, recession, bottom and recovery. Each phase is characterized by different economic conditions.

PEAK (TOP)

The **PEAK** *is the highest point in a new business cycle, and is usually higher than the peak of the previous cycle.* It is the upper or top part of the business cycle. Goods sell briskly and inventory selection is good. Good jobs are available and unemployment is low.

RECESSION (CONTRACTION OR SLUMP)

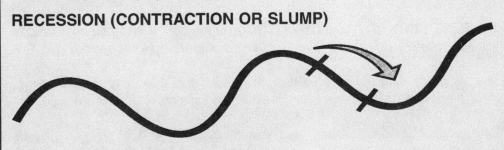

A **CONTRACTION OR SLUMP** *is the period in the business cycle from the peak down to a trough, during which output and employment fall.*

Recession follows the peak with a slow downturn in business activity. Interest rates may be increasing. People are experiencing job losses as inventories are reduced and production is cut back to reduce operating costs.

As unemployment increases, the demand for goods and services also decreases, which can result in even further cutbacks in business.

BOTTOM (TROUGH)

The **BOTTOM (TROUGH)** *is evidenced by a fall in output and employment, followed by an increase in business activity.* At the end of the bottom, interest rates usually have been lowered by the Fed and remain low in order to stimulate a recovery.

RECOVERY (EXPANSION OR BOOM)

The **RECOVERY (EXPANSION or BOOM)** *is the period in the business cycle from the bottom up to a peak, during which output and employment rise.*

The recovery is a happy period during which the economy is expanding. People are purchasing more from an expanding inventory of consumer goods.

Even political elections follow the business cycle. In a recession, politicians in power often get voted out, while they are more likely to remain in office when the economy is strong.

SEASONAL VARIATIONS AND TRENDS

One must realize that seasonal patterns and long-term trends will disturb the business cycle. Retail sales go up every Christmas and beach area hotels are crowded every summer. Long-term trends, such as the automobile industry trends, are on the rise and must be taken into consideration when evaluating the business cycle. Business conditions never remain static. Prosperity is eventually followed by an economic recession. Although in good times, people tend to expect prosperity to continue unabated.

case home builders, to increase production. As production increases, more of the demand is satisfied until a point is reached where production outstrips demand. *At that point, prices begin to fall and production will taper off until demand catches up with supply, and the cycle begins again. This period is called a BUYER'S MARKET.*

B. BALANCE

Economic theory holds that in a healthy economy, supply and demand should be in balance.

BALANCE is the economic principle that value is created and maintained when opposing economic market forces are in a state of equilibrium. In the real world however, this is an idealized situation. The forces that affect supply and demand are constantly changing and thereby constantly shifting supply and demand out of balance. However, as long as supply and demand are reasonably close to balanced, the economy will function quite well. The economy will suffer when either supply or demand greatly exceeds one another (**See Figure 2-2**).

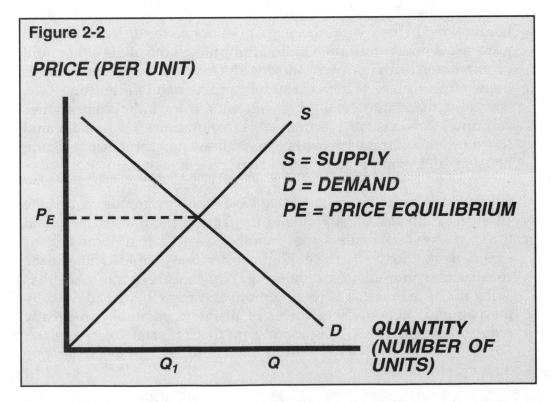

Figure 2-2

PRICE (PER UNIT)

S = SUPPLY
D = DEMAND
PE = PRICE EQUILIBRIUM

P_E

Q_1 Q

QUANTITY (NUMBER OF UNITS)

II. Factors Influencing Real Estate Cycles

Imbalances in supply and demand may be either short-term or long-term, depending on their causes.

It is not always possible to know whether a particular cycle is short-term or long-term, because a number of different factors interact to create the cycles. Among the causes that influence the cycle are the availability of mortgage funds, demographic changes within the population, the state of local and national economies, the cost of labor and materials, and finally political and social attitudes.

A. MORTGAGE FUNDS

The availability of mortgage funding affects both supply and demand for housing.

While there are buyers and sellers at all points along the real estate cycle, they are all affected by the availability of mortgage funds. A house is generally the largest purchase a consumer will make in his or her lifetime. In most cases the buyer does not have sufficient assets to purchase a house outright. Quite simply, most housing is either built or purchased with borrowed money. The availability and cost of this money directly affects both the supply and demand for housing. The source of these mortgage funds can vary from individual savings accounts to invested profits from large corporations. There is demand for mortgage funds to finance new housing, refinance existing housing, and to improve or upgrade existing housing.

For many years it was assumed that local economic trends created the strongest influence on supply and demand in the market place and thus on the real estate cycle. In other words, if a local area is experiencing prosperity there should be funds available to finance the construction and purchase of housing. While local economic health is still a major factor, it is becoming more and more overshadowed by the national economy. The forces of disintermediation can greatly reduce the impact of local economics on the real estate market place. *DISINTERMEDIATION is a loss of savings deposits to higher yielding competitive investments.*

Real Estate Cycle and the Secondary Market

The availability of high interest return, non-real estate related investments can diminish the availability of mortgage funds for investment in real estate, even in very prosperous local areas. This was seen nationally during the second half of the 1990s when there was a rush to invest funds in the high flying stock market, and in technical stocks in particular. Putting money into real estate at 6-8% returns did not make sense to individual or institutional investors when they could make an 18-20% a year rate of return on mutual funds. Of course even greater returns could be made on the so-called "dot com stock."

The collapse of the "dot com" market, and a general downturn in stock market prices, has made money available at lower rates for real estate loans.

However, after the events of September 11, 2001, the economy has weakened. This has created other problems for prospective homebuyers. While rates remain low, many are jobless or unable to save the necessary down payment to purchase a house.

As previously mentioned, housing is the highest cost purchase made by most consumers. The high interest rates provided nationally by other forms of investment tend to limit the amount of money available to the housing market. The housing market is itself very sensitive to minor changes in the interest rate. A very small upward change in either the interest rate or the price of housing can cause home ownership to become unaffordable for many.

Example: Let us assume that a house has a sale price of $100,000. The buyer puts down 20% of the sale price as a down payment. The monthly payment for an $80,000 thirty-year mortgage on the house at 7.5% interest is $559.37. Now let's assume that the price of the house increases to $150,000 and the rate remains the same. The down payment is still $20,000. The monthly payment for a thirty-year mortgage on $130,000 at 7.5% will be $908.98. A one percent increase to an 8.5% rate would make the payment $999.59.

The example above does not exaggerate what has happened in many areas of the country. Typically, lenders expect the borrower to pay a

down payment of from 10-20% of the sales price on the purchase of a house. In addition, most lending guidelines note that the monthly payments should not exceed 25% of the buyer's monthly income. Thus, for the example above at $559.37, the buyer should have a monthly income of approximately $2,400 per month. At $908.98, that qualifying income would increase to $3,900 per month. The one percent increase in rate would require an additional $400 per month in qualifying income.

Many prosperous local markets have seen a rapid growth in employment, along with a huge demand for housing.

As expected, this has caused existing housing prices to rise rapidly in those areas, in many cases far exceeding the ability of buyers to afford them. In the past this acted as a magnet to builders who would start up new construction of both single-family homes and apartment rental units to meet the increased demand and thus "cool off" home prices and help assure affordability. These, in turn, would create demand for more commercial support facilities and provide more jobs and more demand for housing. Yet, in some areas this has not occurred and, as a result, has threatened these prosperous local economies. To fully understand these phenomena we need to examine some of the other factors that influence the real estate cycle.

B. POPULATION

Population demographics are an important factor in the success of a local real estate market.

DEMOGRAPHICS *refer to the study and description of the population of an area.* Demographics include such factors as age, education, gross income, disposable income, number of family members, and savings and spending patterns. Also studied are patterns of migration and establishment of employment centers. Demographic data at the national level may be obtained from the Bureau of the Census. Many local communities and chambers of commerce also are sources of demographic data.

www.census.gov
U.S. Census Bureau

The nation has undergone enormous changes within the past two decades. We have changed from a "smokestack" industrial nation to a technical and service-oriented nation. This has created tremendous dislocation within communities that were factory-oriented due to plant closings and job lay-offs. In addition, many smaller rural farming communities have experienced a loss in population as a result of the growth of agri-business and the closing down of family farms. At the same time, those communities that were successful in attracting the new technical and service-oriented businesses often found that their infrastructures were overwhelmed by the sudden influx of population that these new businesses attracted. While many industrial towns and farming areas had more housing stock than they needed, the new technical communities were often totally lacking in housing stock altogether.

Another demographic factor that is affecting housing needs is a population that is gradually growing older.

Demographic data is important to community planners, developers, politicians, and real estate professionals in order to recognize and plan for changing trends in their areas and communities.

C. SOCIAL ATTITUDES

A major factor that has impacted both the availability of housing and mortgage funding has been the changing social behavior patterns of the population. A modern example is the increase in the portion of the population that is in its prime home buying years. Both baby boomers and their children are now seeking housing, which has been a major factor in the overwhelming demand for housing that has pushed up prices so drastically in the past decade. High divorce rates and a trend toward later marriages have also stimulated demand because there are fewer people per household. These trends, along with a gradually aging population of baby boomers, have been a significant factor in creating the modern phenomenon of condominiums.

While demand has been stimulated dramatically, the ability of builders to satisfy this demand has often been hampered by environmental, political, and social forces.

D. POLITICAL ACTIVITY

The supply and demand for housing and credit depends on notoriously unpredictable political forces.

Because the national government is the largest borrower in the country, its activities have a huge influence on the economy. **DEFICIT SPENDING** *by Congress forces the government to borrow money, making less money available for construction and home loans.* On the other hand, action by the Federal Reserve to loosen credit will rapidly increase available loan money supplies. If the Federal Reserve lowers interest rates too much, it may create inflationary pressure that will only serve to increase the price of housing.

E. REGULATION

Regulation by local, state, and federal governments is pervasive in almost every activity engaged in by our citizenry. The real estate and financial markets are no exception.

This regulation takes the form of federal, state and local tax laws, environmental regulations, lending laws, and local zoning and building codes. The vast majority of these laws and regulations have been enacted to protect the environment, promote public safety, or to protect consumers from predatory loan practices. **PREDATORY LOAN PRACTICES** *include usury, deception, and fraud.*

Individual home ownership is encouraged at the federal and state levels by the provision for the home mortgage interest deduction in the income tax codes. However, at the local level, homes are subject to property taxes. These taxes are necessary to provide local services such as streets, lighting, schools, and fire and police protection. In some areas, these local property taxes have become oppressive. Some communities have implemented so-called "impact fees" in addition to the regular property taxes collected. **IMPACT FEES** *are charged to all new housing that is developed within the community and are levied to pay for community infrastructure.* Often, these fees are really a part of "no-growth" attitudes on the part of a segment of the population that is already living in the community. The fees are often so high that any new construction is totally discouraged.

Environmental regulations have often worked to remove large segments of land that would have been available for development. Additionally, builders are often forced to commission studies or environmental impact reports (EIRs) before development of a housing tract can begin. Builders must also undergo review of their plans by local building and planning commissions. The bottom line, even in a community that does not discourage development, is that the process is often expensive and lengthy for the builder. Projects are often cancelled because the process has taken so long that the economic conditions that supported development have changed for the worse. Compliance with real estate and lending consumer protection laws adds hidden costs to the price of housing and to the mortgage loan as well. Builders, real estate professionals, and lenders are required to generate additional paper work and carry out due diligence procedures to insure that they do not run afoul of the various laws and regulations. This requires additional overhead expense on their part. All of the costs of compliance with political factors are passed along to the consumer.

In some areas of the country it is estimated that the cost of compliance with political, environmental, and regulatory rules adds from $30,000 to $50,000 to the final price of a new home.

III. The Role of the Secondary Market

The supply of funds available for investment in real estate mortgages is channeled into either the primary or secondary market. The *PRIMARY MARKET, made up of the various lending institutions that exist in a local community, is the most familiar market to the general public.* For example, if a borrower wishes to borrow money to finance the purchase of a home, he or she will seek a loan from a local bank, savings bank, or mortgage company. The source of funds for the loan will largely be made up of the savings from individuals and businesses from the local area. These funds would soon dry up if the lending institution were not able to sell some of the mortgage loans it has already made to other investors. The ability to sell off these mortgage loans frees up additional money for lending, which allows the institution to continue providing continuous services to the community by being able to provide additional real estate financing.

Primary lenders sell their mortgages into the secondary market. The **SECONDARY MARKET** *consists of private, quasi-public, and government agencies that buy and sell real estate mortgages from primary lenders.* Presently, private investors do not have the same influence on the real estate market that the agencies created by the government have. Therefore, we will focus our discussion on them.

> *A real estate loan is an investment, just like stocks or bonds.*

The lender (be it a bank, savings bank, or private party) commits its funds to an enterprise (in this case the purchase or construction of a home) in the expectation that the money will generate a return in the form of interest payments. Real estate loans can be bought and sold just like other investments. The present value (cash today) of the lender's right to receive future payments over the life of the loan can be calculated by comparing the rate of return on the loan to the rate of return on other investments with the same degree of risk.

> **Example:** A bank makes a home loan of $135,000 at 11% interest, secured by a deed of trust. One year later, approximately $134,500 of principal remains to be paid on the loan. If market interest rates have gone up to 12.5% for similar quality investments, then the present value of the loan is less than $134,500. The present value is the total amount of cash today it would take to generate the same amount of income at a 12.5% rate of return. An 11% return on $134,500 would be $14,795 per year. This same return could be achieved by investing $118,360 at 12.5% interest, so the present value of the loan (all other factors being equal) is $118,360, rather than its face value of $134,500.

It should be noted that many other factors can influence the value of a loan. A primary influence is the degree of risk associated with the loan. The **DEGREE OF RISK** *refers to the likelihood of default by the borrower and also to the ability of the lender to recover the loan proceeds by selling (foreclosing) the security property.*

> *The degree of risk in real estate loans is controlled mainly by qualifying the buyer and the property before the loan is made.*

To **QUALIFY A BORROWER** *is to insure that he or she has a large enough and stable enough income to minimize the risk of default.* To **QUALIFY A PROPERTY** *is to make sure the property is worth enough to satisfy the loan in the event of default and foreclosure.*

Why buy and sell loans? The secondary market serves two vital functions: it promotes investments in real estate by making funds available for real estate loans, and it provides a measure of stability in the primary (local) market by moderating the adverse effects of real estate cycles. Consider the following examples.

> **Example:** A-1 Savings Bank has a long list of prospective borrowers who need funds for the purchase of homes. A-1's problem is that all of its deposits are already tied up in real estate loans. But, by selling its existing mortgage loans to a secondary market investor, A-1 can get the funds it needs to make the new loans and thereby satisfy its credit-hungry customers. The effects of a tight money market in A-1's local community are moderated because A-1 can get funds in the national market.

> **Example:** If A-1 Savings Bank had a surplus of deposits instead of a shortfall, it might encounter difficulty finding enough local investments to absorb its funds. In this case, A-1 could buy real estate loans on the secondary market, in essence investing in real estate located all over the country. Because of the uniform standards applied to secondary market loans, A-1 can feel fairly secure in its investments, even though it may never see the actual borrowers and properties it is helping to finance.

The availability of funds in the primary market depends on the existence of the secondary market.

This can be seen by taking a brief look at the flow of mortgage funds: first, mortgage funds are given to the homebuyer by a lending institution in the primary market; the mortgage is then sold to a secondary market agency, which may in turn sell it to other investors in the form of mortgage-backed securities. As mortgage-backed securities are sold by the agency, more funds (cash) become available to the secondary market for the purchase of new mortgages from the primary market. As more

mortgages are purchased from the primary market, more funds become available for lenders to pass on to borrowers.

The secondary market provides cash liquidity to primary lenders through the purchase of mortgages. These mortgages are then used as collateral for the sale of mortgage-backed bonds to investors by the secondary market institutions.

IV. Agencies of the Secondary Market

For the purposes of our discussion, the secondary market may be said to include three agencies:

1. The Federal National Mortgage Association (FNMA or "Fannie Mae")

2. The Government National Mortgage Association (GNMA or "Ginnie Mae")

3. The Federal Home Loan Mortgage Corporation (FHLMC or "Freddie Mac")

The secondary market is able to function as it does because of the standardized underwriting criteria applied by these agencies. **UNDERWRITING CRITERIA** *are used to qualify the borrower and the property and include such items as loan-to-value ratios and income-to-expense ratios.* Every mortgage issued by each individual lender must conform to the secondary market. These standards assure a uniform quality control which inspires confidence in the purchasers of the mortgage-backed securities. The purchasers know that the mortgages which back the securities must be of a minimum quality. This lessens their risk in investing in properties they cannot view or assess for themselves. Without the assurance of the underlying underwriting standards, someone in California would be unlikely to invest in sight-unseen property in New Jersey.

Because the secondary market performs such an important function in providing liquidity of mortgage funds, the standards set by the secondary market have a large influence on lending activities in the primary market.

As an example, once secondary agencies began accepting adjustable rate mortgages (ARMs), 15-year fixed-rate mortgages, and convertible ARMs, these types of financing became more readily available in the primary market. Lenders were more willing to make these kinds of loans when they knew the loans could be sold to the secondary market.

A relatively recent development in the activities of the secondary market is the current streamlined online underwriting programs (loans) developed by "Fannie Mae" and "Freddie Mac," thus further expanding the availability of funds available for mortgage lending purposes.

A. FEDERAL NATIONAL MORTGAGE ASSOCIATION (FNMA)

FNMA or, "Fannie Mae," is the nation's largest investor in residential mortgages.

The **FEDERAL NATIONAL MORTGAGE ASSOCIATION (FNMA)** *was created in 1938 as the first government-sponsored secondary market institution.* It was originally formed as a wholly-owned government corporation. While the specific purpose of FNMA was to provide a secondary market for FHA-insured mortgages, FNMA did not start buying FHA mortgages on a large scale until 1948. At that same time, FNMA was also authorized to purchase VA-guaranteed loans.

FNMA underwent several reorganizations and is now a privately owned and managed corporation, although it is still supervised by the Department of Housing and Urban Development (HUD).

The role of FNMA was further expanded in 1970 (after it became a private corporation) with the passage of the **EMERGENCY HOME FINANCE ACT,** *which permitted FNMA to purchase conventional mortgages as well as FHA and VA mortgages.*

FNMA funds its operation by selling securities which are backed by its pool of mortgages to the public. It buys the mortgages from lenders. Lenders who wish to sell loans to FNMA are required to own a certain amount of stock in FNMA, the required amount being based on the principal balance of mortgage loans. FNMA posts the prices

daily that it is willing to pay for the standard loan programs approved for purchase. The required yield and process may also be obtained from a hotline operated by FNMA and from various financial services and publications. Loans sold to FNMA may be serviced by FNMA or by the originating lender. FNMA pays a service fee to the lender if it continues to service the loan.

In 1981, FNMA started a participation program with lenders. A master participation agreement is entered into between a lender and FNMA. The lender than assembles a pool (collection) of loans and a participation interest in that pool (50%-95%) is then sold to FNMA. In this way, both the lender and FNMA own an interest in the loans, instead of the lender selling them outright. In that same year, FNMA also announced the sale of conventional mortgage-backed securities that are guaranteed by FNMA as to full and timely payments of both principal and interest. A service fee is charged by FNMA for issuing securities backed by the mortgage pool, as well as a monthly fee for the guarantee provision.

The most recent development by FNMA is the ***DESKTOP UNDERWRITER®, an automated online underwriting system that is intended to reduce the time, cost, and subjectivity associated with the traditional process.*** The system permits brokers to go online and submit a borrower's application and loan request. The system will then analyze the borrower's credit history and ability to pay, as well as whether the loan meets FNMA's eligibility requirements. The system will then provide either an immediate loan approval, referral to a traditional underwriter, or will reject the loan as out of the scope of FNMA's lending criteria.

In those cases requiring traditional underwriting and assessment of the loan collateral, the process has been shortened as well. In assessing the collateral, the system will determine if a full appraisal is warranted or if the new streamlined **Limited Appraisal (Form 2055)** can be used. Often, the appraisal is also submitted online to the lender by the appraiser. Lastly, Desktop Underwriter® provides access to the proprietary automated underwriting systems of Countrywide Home Loans and GMAC Residential Funding Corporation to underwrite case files for jumbo and other non-conforming loans that do not meet FNMA's eligibility requirements. FNMA provides both online registration and training for lending institutions and brokers, as well as regional classes and in-office training.

www.fanniemae.com
Fannie Mae

B. GOVERNMENT NATIONAL MORTGAGE ASSOCIATION (GNMA)

The *GOVERNMENT NATIONAL MORTGAGE ASSOCIATION (GNMA), or "Ginnie Mae," was created with the passage of the **Housing and Urban Development Act (1968)**.* It is a wholly-owned government corporation which, in effect, replaced FNMA when FNMA became privately owned.

GNMA operates under the Department of Housing and Urban Development (HUD).

At the time of its creation, GNMA was given the responsibility for managing, and eventually liquidating, the remaining FNMA mortgages. Another function of GNMA is that of "special assistance": GNMA assists the financing of urban renewal and housing projects by providing below-market rates to low-income families.

A primary function of GNMA is to promote investment by guaranteeing the payment of principal and interest on FHA and VA mortgages. GNMA carries out this function through its mortgage-backed securities program. GNMA's activities in the "special assistance" area have lessened in importance as activities in its mortgage-backed securities program have increased. This program, supported by the federal government's borrowing power, guarantees timely interest and principal mortgage payments to the mortgage holders. The added security of the guarantee enables the mortgage holders to pledge a pool of their loans as collateral for securities. The repayment of the mortgages is the source of the funds used to pay off the securities when they become due. The mortgage-backed securities offer safety to investors, they can be easily traded, and they can be purchased in smaller denominations than many comparable investment instruments.

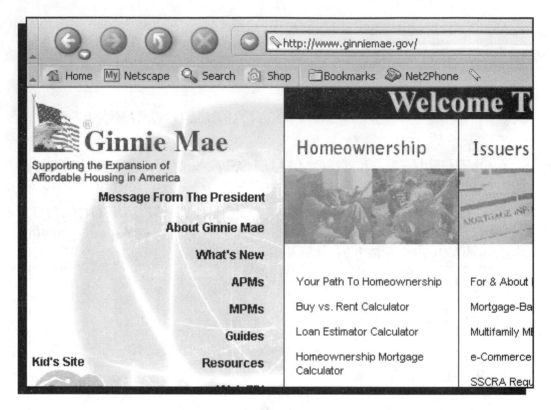

In order to issue GNMA mortgage-backed securities, the issuer must be an FHA or VA-approved mortgagee, be an acceptable GNMA servicer-seller, and have a specified net worth. A fee is paid for the GNMA commitment to guarantee the mortgage pool. The issuer (lender) continues to service the mortgage.

Mortgage-backed securities fall into two general types: bond-type securities and pass-through securities. *BOND-TYPE SECURITIES are long-term, pay interest semi-annually, and provide for repayment at a specified redemption date. PASS-THROUGH SECURITIES pay interest and principal on a monthly basis.*

Pass-through securities are the more prevalent.

FULLY MODIFIED PASS-THROUGH SECURITIES pay interest and principal monthly, regardless of whether the payments have been collected from the mortgagors. Any proceeds from foreclosure or prepayment are also passed on to the security holder as soon as received. If the issuer of the security (the lender) fails to make the payments, GNMA takes over the mortgage pool and makes the payments. *STRAIGHT PASS-THROUGH SECURITIES* *pay monthly interest and principal only when they are collected from the mortgagor.*

C. FEDERAL HOME LOAN MORTGAGE CORPORATION (FHLMC)

The *FEDERAL HOME LOAN MORTGAGE CORPORATION (FHLMC), which is also known as "Freddie Mac," was created through the Emergency Home Finance Act (1970).* Initially, FHLMC was a nonprofit, federally-chartered institution which was controlled by the Federal Home Loan Bank System. The primary function of FHLMC was to aid savings and loan associations who were hit particularly hard by the recession of 1969-1970. FHLMC helped S&Ls acquire additional funds for lending in the mortgage market by purchasing the mortgages they already held. FHLMC was authorized to deal in FHA, VA, and conventional mortgages. In 1989, FHLMC became a private corporation and basically operates in a manner that is similar to FNMA.

FHLMC is now regulated by the U.S. Department of Housing and Urban Development (HUD).

FHLMC emphasizes the purchase of conventional mortgage loans, and also actively sells the mortgage loans from its portfolio, thus acting as a conduit for mortgage investments. The funds which are generated by the sale of the mortgages are then used to purchase more mortgages.

FHLMC has been actively involved in developing underwriting standards for conventional mortgage loans, furthering assistance to savings banks who deal chiefly in conventional mortgages. All members of the Federal Home Loan Bank System, now under the Office of Thrift Supervision, are eligible to sell mortgages to FHLMC. Commercial banks, credit unions, and other non-members may be approved by FHLMC as eligible sellers. Non-member sellers are charged an additional fee for the mortgage purchase.

FHLMC issues its own mortgage-backed securities, which are backed by the conventional mortgages it purchases. FHLMC purchases

mortgages through its immediate delivery program or its forward commitment purchase program. In the *IMMEDIATE DELIVERY PROGRAM, sellers have up to 60 days in which to deliver the mortgages FHLMC has agreed to purchase.* Failure to deliver can mean that the seller will be banned from making sales to FHLMC for two years. The immediate loan delivery program can involve either whole loan purchases or participation purchases. Under the *FORWARD COMMITMENT PURCHASE PROGRAM, commitments are made for six- and eight-month periods.* Delivery of the mortgages is at the option of the seller. There is a non-refundable commitment fee payable to FHLMC.

FHLMC also has an automated underwriting process. This system, established in 1996, is similar to that of FNMA.

www.freddiemac.com
Freddie Mac

V. Quality Control

The secondary market has an enormous influence on the primary market, not only because of the increased availability of funds that it provides, but also because of the standards of quality it imposes on lenders. Because lenders wish to be able to sell their loans to the secondary agencies, they must follow the underwriting guidelines of those agencies. In the 1980s and early 1990s, the rate of mortgage delinquencies and foreclosures rose sharply. In response to this higher loss rate, both FNMA and FHLMC implemented changes in their underwriting guidelines. The secondary market is trying to improve the quality of the loans it purchases and ensure the reputation of residential mortgages as a safe investment.

In their efforts to increase the quality of the loans they purchase, the agencies necessarily force the lenders to upgrade the quality of the loans they make. Not only can the agencies refuse to purchase loans that do not follow their underwriting guidelines, they can also request lenders to repurchase loans already sold if it is later discovered the lender violated an underwriting guideline.

The secondary market encourages lenders to implement their own quality control programs.

The secondary market considers it the lender's responsibility to submit investment quality loans for purchase. According to FHLMC, an investment quality loan is "a loan from a borrower whose timely repayment of the debt can be expected, that is secured by a property of sufficient value to recover the lender's investment if a mortgage default occurs." By encouraging lenders to carefully review property appraisals, legal documentation (e.g., the mortgage instrument), origination documentation (e.g., the loan application, credit report, and employment verification), and the ultimate underwriting decision, the secondary market exerts its influence to increase the overall quality of loans made and to decrease the rate of delinquency and foreclosure.

VI. SUMMARY

The real estate cycle has four phases, beginning with an expansion of real estate activity that leads to a peak, and then a decline to a bottom or trough. Expansion then begins again, leading to another peak and the completion of the cycle. The cycle is driven by supply and demand. Supply and demand for both real estate and mortgage money is affected by economic, social, and political factors. Political regulation of housing and lending, while intended to protect consumer health, safety, and quality of life, has often tended to increase the price of housing for consumers. Supply and demand are seldom in balance, however, balance is critical to maintaining the value of real estate. The establishment of a national secondary market to buy and sell mortgages has worked to soften drastic swings in the real estate cycle by insuring that mortgage money is available at all stages within the cycle. The major players in the secondary market are FNMA, FHLMC, and GNMA. These institutions have recently utilized the Internet to streamline the mortgage lending process and lower both the costs and time required to obtain a loan.

VII. CHAPTER TERMS

Balance	GNMA
Bond-Type Securities	Immediate Delivery Program
Buyer's Market	Pass-Through Securities
Demand	Predatory Lending
Demographics	Primary Market
Disintermediation	Real Estate Cycle
FHLMC	Secondary Market
FNMA	Seller's Market
Forward Commitment Program	Supply

VIII. CHAPTER 2 QUIZ

1. Predatory loan practices include:

    a. usury.
    b. deception.
    c. fraud.
    d. all the above.

2. When the demand for housing increases:

    a. it is a buyer's market.
    b. prices decrease.
    c. prices increase.
    d. prices remain in balance.

3. Value is created and maintained by:

    a. buyers.
    b. political regulation.
    c. the secondary market.
    d. balance.

4. The study and description of the population of an area is called:

    a. disintermediation.
    b. demographics.
    c. demand analysis.
    d. population analysis.

5. FHLMC and FNMA are:

    a. government agencies.
    b. primary lenders.
    c. part of the secondary market.
    d. regulatory bodies.

6. Pass-through securities pay interest:

    a. annually.
    b. quarterly.
    c. semi-annually.
    d. monthly.

7. Disintermediation is:

    a. a loss of savings deposits to higher paying investments.
    b. a gain of savings deposits by local lenders.
    c. mortgage securities sales to investors by the secondary market.
    d. the sale of mortgages to the secondary market by primary lenders.

8. The primary market is made up of:

    a. local lending institutions.
    b. first time homebuyers.
    c. federal agencies.
    d. all the above.

9. Which of the following is false statement regarding political regulation of the housing market?

    a. Regulation serves to protect consumers from deceptive practices.
    b. Regulation helps keep housing prices low.
    c. Regulation increases housing prices.
    d. Regulation protects health and safety.

10. Which of the following is a government agency?

    a. FHLMC
    b. FNMA
    c. GNMC
    d. GNMA

ANSWERS: 1. d; 2. c; 3. d; 4. b; 5. c; 6. d; 7. a; 8. a; 9. b; 10. d

SOURCES OF FUNDS: THE PRIMARY MARKET

The discussion in this chapter will focus on the individuals and institutions that make loans directly to borrowers. As noted in the previous chapter, many of these lenders are local in nature and obtain their funds from the deposits of local savers and businesses. However, some mortgage firms have established a national presence in the marketplace.

I. Traditional Direct Lenders

The market for real estate loans dates back to the establishment of the original building and loan societies in the 1830s. The modern market did not begin until the great depression a hundred years later. It was during this time that the beginnings of a viable secondary market were established. This encouraged the traditional banks and savings and loans to expand their real estate activities. This period was marked by a generally well regulated, stable, and predictable market. The 1980s saw many changes in both the attitudes and practices of the real estate lending institutions.

I. TRADITIONAL DIRECT LENDERS (p. 51)

These changes were brought about by several factors. The first of these was that economic conditions were constantly fluctuating. The forces of disintermediation created by these conditions made it difficult for traditional lending institutions to maintain the stable interest rates that had formerly prevailed. They lobbied for deregulation so that they could compete with other forces in the marketplace. They were successful, for the most part, in obtaining much of the regulatory relief that they sought. By the end of the decade, many of the traditional institutions were victims of the old axiom "be careful what you wish for, you just might get it!"

A. SAVINGS AND LOANS

The savings and loan associations (S&Ls) were the oldest and largest source of funds for financing residential property.

Over the years, *SAVINGS AND LOANS carried out their historic function of investing on average 75% of their funds in the single-family residential market*. They were able to dominate local mortgage markets despite the fact that commercial banks had more assets. The deposits placed with the savings and loans were in the form of savings accounts that were less susceptible to immediate withdrawal than the demand (checking) deposits held by commercial banks.

Between 1945 and the late 1970s, the S&Ls expanded their mortgage loan operations aggressively. While other lenders were afraid of the inherent risk associated with long-term conventional loans, the S&Ls believed that they could succeed based on their intimate knowledge of local market conditions and their ability to attract long-term deposits. Because they were able to offer higher interest rates than the commercial banks, they had no trouble attracting deposits during the period of prosperity from World War II until the 1970s. However, the surge in interest rates in the late 1970s and early 1980s turned the tables on this strategy. Because the savings and loans were restricted by law with respect to how much interest they could pay to their depositors, they found themselves in the unfamiliar and uncomfortable position of being unable to offer attractive enough rates of return to their depositors. The result was that they lost a large portion of their deposits to competing investments, such as money market funds and

government bonds that offered much higher rates of return. *MONEY MARKET FUNDS are private, non-insured investment accounts.*

To make matters worse, the S&Ls found themselves holding long-term, non-liquid mortgages at low rates of interest (by 1980s standards). These loans could not be liquidated into the secondary market and had to be held in portfolio. A *PORTFOLIO loan is a loan held by a lender rather than sold into the secondary market.* The reason for this was that historically the savings and loans had set their own property and borrower standards based on what they considered to be their superior knowledge of the local market. In many cases, those standards were not of a level that was acceptable to the national secondary market.

The S&Ls attacked the problem on two fronts. The first was to ask for deregulation so that they could compete with the money market funds by being able to invest in other areas. The second was the gradual adoption of the secondary market procedures for new real estate loans to enable them to sell into the secondary market.

With banking deregulation, S&Ls were now free to compete with alternative investments.

For many S&Ls, this was a green light to pour money into the most risky investments.

In the heady rush to increase returns, S&Ls forgot the first rule of interest returns: the higher the rate of return the greater the risk.

Often the investments were made in areas that neither the S&Ls nor their regulators had any ability to evaluate. The industry was led by a group of managers with a "good old boy mentality" who were, at best, incompetent and, at worst, fraudulent. The result was a rapid increase in the rate of failure of savings and loans. By late 1986 and early 1987, the problem had reached such epic proportions that it attracted the attention of the U.S. Congress, who held hearings to determine how to rescue the nation's financial system. The result of these hearings was The Financial Institutions Reform, Recovery and Enforcement Act (FIRREA).

1. Financial Institutions Reform, Recovery and Enforcement Act of 1989 (FIRREA)

The Financial Institutions Reform, Recovery and Enforcement Act (FIRREA) governs all federally related transactions.

FIRREA would do more than just address the savings and loans problems. It would affect every institution and every person who deals in a federally related transaction. A **FEDERALLY RELATED TRANSACTION** *is any transaction in which the federal government is involved.* Any real estate transaction, or any loan in which there is federal involvement of any kind, is affected.

FIRREA protects the federal deposit insurance funds.

www.fear.org/fedstat2.html
FIRREA (18 U.S.C.)

Another result of the bill was that minimum standards for lending, underwriting, and appraisal were set in place for all lending institutions that are either regulated by the federal government or have access to federal funds.

Under FIRREA, the **OFFICE OF THRIFT SUPERVISION (OTS)** *was formed to regulate the S&Ls.* This had been handled by the Federal Home Loan Bank Board (FHLBB), which was eliminated by FIRREA. The Federal Deposit Insurance Corporation (FDIC) was granted initial responsibility for the **RESOLUTION TRUST CORPORATION (RTC),** *which was formed to liquidate the assets of fraudulent and failed S&Ls.* By the time this was complete, hundreds of S&Ls had ceased to exist. FIRREA also eliminated the old Federal Savings and Loan Insurance Corporation (FSLIC), granting the FDIC permanent responsibility for managing the **SAVINGS ASSOCIATION INSURANCE FUND (SAIF),** *which replaced the old FSLIC in insuring savings banks (the new name for S&Ls).*

www.fdic.gov/bank/historical/history/vol1.html
History of the '80s — Lessons for the Future

The FIRREA changes reaffirmed the federal government's commitment to insure the safety of all federally insured deposit accounts.

It also set procedures for lending in federal transactions. As a result, depositors were reassured and many again began to invest in the savings and loans. As a result of the massive failures and the reorganizations, the number of savings and loans decreased drastically. Financially secure organizations survived (now known as savings banks), and continue to play an important role in real estate finance.

B. COMMERCIAL BANKS

Commercial banks remain the largest source of investment funds in the country today.

As their name implies, **COMMERCIAL BANKS** *are oriented towards commercial lending activities, supplying capital for business ventures and construction activities on a comparatively short-term basis.* Until relatively recently, residential mortgages were not a major part of their business, primarily because of government limitations on the amount of long-term investments they could make. Those limitations were imposed because the vast majority of deposits held by commercial banks are **demand deposits** or **checking accounts**, which are payable on demand whenever a depositor elects.

Demand deposits are considered less reliable for re-investment in long-term real estate loans than the more stable savings deposits.

Nevertheless, within the past decade, commercial banks have increased their participation in home mortgage lending. The S&L crisis allowed them to gain an increased market share of new depositors at the expense of the S&Ls. At the same time, the banks wanted to be able to offer their customers mortgage loans rather then send them off to competing lenders. Frequently, the bank is able to sell the loan into the secondary market while retaining the servicing of the loan. **SERVICING A MORTGAGE LOAN** *means that the bank collects the mortgage payments for the loan even though it has been sold into the secondary market.* The bank receives a fee for doing this and the borrower remains happy in the belief that his or her loan is still held by the bank.

By offering mortgage loans, the bank is able to attract new customers for its other services such as checking accounts, credit cards, and equity lines of credit.

In the past few years, banks have seen growth in consumer loans, while business loans have remained stable at best. Because of the tax deductibility of mortgage loan interest, banks expect mortgage loans to make up a larger portion of their consumer loan business.

Changes in government banking regulations have also spurred commercial banks to engage in more mortgage lending activity.

Government regulations require that banks hold different percentages of funds on reserve for different types of loans, based on the perceived risk of the loans. First lien home mortgages are in the lowest risk category. That means that banks have to maintain less money on reserve for home mortgage loans than for other types of loans. This leaves more funds available for additional loans or for other investments. All commercial banks are part of the Federal Reserve System and have the ability to borrow funds from that system. This gives them more flexibility in changing markets than other types of lenders.

C. CREDIT UNIONS

Credit unions are one of the relatively new kids on the block in the field of mortgage lending.

CREDIT UNIONS *were set up in 1970 as membership associations made up of employees who worked for individual institutions with a common association of interest.* These members invested savings and could then borrow against the membership funds to finance purchases of goods and services. Generally, only personal property items were loaned upon. Interest rates were low and served to pay expenses, with any remaining profit credited to each individual member's account at quarterly intervals.

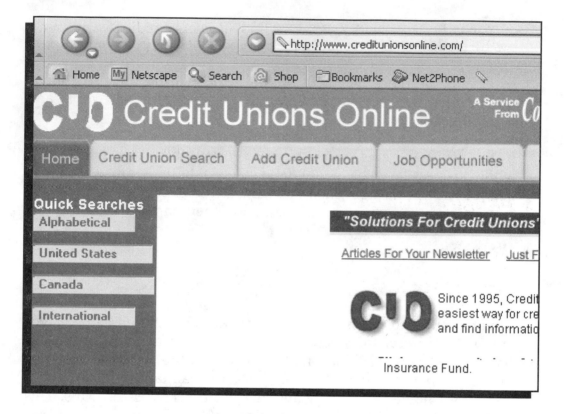

The deregulation of the banking industry provided a growth opportunity for credit unions.

First, many of them started to combine. Thus, the Students Credit Union would merge with the Teachers Credit Union. It then became the Students and Teachers Credit Union and vastly increased its membership. The new deregulation of the banking laws allowed credit unions to enter the mortgage field in direct competition with the banks and S&Ls. At the same time, the credit unions began to combine organizations of differing interests. For example, the Firefighters Credit Union would merge with the Aircraft Workers Credit Union. At this point the banks attempted to kill off the new competition through a series of lawsuits, claiming that the regulations required a common association of interest. While students and teachers could have a common association of interest, it was difficult to say the same of firefighters and aircraft workers. While the lawsuits have slowed down the process of consolidation, it is still ongoing. There is, after all, no rule that says that the Students and Teachers Credit Union cannot merge with any and all education related credit unions in the country.

While credit unions have definitely entered the field of mortgage lending, at this time their overall share of the market remains small.

II. Indirect Lenders

A. PENSION FUNDS

Pension plans were an outgrowth of the economic uncertainty of the 1930s.

American workers insisted on plans that allowed them to set aside a portion of their paychecks to save for retirement. Large corporations discovered the tax advantages of contributing to such plans, and that such contributions resulted in worker retention. With the enactment of the **Employee Retirement Income Security Act of 1974 (ERISA)**, all such plans became relatively well managed and safe. New tax laws that permitted self-employed workers to establish their own pension savings plans have given pension fund managers even more funds to invest. The popularity of these funds has actually adversely impacted other forms of savings.

Traditionally, pension funds have participated in the market place in two areas. The first of these is by direct investment in commercial real estate development. They are an important source of funds for developers and builders. The second of these are pension funds invested in the bond issues of the secondary market. However, the conservative managers of most funds have been unwilling to directly enter the mortgage lending market.

With their ever increasing supply of funding, those who run pension plans have the potential of becoming major players in the field.

B. INSURANCE COMPANIES

INSURANCE COMPANIES control vast amounts of capital, in the form of insurance premiums, which are held for relatively long terms. Money

invested in insurance policies is generally not subject to early or sudden withdrawal (as are the deposits in banks or savings banks) and does not earn the high interest returns that are now common in other investment forms. For these reasons, insurance companies are able to safely invest large sums of money in long-term real estate loans.

In the past, insurance companies preferred direct investments in large scale commercial projects, as opposed to investment in residential lending. Often, the insurance companies would engage in participation loans with commercial developers as well to increase their rate of return. A **PARTICIPATION LOAN** *is one in which the lender assumes a percentage of ownership in addition to the loan proceeds.* This gives them an ongoing permanent share of the profits of the business to which they have loaned the money.

Insurance companies have a lower cost of funds than their competitors in the mortgage lending business.

In addition to whole life policies, which pay minimal dividends or interest, they have even greater sums of money to invest from term policies, on which they pay no interest at all. This has given them a formidable advantage in the investment market place.

For many years, insurance companies have been major players in the secondary market through the purchase of bonds issued against mortgages issued by FHLMC, FNMA, and others. Recently, some insurance companies have entered the primary market by establishing subsidiary multi-tiered mortgage companies that allow them to compete directly in the primary market.

III. The Role of the Correspondent

A. MORTGAGE BROKERS

Mortgage brokers fill a role in the marketing of loans to consumers. *MORTGAGE BROKERS are financial "go-betweens" or coordinators.* The mortgage broker does not loan his or her own funds. He or she is a knowledgeable real estate and loan professional who handles the origination of a loan with the consumer. The broker than "shops" the loan with a variety of primary mortgage lenders who have programs that the borrower will qualify for. The broker then matches the borrower with the lender that will provide the best program at the best price to the consumer. The broker handles all the paperwork involved, helps the lender and the borrower set up escrow, orders the appraisal for the lender, and takes care of the closing paperwork for the lender and the borrower after the loan is funded. The mortgage broker provides an important service to both borrowers and lenders. By acting as a go-between, the broker frees up valuable time for the primary lender, reduces their need for personnel, and is able to advise and guide the borrower through an often lengthy and complex process.

B. MORTGAGE BANKER/MORTGAGE COMPANIES

Mortgager bankers, or mortgage companies, also act in the role of intermediaries in the lending of capital. *MORTGAGE BANKERS/MORTGAGE COMPANIES can both originate and loan funds.* They are often local in nature, and receive lending funds from large national investors, such as insurance companies and pension plans. The major national investors often are not aware of local market conditions and depend on the mortgage bankers to make stable loans for them in the local markets. While the mortgage bankers originate loans themselves, they also work with mortgage brokers. The mortgage bankers do not keep portfolio loans. They will sell their loans into the secondary market as soon as they have "seasoned." A *SEASONED LOAN is one that has been held for a sufficient time to establish that the borrower is making their payments in a timely manner, often 6-12 months.* Often, the mortgage banker will retain or sell the servicing of the loan separately from the loan itself.

Because mortgage bankers/mortgage companies invest little of their own money, their activities are largely controlled by the availability of capital in the secondary market.

As might be expected, their loan qualification criteria must reflect the standards of the national market in order to resell their loans into the secondary market.

IV. The Role of the Private Investor

A. *REAL ESTATE INVESTMENT TRUST (REITs)*

A *REAL ESTATE INVESTMENT TRUST (REIT) is an unincorporated association of real estate investors managed by a trustee.* In 1960, by means of the **Real Estate Investment Trust Act**, Congress made it possible for investors to enjoy the flow-through tax advantages of a partnership, while retaining some of the more important qualities of a corporate operation. The Act allows investors who prefer real estate as an investment to receive tax benefits similar to those granted to mutual funds and other regulated investment companies. Unlike ordinary corporations, whose earnings are subject to double taxation (first at the corporate level and again as personal income when distributed to stockholders), the real estate investment trust earnings are taxed only once; after they have been distributed to their investors. There are several requirements for a REIT:

1. It cannot hold property primarily for sale to customers.
2. It must have at least 100 beneficial owners.
3. No five persons or less can hold over 50% of the beneficial interest.
4. It must issue shares or certificates of interest.
5. Each share must have a proportionate vote in trust policy decisions.
6. 95% of its gross income must be from investments.
7. 75% of its income must be from real estate investments.

B. *PRIVATE INDIVIDUALS*

Private individuals have always been a force in the world of real estate finance.

The majority of these individuals are sellers who extend credit to their purchasers. This is referred to as "taking back" or "carrying back" a part of the sales price, often in the form of a second mortgage. A *SECOND MORTGAGE is often a source of funds when a lender will not loan the full amount of the purchase price of a residence. It may also be a source of funds for home repairs for a homeowner who does not wish to renegotiate the terms of his original mortgage.*

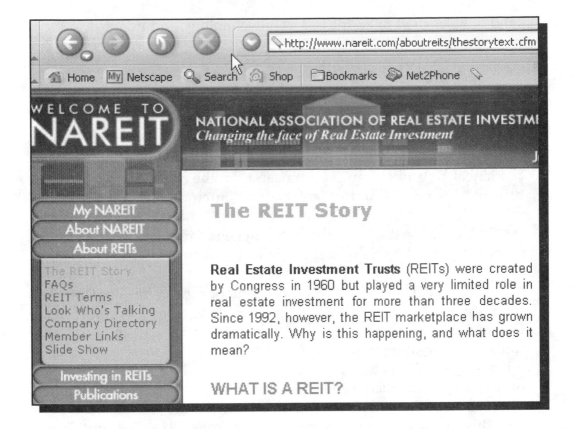

"Seconds" are generally for shorter periods of time and at higher rates than "Firsts."

When interest rates are high or money is in short supply, a buyer may be inclined to ask a property owner to sell his or her property on installment terms.

Private financing becomes much more prevalent when funds from traditional lenders are scarce, too expensive, or both.

C. THE INTERNET

The authors would be remiss if the effect of the Internet on lending was not discussed. Over the past ten years the use of both home computers and of the Internet has become available to virtually every American household. This fact has not been lost on primary lenders,

who have rushed to adopt this new technology and adapt it to their purposes.

The greatest effect of the Internet has been on how fast transactions can take place.

Some primary lenders viewed the Internet as a means to both speed up transactions and remove what some of them viewed as bottlenecks (brokers and appraisers) in the loan process. Many brokers, appraisers, and others saw this attempt at direct electronic marketing as a threat to their livelihoods and worked to use the Internet to advertise their services to clients, reduce their overhead costs, and speed up their part of the loan process.

It is still too early to assess the full impact of the computer/Internet revolution, but after ten years, several trends have become clear. Consumers do use the Internet to view properties and shop for loan rates and other information. However, many of these consumers, when they wish to obtain a loan, prefer to use their local loan broker or lender rather than some "faceless" national Internet company. These local brokers now are dealing with more knowledgeable clients and this factor has actually made the broker's job easier and faster. Appraisers have discovered that their lenders have *investors* who feel that the appraiser is a trusted and important part of the process that *they* do not wish to go away.

The adoption of computerization and the Internet has both lowered consumer costs and increased productivity throughout the industry.

1. Online Loan Applications - A Good Start

Like many aspects of the loan industry, the application process can be started online. An applicant accessess a website and fills out a simple form to begin the process. In theory, the applicant will receive a number of offers. It has been the author's experience that most loans cannot be fully completed through the Internet. It usually takes at least one face-to-face meeting, as well as other correspondence, to complete the process.

Don't assume that loans generated online will be at the lowest net cost to the consumer. The Internet is a good starting point for the shopping around process, but other avenues should explored to find the best deal. It would be ill-advised to automatically rule out your local savings bank or credit union and real estate agents. With their experience and expertise, they can be excellent resources and a place to start the shopping process.

www.lendingtree.com
www.countrywide.com
www.bloomberg.com
www.indymacmortgage.com
http://quickenloans.quicken.com

V. SUMMARY

The primary market is mostly made up of local banks, savings banks, and mortgage companies. Funds for the primary market come from savings by local businesses, local deposits, and individual investors. For many years residential lending was dominated by the savings and loans. Banking deregulation had an adverse effect on the S&Ls and permitted other lenders to take over part of their market share. This same deregulation has allowed other institutions, such as credit unions, insurance companies, and pension plans to enter the primary market. Real Estate Investment Trusts allow ordinary individual investors to invest in real estate loans and provide a tax advantage for their investments. Loans by private individuals have always been a part of the primary mortgage loan market. These loans are primarily in the form of second trust mortgages. The Internet has helped to shorten the length of the loan process, reduce consumer expense, and increase industry productivity.

VI. CHAPTER TERMS

Federally Related Transaction	Portfolio Loan
FIRREA	REIT
Money Market Funds	SAIF
Mortgage Banker	Second Mortgage
Mortgage Broker	Servicing
Participation Loan	

VII. CHAPTER 3 QUIZ

1. What percentage of its assets must a REIT have invested in real estate?

    a. 95%
    b. 75%
    c. 50%
    d. 100%

2. The collection of principle and interest payments by one lender on behalf of another is called:

    a. loan seasoning.
    b. loan participation.
    c. loan portfolio.
    d. loan servicing.

3. A federally related transaction is:

    a. any transaction that involves the federal government.
    b. any loan by a bank or savings bank.
    c. any loan by a credit union.
    d. all the above.

4. A mortgage broker:

    a. acts as a loan coordinator.
    b. loans his/her own money.
    c. services loans.
    d. all of the above.

5. The practice of holding a loan for a specified period before it may be sold into the secondary market is called:

    a. loan seasoning.
    b. loan participation.
    c. loan portfolio.
    d. loan servicing.

6. The deposit insurance fund for both banks and savings banks is managed by:

   a. FSLIC.
   b. FNMA.
   c. FDIC.
   d. None of the above.

7. Requiring a percentage of a developer's profit, as well as principle and interest, is known as:

   a. loan seasoning.
   b. loan participation.
   c. loan portfolio.
   d. loan servicing.

8. Money Market funds are:

   a. privately insured.
   b. federally insured.
   c. not insured.
   d. none of the above.

9. Loans that are not sold into the secondary market are called:

   a. seasoned loans.
   b. participation loans.
   c. portfolio loans.
   d. serviced loans.

10. The usage of computers and the Internet:

   a. increases productivity.
   b. saves time.
   c. lowers consumer cost.
   d. all the above.

ANSWERS: 1. b; 2. d; 3. a; 4. a; 5. a; 6. c; 7. b; 8. c; 9. c; 10. d

— PART II —
CHAPTERS 4, 5, AND 6
LENDING RULES

CHAPTER 4 - THE SECONDARY MARKET AND FEDERAL CREDIT AGENCIES

While loans are made directly to borrowers at the local level by savings banks, banks, credit unions, and mortgage bankers from local deposits by individuals and businesses, these sources of funds are often not enough to maintain continued lending, especially during periods of high demand. The establishment of the secondary market has provided these lenders with a stable market in which to sell their mortgages.

CHAPTER 5 - FEDERAL REGULATION AND CONSUMER PROTECTION

The federal government has long taken an active role in assuring that all citizens will be able to enjoy the benefits of property ownership. In addition to support of the capital markets that make real estate loans possible, particular care has been taken to assure that no citizen will be discriminated against on the basis of race, religion, sex, disability, or ethnicity.

CHAPTER 6 - STATE REGULATION OF LENDING

The 10th Amendment to the U.S. Constitution reserves all powers to the states that are not specifically given to the federal government in the Constitution. As a result, the states have regulated by law the form and manner of property ownership, as well as the documentation required for ownership.

CHAPTER 4

SECONDARY MARKET AND FEDERAL CREDIT AGENCIES

In Chapter 2 we discussed the history of some of the major agencies that make up the secondary market, and their interaction with the primary market. In this chapter we will discuss the interaction of the secondary market with the investment community. As we have seen, mortgages that originate in the primary market are sold into the secondary market and the funds received from them by the primary lenders are the source of new mortgage loans to borrowers.

I. The Secondary Market

The participants who make up the secondary mortgage market must themselves raise the necessary funds to purchase the mortgages from the primary lenders.

This is generally accomplished by issuing bonds. *The mortgages that have been purchased by the participants in the secondary market act as collateral for the bonds they issue. These bonds are referred to as MORTGAGE RELATED SECURITIES.* These bonds, or securities, have found a ready market for several reasons. The first is that the mortgage pools that underlie the bonds

Chapter 4

CHAPTER 4 OUTLINE

are broad based. The mortgages that make up a pool are national in scope, rather than regional. Thus, even though one region of the country might be experiencing the sort of economic difficulties that could lead to default, the rest of mortgages in the pool are from regions that are stable. *DEFAULT is the non-payment of the mortgage by the borrower*. The effects of defaults are diluted by the number and mix of mortgages in the pool.

The second reason that the bonds are attractive to investors is the establishment of underwriting guidelines by the agencies that participate in the market. This provides assurance to the investors that the mortgages rest on credit-worthy borrowers and sound collateral from the underlying real estate. The third reason that these bonds are popular is that in most cases they are not double taxed. Also, each offering of bonds is rated for overall credit quality by such agencies as Standard & Poor's and Moody's. Lastly, there is the perception (which may or may not be true) that some of these bonds, such as those offered by FNMA and FHLMC, are protected by the government.

A. PASS-THROUGH SECURITIES

The first popular mortgage-backed security was the pass-through security. These were securities offered by the Government National Mortgage Association or GNMA. GNMA ("Ginnie Mae") is a government agency within the Department of Housing and Urban Development (HUD). *PASS-THROUGH SECURITIES provide the investor with an "undivided interest" in the mortgage pool. In essence, the investor is an owner and will receive the principal and interest on their share of the mortgages plus any prepayments of the mortgage.* These payments are guaranteed by GNMA. Pass-through securities have a relatively high yield when compared to other investments that are considered safe, such as treasury bonds, are liquid, and as they are guaranteed by a government agency, risk-free. A *LIQUID investment may be instantly sold into an established market place*. Stocks and bonds are examples of liquid investments. All of these factors contribute to popularity with investors.

However there is also a downside to pass-through securities. Cash flows are often not predictable due to the propensity of borrowers to prepay their mortgages. This tends to happen when interest rates decline and borrowers refinance to obtain the lower rates. This means

that investors must re-invest the funds obtained from the prepayments at lower rates as well.

In addition to the GNMA pass-through securities, there are also similar programs that are offered by private entities. These programs meet the expectations of investors for safety in two ways. First, the collateral properties are evaluated by a rating service, such as Standard & Poor's or Moody's. Secondly, the issuing entity also receives a rating based on its ability to pay the principal and interest on any defaulted loans. This rating is based on property type and loan-to-value (LTV) ratio as well as whether or not the properties involved are covered by government insurance or private mortgage insurance. **Private mortgage insurance (PMI)** is required on loans that exceed 80% of the value of the property.

Very often, the issuing entity will "over-collateralize" the securities package. For example, the private secondary lender may issue a securities pool with a principal balance of $100 million. However, the pool will contain $110 million worth of mortgages. *The $100 million principal balance would be called a SENIOR PASS-THROUGH. The additional $10 million in mortgages would be called a SUBORDINATE PASS-THROUGH.* Thus, payments on $110 million in mortgages are used to pay off the $100 million in the securities issue. This provides safety from defaults or early payoffs for the investor.

B. MORTGAGE-BACKED SECURITIES

MORTGAGE-BACKED SECURITIES are instruments issued by various agencies, such as GNMA, to raise investment funds. These securities are similar to the familiar corporate bond. They pay interest at intervals until maturity, at which time the face value of the bond is paid to the holder. They differ from the pass-through in that the investor does not have any ownership interest in the mortgages themselves. Generally, the interest amount will be below the interest rates of the underlying mortgages which back the bonds. These bonds also rely on over-collateralization of the mortgages which back them to provide safety to the investors. The mortgages are held by a trustee who will track the interest rates in the market, as well as the interest rates paid on the bonds. When market rates decline to a point where the investment safety of the pool might be endangered, the trustee will require that the issuing entity purchase more mortgages to place into the pool. This process is called marking to market. *MARKING TO MARKET is the process of tracking and comparing mortgage interest rates held in a pool to current market interest rates.*

These bonds are also rated by the ratings agencies. Ratings are based on the quality, quantity, and diversification of the mortgages held in the individual investment pool.

C. COLLATERALIZED MORTGAGE OBLIGATIONS (CMOs)

The *COLLATERALIZED MORTGAGE OBLIGATION allows the creation of multi-class mortgage securities.* These mortgage securities rearrange the cash flows into a series of securities with different maturity dates. *The different classes of securities are called TRANGHES.* An investor can select either a long-term tranch or a short-term tranch with or without pass-through privileges. There are also interest-only and principal-only securities. One class of investors receives payment from principle on the mortgages only and the other class receives payments from the interest on the mortgages only. These complex securities initially ran into the problem of double taxation by the Internal Revenue Service (once at the corporate level and again at the individual investor level). In 1986, Congress addressed this problem and created the Real Estate Mortgage Investment Conduit. A *REAL ESTATE MORTGAGE INVESTMENT CONDUIT (REMIC) is an entity that can issue CMO securities without double taxation.*

A partnership, corporation, or trust may issue collateralized mortgage obligations if it establishes itself as a REMIC.

At this point, it will not be subject to the double taxation rules for CMO related activity. A REMIC is prohibited from receiving any income from any activity that is not a qualified mortgage in the securities pool. It is not allowed to receive fees or other compensation, other than servicing income from its mortgage portfolio, nor is it allowed to buy or sell mortgages outside of the established pool. Proceeds from sales of securities within the pool must be disbursed to investors within 90 days.

II. FNMA and FHLMC

We have noted that the Federal National Mortgage Association (FNMA) and the Federal Home Loan Mortgage Corporation (FHLMC) were originally set up by the federal government to establish a strong secondary market. They are not, however, agencies of the federal government. While they are chartered by Congress, they are private corporations. The government does not guarantee their obligations in any manner. However, the public, both borrowers and investors, have the perception that somehow they are federal agencies. This perception has been bolstered by the fact that Congress has expressed the intention of federal support in the case of a default on the part of either of the agencies. To back up this statement of intent, Congress passed the *FEDERAL HOUSING ENTERPRISE FINANCIAL SAFETY AND SOUNDNESS ACT in 1992. This act set capital guidelines for both FNMA and FHLMC.* The act also established the *OFFICE OF SECONDARY MARKET EXAMINATION AND OVERSIGHT (OSMEO) as an agency within the Department of Housing and Urban Development to monitor the capital requirements of both FNMA and FHLMC.*

> *While "Fannie Mae" and "Freddie Mac" both enjoy unprecedented success at the moment, there is always the chance that poor management, interest rate risk, and loan defaults could place them in the position of the S&Ls in the 1980s.*

In essence, Congress has established the framework for changing regulation of FNMA and FHLMC if it becomes necessary.

III. Federal Credit Agencies

There are a number of federal agencies that provide both primary and secondary market support. Many of these agencies were formed paticularly to support mortgage loans in the agricultural sector of the economy. Typically, conventional lenders are reluctant to loan on farms, as income from agriculture is highly dependent on a number of variables. Among these are: weather, crop yields, and national and world market prices at time of harvest (food is highly perishable and must be immediately

processed). All of those inherently uncertain factors contribute to the lender's concern regarding the borrower's ability to repay the loan.

A. FARM SERVICE AGENCY (FSA)

The mission of the U.S. Department of Agriculture's *FARM SERVICE AGENCY (FSA) is to stabilize farm income, help farmers conserve land and water resources, provide credit to new or disadvantaged farmers and ranchers, and help farm operations recover from the effects of disaster.*

FSA was set up when the Department was reorganized in 1994, incorporating programs from several agencies, including the Agricultural Stabilization and Conservation Service, the Federal Crop Insurance Corporation (now a separate Risk Management Agency), and the Farmers Home Administration. Though FSA's name has changed over the years, the Agency's relationship with farmers goes back to the 1930s.

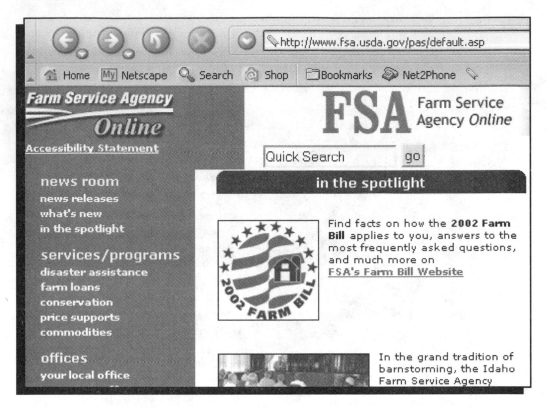

In the 1930s, Congress set up a unique system under which federal farm programs are administered locally. Farmers who are eligible to participate in these programs elect a three-to-five person county committee which reviews county office operations and makes decisions on how to apply the programs. This grassroots approach gives farmers a much-needed say in how federal actions affect their communities and their individual operations. After more than 60 years, it remains a cornerstone of FSA's efforts to preserve and promote American agriculture.

The Farm Service Agency was set up to provide relief and emergency farm financing. The agency requires that a borrower be unable to obtain funds from more traditional lending sources before they will finance or insure a loan. Direct loans may be made at lower-than-market rates to those who qualify.

In general, the agency serves low income family farmers and the elderly, or veterans who are farmers.

B. FARM CREDIT SYSTEM (FCS)

The *FARM CREDIT SYSTEM (FCS) specializes in providing credit and related services to farmers, ranchers, and producers or harvesters of aquatic products.* FCS is a network of borrower-owned lending institutions and related service organizations serving all 50 states and the Commonwealth of Puerto Rico. Loans may also be made to finance the processing and marketing activities of these borrowers. In addition, loans may be made to rural homeowners, certain farm-related businesses, and agricultural, aquatic, and public utility cooperatives.

The Farm Credit Administration (FCA) is responsible for the regulation and examination of all institutions in the Farm Credit System.

All FCS banks and associations are governed by boards of directors elected by the stockholders who are farmer-borrowers of each institution. Additionally, federal law requires that at least one member of the board be elected from outside the FCS by the other directors.

FCS institutions, unlike commercial banks or thrifts, do not take deposits.

On April 1, 2002, the FCS was composed of the following lending institutions:

1. Six Farm Credit Banks (FCBs) that provide loan funds to 6 Production Credit Associations (PCAs), 80 Agricultural Credit Associations (ACAs), and 18 Federal Land Credit Associations (FLCAs). PCAs make short and intermediate-term loans, ACAS make short, intermediate, and long-term loans, and FLCAs make long-term loans.

2. One Agricultural Credit Bank (ACB), which has the authority of an FCB and provides loan funds to four ACAs. In addition, the ACB makes loans of all kinds to agricultural, aquatic, and public utility cooperatives and is authorized to finance U.S. agricultural exports and provide international banking services for farmer-owned cooperatives.

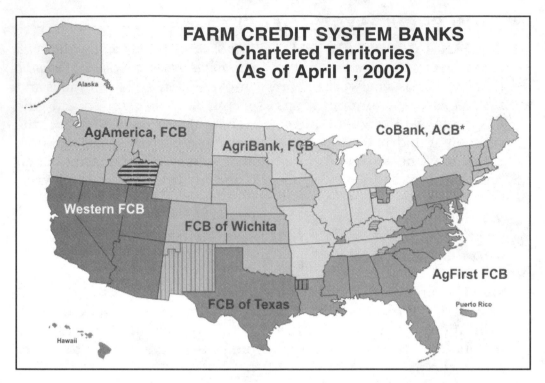

FARM CREDIT SYSTEM BANKS
Chartered Territories
(As of April 1, 2002)

Alaska

AgAmerica, FCB

AgriBank, FCB

CoBank, ACB*

Western FCB

FCB of Wichita

AgFirst FCB

Puerto Rico

FCB of Texas

Hawaii

1. Federal Credit System Financial Assistance Corporation

The **FEDERAL CREDIT SYSTEM FINANCIAL ASSISTANCE CORPORATION** *was created by the Agricultural Credit Act to provide capital to farm credit banks that were in financial difficulty.* Approximately $1.26 billion in funds was provided by the Assistance Corporation before its authority to raise additional funds expired on December 31, 1992. It will continue to operate until all funds used to provide the assistance are repaid.

2. Federal Agricultural Mortgage Corporation (FAMC)

The Federal Agricultural Mortgage Corporation is better known as "Farmer Mac."

The **FEDERAL AGRICULTURAL MORTGAGE CORPORATION (FAMC)** *was also created as a charted corporation by the Agricultural Credit Act. It is similar in concept to the Government National Mortgage Corporation in operation but exists solely to provide a secondary market for farm mortgages.* The agency is part of the Farm Credit System. It examines mortgage pools and provides a guarantee on repayment

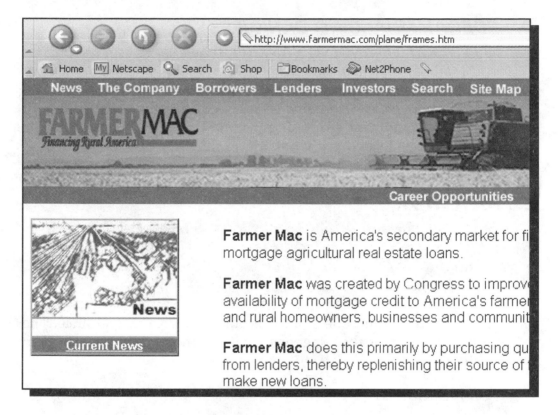

http://www.farmermac.com/plane/frames.htm

Home · My Netscape · Search · Shop · Bookmarks · Net2Phone

News | The Company | Borrowers | Lenders | Investors | Search | Site Map

FARMER MAC
Financing Rural America

Career Opportunities

News
Current News

Farmer Mac is America's secondary market for fi
mortgage agricultural real estate loans.

Farmer Mac was created by Congress to improv
availability of mortgage credit to America's farmer
and rural homeowners, businesses and communit

Farmer Mac does this primarily by purchasing qu
from lenders, thereby replenishing their source of
make new loans.

of principle and interest by the borrowers. The mortgages in the pools are then used as the basis for pass-through securities to be sold to investors. However, there is a basic difference between the guaranties issued by FAMC and GNMA. Farmer Mac will only guarantee up to 90 percent of the principle and interest. However, that guarantee is backed by a direct line of credit with the U.S. Treasury, which has, as yet, never been needed.

C. FINANCING CORPORATION (FICO)

The *FINANCING CORPORATION (FICO) was chartered by the Federal Home Loan Bank Board in 1987 to help resolve the crisis created by the widespread collapse of the savings and loans.* The purpose of the agency was to stabilize and recapitalize the FSLIC (later replaced by SAIF) which had virtually exhausted its funds and was at the point of bankruptcy. FICO was authorized to issue bonds. The proceeds of the bonds were to be used by the FSLIC to resolve the S&L insolvencies. The bonds had no federal guarantee.

D. FEDERAL FINANCING BANK (FFB)

The *FEDERAL FINANCING BANK (FFB) came about as a result of the passage of the Federal Financing Act of 1973. The purpose of this agency was to consolidate the financing activities of a number of different federal agencies in one place.* The bank issues securities for many different agencies. Among them are NASA and the U.S. Postal Service. While most mortgage related activities are excluded, FFB does purchase HUD Section 108 guaranteed loans.

E. FHA AND VA

While it is commonplace for brokers, borrowers, lenders, and investors to refer to "FHA loans" or "VA loans" neither of these government agencies buys or sells mortgage loans.

The FHA and VA are issuers of government mortgage insurance. The activities of both of these agencies will be more fully discussed in Chapter 11.

IV. SUMMARY

Loans are made directly to borrowers by savings banks, banks, credit unions, and mortgage bankers from local deposits by individuals and businesses. However, these sources of funds are often not enough to maintain continued lending, especially during periods of high demand. The establishment of the secondary market has provided these lenders with a stable market in which to sell their mortgages. This secondary market has to raise the necessary funds to provide this essential service to the primary market. This has been accomplished by the establishment of both private firms and government agencies for this purpose.

The firms and agencies have been successful for a number of reasons. The most important of these has been the creation of national mortgage loan underwriting guidelines that assure investors of the quality of the mortgage loans that back the investment pools. The members of the secondary market issue mortgage-related securities and bonds that are attractive to investors because the underlying mortgages are broad based, have sound collateral, and are often free from double taxation unlike other investments such as stocks and bonds. Securities issued by private firms in this market are often covered by private mortgage insurance as well as over-collateralized to enhance their safety as investments. The securities of the secondary market are also rated by third party investment rating services.

FNMA, FHLMC, and GNMA are the major issuers of residential mortgage-related securities. The three major types of securities that are issued are: pass-through securities, mortgage-backed bonds, and collateralized mortgage obligations. The federal government has been an active supporter of this market, either through direct federal agency support or beneficial regulation. In addition, a number of federal agencies have been established to provide mortgage lending for farm and rural areas. The best known of these are the Farm Service Agency (FSA) and the Federal Agricultural Mortgage Corporation (FAMC) or "Farmer Mac." The secondary market has made home ownership a realization for millions of Americans, rather than just a dream.

V. CHAPTER TERMS

Agricultural Credit Act	Marking to Market
Default	Mortgage Related Securities
FAMC	Pass-Through Securities
FICO	Private Mortgage Insurance (PMI)
FCA	REMIC
FSA	Senior Pass-Through
Liquidity	Subordinate Pass-Through

Secondary Market and Federal Credit Agencies

VI. CHAPTER 4 QUIZ

1. An investment is said to be liquid when:

    a. it is guaranteed by the government.
    b. it can be readily sold.
    c. it is worthless.
    d. it is difficult to sell.

2. Mortgage-related securities are:

    a. easily bought and sold.
    b. issued by participants in the secondary market.
    c. have real estate mortgages as their collateral.
    d. all the above.

3. When a borrower prematurely stops making loan payments, the loan is said to be:

    a. paid off.
    b. in arrears.
    c. in suspense.
    d. in default.

4. Standard and Poor's and Moody's are:

    a. primary lenders.
    b. private secondary lenders.
    c. rating services.
    d. mortgage insurance companies.

5. FNMA and FHLMC are:

    a. government agencies.
    b. government chartered private corporations.
    c. primary lenders.
    d. funded by the U.S. Treasury.

6. If $100 million worth of mortgages are used to collateralize $90 million of securities, the additional $10 million is known as a(n):

    a. subordinate pass-through.
    b. senior pass-through.
    c. over-capitalized pass-through.
    d. junior pass-through.

7. Private Mortgage Insurance is required on loans that exceed what percentage of the value of the property?

    a. 60%
    b. 70%
    c. 80%
    d. 90%

8. The process of tracking mortgages in a pool and comparing their rates to current market rates is called:

    a. an investment rating.
    b. pool analysis.
    c. market analysis.
    d. marking to market.

9. A tranch is a(n):

    a. rating.
    b. investment pool.
    c. portion of a multi-class security.
    d. REMIC

10. The Agricultural Credit Act:

    a. provides direct farm loans.
    b. superceded and consolidated previous farm credit legislation.
    c. forbids the sale of farm-based mortgage securities.
    d. was passed to rescue the failing Department of Agriculture.

ANSWERS: 1. b; 2. d; 3. d; 4. c; 5. b; 6. a; 7. c; 8. d; 9. c; 10. b

Secondary Market and Federal Credit Agencies

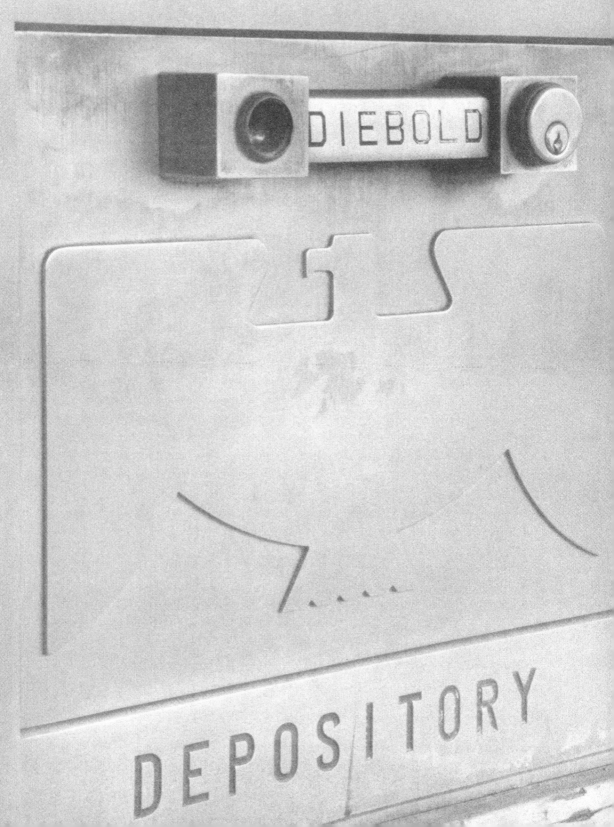

CHAPTER 5

FEDERAL REGULATION AND CONSUMER PROTECTION

The federal government has a long history of legislation that protects property ownership and prohibits discrimination. The U.S. Constitution severely limits the government's ability to take the private property of citizens, except for public use. In addition, the Bill of Rights assures the citizens of the United States extraordinary personal freedom. These freedoms were expanded by the adoption of the 13th, 14th, and 15th Amendments to the Constitution immediately after the Civil War. These amendments not only did away with slavery, but addressed the concept of anti-discrimination as well.

Additionally, during this period, Congress also passed specific anti-discriminatory legislation that addressed ownership of real estate. Since that time, Congress has strengthened that original legislation with additional laws that cover real estate sales, ownership, rental, lending, and appraisal. In addition to laws prohibiting discrimination, there are laws that prohibit abusive sales and loan practices, as well as legislation that addresses disclosure. *DISCLOSURE requires that all pertinent information about a property or a loan be provided to enable a consumer to make informed choices in the lending process.* It is important that professional real

CHAPTER 5 OUTLINE

estate and finance practitioners should be aware of, understand, and comply with all these federal laws.

I. Anti-Discrimination Legislation

A. CIVIL RIGHTS ACT OF 1866

The Civil Rights Act of 1866 was the first piece of legislation passed by Congress after the Civil War that dealt with real estate in particular.

The **CIVIL RIGHTS ACT OF 1866** *provides that "all citizens of the United States shall have the same right, in every state and territory, as is enjoyed by white citizens thereof to inherit, purchase, lease, sell, hold, and convey real and personal property." The act specifically prohibits any discrimination based on race or ancestry.* The law was not really enforced after the latter part of the 19th Century, and it was not challenged in court until 1968. In the historic *Jones v. Mayer* case, the U.S. Supreme Court ruled that the 1866 federal law "prohibits all racial discrimination, private or public, in the sale or rental of property." The court upheld the constitutionality of the law based on the 13th Amendment to the U.S. Constitution which prohibits slavery.

B. FEDERAL FAIR HOUSING ACT

The Federal Fair Housing Act is contained in Title VIII of the Civil Rights Act of 1968.

With this law, congress broadened the protections of the Civil Rights Act of 1866. The **FEDERAL FAIR HOUSING ACT** *makes it illegal to discriminate on the basis of race, color, religion, sex, national origin, or handicap, or against families with children, in the sale or lease of residential property or in the sale or lease of vacant land for the construction of residential buildings.*

Some residential sales and leases are exempt from the provisions of the Fair Housing Act. The sale of a single-family home is exempt if three conditions are met:

1. the owner does not own more than three such homes at one time;

2. there is no real estate broker or agent involved in the transaction; and

3. there is no discriminatory advertising.

This exemption is limited to one transaction in any 24-month period, unless the owner was the most recent occupant of the home.

Religious discrimination is permitted, with respect to rentals, in dwellings owned by religious organizations. Lodging in private clubs is also exempt from the anti-discrimination law if the club is truly private and non-commercial. Discrimination against families with children is permitted by apartment complexes, condominiums, and other developments that qualify as "housing for older persons" under the act. These exemptions were permitted in order to allow the constitutional guarantee of "freedom of association."

Violations of the act include: refusing to sell, rent, or negotiate the terms of a sale or lease for residential property; changing the terms of a sale or lease for different people; discriminating in advertising; making false representations regarding the availability of property; blockbusting; steering; and limiting participation in a multiple listing service (MLS).

BLOCKBUSTING is inducing property owners in a neighborhood to sell by predicting the entrance of minorities into the neighborhood. The person making the prediction buys the property and then resells it for a profit. *STEERING is the channeling of various applicants to specific areas in order to maintain or change the character of those neighborhoods.*

The Fair Housing Act also makes it unlawful to discriminate in lending practices based on a borrower's race, color religion, sex, national origin, or handicap. In addition, it specifically prohibits redlining. *REDLINING is the refusal to make loans on properties in a particular area based on racially discriminatory reasons.*

C. EQUAL CREDIT OPPORTUNITY ACT

The *EQUAL CREDIT OPPORTUNITY ACT is a federal law prohibiting those who lend money from discriminating against borrowers based on their race, sex, color, religion, handicap, national origin, age, or marital status.*

Federal Regulation and Consumer Protection

Enacted in 1974, this Act was a result of hearings by the National Commission on Consumer Finance in 1972 that focused on the denial of credit to women. Married women were often denied credit in their own name, even when they were the principal breadwinner in the family. If they should divorce their husbands, all credit was in the husbands' names and thus the women had no credit history and, by extension, no credit-worthiness. The information gathered in this series of hearings was utilized by both Houses of Congress to develop a bill to protect the rights of women, both married and unmarried, in the lending process. This initial law went into effect in 1974. Congress revisited the bill and expanded it to include additional protections based on age, race, color, religion, and those on welfare. This revised legislation became law in 1976.

The law has several provisions that attempt to remove discrimination from the process and provide regulatory oversight of lenders efforts to be non-discriminatory in the lending process. Lenders are required to notify loan applicants within thirty days of their decision as to whether or not to extend credit. If credit is denied, the lender must state the reasons for the denial in writing to the borrower. Questions regarding sex, marital status, religion, national origin, and welfare status on an application are forbidden. For loan purposes, a married woman has the right to maintain a separate credit history and have it considered separately from her husband's credit, regardless of his creditworthiness.

While the attempt to provide inclusiveness to minority and underrepresented groups in the lending process is laudable, it sometimes flies in the face of simple economics. Minorities are indeed underrepresented in the ability to acquire credit. However, many lenders argue that this is because they do not meet the credit guidelines that have been established to properly qualify borrowers for a loan, and not from some hidden agenda to deny them credit because they are a member of a minority group. The lenders argue, quite reasonably, that the same federal government that requires minority inclusiveness sets many of the lending guidelines that protect both the federal insurance programs and the investors in the marketplace. They further argue that they are in the business of making money. Good loans to creditworthy borrowers, regardless of their minority status, help them to make money. Loans to borrowers

who are not creditworthy are risky and prone to foreclosure, thereby driving the price of credit up for everyone. These arguments are certainly valid and have been considered in the oversight of the law by the Federal Reserve Board.

The Federal Reserve Board oversees compliance with the Equal Credit Opportunity Act.

The Federal Reserve Board issued Regulation B to provide guidelines for lenders in this sensitive area. *REGULATION B notes that it is illegal to discriminate by "intent," by "practice," or by "effect."* It is often virtually impossible to prove discrimination by intent without clear written or taped evidence. However, the board's guidelines focus on practices through the implementation of guidelines that force the lenders to treat each application in a uniform manner. The board also addresses effects through periodic reviews of a lender's records in an attempt to uncover evidence of loan redlining.

D. HOME MORTGAGE DISCLOSURE ACT

The *HOME MORTGAGE DISCLOSURE ACT (1975) was specifically passed by Congress to deal with the problem of redlining.* As previously noted, redlining is the practice by lenders of refusing to make loans in certain neighborhoods based on neighborhood decline that is attributed to racial composition or a perception of higher crime rates. The lenders often justified "redline areas" by incorrectly analyzing both census data and the contents of appraisal reports in their possession. This improper application of data was then used to deny loans to borrowers who lived in those areas.

The new law would use the very same data collection by the Bureau of the Census, and the information that it contains, to correct lending inequity. The law requires any lender with assets of $10 million or more to make a report of all of its loans both within and outside of the Standard Metropolitan Statistical Area in which it has either a main office or a branch office. A *STANDARD METROPOLITAN STATISTICAL AREA (SMSA) is a city and its suburbs having a population of 50,000 persons or more.* The distribution of loans must be indicated by the census tracts in which they were made. A *CENSUS TRACT is the smallest demographic area used by the Bureau of the Census. It consists of areas of approximately 4,000 persons in neighborhoods of similar economic conditions.* The law requires use of current census data. This means that the SMSAs and census tracts must be drawn from the 2000 census. State chartered lenders are exempt only if their state has similar requirements. In other words, they are not really exempt.

It is easy for the regulators to determine if a lender is not making loans in any nearby census tract area and to initiate inquiries to determine why they are not.

E. COMMUNITY REINVESTMENT ACT

The *COMMUNITY REINVESTMENT ACT (1978) was passed to make all federally regulated institutions responsive to the needs of their communities by requiring them to publicize how well they were serving their local communities.* To properly comply with the act, the institutions must define the area from which it accepts deposits and to which it makes loans. It must provide the public with information about all the types of loans and accounts available. The institution must post a notice in all its places of business that notifies the public who it is regulated by and that the public is invited to comment on its practices at any appropriate hearing. Finally, it must make periodic reports to its regulators about its efforts to make credit available to the community that it serves. This report is called a community support statement. A *COMMUNITY SUPPORT STATEMENT is a report to federally regulated institutions regulators that details exactly how well the institution serves its community.* Based on the community support statement, as well as input from the community itself, the regulators may or may not permit the further expansion of a particular lending institution.

F. FINANCIAL INSTITUTIONS REFORM, RECOVERY AND ENFORCEMENT ACT (FIRREA)

The *FINANCIAL INSTITUTIONS REFORM, RECOVERY AND ENFORCEMENT ACT (FIRREA) of 1989 was a response to the failure of the savings and loan industry in the 1980s. It revised the regulation of thrift organizations and created several new agencies, such as the Office of Thrift Supervision (OTS) and the Resoluton Trust Corporation (RTC).* It would make sweeping changes in the operations of all individuals and institutions involved in federally related lending transactions.

FIRREA defines a federally related transaction as any transaction that involves the use of federal monies or access to federal monies.

The Act includes all mortgage lenders, including the primary and secondary market, that are not affiliated with depository institutions, as well as mortgage brokers and appraisers. FIRREA requires mortgage and home improvement lenders to report the sex, race, and income levels of loan applicants. In particular, the law requires that all data on rejected applications submitted by mortgage loan brokers be filed with the regulators.

The purpose of the FIRREA regulations is to insure that redlining and other discriminatory acts do not occur at any level in the lending process.

Under the Act, lenders are evaluated publicly on how well they meet a community's lending needs. The evaluations consist of "outstanding," "satisfactory," "in need of improvement," or "in non-compliance." Any rating of "less-than-satisfactory" will require immediate remedy on the part of the lender to maintain access to the federal credit market. The Act also requires that regulators keep secret the names of any persons who lodge complaints of possible discrimination with an institution's regulators.

FIRREA requires the licensing of appraisers by all fifty states and sets up the *APPRAISAL SUB-COMMITTEE as a federal agency to monitor the actions of lenders, state regulators, the Appraisal Foundation, and other federal regulatory agencies*. The agency has representatives from all federal financial regulatory agencies on its board. The agency is concerned with: safe-guarding the financial security of financial institutions, uniformity of regulations among its member regulatory agencies, and anti-discriminatory practices and competency in the appraisal process.

FIRREA applies to everyone associated with a federally related transaction.

The Federal Reserve Board is charged with implementing regulations as needed for lenders. FIRREA carries both civil and criminal penalties for violations of the Act.

G. REAL ESTATE SETTLEMENT PROCEDURES ACT (RESPA)

*The **REAL ESTATE SETTLEMENT PROCEDURES ACT (RESPA)** of 1974 was passed to protect consumers from abusive practices by lenders.*

Consumers had long complained about the various fees and commissions paid in the loan process. A home purchase can be an unsettling experience. For many consumers, it is one of the most confusing transactions that they will undertake in a lifetime. The settlement charges on a loan seem endless. Among the charges are: fees for a credit report, appraisal, termite inspection, title search and insurance, escrow, recording and transfer fees, taxes, pre-paid interest, and various lender fees (also known as "garbage fees"). How is a consumer to know if the fees are valid and customary or if he or she is being overcharged? How can a consumer shop intelligently for the best deal?

Congress asked themselves the same questions. In addition, Congress was concerned that the potential existed for lenders to provide kickbacks to real estate agents who steered clients towards them. The potential for this sort of activity existed throughout the process. For example, lenders might receive kickbacks from appraisers, escrow companies, and title companies for using their services. The kickbacks could then be concealed as charges for services in the settlement statements provided by the lenders to the borrowers.

RESPA dealt with these problems by requiring all lenders to provide three disclosure statements to the borrower:

1. A HUD booklet that explains the loan settlement process and outlines standard procedures.

2. A **Good Faith Estimate** of all settlement charges.

3. A **Uniform Settlement Statement** prior to close of escrow.

The HUD booklet not only explains the loan process and the standard procedures and documentation required, but also provides the borrower with information about the various remedies that he or she

may seek if RESPA has been violated. A *GOOD FAITH ESTIMATE is provided to the borrower at the beginning of the loan process. This document lists estimates of the charges that the borrower will have to pay and whether or not any special relationship exists between any of the parties to the transaction.* (**See Figure 5-1.**) Charges listed must be for actual services provided and must be based on actual current market costs. The *UNIFORM SETTLEMENT STATEMENT must be provided to the borrower before the settlement. This document provides a complete statement of all charges and may contain no estimates.* The lender must keep a copy on file for at least two years after the settlement. The lender is not allowed to charge any fee for completing the forms.

RESPA forbids kickbacks or the use of required title companies, and limits the amount of funds required to be deposited to escrow accounts.

No more than 1/12 of annual taxes or insurance may be required to be deposited in escrow. Additionally, the lender is required to tell the borrower if the lender intends to sell the mortgage, what percentage of its loans were sold in the preceding year, and how many it plans to sell in the next year. RESPA provides for both civil and criminal penalties for violations of the Act. A borrower may obtain up to three times the actual damages incurred, as well as attorney and court costs.

The advent of the Internet has actually been a boon to consumers as major primary lenders have rushed to advertise their rates and charges almost on an hourly basis.

This permits consumers to shop rates and fees between the various lenders. It has also serves to make borrowers more familiar with the entire process. Many traditional loan brokers at first believed Internet advertising might have a detrimental effect on their business. Research has shown, however, that there is enough business to go around and that consumers like a familiar person that they can interact with to handle their loans. Informed consumers have lightened the workload of many brokers by familiarizing themselves with the process, fees, and necessary required documentation that they must provide before they arrive at their local loan broker's office to begin the process.

Figure 5-1

MORTGAGE LOAN DISCLOSURE STATEMENT/GOOD FAITH ESTIMATE   Date Prepared:

Borrower's Name(s): _____

Real Property Collateral: the intended security for this proposed loan will be a Deed of Trust on (street address or legal description)

This joint Mortgage Loan Disclosure Statement/Good Faith Estimate is being provided by __UNITED CALIFORNIA FINANCIAL__ a real estate broker acting as a mortgage broker, pursuant to the Federal Real Estate Settlement Procedures Act (RESPA) and similar California law. In a transaction subject to RESPA, a lender will provide you with an additional Good Faith Estimate within three business days of the receipt of your loan application. You will also be informed of material changes before settlement/close of escrow. The name of the intended lender to whom your loan application will be delivered is:

☑ Unknown   ☐ _____ (Name of lender, if known)

GOOD FAITH ESTIMATE OF CLOSING COSTS

The information provided below reflects estimates of the charges you are likely to incur at the settlement of your loan. The fees, commissions, costs and expenses listed are estimates; the actual charges may be more or less. Your transaction may not involve a charge for every item listed and any additional items charged will be listed. The numbers listed beside the estimate generally correspond to the numbered lines contained in the HUD-1 Settlement Statement which you will receive at settlement if this transaction is subject to RESPA. The HUD-1 Settlement Statement contains the actual costs for the items paid at settlement. When this transaction is subject to RESPA, by signing page two of this form you are also acknowledging receipt of the HUD Guide to Settlement Costs.

HUD-1	Item	Paid to Others	Paid to Broker
800	**Items Payable in Connection with Loan**		
801	Lender's Loan Origination Fee	$ _____	$ _____
802	Lender's Loan Discount Fee	$ _____	$ _____
803	Appraisal Fee	$ _____	$ _____
804	Credit Report	$ _____	$ _____
805	Lender's Inspection Fee	$ _____	$ _____
808	Mtg Broker Commission/Fee	$ _____	$ _____
809	Tax Service Fee	$ _____	$ _____
810	Processing Fee	$ _____	$ _____
811	Underwriting Fee	$ _____	$ _____
812	Wire Transfer Fee	$ _____	$ _____
____	_____	$ _____	$ _____
____	_____	$ _____	$ _____
____	_____	$ _____	$ _____
		$ _____	$ _____
900	**Items Required by Lender to be Paid in Advance**		
901	Interest for ____ days at $ _____ per day	$ _____	$ _____
902	Mortgage Insurance Premiums	$ _____	$ _____
903	Hazard Insurance Premiums	$ _____	$ _____
904	County Property Taxes	$ _____	$ _____
905	VA Funding Fee	$ _____	$ _____
		$ _____	$ _____
1000	**Reserves Deposited with Lender**		
1001	Hazard Insurance: ____ months at $ _____ /mo.	$ _____	$ _____
1002	Mortgage Insurance: ____ months at $ _____ /mo.	$ _____	$ _____
1004	Co. Property Taxes: ____ months at $ _____ /mo.	$ _____	$ _____
		$ _____	$ _____
1100	**Title Charges**		
1101	Settlement or Closing/Escrow Fee:	$ _____	$ _____
1105	Document Preparation Fee	$ _____	$ _____
1106	Notary Fee	$ _____	$ _____
1108	Title Insurance:	$ _____	$ _____
		$ _____	$ _____
		$ _____	$ _____
1200	**Government Recording and Transfer Charges**		
1201	Recording Fees:	$ _____	$ _____
1202	City/County Tax/Stamps:	$ _____	$ _____
		$ _____	$ _____
1300	**Additional Settlement Charges**		
1302	Pest Inspection	$ _____	$ _____
____	_____	$ _____	$ _____
____	_____	$ _____	$ _____
		$ _____	$ _____

Subtotal of Initial Fees, Commissions, Costs and Expenses $ _____ $ _____

Total of Initial Fees, Commissions, Costs and Expenses $ _____
Compensation to Broker (Not Paid Out of Loan Proceeds):
Mortgage Broker Commission/Fee: $ _____
Any Additional Compensation from Lender   ☑ No ☐ Yes $ _____ (If known)

RESPA protects consumers from predatory lending practices.

H. CONSUMER CREDIT PROTECTION ACT (TRUTH IN LENDING ACT)

The Consumer Credit Protection Act of 1968 is also called the Truth in Lending Act.

It contains several important provisions that are administered by the Federal Reserve. The Federal Reserve Board of Governors issued Regulation Z to implement the Act. *REGULATION Z requires that the lender provide the consumer with the total of all finance charges and the Annual Percentage Rate (APR) of the loan.* (**See Figure 5-2.**) This disclosure must be in writing and be more prominent than other items in the disclosure. This disclosure must be made to the borrower, in writing, within three business days from the time the lender receives the application.

FINANCE CHARGES include interest charges, discount points, appraisal fees, inspection fees, origination fees, and any credit life or mortgage insurance fees. The *ANNUAL PERCENTAGE RATE (APR) is the effective yield on the loan.* It will be higher than the quoted loan rate if up front charges, such as origination fees and discount points, are included.

Another important borrower right provided by Regulation Z is the *RIGHT OF RESCISSION (RIGHT TO CANCEL), which means that a borrower may cancel any agreement entered into within three business days after the close of the transaction.* (**See Figure 5-3.**) A lender is required to inform the consumer of the right to rescind by providing a notice of rescission. This must be in writing and separate from any other sale or credit document. The rescission document must describe the acquisition of the security interest, how the right of rescission is to be exercised, the effects of the rescission, and the date the right of rescission expires. This allows a borrower to back out of any transaction into which they have either been pressured or have "buyer's remorse" over. The borrower may not waive his or her right of rescission. The right of rescission does not apply to the purchase of any property other than their principal residence.

Figure 5-2

FEDERAL TRUTH-IN-LENDING DISCLOSURE STATEMENT
(THIS IS NEITHER A CONTRACT NOR A COMMITMENT TO LEND)

Applicants: Prepared By:

Property Address:

Application No: Date Prepared:
Check box if applicable:

ANNUAL PERCENTAGE RATE The cost of your credit as a yearly rate	FINANCE CHARGE The dollar amount the credit will cost you	Amount Financed The amount of credit provided to you or on your behalf	Total of Payments The amount you will have paid after making all payments as scheduled
%	$	$	$

☐ REQUIRED DEPOSIT: The annual percentage rate does not take into account your required deposit
PAYMENTS: Your payment schedule will be:

Number of Payments	Amount of Payments **	When Payments Are Due	Number of Payments	Amount of Payments **	When Payments Are Due	Number of Payments	Amount of Payments **	When Payments Are Due
		Monthly Beginning:			Monthly Beginning:			Monthly Beginning:

☐ DEMAND FEATURE: This obligation has a demand feature.
☐ VARIABLE RATE FEATURE: This loan contains a variable rate feature. A variable rate disclosure has been provided earlier.

INSURANCE: The following insurance is required to obtain credit:
☐ Credit life insurance and credit disability   ☐ Property insurance   ☐ Flood insurance
You may obtain the insurance from anyone you want that is acceptable to creditor
☐ If you purchase   ☐ property   ☐ flood insurance from creditor you will pay $ for a one year term.
SECURITY: You are giving a security interest in:
☐ The goods or property being purchased   ☐ Real property you already own.
FILING FEES: $
LATE CHARGE: If a payment is more than   days late, you will be charged   % of the payment.
PREPAYMENT: If you pay off early, you
☐ may   ☐ will not   have to pay a penalty.
☐ may   ☐ will not   be entitled to a refund of part of the finance charge.
ASSUMPTION: Someone buying your property
☐ may   ☐ may, subject to conditions   ☐ may not   assume the remainder of your loan on the original terms.
See your contract documents for any additional information about nonpayment, default, any required repayment in full before the scheduled date and prepayment refunds and penalties
☐ * means an estimate   ☐ all dates and numerical disclosures except the late payment disclosures are estimates.

THE UNDERSIGNED ACKNOWLEDGE RECEIVING A COMPLETED COPY OF THIS DISCLOSURE.

_____   _____
(Applicant)   (Date)   (Applicant)   (Date)

_____   _____
(Applicant)   (Date)   (Applicant)   (Date)

_____
(Lender)   (Date)

* * NOTE PAYMENTS SHOWN ABOVE DO INCLUDE RESERVE DEPOSITS FOR MORTGAGE INSURANCE (IF APPLICABLE) BUT NOT PROPERTY TAXES OR INSURANCE.

Figure 5-3   **NOTICE OF RIGHT TO CANCEL**

Name(s) of Customer(s) _____

Type of Loan _____

Amount of Loan _____ $ _____

You have entered into a transaction which will result in a deed of trust or mortgage on your home. You have a legal right under federal law to cancel this transaction, without cost, within three business days from whichever of the following occurs last:

1. the date of the transaction, which is _____ : or

2. the date you received your Truth in Lending disclosures: or

3. the date you received this notice of your right to cancel.

If you cancel the transaction, the deed of trust or mortgage is also cancelled. Within 20 calendar days after we receive your notice, we must take the steps necessary to reflect the fact that the deed of trust or mortgage on your home has been cancelled, and we must return to you any money or property you have given to us or to anyone else in connection with this transaction.

You may keep any money or property we have given you until we have done the things mentioned above, but you must then offer to return the money or property. If it is impractical or unfair for you to return the property, you must offer its reasonable value. You may offer to return the property at your home or at the location of the property. Money must be returned to the address below. If we do not take possession of the money or property within 20 calendar days of your offer, you may keep it without further obligation.

ACKNOWLEDGEMENT OF RECEIPT

I hereby acknowledge receipt of TWO copies of the foregoing Notice of Right to Cancel.

_____ ,20_____   _____
       (Date)   (Customer's Signature)

                                       _____
                                      (All joint owners must sign)

HOW TO CANCEL

If you decide to cancel this transaction, you may do so by notifying us in writing. at the following address:

_____
(Creditor's Name)

_____
(Address)

_____
(City, State. Zip Code)

You may use any written statement that is signed and dated by you and states your intention to cancel, or you may use this notice by dating and signing below. Keep one copy of this notice because it contains important information about your rights.

If you cancel by mail or telegram, you must send the notice no later than midnight of _____ _____ (or midnight of the third business day following
                  (date)
the latest of the three events listed above). If you send your written notice to cancel some other way, it must be delivered to the above address no later than that time.

_____ ,20_____   _____
       (Date)   (Customer's Signature)

Business or corporate entities do not qualify for the right of rescission.

Regulation Z also contains provisions that apply to advertising. Prior to passage of the Act, an advertiser might have disclosed only the most attractive credit terms, thus distorting the true costs of the financing.

Regulation Z requires that advertisers disclose all the terms of the financing if the ad contains any information about a single financing term.

These terms include, but are not limited to, the cash price, interest rate, or payment amounts. *These are known as* **TRIGGERS**. If any trigger is used, the advertiser must disclose all the terms of the financing. Such information is not allowed to be contained in a "fine print" section of the advertisement. (See **Figures 5-4** and **5-5**.)

Anyone who places an advertisement for consumer credit must comply with the provisions of the Act; this includes lenders, real estate agents, and builders.

Figure 5-4

WRONG

Now Get A Home Equity Loan With No Application Fee, No Appraisal Fee And No Points.

BUT ONLY UNTIL

If you own a house, a condo, or a co-op,   can save you a lot of money on a Home Equity Loan.

There's no application fee. Saving you up to $200.

There's no appraisal cost. Saving you up to $250.

And there are no points at closing for an additional savings.

Also, your Home Equity Loan or Home Equity Line of Credit can be used for almost any purpose and your interest payments may be 100% tax-deductible. (Consult your tax advisor.)

To apply for a loan or to find out how much you can borrow, visit any of our   branches. Or call at   But do it soon. Offer ends

All loans are secured by a mortgage on your home and are subject to credit approval
Available through   Applications must be received by

Triggering Terms

Required Disclosures Needed

Figure 5-5

OUR VALUE IS DOUBLED IN STAFFORD COUNTY

The Bunker Hill – 3 bedroom split level with expandable lower level.

Two exceptional Virginia communities with large wooded lots.

Hickory Ridge Priced from $46,200. Large wooded lots close to major shopping, schools and commuter transportation. And you'll love the low taxes. The Bunker Hill 3 bedroom pictured above—from $49,800. Directions:

Patriot's Landing Priced from $50,600. Our new community of 3, 4 and 5 bedroom quality homes, tucked away in the woods, just off I-95. The Bunker Hill 3 bedroom pictured above.—from $54,400. Directions:

Proper disclosure

Typical financing: The Bunker Hill – (Hickory Ridge) – cash price $49,800, $2,500 down payment (5%) at 9-7/8% interest (10½ annual percentage rate). Mortgage $47,300 to be paid in 360 equal and consecutive monthly installments of $411 plus taxes and insurance.

We pay all closing costs except prepaid items and loan origination fees.

Triggering term

VA Financing and 5% down* Conventional Financing 9-7/8% Interest (10-1/2% Annual Percentage Rate)

Proper disclosure of the rate of finance charge

...talk to in Stafford

II. SUMMARY

The federal government has long taken an active role in assuring that all citizens will be able to enjoy the benefits of property ownership. In addition to support of the capital markets that make real estate loans possible, particular care has been taken to assure that no citizen will be discriminated against on the basis of race, religion, sex, disability, or ethnicity. In addition, the government has sought to curb both abusive and predatory sales and lending practices. The government has required full disclosure throughout the lending process, both to protect consumers and to allow them to be well informed. This legislation has also benefited lenders, as it has rooted out anti-competitive lending practices.

III. CHAPTER TERMS

APR	Finance Charges
Blockbusting	FIRREA
Census Tracts	Good Faith Estimate
Civil Rights Act of 1866	Home Mortgage Disclosure Act
Civil Rights Act of 1968	Redlining
Consumer Credit Protection Act	Regulation Z
Community Reinvestment Act	RESPA
Community Support Statement	Right of Rescission
Disclosure	Steering
Equal Credit Opportunity Act	Triggers
Federal Fair Housing Act	Uniform Settlement Statement

IV. CHAPTER 5 QUIZ

1. RESPA is the:

    a. Real Estate Security and Procedures Act.
    b. Real Estate Safety and Practices Act.
    c. Real Estate Settlement and Practices Act.
    d. Real Estate Settlement Procedures Act.

2. The Civil Rights Act of 1866:

    a. requires disclosure.
    b. prevents discrimination in real property ownership.
    c. requires lenders to publish information on loans to minority borrowers.
    d. does not apply to modern lending.

3. Redlining is:

    a. refusal to loan in certain neighborhoods.
    b. marking boundaries of census tracts.
    c. not lending to bad credit consumers.
    d. not lending on insufficient collateral.

4. The Federal Fair Housing Act prohibits acts based on:

    a. blockbusting.
    b. steering.
    c. redlining.
    d. all the above.

5. The Consumer Protection Act:

    a. contains the truth in lending laws.
    b. defines abusive practices.
    c. requires a good faith estimate.
    d. none of the above.

6. FIRREA applies to:

    a. appraisers only.
    b. lenders only.
    c. everyone involved in a federally related transaction.
    d. regulators only.

7. A Community Support Statement is provided by:

   a. lenders to their local news media.
   b. lenders to the borrower.
   c. lenders to their regulators.
   d. community leaders to the lender.

8. A good faith estimate is:

   a. provided at the end of the loan process.
   b. provided at the beginning of the loan process.
   c. an estimate of the annual percentage rate only.
   d. an estimate of the time it will take to complete the loan.

9. It is illegal to discriminate:

   a. by intent.
   b. by effect.
   c. by practice.
   d. all the above.

10. Regulation Z:

    a. prohibits redlining.
    b. prohibits racial discrimination.
    c. allows a married woman to maintain separate credit.
    d. is overseen by the Federal Reserve Board.

ANSWERS: *1. d; 2. b; 3. a; 4. d; 5. a; 6. c; 7. c; 8. b; 9. d; 10. d*

CHAPTER 6

STATE REGULATION OF LENDING

This chapter will examine the role played by state governments in the lending process.

The 10th Amendment to the U.S. Constitution reserved all powers not specifically enumerated (listed) in the Constitution to the states. A read of the Constitution would make apparent to the reader that the states seemed to retain more powers than they gave up.

The U.S. Constitution and the first ten amendments do not specifically address the issues of banking, finance, real estate law, or consumer legislation. In the beginning, Congress was content with the power to coin money and provide a uniform money system through the establishment of the Bank of the United States. As we saw in the last chapter, federal interest in discrimination, consumer rights, and lending did not really begin until after the Civil War. Even then the amount of federal involvement was minor until the era of the great depression and later. It was left up to the states to develop laws that would protect consumers from usury, develop mortgage and real estate laws, and charter local banking institutions.

CHAPTER 6 OUTLINE

I. Real Estate Laws

The United States was initially made up of a group of former English colonies that had become states within the constitutional union. It is therefore not surprising that they would, for the most part, adopt the British common law systems of legal Real Property and Real Estate ownership. **REAL ESTATE** *is the ownership of the physical land itself.* **REAL PROPERTY** *consists of those rights that come with the ownership of the real estate.* Very often, real property rights are more valuable than the physical property itself. Real property rights are often stated as:

1. The right to possess.
2. The right to use.
3. The right to borrow money against.
4. The right to rent to others.
5. The right to dispose of (by, sale, will, or transfer).
6. The right to quiet enjoyment.
7. The right to exclude others.
8. The right to do nothing at all.

These real property rights are often referred to as the **BUNDLE OF RIGHTS**. *An individual in control of all those rights is said to own the property in* **FEE SIMPLE**. These rights are limited by the power of eminent domain under the Constitution and by zoning laws in most jurisdictions. As our pioneering ancestors spread outward into the territories, they brought this imminently sensible system of ownership with them. This is the system of land and real property ownership throughout the United States, with only minor variations from state to state

A. ESTATES

An **ESTATE** *is a possessory interest in real estate or real property.*

Fee Simple is the highest form of possessory interest.

There are several estates that have less than the full possessory rights. The most important of these is the **LEASED FEE ESTATE**, *which is the interest held by a landlord.* In essence, a landlord has given up his right of possession to the property to a tenant for a specified period. Both the right to the rents and the right to the **REVERSION** *(return of the*

property) at the end of the lease may be sold or lent upon. Additionally, *the tenant's possessory interest, called the LEASEHOLD ESTATE*, may also have loan or sale value, particularly if the tenant's rents are below market. This could easily happen in the case of a long-term lease. While the various states and territories of the United States recognize a number of other forms of ownership estates, they are, for the most part, beyond the scope of this book.

B. DEEDS

TITLE is a term that signifies the proof of ownership. The title to a property is based on the legal chain of documents that show ownership interests and transfers from owner to owner. *Title to real estate and real property is transferred from one person to another by use of a legal document called a DEED. The owner who is making the transfer is called the GRANTOR. The person receiving title is called the GRANTEE.* A deed must be in writing in all jurisdictions and must meet all requirements of the state in which the property is located.

Originally, title was researched and individual deeds were drawn up by attorneys. Over time, and with the advent of title insurance, this practice has been reduced somewhat. *TITLE INSURANCE is insurance written by a title company to protect the property owner against loss if the title is imperfect.* Individual deeds, however, are still widely used today in the east and the south. The acceptance of pre-printed legal form deeds by many states has also served to reduce the need for the services of attorneys.

The advantage of title insurance is that it also protects against hidden or unknown claims against title.

The use of title insurance is required for any loan that is sold into the secondary market. Title companies are supervised by agencies of the states in which they operate.

1. General Warranty Deeds

In most states, general warranty deeds are the most commonly used deeds in real estate transactions.

A *GENERAL WARRANTY DEED offers the most complete warranty regarding the quality of the title. The grantor warrants that the title he or she is conveying is free and clear of all claims except those specifically listed in the deed.* Specifically, the deed will guarantee free and clear legal title to the property, that the grantor has the right to convey the property, and that the grantor will compensate the grantee for loss of property or eviction if it is discovered that someone else has any claim to the property.

A general warranty deed covers all transfers of the property from the original source of title to the present.

2. Special Warranty Deeds

A *SPECIAL WARRANTY DEED makes the same warranties as a general warranty deed except it limits the application of defects to the title to those discovered while under ownership of the grantor.* It does not apply to title problems caused by owners previous to the current grantor.

3. Grant Deeds

The grant deed is very popular in the western states.

A *GRANT DEED transfers absolute legal title to a property.* It is sometimes called a "naked title deed." (**See Figure 6-1**.) A grant deed carries only two *implied* warranties: 1) that the grantor has not transferred title to anyone else at the same time, and 2) that the grantor is transferring the estate free of any encumbrances made by the grantor other than those disclosed to the grantee. The interesting thing about this form of transfer is that the deed does not state that the grantor is the owner of the property or that the property is not encumbered by debt or liens not made by the grantor. It merely implies that the grantor has not made a deed to others and that the grantor has not encumbered the property with debt or liens. As a result, it is absolutely necessary to obtain a policy of title insurance at the time of any transfer. However, the beneficial result is that the title insurance company carries the full legal liability for any title claims against the property rather than the grantor, grantee, or previous owners.

Figure 6-1

RECORDING REQUESTED BY

320

827367

WHEN RECORDED MAIL TO

NAME Philip S. Dockter
Street Address 1212 Lincoln Avenue
City & State Pomona, California 91767

#61638

MAIL TAX STATEMENTS TO

NAME SAME AS SHOWN ABOVE:
Street Address
City & State

RECORDED IN OFFICIAL RECORDS
OF LOS ANGELES COUNTY, CALIF.
FOR TITLE INSURANCE & TRUST CO
MAY 19 1971 AT 8 A.M.
Registrar-Recorder

FEE $2 C

SPACE ABOVE THIS LINE FOR RECORDER'S USE

DOCUMENTARY TRANSFER TAX $33.00
Computed on full value of property conveyed
Or computed on full value less liens and encumbrances remaining at time of sale.
WILSHIRE ESCROW COMPANY
Signature of Declarant or Agent determining tax. Firm name

Grant Deed

FOR A VALUABLE CONSIDERATION, receipt of which is hereby acknowledged,

HENRY W. SPLITTER, a widower, who acquired title as HENRY SPLITTER, does hereby

GRANT to   Philip S. Dockter , a single man,

the real property in the   City of Los Angeles   County of   Los Angeles
State of California, described as:

Lot 22 in Block 21 of Short Line Beach Subdivision No. 2, as per map recorded in
Book 4 Page 42 of Maps, in the office of the County Recorder of said County.

RESERVING UNTO THE GRANTOR 50% of all oil, minerals, coals, petroleum, gas and
kindred substances in and under said land, from a depth below 500 feet from the
surface of said land, but without the right of entry of the surface thereof.

SUBJECT TO:
1. General and Special Taxes for the fiscal year 1971-72.
2. Covenants, conditions, restrictions, reservations, easements, rights and rights
    of way of record, if any.
3. Trust Deed to file concurrently herewith.

Dated   April 15, 1971

Henry W. Splitter
Henry W. Splitter

STATE OF CALIFORNIA
COUNTY OF Los Angeles }SS.
On   May 4, 1971   before me, the undersigned, a Notary Public in and for said State, personally appeared
Henry W. Splitter

, known to me
to be the person whose name is subscribed to the within
instrument and acknowledged that he executed the same.
WITNESS my hand and official seal.

Signature Donald R. Shewfelt
Name (Typed or Printed)

OFFICIAL SEAL
DONALD R. SHEWFELT
NOTARY PUBLIC — CALIFORNIA
PRINCIPAL OFFICE IN
LOS ANGELES COUNTY
My Commission Expires Aug. 17, 1971

(This area for official notarial seal)

320

MAIL TAX STATEMENTS AS DIRECTED ABOVE

4. Quitclaim Deed

The **QUITCLAIM DEED** *is most often used to remove items from the public record, such as easements or recorded restrictions.* It merely says that the grantor is relinquishing any interest that he or she has in the property. (**See Figure 6-2.**)

A quitclaim deed contains no warranties, written or implied.

5. Gift Deed

A **GIFT DEED** *is often used to transfer real estate to children or other loved ones.* Generally, no monetary legal consideration is required to transfer the property.

A gift deed can be invalidated if it is discovered that it was used to defraud creditors.

6. Sheriff's Deed/Commissioner's Deed

A **SHERIFF'S DEED** *is used to transfer property that has been ordered to be sold by a court of law.* This can happen as a result of a monetary judgment against the owner. The property is then sold by the court to satisfy the judgment. In some states this is known as a commissioner's sale and a commissioner's deed.

A sheriff's deed or commissioner's deed carries no warranties.

7. Tax Deed

A **TAX DEED** *is issued by a tax collector after the sale of property that has been seized by the state, county, or local municipality for non-payment of taxes due.* Again no warranty of the deed is expressed or implied.

8. Deed of Trust/Deed of Reconveyance

These deeds are types of financing instruments and will be discussed in the Chapter 7.

All states have laws that require legal delivery of a deed from the grantor to the grantee.

Figure 6-2

RECORDING REQUESTED BY

AND WHEN RECORDED MAIL THIS DEED AND, UNLESS OTHER-
WISE SHOWN BELOW, MAIL TAX STATEMENTS TO:

NAME
ADDRESS
CITY &
STATE
ZIP

Title Order No.   Escrow No.

SPACE ABOVE THIS LINE FOR RECORDER'S USE

Quitclaim Deed

The undersigned declares that the documentary transfer tax is $ .... and is
☐ computed on the full value of the interest or property conveyed, or is
☐ computed on the full value less the value of liens or encumbrances remaining thereon at the time of sale. The land, tenements or realty is located in
☐ unincorporated area   ☐ city of ....

FOR A VALUABLE CONSIDERATION, receipt of which is hereby acknowledged,

do   . hereby remise, release and forever quitclaim to

the following described real property in the   county of
state of California:

Dated ....

STATE OF CALIFORNIA
                      } SS
COUNTY OF ....
On this the .... day of .... 19 ......, before me,
the undersigned, a Notary Public in and for said County and State,
personally appeared ....
....
....
...., personally known to me
or proved to me on the basis of satisfactory evidence to be the
person.......... whose name.......... subscribed to the within instrument
and acknowledged that .... executed the same.

....
Signature of Notary

FOR NOTARY SEAL OR STAMP

MAIL TAX STATEMENTS TO PARTY SHOWN ON FOLLOWING LINE; IF NO PARTY SO SHOWN, MAIL AS DIRECTED ABOVE

Name   Street Address   City & State
SAFECO Stock No. **CAL-0011A** ′

In general, all states have laws that will invalidate a deed if the grantor is incompetent at the time the deed is made, if the deed is never delivered, or if the deed is a forgery or fraudulently altered. Case law in each state prescribes how the validity of a deed is determined and what other provisions may apply to property transfers.

C. MORTGAGES

A *MORTGAGE is a legal document that pledges the property of the borrower to a lender as security for a loan.* This, again, was an area that was originally the exclusive domain of attorneys. While attorneys are still engaged in drawing up some mortgages, the advent of pre-printed legal forms for residential transactions has served to lesson the involvement of attorneys in this area. Mortgage law has traditionally been within the jurisdiction of state law. To be valid, a mortgage must meet the requirements of the state in which it is drawn up. The federal government, as we have seen, has become more involved in the field of mortgage lending in the past century and has acted to pre-empt certain state laws. The federal government has overturned state laws restricting the "due on sale" clause, some usury laws, established conditions that allow prepayment of mortgages, and set ceilings on pre-payment penalties.

D. RECORDING

All the states have enacted laws known as recording acts. These vary by individual state.

The general intent of recording is to create a publicly available record that establishes the chain of ownership of any individual property.

These laws were enacted to protect the claims of owners and to protect prospective purchasers. Virtually all states require recording to protect an ownership claim. The places and methods of recordation vary from state to state.

E. STATE CHARTED BANKS

As we saw in Chapter 1, banking in general was unregulated in the early nation, with the exception of the establishment of the Bank of

the United States. The states established banking laws and regulations at a very early period to protect the public. While state laws still govern state chartered institutions, the effect of their regulation has been tempered by the fact that most real estate lending is now governed by federal laws and regulations.

F. USURY LAWS

Beginning in the 1830s, many states passed laws to limit the interest charges that individual lenders and banks operating within their states could charge a borrower. Implementation of these laws became very popular during the great depression. The laws were designed to protect consumers from grossly unfair interest rates charged by lenders. Lenders argued that in many cases such state-regulated rates were set at levels that made lending impossible during times of high interest rates. The lenders found a sympathetic ear in the federal government, at least in the case of real estate loans.

The establishment of the Federal Reserve and the secondary markets put the federal government in the rate-setting business.

To insure that the system works smoothly and provides reasonable rates to all, the federal courts overturned many state usury laws, or at least those sections dealing with federally-related real estate transactions. Most states still have usury laws that deal with other types of consumer credit.

II. The Rise of Federalism

Over the last century, the federal government has gradually extended its control of lending within the United States.

Federal authorities have virtually taken over the entire banking system. Many real estate loans are now subject to federal loan guarantees. This makes the loans subject to federal regulation. The federal government has also entered the domain of consumer law. This has been carried out by utilizing laws that were designed to prohibit discrimination and were themselves based on the 13th, 14th, and 15th Amendments to the U.S. Constitution. The beneficial effect has been that the process of the law in the nation has become more uniform and the lending system has been protected.

The adverse effect of federal regulation has been that federal incursion has come at the expense of the states and property owners.

The demise of usury laws has created a system in which the federal government sets interest rates. The passage of the **Garn-St. Germaine Act** in 1982 set the stage for the enforcement of the "due on sale clause." A *DUE ON SALE CLAUSE in a mortgage allows the lender to demand payment in full if the property is sold.* It also means that many real estate loans are not assumable. An *ASSUMABLE LOAN allows the owner to take a down payment for his equity and permits the purchaser to assume the current loan on the property.* Lenders are perfectly willing in times of low rates to allow a new borrower to assume a loan, particularly if the rate on the loan is the same or higher than the current market rates. However, if the rate is below current market, they want the power to force the buyer to have to make a new loan at a new higher rate. The problem with this is that often the buyer will not qualify for the new rate and the sale is lost. When sales are lost the market declines and so do home prices. As home prices decline, more loan defaults take place and the lenders lose money. Before 1982, many states had prohibitions on the due on sale clause.

The effect of the Garn-St Germaine Bill was to transfer a part of a property owner's rights to the lenders.

III. The Modern Role of the States

The modern role of the state remains that of a protector of the interests of its citizens.

States still control deeds and recording laws. In addition, they regulate appraisers, real estate agents, and loan brokers. In the areas of anti-discrimination, consumer law, and anti-redlining, many state laws are actually more severe than federal law. Also, many states have state lending agencies.

The state lending agencies provide state financial assistance at two levels. The first level consists of loans to communities to attract new business to an area and the second level consists of loans to improve housing in local communities. Some states and local communities also have special low interest loan programs for teachers and other professionals that allow the state or community to attract and retain people in designated fields.

IV. SUMMARY

The 10th Amendment to the U.S. Constitution reserves all powers to the states that are not specifically given to the federal government. As a result, the states have regulated by law the form and manner of property ownership, as well as the documentation required for ownership. This law was, for the most part, based on English Common Law and was adopted in each new territory throughout the United States during the past two centuries. The highest and most common form of property ownership is fee simple, which has with it a bundle of rights. This bundle of rights consists of real property rights.

Title to real estate is generally transferred by a deed. The most common form of deed used in the United States is the general warranty deed. This form of deed is the most comprehensive and assures a grantee (buyer) that the title to the property is free and clear and that the warranty extends back through the entire chain of ownership. In the western states, the grant deed is popular. This deed, when used in conjunction with title insurance, shifts any title liability to the title insurance company.

States have also carried out the very important function of publicly recording all documents relating to real estate, such as deeds and mortgages. While federal lending laws have, in some cases, adversely impacted a states ability to regulate real estate lending, the states have retained their role as regulators of agents, brokers, and appraisers.

V. CHAPTER TERMS

Deed	Leased Fee Estate
Due on Sale Clause	Leasehold Estate
Estate	Mortgage
Fee Simple	Real Estate
Garn-St Germaine Act	Real Property
General Warranty Deed	Recording Acts
Grant Deed	Reversion
Grantee	Special Warranty Deed
Grantor	Title

VI. CHAPTER 6 QUIZ

1. A grantor is:

    a. one who sells or transfers property.
    b. one who receives property by deed.
    c. an agency that guarantees title.
    d. none of the above.

2. A Special Warranty Deed:

    a. warranties the title for the entire chain of ownership.
    b. does not carry any warranty of title by the grantor.
    c. warranties the title only for actions of the grantor.
    d. warranties actions of the grantee.

3. A landlord holds title in:

    a. fee simple estate.
    b. leasehold estate.
    c. leased fee estate.
    d. life estate.

4. The return of property to the landlord at the end of a lease is called a:

    a. reversion.
    b. release.
    c. transfer.
    d. none of the above.

5. A grant deed is also called:

    a. a special warranty deed.
    b. a title deed.
    c. a non-warranted deed.
    d. a naked title deed.

6. Real property is:

    a. the physical land only.
    b. the rights of property ownership.
    c. tangible.
    d. none of the above.

7. The constitutional amendment that reserves all powers not granted to the federal government to the states is the:

    a. 10th amendment.
    b. 11th amendment.
    c. 12th amendment.
    d. 13th amendment.

8. An estate is a:

    a. form of ownership interest.
    b. type of deed.
    c. type of mortgage.
    d. type of sales contract.

9. The most common form of deed in the U.S. is the:

    a. General Warranty deed.
    b. Special Warranty Deed.
    c. Grant Deed.
    d. Quitclaim Deed.

10. A lender's right to limit or deny a buyer's ability to assume a loan is called:

    a. the Garn-St Germaine Bill.
    b. the due on sale clause.
    c. a trust deed.
    d. a special warranty deed.

ANSWERS: 1. a; 2. c; 3. c; 4. a; 5. d; 6. b; 7. a; 8. a; 9. a; 10. b

SEARS SAVINGS BANK

GLENDALE
PLAZA
BRANCH

HOURS
MONDAY-THURSDAY
9:00 TO 4:00
FRIDAY
9:00 TO 6:00

NO SOLICITING

FSLIC
MEMBER
Federal Savings & Loan Insurance Corp.
Your Savings Insured to $100,000

A MEMBER OF THE
SEARS FINANCIAL NETWORK

— PART III —
CHAPTERS 7, 8, AND 9
HOW THE LOAN PROCESS WORKS

CHAPTER 7 - FINANCE INSTRUMENTS

Instruments of real estate finance are documents that provide evidence of debt and give the lender the right to proceed against the collateral property if the borrower defaults on the loan. The promissory note is the basic instrument of debt. Mortgages, deeds of trust, and real estate contracts give the lender or seller the right to foreclose against or repossess the property if the buyer defaults. The deed of trust provides a speedier method of foreclosure than does a mortgage.

CHAPTER 8 - OVERVIEW OF THE LOAN PROCESS

The loan process consists of four general steps. By supplying all the necessary data the lender needs, the borrower can ensure a much smoother loan process for all concerned.

CHAPTER 9 - CONVENTIONAL FINANCING

The majority of conventional loans are fixed-rate, fully amortized 30-year loans. However, 15-year loans have been gaining in popularity because of the significant savings in interest payments. Also, loans may be fully amortized, partially amortized, or interest only with a balloon payment.

FINANCE INSTRUMENTS

This chapter on real estate finance instruments is an introduction to the contents and operation of these instruments. It is not intended as a substitute for competent professional advice and it should not be used as the basis for personal action, or to advise clients or customers regarding the operation of particular documents. The laws governing creditor-debtor relations are subject to change by judicial or legislative action. Therefore, it is advisable to consult an attorney for current, local advice concerning the effect of these instruments in any particular transaction.

The "instruments" that will be discussed in this chapter are written documents.

Written agreements are an integral part of most real estate financing transactions.

This chapter will discuss promissory notes, mortgages, deeds of trust (or trust deeds), real estate contracts, and some of the more common and, for the real estate practitioner, more significant clauses found in those documents.

CHAPTER 7 OUTLINE

I. Promissory Notes

Before a lender will finance the purchase of a house, the borrower must promise to repay the funds. That promise is put in writing in the form of a promissory note. (**See Figure 7-1**.) A *PROMISSORY NOTE is a written promise to pay money. The one promising to pay the money is called the MAKER of the note.* Usually, the maker is the homebuyer. *The one promised payment is called the PAYEE.* Usually, the payee is either a lender (if the purchaser has borrowed money from a bank or other lender to buy the property) or a seller (if the seller is financing the transaction in whole or in part by taking back a promissory note and mortgage or deed of trust).

The promissory note is the basic evidence of debt: it shows who owes how much money to whom.

Promissory notes are usually brief and simple documents. They normally are less than a page long and state:

1. the names of the parties,
2. the amount of the debt,
3. how and when the money is to be paid,
4. whether there is an acceleration clause (discussed below),
5. the payee's remedies if the money is not properly repaid, and
6. the signature of the maker.

Other provisions of the financing agreement between the debtor (maker or buyer) and the creditor (payee or lender/seller) are found in the mortgage or deed of trust.

A. NEGOTIABLE INSTRUMENTS

Virtually all promissory notes used in real estate financing are negotiable instruments.

Negotiable instruments are promissory notes that are freely transferable. *FREELY TRANSFERABLE means a bank or other creditor can sell the note and obtain immediate cash.* The sale is usually made at a discount, meaning the note is sold for a cash amount that is less than the face value of the note. The **Uniform Commercial Code (UCC),** which governs negotiable instruments, defines a *NEGOTIABLE INSTRUMENT as a written,*

Figure 7-1

NOTE

...., 19.........   ...., ...
                                                   [City]   [State]

....
                                           [Property Address]

1. BORROWER'S PROMISE TO PAY

In return for a loan that I have received. I promise to pay U.S. $...................(this amount is called "principal"), plus interest, to the order of the Lender. The Lender is ....' Savings and Loan Association I understand that the Lender may transfer this Note. The Lender or anyone who takes this Note by transfer and who is entitled to receive payments under this Note is called the "Note Holder".

2. INTEREST

Interest will be charged on unpaid principal until the full amount of principal has been paid. I will pay interest at a yearly rate of ....%.

The interest rate required by this Section 2 is the rate I will pay both before and after any default described in Section 6(B) of this Note.

3. PAYMENTS

(A) Time and Place of Payments

I will pay principal and interest by making payments every month.

I will make my monthly payments on the 1st day of each month beginning on .... 19........ I will make these payments every month until I have paid all of the principal and interest and any other charges described below that I may owe under this Note. My monthly payments will be applied to interest before principal. If, on .... I still owe amounts under this Note. I will pay those amounts in full on that date. which is called the "maturity date".

I will make my monthly payments at .... or at a different place if required by the Note Holder.

(B) Amount of Monthly Payments

My monthly payment will be in the amount of U.S. $..

4. BORROWER'S RIGHT TO PREPAY

I have the right to make payments of principal at any time before they are due. A payment of principal only is known as a "prepayment." When I make a prepayment, I will tell the Note Holder in writing that I am doing so.

I may make a full prepayment or partial prepayments without paying any prepayment charge. The Note Holder will use all of my prepayments to reduce the amount of principal that I owe under this Note. If I make a partial prepayment, there will be no changes in the due date or in the amount of my monthly payment unless the Note Holder agrees in writing to those changes.

5. LOAN CHARGES

If a law, which applies to this loan and which sets maximum loan charges, is finally interpreted so that the interest or other loan charges collected or to be collected in connection with this loan exceed the permitted limits, then: (i) any such loan charge shall be reduced by the amount necessary to reduce the charge to the permitted limit; and (ii) any sums already collected from me which exceeded permitted limits will be refunded to me. The Note Holder may choose to make this refund by reducing the principal I owe under this Note or by making a direct payment to me. If a refund reduces principal, the reduction will be treated as a partial prepayment.

6. BORROWER'S FAILURE TO PAY AS REQUIRED

(A) Late Charge for Overdue Payments

If the Note Holder has not received full amount of any monthly payment by the end of the 16th calendar day after the date it is due, I will pay a late charge to the Note Holder. The amount of the charge will be 5% of my overdue payment of principal and interest. I will pay this late charge promptly but only once on each late payment.

(B) Default

If I do not pay the full amount of each monthly payment on the date it is due, I will be in default.

(C) Notice of Default

If I am in default, the Note Holder may send me a written notice telling me that if I do not pay the overdue amount by a certain date, the Note Holder may require me to pay immediately the full amount of principal which has not been paid and all the interest that I owe on that amount. That date must be at least 30 days after the date on which the notice is delivered or mailed to me.

(D) No Waiver By Note Holder

Even if, at a time when I am in default, the Note Holder does not require me to pay immediately in full as described above, the Note Holder will still have the right to do so if I am in default at a later time.

(E) Payment of Note Holder's Costs and Expenses

If the Note Holder has required me to pay immediately in full as described above, the Note Holder will have the right to be paid back by me for all of its costs and expenses in enforcing this Note to the extent not prohibited by applicable law. Those expenses include, for example, reasonable attorneys' fees.

7. GIVING OF NOTICES

Unless applicable law requires a different method, any notice that must be given to me under this Note will be given by delivering it or by mailing it by first class mail to me at the Property Address above or at a different address if I give the Note Holder a notice of my different address.

Any notice that must be given to the Note Holder under this Note will be given by mailing it by first class mail to the Note Holder at the address stated in Section 3(A) above or at a different address if I am given a notice of that different address.

MULTISTATE FIXED RATE NOTE—Single Family—**FNMA/FHLMC UNIFORM INSTRUMENT**

8. OBLIGATIONS OF PERSONS UNDER THIS NOTE

If more than one person signs this Note, each person is fully and personally obligated to keep all of the promises made in this Note, including the promise to pay the full amount owed. Any person who is a guarantor, surety or endorser of this Note is also obligated to do these things. Any person who takes over these obligations, including the obligations of a guarantor, surety or endorser of this Note, is also obligated to keep all of the promises made in this Note. The Note Holder may enforce its rights under this Note against each person individually or against all of us together. This means that any one of us may be required to pay all of the amounts owed under this Note.

9. WAIVERS

I and any other person who has obligations under this Note waive the rights of presentment and notice of dishonor. "Presentment" means the right to require the Note Holder to demand payment of amounts due. "Notice of dishonor" means the right to require the Note Holder to give notice to other persons that amounts due have not been paid.

10. UNIFORM SECURED NOTE

This Note is a uniform instrument with limited variations in some jurisdictions. In addition to the protections given to the Note Holder under this Note, a Mortgage, Deed of Trust or Security Deed (the "Security Instrument"), dated the same date as this Note, protects the Note Holder from possible losses which might result if I do not keep the promises which I make in this Note. That Security Instrument describes how and under what conditions I may be required to make immediate payment in full of all amounts I owe under this Note. Some of those conditions are described as follows:

Transfer of the Property or a Beneficial Interest in Borrower. If all or any part of the Property or any interest in it is sold or transferred (or if a beneficial interest in Borrower is sold or transferred and Borrower is not a natural person) without Lender's prior written consent, Lender may, at its option, require immediate payment in full of all sums secured by this Security Instrument. However, this option shall not be exercised by Lender if exercise is prohibited by federal law as of the date of this Security Instrument.

If Lender exercises this option, Lender shall give Borrower notice of acceleration. The notice shall provide a period of not less than 30 days from the date the notice is delivered or mailed within which Borrower must pay all sums secured by this Security Instrument. If Borrower fails to pay these sums prior to the expiration of this period, Lender may invoke any remedies permitted by this Security Instrument without further notice or demand on Borrower.

WITNESS THE HAND(S) AND SEAL(S) OF THE UNDERSIGNED.

....(Seal)
-Borrower

....(Seal)
-Borrower

....(Seal)
-Borrower

[Sign Original Only]

unconditional promise or order to pay a certain sum of money, either on a certain date or on demand, payable either to order or to bearer, and signed by the maker.

The promissory note is almost always accompanied by a security instrument. A *SECURITY INSTRUMENT gives the creditor the right to have the security property sold to satisfy the debt if the debtor fails to pay the debt according to the terms of the agreement.* The security instrument may be either a deed of trust or a mortgage. The relative rights of the creditor and debtor under these security instruments vary according to whether it is a deed of trust or a mortgage. The next two sections of this chapter will cover deeds of trust and mortgages, the rights of the parties, the methods of foreclosure, and the advantages and disadvantages of the two documents.

II. The Deed of Trust (Trust Deed)

The *DEED OF TRUST (or TRUST DEED) is a commonly used security device. It is a three-party device. The borrower is called the GRANTOR or TRUSTOR; the lender is called the BENEFICIARY; and there is an independent third party, the TRUSTEE.* The trust deed was originally designed to convey naked title (legal title with no rights to possession) to the trustee throughout the period of indebtedness. *In some states, called TITLE THEORY STATES, the trust deed still conveys title. In most states, called LIEN THEORY STATES, the deed of trust creates a lien against the property in favor of the beneficiary.*

> *The deed of trust (lien) gives the creditor the right to force the sale of the property if the debtor defaults on the obligations under the promissory note or the trust deed.*

A. REQUIREMENTS FOR A VALID TRUST DEED

To be valid, a deed of trust must contain certain provisions. These include:

1. A statement pledging the property as collateral for a debt (a granting clause).

2. A complete and unambiguous property description.

3. The amount of the debt.

4. The maturity date of the debt.

5. A defeasance clause (stating that the trust deed will be cancelled when the debt is paid).

6. A power of sale clause.

When the debt is paid in full, the beneficiary directs the trustee to reconvey the title to the trustor (maker). The trustee releases the lien of the trust deed by signing and recording a deed of reconveyance. A *DEED OF RECONVEYANCE returns full title to the maker (trustor) of the debt.*

When a beneficiary fails to release a trustor in a timely manner, the beneficiary is liable in an action for damages and subject to statutory penalties.

The first page of a standard deed of trust is shown in **Figure 7-2**. Most lenders use this standard FNMA/FHLMC trust deed form so the loan will be easily salable to these agencies. If FNMA or FHLMC had to carefully inspect the provisions of each individual deed of trust they purchase, it would be an impractical, time-consuming process. When all lenders use a standard form, secondary investors can be assured of receiving a deed of trust with acceptable provisions.

B. FORECLOSURE

A deed of trust allows the beneficiary to foreclose the lien without the burden of bringing a legal action. This is called a *NON-JUDICIAL FORECLOSURE, that is, foreclosure without having to go to court.*

C. POWER OF SALE

The deed of trust contains a power of sale clause which authorizes the trustee to sell the property without court supervision if the debtor defaults. A typical power of sale clause might read as follows:

If the default is not cured on or before the date specified in the notice, lender, at its option, may require immediate payment in full of all sums secured by this security instrument without further demand and may invoke the power of sale. If lender invokes the power of sale, lender shall execute or cause trustee to execute a written notice of the occurrence of an event of default and of lenders election to cause the property to be sold.

Figure 7-2

——————————————————————————— [Space Above This Line For Recording Data] ———————————————————————————

DEED OF TRUST

THIS DEED OF TRUST ("Security Instrument") is made on ....,
19.......... The trustor is ....
.... ("Borrower"). The trustee is ....
.... ("Trustee"). The beneficiary is
...., which is organized and existing
under the laws of ...., and whose address is ....
.... ("Lender").
Borrower owes Lender the principal sum of ....
.... Dollars (U.S. $................................). This debt is evidenced by Borrower's note
dated the same date as this Security Instrument ("Note"), which provides for monthly payments, with the full debt, if not
paid earlier, due and payable on .... This Security Instrument
secures to Lender: (a) the repayment of the debt evidenced by the Note, with interest, and all renewals, extensions and
modifications; (b) the payment of all other sums, with interest, advanced under paragraph 7 to protect the security of this
Security Instrument; and (c) the performance of Borrower's covenants and agreements under this Security Instrument and
the Note. For this purpose, Borrower irrevocably grants and conveys to Trustee, in trust, with power of sale, the following
described property located in .... County, California:

which has the address of ...., ...,
                                           [Street]   [City]
California .... ("Property Address");
                   [Zip Code]

TOGETHER WITH all the improvements now or hereafter erected on the property, and all easements, rights,
appurtenances, rents, royalties, mineral, oil and gas rights and profits, water rights and stock and all fixtures now or
hereafter a part of the property. All replacements and additions shall also be covered by this Security Instrument. All of the
foregoing is referred to in this Security Instrument as the "Property."

BORROWER COVENANTS that Borrower is lawfully seised of the estate hereby conveyed and has the right to grant
and convey the Property and that the Property is unencumbered, except for encumbrances of record. Borrower warrants
and will defend generally the title to the Property against all claims and demands, subject to any encumbrances of record.

THIS SECURITY INSTRUMENT combines uniform covenants for national use and non-uniform covenants with
limited variations by jurisdiction to constitute a uniform security instrument covering real property.

CALIFORNIA—Single Family—FNMA/FHLMC UNIFORM INSTRUMENT   Form 3005 12/83

D. TRUSTEE'S SALE

At the direction of the beneficiary, the trustee conducts an out-of-court sale, or auction, called a TRUSTEE'S SALE. The proceeds from the sale are used to pay off the trustor's debt.

However, before the trustee can sell the property, certain legal requirements must be met. First, the beneficiary (lender) prepares a document called the **Declaration of Default**, requesting the trustee to begin the foreclosure proceedings. The trustee then prepares a **Notice of Default and Election to Sell**, which is sent to the borrower. The trustee also notifies anyone who has subsequently recorded a request for notice of default and sale. The trustee is required to provide notice to all lien holders.

The borrower can prevent the sale of the property by **reinstating** the loan. A loan is reinstated by paying all past due installments, plus late charges, interest, and other costs.

A borrower may reinstate the loan at any time from the notice of default until five business days before the sale date.

If the loan is not reinstated within three months of the notice of default, the trustee publishes a Notice of Sale of the property in a newspaper of general circulation. A *NOTICE OF SALE warns not only the borrower, but also other lien holders that the property is being sold to recover the monies owed against it.* The notice must appear weekly and the sale cannot take place until at least 20 days have elapsed from the first date of publication. Additionally, a notice of sale must be sent to the borrower, and posted on the property.

At the sale (usually a public auction), any person, including the debtor or creditor, may bid. The trustee can reject any or all inadequate bids and can postpone the sale if there are no acceptable bids. Otherwise, the sale is made to the highest bidder. The purchaser receives a *TRUSTEE'S DEED, which eliminates all liens junior to the trust deed being foreclosed, and any interest the debtor had in the property.* The trustee applies the sale proceeds in the following order:

1. To pay the trustee's costs and sale expenses.
2. To satisfy the beneficiary's debt.
3. To junior lien holders in order of priority.
4. To the debtor, if any surplus.

The entire process of selling property through the power of sale clause in a deed of trust may be accomplished in well under a year, without the expenses involved in court proceedings. There are, of course, expenses connected with a trustee's sale, but these are usually substantially less than those connected with a court-ordered sheriff's sale.

The relative speed and economy of the trustee's sale has caused trust deeds to all but replace mortgages in many states.

Because no court is involved in the trust deed foreclosure process, it is impossible to obtain a deficiency judgment in a trustee's sale.

A deficiency judgment may only be granted by a court of law. The courts are not involved in the trustee's sale process.

If the sale of the property fails to cover the debt, the beneficiary cannot then sue the debtor for the remainder. He or she must be satisfied with the proceeds of the trustee's sale. However, it is possible to foreclose a deed of trust like a mortgage, whereby all the procedures and rights relating to mortgages are applicable.

E. ADVANTAGES AND DISADVANTAGES OF THE TRUST DEED

For the creditor, the primary advantage of the deed of trust is the quick and inexpensive non-judicial sale process, with no post-sale right of redemption for the borrower. The primary disadvantage is that a deficiency judgment is unobtainable after a non-judicial foreclosure.

From the borrower's point of view, the protection against deficiency judgements is probably the main advantage of the trust deed. The speed of the process, the lack of judicial supervision, and the lack of redemption rights following the trustee's sale are all disadvantages for the borrower.

III. Mortgages

A **MORTGAGE** *is a two-party instrument in which the borrower (called the* **MORTGAGOR)** *mortgages his or her property to the lender (called the* **MORTGAGEE).**

For the most part, lenders prefer the deed of trust to the mortgage.

A. FORECLOSURE

A foreclosure under a mortgage requires a court-ordered sale conducted by the sheriff or other court-appointed official. This type of foreclosure process is called **JUDICIAL FORECLOSURE**. In the event of default, the mortgagee accelerates the due date of the debt to the present and notifies the defaulting debtor to pay off the entire outstanding balance at once. *If the debtor fails to do so, the mortgagee initiates a lawsuit, called a* **FORECLOSURE ACTION**, *in the county where the land is located.* The purpose of this legal proceeding is to get a judge to order the county sheriff to seize and sell the property. *The judge's order is called an* **ORDER OF EXECUTION**. Acting under the order of execution, the sheriff notifies the public of the place and date of the sale. This requires posting notices at the property and the courthouse and running an advertisement of the sale in a newspaper circulated in the county. This process takes several weeks.

1. Redemption

At any time up until the sheriff's sale, the debtor may save the property by paying the mortgagee what is due. *This right to save or redeem the property before the sale is called the* **EQUITABLE RIGHT OF REDEMPTION**. The debtor may also be obligated to pay delinquent interest, court costs, attorney's fees, and sheriff's fees in order to redeem the property.

2. Sheriff's Sale

The **SHERIFF'S SALE** *is a public auction, normally held at the courthouse door, and anyone can bid on the property.* The property is sold to the highest bidder and the proceeds are used to pay for the costs of the sale and to pay off the mortgage. As with the trust deed, any surplus goes to the debtor.

If the property does not bring enough money at the sale to pay off the mortgage, the debtor may be able to obtain a deficiency judgment against the debtor for the remaining debt. To obtain a deficiency judgment, the creditor must apply to the court within three months of the judicial sale.

In some states, such as California, deficiency judgments are prohibited if the mortgage secured a loan to purchase a one-to-four unit personal residence occupied by the owner.

3. Post-Sale Redemption

After the sale, the debtor has another opportunity to save or redeem the property. The debtor can do this by paying the purchaser the amount paid for the property plus accrued interest from the time of the sale. *This right to redeem the property following the sheriff's sale is called the* **STATUTORY RIGHT OF REDEMPTION**.

Depending on the court congestion and the availability of the sheriff for foreclosures, a judicial mortgage foreclosure may take anywhere from several months to several years from the time of default until a sheriff's deed is delivered to the purchaser, which finally divests the debtor of title.

The period of post-sale redemption lasts one year in some states, if the proceeds are less than the amount needed to satisfy the indebtedness, or three months if the proceeds satisfy the indebtedness. This period varies in other states.

B. ADVANTAGES AND DISADVANTAGES OF THE MORTGAGE

For the creditor (mortgagee), the main advantage of a mortgage is the right to obtain a personal judgment against the debtor (mortgagor) for any deficiency if the property does not bring enough at the sheriff's sale to satisfy the debt.

The main disadvantages to the creditor concern the time and expense involved in executing a judicial foreclosure. Legal fees and court costs may easily amount to several thousand dollars, which must be paid out of the creditor's pocket, and may or may not be recovered at the sale. The entire process, as has already been mentioned, can take a long time to complete.

The advantages and disadvantages of a mortgage for the debtor (mortgagor) generally correspond to those for the creditor, but in reverse. Because court proceedings are slow, a mortgagor usually has a longer time to get the money together to prevent the foreclosure than a trust deed borrower. And even after the foreclosure sale, the mortgagor still has a chance to redeem the property. On the other hand, the mortgagor faces the possibility of a deficiency judgment, even after the foreclosure has taken place and the property is lost for good, a portion of the debt may have to be repaid.

IV. Real Estate Contracts

Real estate contracts are also called contracts for deed, installment sales contracts, conditional sales contracts, and land contracts.

Real estate contracts differ significantly from mortgages and deeds of trust. Under both mortgage and trust deed security arrangements, the debtor acquires title to the property. Under a *REAL ESTATE CONTRACT, the seller (VENDOR) retains legal title until the buyer (VENDEE) pays off the entire contract*. During the period the purchaser is paying on the contract (which may be many years), the purchaser has the right to possess and enjoy the property, but is not the legal owner.

In some states, real estate contracts often provide that if the buyer defaults on the contract obligation, all the buyer's rights in the property are forfeited, any payments made may be retained by the seller as liquidated damages, and the seller has a right to retake possession of the property immediately. In other states, such as California, such provisions are no longer enforceable. In these states, the seller is required to reimburse the buyer when repossessing the property, although the reimbursement may be reduced by any damages the seller incurred. The buyer has the right to reinstate the contract after default, and once a substantial portion of the contract price has been paid, the buyer gains a right of redemption.

A. ADVANTAGES AND DISADVANTAGES OF REAL ESTATE CONTRACTS

For the seller (vendor), one advantage of contract sales is the personal satisfaction or security that the seller may feel by remaining the title owner—by not giving the buyer (vendee) a deed until the entire purchase price has been paid. However, since it may be necessary to file a quiet title action to regain the property, this feeling of security may be largely illusory. A **QUIET TITLE** *is a title granted by a court that clears away all liens and other claims against a title.*

The main disadvantage for the vendor under a real estate contract is similar to the main disadvantage for the creditor under a mortgage: the expense and time required for terminating the contract and retaking possession of the property.

A serious disadvantage for the vendee under the contract is the fact that the vendor remains the legal owner, unlike mortgages or deeds of trust.

This often makes it difficult, if not impossible, for the vendee to obtain bank financing for construction or improvements. Banks are usually reluctant to lend to persons who do not have legal title because the vendor remains the legal owner.

V. Typical Clauses in Security Instruments

We will now take a brief look at some clauses commonly used in real estate finance instruments. These clauses are generally used to safeguard the interests of the lender in the event of a default by the borrower. They are also often used to insure that the lender receives additional monies in the event of a pre-payment of the mortgage debt.

A. ACCELERATION CLAUSE

Almost all promissory notes, mortgages, deeds of trust, and many real estate contracts contain an acceleration clause. An **ACCELERATION CLAUSE** *allows the creditor or seller to accelerate the debt, that is, to declare the entire outstanding balance immediately due and payable in the event of default.* This means that a debtor who misses one payment may discover the following month that he or she does not owe just two payments, but rather the entire remaining balance. Most lenders will wait until payments are at least 90 days delinquent before they enforce an acceleration clause. The following is a typical acceleration clause:

In case the mortgagor (or trustor) shall fail to pay any installment of principal or interest secured hereby when due to keep or perform any covenant or agreement aforesaid, then the whole indebtedness hereby secured shall forthwith become due and payable, at the election of the mortgagee (or beneficiary).

B. PREPAYMENT CLAUSE

Many conventional loans have prepayment provisions. (They are prohibited on FHA and VA loans.) While the time periods and the amount of payment vary considerably, the basic effect of a prepayment provision is to charge the debtor for paying off the loan too early and depriving the lender of receiving the anticipated interest. An example might be a provision which charges the debtor 3% of the original loan amount if more than 20% of the principal is repaid in any one of the first five years of the loan. An example of the wording of a typical prepayment penalty clause is as follows:

If, within five years from the date of this note, borrower makes any prepayments of principal in excess of twenty percent of the original

principal amount in any 12-month period beginning with the date of this note or anniversary dates thereof ("loan year"), borrower shall pay the note holder three percent of the original principal amount.

Under California law, if the loan is secured by owner-occupied residential property (one-to-four units), the borrower must be allowed to prepay up to 20% of the original loan amount in one year without penalty. (Exception for seller financing: a seller can prohibit prepayment in the year of sale.) Any penalty imposed may not be more than six months' interest on the amount of prepayment over 20%. Once the loan has been in place for five years, no further prepayment penalties can be charged. Other states have slightly differing requirements.

C. ALIENATION CLAUSE

Alienation refers to transfer of ownership.

ALIENATION CLAUSES *in loan documents limit the debtor's right to transfer the property without the creditor's permission.* Depending on the clause, it may be triggered by a transfer of title or the transfer of any interest in the property (such as a land contract, a long-term lease, or even a lease with an option to purchase). *The alienation clause may give the lender the right to declare the entire loan balance due immediately, in which case it is called a* **DUE ON SALE CLAUSE**, to raise the interest rate if current rates are higher than the loan's rate, or to do either at its option.

Although alienation clauses are common in fixed rate loans, Adjustable Rate Mortgage loans (ARMs) seldom include them.

An ARM's rate adjustment feature allows the lender to keep the interest rate at or near market rates, even if ownership does change hands. The following is a typical due-on-sale clause:

If all or any part of the property, or an interest therein, is sold or transferred by borrower without lender's prior written consent, lender may, at lender's option, declare all the sums secured by this instrument to be immediately due and payable.

Before 1982, the enforceability of such clauses varied widely from state to state. Some states regarded such provisions as enforceable according to their terms. Other states refused to enforce them unless the lender could show that its security was impaired by the transfer. Still other states distinguished between the various types of clauses, regarding some as enforceable and others as unenforceable.

In 1982, two actions on the federal level had the effect of limiting the power of the states with respect to the enforceability of due-on-sale clauses. The first action resulted from a lawsuit involving the enforceability of alienation clauses by a savings and loan association in California (*Fidelity Savings and Loan Association v. De La Cuesta, et al.*). In that case, the U.S. Supreme Court upheld a Federal Home Loan Bank Board regulation which pre-empted state law and permitted federally chartered savings and loans to enforce due-on-sale clauses, regardless of whether such clauses were enforceable under state law.

This decision affected only the enforceability of alienation clauses by federal savings and loans; it was not directly applicable to actions by other lenders. However, passage of the Deposit Insurance Flexibility Act (**Garn-St. Germain Act**) in the same year gave all lenders the right to enforce due-on-sale clauses in their security instruments. The act provided for a three-year transition period from October 15, 1982, to October 15, 1985, to phase in enforceability of alienation clauses in states where they had previously been unenforceable. In those states, the enforceability of due-on-sale clauses in loans, which had been made during the period beginning when state law declared alienation clauses unenforceable and ending with passage of the Garn-St. Germain Act, was delayed until October 15, 1985. The states where the window period applied were given the right to extend the window period by action of their state legislature.

In California, the window period ran between August 1978 (the date of California Supreme Court decision ruling alienation clauses unenforceable) and October 1982.

NOTE: If the seller decides to sell the property without assuming the existing mortgage (e.g., the buyer takes out a new mortgage, the proceeds of which are used to pay off the seller's mortgage), any prepayment penalty provision may then apply. This "due-on-sale catch-22" is something the seller should be aware of.

In California, a lender may not enforce the alienation clause and also the prepayment penalty on one-to-four unit dwellings. On other properties, the lender may enforce both clauses only if the borrower has separately agreed to pay a prepayment penalty on acceleration.

D. SUBORDINATION CLAUSE

Generally, the priority among mortgages, trust deeds, and real estate contracts is determined by the date of recording, the first recorded instrument being the first in priority. In some situations, however, the parties may desire that a later recorded instrument have priority over an earlier recorded instrument. This is particularly common in construction financing. Due to the high-risk nature of construction loans, construction lenders frequently refuse to lend any money unless they can be assured of first lien priority. Because the developer, in many circumstances, has purchased the land on some sort of deferred payment plan, there is often a security instrument (mortgage, trust deed, or contract) which has already been recorded. In order for the later construction loan mortgage or trust deed to take priority over the earlier instrument, the earlier instrument must contain a subordination clause, or the earlier lender must sign a separate subordination agreement.

A *SUBORDINATION CLAUSE states that the instrument in which it is contained will be subordinate (junior) to a construction loan lien (mortgage or deed of trust) to be recorded later.* A subordination agreement accomplishes the same thing, but may be executed at any time (for example, when the later loan is made). The following is a typical subordination clause:

Lender agrees that this instrument shall be subordinate to a lien given by borrower to secure funds for the construction of improvements on the property, provided said lien is duly recorded and also provided that the amount secured by said lien does not exceed $95,000.00.

E. PARTIAL RELEASE, SATISFACTION, OR RECONVEYANCE CLAUSE

A *PARTIAL RELEASE, SATISFACTION, OR RECONVEYANCE CLAUSE obligates the creditor to release part of the property from the lien when part of the debt has been paid.*

Example: A real estate contract for the purchase of five acres of land may contain a clause stating that when the vendee has paid 20% of the purchase price, the vendor will execute a deed to the vendee for one acre of the land. This would allow the vendee to acquire clear title to one acre, which may then be used to build upon.

The fact that the vendee has title will make it much easier to obtain construction financing. Such clauses are also frequently found in blanket mortgages or trust deeds covering subdivisions in the process of being developed and sold.

The partial release (for real estate contracts), partial satisfaction (for mortgages), or partial reconveyance (for trust deeds) clause permits the developer to acquire, and therefore convey, clear title to one lot for which he or she has a purchaser, without having to pay off the entire lien against the development.

The following is a typical partial release clause:

Upon payment of all sums due with respect to any lot subject to this lien, lender shall release said lot from the lien at no cost to the borrower.

VI. SUMMARY

Instruments of real estate finance are documents that provide evidence of debt and give the lender the right to proceed against the collateral property if the borrower defaults on the loan. The promissory note is the basic instrument of debt, signed by the borrower and showing the amount of the loan, interest rate, method and manner of repayment, and the borrower's promise to repay the debt. Mortgages, deeds of trust, and real estate contracts give the lender or seller the right to foreclose against or repossess the property if the buyer defaults. The deed of trust provides a speedier method of foreclosure than does a mortgage.

Some particular clauses found in many mortgages, trust deeds, and installment contracts include acceleration clauses, prepayment provisions, and alienation (due-on-sale) clauses. Subordination agreements and partial release or satisfaction clauses are less common in residential loans, but are frequently found in construction or development loans.

VII. CHAPTER TERMS

Beneficiary	Non-Judicial Foreclosure
Declaration of Default	Notice of Default and Election to Sell
Deed of Reconveyance	Notice of Sale
Deficiency Judgment	Payee
Equitable Right of Redemption	Promissory Note
Grantor	Quiet Title
Judicial Foreclosure	Trustee
Maker	Trustor
Mortgagee	Vendee
Mortgagor	Vendor

VIII. CHAPTER 7 QUIZ

1. In a promissory, note the borrower is called the:

   a. payee.
   b. maker.
   c. trustee.
   d. beneficiary.

2. A deed of reconveyance is provided by the:

   a. trustee.
   b. trustor.
   c. beneficiary.
   d. payee.

3. A deficiency judgment:

   a. is part of a deed of reconveyance.
   b. is exercised by the vendee.
   c. may only be granted by a court of law.
   d. none of the above.

4. The seller of a real estate contract is known as the:

   a. payee.
   b. vendee.
   c. payer.
   d. vendor.

5. The right of a borrower to redeem property after a sheriff's sale is called:

   a. the equitable right of redemption.
   b. the statutory right of redemption.
   c. a deficiency judgment.
   d. a quiet title action.

6. A lender's right to declare a balance immediately due and payable in the event of default is called:

   a. prepayment.
   b. acceleration.
   c. alienation.
   d. duc-on-sale.

7. A mortgage that is junior to another is called:

    a. a priority lien.
    b. a non-priority lien.
    c. subordinate.
    d. none of the above.

8. A foreclosure that does not have to be taken to court is called:

    a. non-judicial.
    b. judicial.
    c. a reconveyance deed.
    d. a non-recurring foreclosure.

9. A declaration of default is prepared by a:

    a. judge.
    b. trustee.
    c. lender.
    d. borrower.

10. A notice of sale:

    a. requires a 30-day notice.
    b. must be approved by a judge.
    c. is sent by the county sheriff.
    d. is published in a newspaper.

ANSWERS: 1. b; 2. a; 3. c; 4. d; 5. b; 6. b; 7. c; 8. a; 9. c; 10. d

HERE

Countrywide®
HOME LOANS

JOB
POSTINGS

OVERVIEW OF THE LOAN PROCESS

While the principles behind real estate finance are fairly straightforward, they will be easier to understand after taking a brief look at the financing process. The procedures for financing real estate can be conveniently broken down into four steps:

1. Loan application
2. Analysis of the borrower and property
3. Processing the loan application
4. Closing the loan

A fifth step could be added: servicing and sale to the secondary market. However, because this step takes place after the loan has been placed, it is primarily a matter of administration rather than analysis and judgment.

I. The Loan Process

This chapter will provide an overview of the steps in the process. A more detailed analysis of the process will be provided in chapters 13 and 14.

Chapter 8

CHAPTER 8 OUTLINE

These chapters deal with the qualification of the borrower and the qualification of the property.

A. THE LOAN APPLICATION

The first step in obtaining a real estate loan is to fill out the **Loan Application**. The loan application is not designed for those merely inquiring about real estate loans, but for those who will follow through and actually borrow the funds (provided the loan is approved). The home buyer (or the real estate agent on behalf of the buyer) sets up an appointment with the lender. The buyer will attend this appointment armed with a good deal of personal and financial data which will be the basis of the lender's decision whether or not to make the loan. The types of information the buyer should take to this interview will be discussed shortly. It should be noted that if the buyer does not have all the necessary data at the interview, it will be necessary to provide the missing information at a later date, which will cause a delay in the loan application process.

A borrower must provide personal and financial information when applying for a loan.

During the initial interview, the buyer will learn about the various types of financing programs offered by the lender. These will probably include 30-year, fixed rate mortgages, 15-year, fixed rate mortgages, and adjustable rate mortgages (ARMs). Based on the information given by the lender and the buyer's own personal circumstances, the buyer will decide which program best suits his or her needs.

The lender will also require a deposit to cover the expenses that must be paid up front. These include the costs of the credit report, property appraisal, and preliminary title report. This deposit will assure the lender that these fees will be paid for, even if the loan does not close.

A borrower pays for a credit report, property appraisal, and preliminary title report up front.

The **deposit receipt** will be examined at this interview as well. This is so the lender can be sure that the terms of the agreement are in keeping with the terms of the loan the lender can offer (e.g., interest

rate and length of the term of the loan). Of particular concern is the agreed-upon closing date. Often, the deposit receipt will provide for a closing date which is far too early to be realistic. If it is impossible for the lender to meet the closing date, a more feasible one can be agreed on and later frustration avoided.

A deposit receipt is given to a home purchaser by the seller; it contains the sale terms and the date that the parties expect the transaction to close.

B. ANALYSIS OF THE BORROWER AND THE PROPERTY

Once the application has been properly filled out, the lender can begin gathering other pertinent information on the buyer. Verification forms will be sent out to the buyer's employer, banks or other financial institutions, and any previous mortgage lender. The lender will order a credit report and have a preliminary title report prepared. A **CREDIT REPORT** *verifies the borrower's good credit standing.* An approved appraiser will also be contacted to have an appraisal done on the property. An *APPRAISAL provides a professional third party opinion of the value of the property.*

After examining the application, the lender may also ask the buyer to submit further information, including:

1. a copy of any divorce decree (to verify any child support or alimony obligations and any settlement agreement that may be the source of the down payment);

2. an investment account record;

3. pension plan documentation;

4. tax returns (if the buyer is self-employed or retired and living on investment income); and

5. any other documentation that may have an effect on the buyer's income or credit status.

The lender will be very concerned with the source of the buyer's down payment. Personal savings, the previous sale of a home, or gifts are all acceptable sources of the down payment.

*Using borrowed funds for the down payment is usually
not permitted.*

1. Equal Credit Opportunity Act

The federal *EQUAL CREDIT OPPORTUNITY ACT prohibits
discrimination based on age, sex, race, marital status, color, religion, or
national origin.* Senior citizens, young adults, and single persons
must be considered on the basis of income adequacy, satisfactory
net worth, job stability, and satisfactory credit rating. Lenders
must apply their credit guidelines to each potential borrower in
the same manner.

C. PROCESSING THE LOAN APPLICATION

When the credit report, verification forms, preliminary title report,
and appraisal have all been received by the lender, a loan package is
put together and submitted to the underwriting department. The
loan underwriter thoroughly examines the loan package and then
makes the decision to approve it, reject it, or approve it under certain
conditions. A conditional approval usually requires the submission
of additional information, such as:

1. the closing statement from the sale of the buyer's previous home;

2. pay stubs to verify employment;

3. a final inspection report; and

4. a commitment for private mortgage insurance (PMI) if the down
   payment is less than 20% of the purchase price.

D. CLOSING THE LOAN

After the conditions are met, all the necessary documents are
prepared for closing. The closing process ordinarily takes about one
week if everything goes smoothly.

*The mechanics of closing are normally the responsibility
of the escrow agent.*

This escrow holder may be an "in-house" escrow department of the
lender, an independent escrow company, or a title insurance company

(depending on the region). The escrow agent simultaneously follows the instructions of both the buyer and the seller, and is responsible for providing the lender with a certified copy of the **escrow instructions**. The escrow agent gathers together all the necessary documents (e. g., the promissory note and deed of trust) and makes sure that all the documents are properly signed by the parties. The escrow agent calculates the various prorations, adjustments, and charges to be assessed against each party, makes sure that all required funds and documents are deposited, and furnishes each party with a settlement (for closing) statement.

If there are no unforeseen problems during closing (e.g., the seller does not have title to the property), the loan papers are signed and sent to the funding department. This department makes one final check to be sure that everything is in order and that it has the necessary instructions for the release of the funds. The loan funds are then disbursed to the proper parties.

E. FILLING OUT THE LOAN APPLICATION

As mentioned earlier, the buyer fills out a loan application at the initial interview with the lender. A copy of such a loan application is shown in **Figure 8-1**. This standard loan application is used throughout the United States for a conventional (non-government insured) loan.

Lenders expect the loans they make to be repaid without collection, loan servicing, or foreclosure problems. They are obviously careful to make loans only to those borrowers who can be expected to repay the loan in a timely manner. Therefore, employment stability, income potential, history of debt management, and net worth are important considerations to the lender. These are the types of information the loan application is designed to elicit.

1. Property Information

The application begins with a section on the property. Questions as to the type of loan sought, the terms of the loan, location and legal description of the property, the property's value, and the manner of taking title must be completed. This information is used to determine how much security for the loan will be provided.

Figure 8-1

Uniform Residential Loan Application

This application is designed to be completed by the applicant(s) with the Lender's assistance. Applicants should complete this form as "Borrower" or "Co-Borrower," as applicable. Co-Borrower information must also be provided (and the appropriate box checked) when ☐ the income or assets of a person other than the "Borrower" (including the Borrower's spouse) will be used as a basis for loan qualification or ☐ the income or assets of the Borrower's spouse will not be used as a basis for loan qualification, but his or her liabilities must be considered because the Borrower resides in a community property state, the security property is located in a community property state, or the Borrower is relying on other property located in a community property state as a basis for repayment of the loan.

I. TYPE OF MORTGAGE AND TERMS OF LOAN

| Mortgage Applied for: | ☐ VA   ☐ Conventional   ☐ Other (explain): | Agency Case Number | Lender Case Number |
| | ☐ FHA   ☐ USDA/Rural Housing Service | | |

| Amount $ | Interest Rate % | No. of Months | Amortization Type: | ☐ Fixed Rate   ☐ Other (explain): ☐ GPM   ☐ ARM (type): |

II. PROPERTY INFORMATION AND PURPOSE OF LOAN

| Subject Property Address (street, city, state, & ZIP) | No. of Units |

| Legal Description of Subject Property (attach description if necessary) | Year Built |

Purpose of Loan ☐ Purchase ☐ Construction ☐ Other (explain): ☐ Refinance ☐ Construction-Permanent

Property will be: ☐ Primary Residence ☐ Secondary Residence ☐ Investment

Complete this line if construction or construction-permanent loan.

| Year Lot Acquired | Original Cost $ | Amount Existing Liens $ | (a) Present Value of Lot $ | (b) Cost of Improvements $ | Total (a + b) $ |

Complete this line if this is a refinance loan.

| Year Acquired | Original Cost $ | Amount Existing Liens $ | Purpose of Refinance | Describe Improvements ☐ made ☐ to be made Cost: $ |

| Title will be held in what Name(s) | Manner in which Title will be held | Estate will be held in: ☐ Fee Simple ☐ Leasehold (show expiration date) |

Source of Down Payment, Settlement Charges and/or Subordinate Financing (explain)

III. BORROWER INFORMATION

Borrower	Co-Borrower
Borrower's Name (include Jr. or Sr. if applicable)	Co-Borrower's Name (include Jr. or Sr. if applicable)

| Social Security Number | Home Phone (incl. area code) | DOB (MM/DD/YYYY) | Yrs. School | Social Security Number | Home Phone (incl. area code) | DOB (MM/DD/YYYY) | Yrs. School |

| ☐ Married ☐ Unmarried (include single, divorced, widowed) ☐ Separated | Dependents (not listed by Co-Borrower) no.   ages | ☐ Married ☐ Unmarried (include single, divorced, widowed) ☐ Separated | Dependents (not listed by Borrower) no.   ages |

| Present Address (street, city, state, ZIP) ☐ Own ☐ Rent ____ No. Yrs. | Present Address (street, city, state, ZIP) ☐ Own ☐ Rent ____ No. Yrs. |

| Mailing Address, if different from Present Address | Mailing Address, if different from Present Address |

If residing at present address for less than two years, complete the following:

| Former Address (street, city, state, ZIP) ☐ Own ☐ Rent ____ No. Yrs. | Former Address (street, city, state, ZIP) ☐ Own ☐ Rent ____ No. Yrs. |

IV. EMPLOYMENT INFORMATION

Borrower	Co-Borrower
Name & Address of Employer ☐ Self Employed	Yrs. on this job	Name & Address of Employer ☐ Self Employed	Yrs. on this job
	Yrs. employed in this line of work/profession		Yrs. employed in this line of work/profession
Position/Title/Type of Business	Business Phone (incl. area code)	Position/Title/Type of Business	Business Phone (incl. area code)

If employed in current position for less than two years or if currently employed in more than one position, complete the following:

Name & Address of Employer ☐ Self Employed	Dates (from – to)	Name & Address of Employer ☐ Self Employed	Dates (from – to)
	Monthly Income $		Monthly Income $
Position/Title/Type of Business	Business Phone (incl. area code)	Position/Title/Type of Business	Business Phone (incl. area code)

Name & Address of Employer ☐ Self Employed	Dates (from – to)	Name & Address of Employer ☐ Self Employed	Dates (from – to)
	Monthly Income $		Monthly Income $
Position/Title/Type of Business	Business Phone (incl. area code)	Position/Title/Type of Business	Business Phone (incl. area code)

Freddie Mac Form 65   01/04

Fannie Mae Form 1003   01/04

Gross Monthly Income	Borrower	Co-Borrower	Total	Combined Monthly Housing Expense	Present	Proposed
Base Empl. Income*	$	$	$	Rent	$	
Overtime				First Mortgage (P&I)		$
Bonuses				Other Financing (P&I)		
Commissions				Hazard Insurance		
Dividends/Interest				Real Estate Taxes		
Net Rental Income				Mortgage Insurance		
Other (before completing, see the notice in "describe other income," below)				Homeowner Assn. Dues		
				Other:		
Total	$	$	$	Total	$	$

* Self Employed Borrower(s) may be required to provide additional documentation such as tax returns and financial statements.

Describe Other Income *Notice:* Alimony, child support, or separate maintenance income need not be revealed if the Borrower (B) or Co-Borrower (C) does not choose to have it considered for repaying this loan.

B/C		Monthly Amount
		$

This Statement and any applicable supporting schedules may be completed jointly by both married and unmarried Co-Borrowers if their assets and liabilities are sufficiently joined so that the Statement can be meaningfully and fairly presented on a combined basis; otherwise, separate Statements and Schedules are required. If the Co-Borrower section was completed about a spouse, this Statement and supporting schedules must be completed about that spouse also.

Completed ☐ Jointly ☐ Not Jointly

ASSETS Description	Cash or Market Value	Liabilities and Pledged Assets. List the creditor's name, address and account number for all outstanding debts, including automobile loans, revolving charge accounts, real estate loans, alimony, child support, stock pledges, etc. Use continuation sheet, if necessary. Indicate by (*) those liabilities which will be satisfied upon sale of real estate owned or upon refinancing of the subject property.		
Cash deposit toward purchase held by:	$			
		LIABILITIES	Monthly Payment & Months Left to Pay	Unpaid Balance
List checking and savings accounts below		Name and address of Company	$ Payment/Months	$
Name and address of Bank, S&L, or Credit Union				
		Acct. no.		
Acct. no.	$	Name and address of Company	$ Payment/Months	$
Name and address of Bank, S&L, or Credit Union				
		Acct. no.		
Acct. no.	$	Name and address of Company	$ Payment/Months	$
Name and address of Bank, S&L, or Credit Union				
		Acct. no.		
Acct. no.	$	Name and address of Company	$ Payment/Months	$
Name and address of Bank, S&L, or Credit Union				
		Acct. no.		
Acct. no.	$	Name and address of Company	$ Payment/Months	$
Stocks & Bonds (Company name/number & description)	$			
		Acct. no.		
		Name and address of Company	$ Payment/Months	$
Life insurance net cash value	$			
Face amount: $				
Subtotal Liquid Assets	$			
Real estate owned (enter market value from schedule of real estate owned)	$	Acct. no.		
		Name and address of Company	$ Payment/Months	$
Vested interest in retirement fund	$			
Net worth of business(es) owned (attach financial statement)	$			
Automobiles owned (make and year)	$	Acct. no.		
		Alimony/Child Support/Separate Maintenance Payments Owed to:	$	
Other Assets (itemize)	$			
		Job-Related Expense (child care, union dues, etc.)	$	
		Total Monthly Payments	$	
Total Assets a.	$	Net Worth (a minus b) ▶ $	Total Liabilities b.	$

Schedule of Real Estate Owned (If additional properties are owned, use continuation sheet.)

Property Address (enter S if sold, PS if pending sale or R if rental being held for income)	Type of Property	Present Market Value	Amount of Mortgages & Liens	Gross Rental Income	Mortgage Payments	Insurance, Maintenance, Taxes & Misc.	Net Rental Income
		$	$	$	$	$	$
Totals		$	$	$	$	$	$

List any additional names under which credit has previously been received and indicate appropriate creditor name(s) and account number(s):

Alternate Name	Creditor Name	Account Number

VII. DETAILS OF TRANSACTION

a. Purchase price	$
b. Alterations, improvements, repairs	
c. Land (if acquired separately)	
d. Refinance (incl. debts to be paid off)	
e. Estimated prepaid items	
f. Estimated closing costs	
g. PMI, MIP, Funding Fee	
h. Discount (if Borrower will pay)	
i. Total costs (add items a through h)	
j. Subordinate financing	
k. Borrower's closing costs paid by Seller	
l. Other Credits (explain)	
m. Loan amount (exclude PMI, MIP, Funding Fee financed)	
n. PMI, MIP, Funding Fee financed	
o. Loan amount (add m & n)	
p. Cash from/to Borrower (subtract j, k, l & o from i)	

VIII. DECLARATIONS

If you answer "Yes" to any questions a through i, please use continuation sheet for explanation.

	Borrower Yes	No	Co-Borrower Yes	No
a. Are there any outstanding judgments against you?	☐	☐	☐	☐
b. Have you been declared bankrupt within the past 7 years?	☐	☐	☐	☐
c. Have you had property foreclosed upon or given title or deed in lieu thereof in the last 7 years?	☐	☐	☐	☐
d. Are you a party to a lawsuit?	☐	☐	☐	☐
e. Have you directly or indirectly been obligated on any loan which resulted in foreclosure, transfer of title in lieu of foreclosure, or judgment? (This would include such loans as home mortgage loans, SBA loans, home improvement loans, educational loans, manufactured (mobile) home loans, any mortgage, financial obligation, bond, or loan guarantee. If "Yes," provide details, including date, name and address of Lender, FHA or VA case number, if any, and reasons for the action.)	☐	☐	☐	☐
f. Are you presently delinquent or in default on any Federal debt or any other loan, mortgage, financial obligation, bond, or loan guarantee? If "Yes," give details as described in the preceding question.	☐	☐	☐	☐
g. Are you obligated to pay alimony, child support, or separate maintenance?	☐	☐	☐	☐
h. Is any part of the down payment borrowed?	☐	☐	☐	☐
i. Are you a co-maker or endorser on a note?	☐	☐	☐	☐
j. Are you a U.S. citizen?	☐	☐	☐	☐
k. Are you a permanent resident alien?	☐	☐	☐	☐
l. Do you intend to occupy the property as your primary residence? If "Yes," complete question m below.	☐	☐	☐	☐
m. Have you had an ownership interest in a property in the last three years?	☐	☐	☐	☐
(1) What type of property did you own—principal residence (PR), second home (SH), or investment property (IP)?				
(2) How did you hold title to the home—solely by yourself (S), jointly with your spouse (SP), or jointly with another person (O)?				

IX. ACKNOWLEDGMENT AND AGREEMENT

Each of the undersigned specifically represents to Lender and to Lender's actual or potential agents, brokers, processors, attorneys, insurers, servicers, successors and assigns and agrees and acknowledges that: (1) the information provided in this application is true and correct as of the date set forth opposite my signature and that any intentional or negligent misrepresentation of this information contained in this application may result in civil liability, including monetary damages, to any person who may suffer any loss due to reliance upon any misrepresentation that I have made on this application, and/or in criminal penalties including, but not limited to, fine or imprisonment or both under the provisions of Title 18, United States Code, Sec. 1001, et seq.; (2) the loan requested pursuant to this application (the "Loan") will be secured by a mortgage or deed of trust on the property described herein; (3) the property will not be used for any illegal or prohibited purpose or use; (4) all statements made in this application are made for the purpose of obtaining a residential mortgage loan; (5) the property will be occupied as indicated herein; (6) any owner or servicer of the Loan may verify or reverify any information contained in the application from any source named in this application, and Lender, its successors or assigns may retain the original and/or an electronic record of this application, even if the Loan is not approved; (7) the Lender and its agents, brokers, insurers, servicers, successors and assigns may continuously rely on the information contained in the application, and I am obligated to amend and/or supplement the information provided in this application if any of the material facts that I have represented herein should change prior to closing of the Loan; (8) in the event that my payments on the Loan become delinquent, the owner or servicer of the Loan may, in addition to any other rights and remedies that it may have relating to such delinquency, report my name and account information to one or more consumer credit reporting agencies; (9) ownership of the Loan and/or administration of the Loan account may be transferred with such notice as may be required by law; (10) neither Lender nor its agents, brokers, insurers, servicers, successors or assigns has made any representation or warranty, express or implied, to me regarding the property or the condition or value of the property; and (11) my transmission of this application as an "electronic record" containing my "electronic signature," as those terms are defined in applicable federal and/or state laws (excluding audio and video recordings), or my facsimile transmission of this application containing a facsimile of my signature, shall be as effective, enforceable and valid as if a paper version of this application were delivered containing my original written signature.

Borrower's Signature	Date	Co-Borrower's Signature	Date
X		X	

X. INFORMATION FOR GOVERNMENT MONITORING PURPOSES

The following information is requested by the Federal Government for certain types of loans related to a dwelling in order to monitor the lender's compliance with equal credit opportunity, fair housing and home mortgage disclosure laws. You are not required to furnish this information, but are encouraged to do so. The law provides that a lender may discriminate neither on the basis of this information, nor on whether you choose to furnish it. If you furnish the information, please provide both ethnicity and race. For race, you may check more than one designation. If you do not furnish ethnicity, race, or sex, under Federal regulations, this lender is required to note the information on the basis of visual observation or surname. If you do not wish to furnish the information, please check the box below. (Lender must review the above material to assure that the disclosures satisfy all requirements to which the lender is subject under applicable state law for the particular type of loan applied for.)

BORROWER ☐ I do not wish to furnish this information.	CO-BORROWER ☐ I do not wish to furnish this information.
Ethnicity: ☐ Hispanic or Latino ☐ Not Hispanic or Latino	**Ethnicity:** ☐ Hispanic or Latino ☐ Not Hispanic or Latino
Race: ☐ American Indian or Alaska Native ☐ Asian ☐ Black or African American ☐ Native Hawaiian or Other Pacific Islander ☐ White	**Race:** ☐ American Indian or Alaska Native ☐ Asian ☐ Black or African American ☐ Native Hawaiian or Other Pacific Islander ☐ White
Sex: ☐ Female ☐ Male	**Sex:** ☐ Female ☐ Male

To be Completed by Interviewer This application was taken by: ☐ Face-to-face interview ☐ Mail ☐ Telephone ☐ Internet	Interviewer's Name (print or type)	Name and Address of Interviewer's Employer
	Interviewer's Signature Date	
	Interviewer's Phone Number (incl. area code)	

Freddie Mac Form 65   01/04

Fannie Mae Form 1003   01/04

Because lenders must live with their lending decisions for long periods of time, they are interested in the trend of the collateral's value as well as its current value.

2. Borrower Information

The next section of the application requests the borrower's name, address, telephone number, social security number, marital status, and employer. There is a parallel section for the same information on any co-borrower (e.g., spouse). This information helps the lender determine both the borrower's ability and willingness to repay the loan.

3. Dependents

The lender will want to know how many dependents the borrower must support. Although children help stabilize a borrower, they also add considerably to the financial obligations of the borrower.

4. Employment Information

The next section of the form asks for the borrower's employment information and how to contact the borrower's employer to confirm the information given. If the borrower has been employed less than two years, previous employers must be listed as well.

5. Income

The section regarding income provides spaces for primary employment income, overtime, bonuses, commissions, dividends and interest, net rental income, and information regarding income from any other sources.

6. Monthly Housing Expense

The monthly housing expense is made up of such items as rent, principal and interest payments, any secondary financing payments, hazard insurance premiums, real estate taxes, mortgage insurance premiums, and homeowners' association dues.

7. Assets and Liabilities

In this section of the form, the borrower is required to list all assets and liabilities. Assets include cash deposits, checking and savings accounts, stocks and bonds, life insurance policies, owned real estate, retirement funds, automobiles, and other personal property. Liabilities include any installment debts, automobile loans, real estate loans, alimony, and/or child support payments.

8. Details of Purchase

The next section asks for information on the real estate transaction itself. The buyer is to fill in the purchase price, closing costs, prepaid escrow expenses, mortgage amount, any secondary financing amounts, other equity, amount of cash deposit, closing costs to be paid by the seller, and an estimate of the cash amount that the borrower will be required to pay at the close of the transaction.

9. Declarations

In this section, the buyers are required to note if there have been any legal judgments against them, if they have had a foreclosure within the past seven years, if they have declared bankruptcy within the past seven years, and if they are a party to any lawsuit. The answers to these questions will be of extreme interest to the lender. Obviously, an affirmative answer to any one of them could possibly adversely affect the ability of a borrower to obtain a loan.

10. Borrower's Signature and Information for Government Monitoring Purposes

Finally, there is a space for the buyer to date and sign the application. Below this space is a section that asks for the race, national origin, and sex of the borrower. This information is entirely *voluntary* on the part of the borrower and is collected to carry out the federal government's anti-discrimination laws.

F. LOAN APPLICATION CHECKLIST

In order to properly fill out the loan application, the borrower will need to know a variety of information that may not be easily recalled from memory. To ensure that all necessary data is at the borrower's

fingertips, it would be wise for him or her to take the following information to the initial interview:

1. The deposit receipt.

2. A residence history.

   a. Where the buyer has lived for the past two years.
   b. If the buyer is currently renting, the landlord or rental agency's name, address, and phone number.
   c. If the buyer owns his or her present home, the name, address, and phone number of the lender and the type of loan (e.g., FHA or conventional).

3. Employment history.

   a. Names, addresses, and zip codes of where the buyer has been employed for the last two years; the position held; whether the employment was full-time, part-time or temporary; and the income being earned at the time of departure.
   b. If self-employed or fully commissioned, the tax returns for the past two calendar years, plus a year-to-date income and expense statement.
   c. If a major stockholder in a corporation (owns 25% or more of the stock), three years of corporate tax returns.

4. Income.

   a. The amount and sources, including regular salary and secondary sources, such as:
      1. military retirement,
      2. company pensions,
      3. social security benefits,
      4. disability benefits, and
      5. child support or alimony will require a copy of the divorce decree.

5. A list of assets.

   a. Names, addresses, and account numbers for all bank accounts.
   b. The value of household goods and personal property.
   c. The make, model, year, and market value of automobiles.
   d. The cash and face value of insurance policies.

Figure 8-2

							MORTGAGEE NAME, LOAN NUMBER, &	
ADDRESS	MARKET VALUE	MORTGAGE BALANCE	EQUITY	GROSS RENT	MORTGAGE PAYMENT	INCOME	MAILING ADDRESS	SUBDIVISION NAME & COMMENTS

SCHEDULE OF REAL ESTATE

e. The address, description, and value of any other real estate owned (income properties should have a spread sheet showing relevant data, similar to the one shown in **Figure 8-2**).

6. A copy of a gift letter.

   a. If a gift is the source of the down-payment or closing costs.
   b. The letter must be signed by the donor (a close relative) and state that the funds are not to be repaid.

7. A list of liabilities.

   a. The name, address, and phone number for each creditor and the balance, monthly payment, and account number.
   b. A copy of the divorce decree if there is any child support or alimony obligation.

8. A Certificate of Eligibility for VA loans.

9. If there is to be the sale of a present home.

   a. The net dollar amount from the sale after deducting the sales commission and any expenses.

b. If the buyer is being relocated by an employer who is paying all or part of the closing costs, a letter from the employer stating exactly what costs will be paid by the company.

II. SUMMARY

The loan process consists of four general steps:

1. Filling out the loan application;
2. Analyzing the borrower and property;
3. Processing the loan application; and
4. Closing the loan.

Each of these steps can be simplified if the borrower (and real estate agent) knows what is required of him or her. By supplying all the necessary data the lender needs, the borrower can ensure a much smoother loan process for all concerned. Some of the information the lender will require:

1. The deposit receipt
2. A residence history
3. An employment history
4. Income information
5. A list of assets
6. A copy of any gift letter
7. A list of liabilities

III. CHAPTER TERMS

Appraisal	Escrow Agent
Credit Report	Escrow Instructions
Deposit Receipt	Loan Application

IV. CHAPTER 8 QUIZ

1. An escrow agent:

   a. fills out the loan application.
   b. acts on the instructions of the parties to the loan.
   c. determines the value of the property.
   d. none of the above.

2. An appraiser:

   a. provides an opinion of the value of the loan.
   b. provides an opinion of the value of the borrower's credit.
   c. provides an opinion of the value of the property.
   d. none of the above.

3. A deposit receipt is:

   a. provided by the lender at the close of the loan.
   b. provided by the borrower at the close of the loan.
   c. not required.
   d. a document that shows the terms of sale and expected closing date.

4. A credit report is:

   a. not necessary.
   b. paid for at the time of application.
   c. provided by the borrower.
   d. ordered by the escrow agent.

5. A bankruptcy would be noted on what section of the application?

   a. Assets and liabilities
   b. Borrower information
   c. Declarations
   d. Income

6. Real estate loans would be noted on what part of the form?

   a. Assets and liabilities
   b. Declarations
   c. Details of purchase
   d. Monthly housing expense

7. Information provided for government monitoring purposes is:

   a. required.
   b. voluntary.
   c. highly intrusive.
   d. used to redline borrowers based on their race.

8. A borrower must provide employment status for the past:

   a. one year.
   b. two years.
   c. three years.
   d. five years.

9. Discrimination in the loan process is prohibited by:

   a. the Fair Housing Act.
   b. the Credit Bureau Act.
   c. the Equal Credit Opportunity Act.
   d. none of the above.

10. Bankruptcies and foreclosures must be reported if they have occurred in the past ___ years.

    a. five
    b. three
    c. seven
    d. ten

ANSWERS: 1. b; 2. c; 3. d; 4. b; 5. c; 6. a; 7. b; 8. b; 9. c; 10. c

CHAPTER 9

CONVENTIONAL FINANCING

For the sake of simplicity and organization, we have divided the subject of financing programs into three general categories:

1. Conventional loan programs
2. Creative financing methods
3. Government insured or guaranteed loan programs

Since the Federal Housing Administration (FHA) was formed in 1934, conventional loans, government-sponsored loans, and certain forms of creative financing have provided the solutions to virtually all real estate financing problems.

Until the late 1970s, most real estate loans (conventional, creative, or government-sponsored) involved long-term, fixed rate repayment plans. A *LONG-TERM, FIXED RATE REAL ESTATE LOAN is one that is repaid over 15-30 years at an unchanging rate of interest.*

CHAPTER 9 OUTLINE

The fixed rate mortgage has been the cornerstone financing instrument since the Great Depression.

However, in times of high or volatile interest rates, the fixed rate mortgage is not favored by real estate lenders, due primarily to its slow payback of principal and its inability to keep pace with inflation and rising interest rates. A fixed rate mortgage bearing 7% interest will provide a 7% return throughout its term (up to 30 years), regardless of what happens to the cost of money during that time.

A fixed rate mortgage remains at the same rate of interest for the life of the loan.

If real estate is to attract investment money, it will be on the promise of return yields that are competitive with other investment alternatives. This means homebuyers today, and in the future, will have to pay interest rates that provide a similar return to that of the stock and bond markets. Furthermore, because interest levels are subject to significant change over relatively short periods, it's reasonable to expect lenders to protect themselves by committing their funds for shorter terms (15 years and less), or by offering variable rate loans, like adjustable rate mortgages (ARMs).

I. Conventional Loans

A **CONVENTIONAL LOAN** *is any loan not insured or guaranteed by a government agency.* The best way to explain contemporary non-government financing is to start with a look at conventional loans as they've been structured in the past, and then follow with a recital of the changes that resulted in today's conventional financing programs.

A. AMORTIZED LOANS

Conventional loans made over the past several decades have generally been long-term, fixed rate, fully amortizing loans. An **AMORTIZED LOAN** *is one that provides for repayment within an agreed period (term) by means of regular level payments (usually monthly) which include a portion for principal and a portion for interest.* As each payment is received, the appropriate amount of principal is deducted from the

173

Figure 9-1

Example: $90,000 loan @ 10¼%, 30-year term (figures approximate)					
PYMT. NO.	PRINCIPAL BALANCE	TOTAL PYMT.	INTEREST PORTION	PRNCPL. PORTION	ENDING BALANCE
1	$90,000.00	$806.49	$768.75	$37.74	$89,962.26
2	89,962.26	806.49	768.43	38.06	89,924.20
3	89,924.20	806.49	768.10	38.39	89,885.81
4	89,885.81	806.49	767.77	38.72	89,847.09
5	89,847.09	806.49	767.44	39.05	89,808.04

debt and the remainder of the payment, which represents the interest, is retained by the lender as earnings or profit. With each payment, the amount of the debt is reduced. Every month the interest portion of the payment is reduced and the principal portion is increased. (**See Figure 9-1**.)

The long-term, fully amortized or level payment loan has obvious advantages for the borrower.

1. Its repayment is spread out over 15-30 years, which keeps the monthly payment at a manageable level.

2. It is self-liquidating as the loan balance steadily declines to zero (the borrower is not faced with balloon payments of any kind).

3. The principal and interest payment remains constant for the entire term of the debt.

The long-term, fully amortized, fixed rate real estate loan is the loan type that borrowers are most familiar with and, in most cases, the type they would like to obtain when financing a home.

B. 15-YEAR, FIXED RATE MORTGAGE

The 15-year, fixed rate mortgage has gained increasing popularity over the last few years. Before the advent of the Federal Housing

Administration in 1934, a home loan normally was made for a period of five, seven, or 15 years. However, most of those loans involved partial or no amortization with balloon payments at the conclusion of their terms.

In the past two decades, there has been increased use of fixed rate mortgages that are amortized over a 15-year period. In the late 1980s lenders began to report that as many as 30% of their mortgages were 15-year, fixed rate. The secondary agencies also reported an increase in volume of 15-year mortgages.

1. Advantages of 15-Year Mortgages

A 15-year mortgage saves money.

There are several advantages to the 15-year mortgage. One is that lenders will often offer lower fixed interest rates on a 15-year than a 30-year mortgage because the shorter term means less risk for the lender. A 15-year mortgage also offers free and clear home ownership in half the time. The major benefit is the thousands of dollars that borrowers can save because of lower total payments over the life of the loan. A borrower who can do simple arithmetic will understand that for the relatively small additional monthly payment, the 15-year mortgage offers significant savings over its 30-year counterpart. In **Figure 9-2**, a comparison is made between a $70,000, $100,000, and $125,000 mortgage at 10% for 15-year terms and 10.5% for 30-year terms.

2. Disadvantages of 15-Year Mortgages

The growth in the use of 15-year mortgages has slowed somewhat in the past decade due to several disadvantages. A 15-year mortgage requires higher monthly payments. Larger down payments are often required to reduce the monthly payments. This combination of larger down payment and higher monthly payments has made it difficult for many young first-time buyers to utilize the 15-year mortgage. In addition, the homeowner loses the tax deduction on the interest payments sooner because homeownership is attained sooner. Lastly, because borrowers usually have the option of making extra payments on a 30-year

Figure 9-2

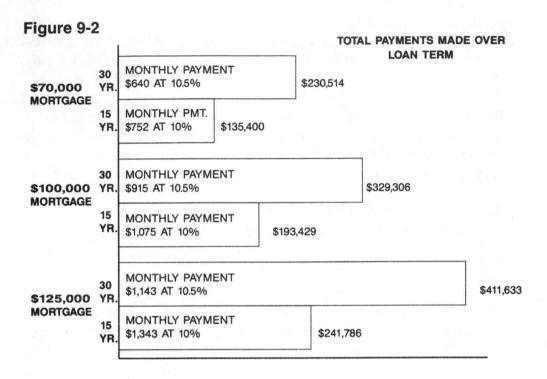

mortgage, they can choose to retire the debt early, without being legally obligated to make the higher payments.

C. CONFORMING VS. NONCONFORMING LOANS

The particulars of the conventional loan programs detailed in this chapter reflect the criteria established by the national secondary market investors, primarily the FNMA and FHLMC. Every conventional lender who has the option of keeping its loans in portfolio (primarily banks and savings banks) can, within the limits of the law, deviate from the standards set by the secondary investors. But when a loan does not meet secondary market criteria, it's considered nonconforming and is not salable on the secondary market. For example, so-called *JUMBO LOANS are loans that exceed the maximum loan amount that FNMA or FHLMC will purchase (currently $359,650) for a single-family residence.* A loan larger than the FNMA/FHLMC maximum would not conform to their standards and could not be sold to FNMA or FHLMC.

A jumbo loan exceeds the amount established by the secondary market and must be retained in the lender's portfolio.

Today the trend is almost exclusively towards **CONFORMING LOANS**; *that is, loans that meet secondary market standards.* While lenders in local communities may occasionally set policies that differ from those explained below, the vast majority of their loans will conform to the policies and standards set by the secondary market.

D. 80% CONVENTIONAL LOAN

For many years now, the standard conventional loan-to-value ratio (LTV) has been 80% of the appraised value or the sales price, whichever is less.

With this type of loan the buyer makes a 20% down payment and obtains a 30-year, fixed rate conventional loan for the balance of the purchase price.

If a buyer does not have enough money for a 20% down payment but still wants a conventional loan, he or she has a number of options, including:

1. A 90% conventional loan with a 10% down payment.

2. A 95% conventional loan with a 5% down payment.

3. A down payment of 10% with a conventional loan for up to 75% and the seller carrying a second mortgage for the remaining portion of the purchase.

Example: $120,000 sales price

$90,000   75% first mortgage
$18,000   15% 2nd mortgage (seller's)
$12,000   10% down payment
$120,000

Chapter 9

Asking the seller to carry a portion of the purchase price on installment has been a popular way to finance conventional transactions ever since the long-term, fully amortized loan came into existence in the 1930s.

Its popularity increases when interest rates are high and money from institutional sources (banks and savings banks) is scarce.

E. LOAN ORIGINATION FEE

To cover the administrative costs of making a real estate loan, the lender will always charge a LOAN ORIGINATION FEE, also called a "loan fee" or "loan service fee." The loan fee is a percentage of the loan amount, not the sales price. On conventional loans it will range from 1% to 3% or more.

Example:

$120,000	sales price
x .80	80% loan-to-value ratio
$96,000	loan amount
x .02	2% loan fee
$1,920	loan fee

The fee is customarily paid by the buyer. The lender generally charges lower loan fees on loans with 80% or lower ratios, and higher fees on the riskier 90% and 95% loans.

F. SECONDARY FINANCING

When a purchaser borrows money from any source to pay a portion of the required down payment or settlement costs, it is called SECONDARY FINANCING. In the preceding example, a 25% down payment would have been $30,000 ($120,000 purchase price less $90,000 loan equals $30,000 down payment). However, the borrower arranged for the seller to "carry" a portion of the purchase price over a period of time. In effect, the borrower has been extended credit by the seller and it's viewed as secondary financing, just as if the money had been borrowed from a lender. Conventional lenders allow secondary financing, provided the following requirements are met.

The borrower must make a 10% down payment. For owner-occupied property, the total of the first and second mortgage must not exceed 90% of the appraised value or the sales price, whichever is less. The borrower must pay the remaining 10% of the purchase price out of his or her own funds. The first mortgage may not exceed 75% loan to value.

Term not to exceed 30 years or to be less than five years. The "term" of a loan, in this context, refers to secondary financing which cannot extend beyond 30 years. The rationale for the 30-year limit is that it should not take longer to pay off a second mortgage than it will take to pay off a first mortgage, and traditionally the repayment period for a long-term, fully amortized first mortgage has been 30 years.

No prepayment penalty permitted. The second mortgage must be payable in part or in full at any time without a prepayment penalty.

Scheduled payments must be due on a regular basis. Payments on the second may be monthly, quarterly, semi-annual, or on any other regular basis. The scheduled payments can be designed to fully amortize the debt during its term or to pay interest only with a balloon payment at the conclusion of the term.

No negative amortization. The payment on the second mortgage must at least equal the interest on the loan. No negative amortization is allowed. *NEGATIVE AMORTIZATION occurs when the monthly payment is insufficient to pay the monthly interest and principle.* Thus, the unpaid interest is added back into the loan and the balance owed increases rather than decreasing.

The buyer must be able to afford the payments on both the first and second mortgages. In other words, the first mortgage lender takes the payments on the secondary mortgage into account when applying the qualifying ratios to the borrower's income.

1. Fully Amortized Second Mortgage

A five-year, $9,000 fully amortized second mortgage bearing 9.25% interest will cost the borrower approximately $190.12 per

month. When underwriting the loan, the lender will include this amount in the borrower's monthly housing expense.

Example:

$632.00   payment on 10%, 30-year, and $60,000 first mortgage (includes principle, interest, real estate taxes, and insurance)

+$190.12   payment on 9.75%, five-year, $9,000 second mortgage (fully amortized)

$822.12   total housing expense

2. Partially Amortized Second Mortgage with Balloon Payment

If a second mortgage is fully amortized (so that the loan is completely paid off by the end of the loan term), the monthly payments will be larger than if it is only partially amortized over the same period (so that the regular payments pay off only part of the loan by the end of the term, and a balloon payment is necessary). The thinking behind the partially amortized mortgage is that the smaller monthly payments make the total housing expense less burdensome for the borrower, and thus easier to qualify for the loan.

Example:

$632.00   payment on 10%, 30-year, $60,000 first mortgage (includes taxes and insurance)

+$77.32   payment on 9.75%, five-year, $9,000 second (partially amortized, based on 30-year repayment schedule)

$709.32

When compared to the example for the fully amortized second mortgage, it's clear the partially amortized second mortgage eases the qualifying burden somewhat. It may be a preferred financing arrangement when a borrower's income is insufficient to qualify for the higher monthly payments.

3. Setting Up a Partial Amortization Schedule

The above example states that the payments for the partially amortized mortgage are based on a 30-year repayment (amortization) plan. This means the payments were scheduled as though the debt would be paid in full over a 30-year period, even though the entire balance would be due and payable after five years. When the repayment term is 30 years, as opposed to five years, the payments are lower and the debt is retired very gradually. In fact, after five years, payments based on 30-year amortization will have reduced the original loan balance by a relatively small amount, and if the second mortgage is to be paid at that time, there will be a substantial balloon payment. The following chart illustrates how the $9,000 second mortgage balance would steadily decline over 30 years if allowed to do so. A 30-year, $9,000 loan at 9.75% will have an $8,677 (approximate) balance at the end of five years. This would be the amount of the balloon payment. (**See Figure 9-3.**)

Figure 9-3

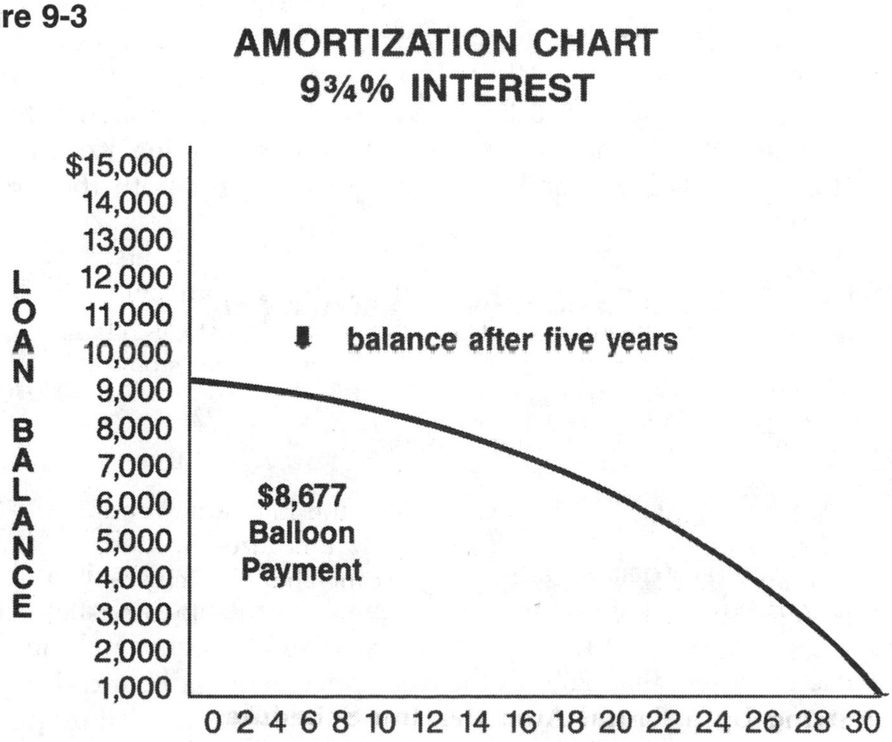

AMORTIZATION CHART
9¾% INTEREST

181

4. Interest-Only Second Mortgage

The second mortgage can call for "interest only," which will reduce the amount of the monthly payments still more. Of course, if no principal is paid during the term of the loan, the balloon payment will be the original amount (in the case of our prior example, $9,000). Monthly interest-only payments are computed by multiplying the mortgage debt by the stipulated interest and dividing that figure by 12 (months).

Example:

$9,000 x .0975 = $877.50
$877.50 ÷ 12 = $73.13 monthly interest payment.

5. Lender First and Lender Second Mortgage

The seller does not necessarily have to carry the second mortgage when secondary financing is included. The lender, for example, can make a normal 80% loan and a 10% second loan. The buyer makes a 10% down payment. A typical lender second under these circumstances might have payments based on 30-year amortization with a five-year *CALL PROVISION (balloon payment in five years)*, or it might be a fully amortized ten-year loan. The repayment plan is a matter of agreement between borrower and lender. Keep in mind, the lender will normally charge a loan fee for both the first and second loans.

G. PRIVATE MORTGAGE INSURANCE (PMI)

Eighty percent conventional loans have traditionally been considered "safe" by the mortgage industry because the substantial equity the borrower has in the property (20% of the purchase price) is a strong incentive to keep mortgage payments current.

Even if there is a default, a foreclosure sale of the property is more than likely to produce enough funds to cover 80% of the original sales price (or appraised value). However, once borrowers begin making down payments of less than 20% of the sales price, lenders regard the loan as more risky. Under these circumstances, the lender will require the borrower to pay for private mortgage insurance as protection against loss.

The presence of mortgage insurance reduces the lender's risk of loss in the event of a borrower default.

Both FNMA and FHLMC require third-party insurance on home loans with less than 20% down payments. Needless to say, the smaller down payment requirement of the 90% loan made it very popular with buyers, sellers, and real estate agents. Mortgage insurance is sometimes available for loans with up to 95% LTV.

1. How Mortgage Insurance Works

When insuring a loan, the mortgage insurance company shares the lender's risk, but actually assumes only the primary element of risk. This is to say the insurer does not insure the entire loan amount, but rather the upper portion of the loan. The amount of coverage can vary, but typically it's 20% to 25% of the loan amount.

Example: 20% coverage

```
$200,000    sales price
     x.90    LTV
$180,000    90% loan
      x.20   amount of coverage
 $36,000    amount of policy
```

In the event of default and foreclosure, the lender, at the insurer's option, will either sell the property and make a claim for reimbursement of actual losses (if any) up to the face amount of the policy, or relinquish the property to the insurer and make a claim for actual losses up to the policy amount. Losses incurred by the lender take the form of unpaid interest, property taxes and hazard insurance, attorney's fees, and costs of preserving the property during the period of foreclosure and resale, as well as the expense of selling the property itself. The following example is an illustration of how a claim is determined:

1. $10,950   unpaid interest
       2,061   unpaid taxes and insurance
       1,750   attorney's fees
       6,075   resale costs
      + 310   miscellaneous expenses
    $21,146   total cost of foreclosure and resale

2. $195,000   resale price
    -187,000   loan balance
      $8,000   gross profit on resale

3. $8,000   gross profit on resale
     -21,146   foreclosure and resale costs
    <$13,146>   net loss—amount of claim

In return for insuring the loan, the mortgage insurance company charges an initial premium at the time the loan is made and a recurring fee, called a RENEWAL PREMIUM, that is added to the borrower's mortgage payment. Real estate agents and lenders refer to the charges as the PMI (private mortgage insurance) or the MIP (MORTGAGE INSURANCE PREMIUM).

The initial premium charged at loan closing for a 90% fixed rate mortgage is generally less than 1% of the loan amount, depending upon the amount of coverage requested. Typical coverage would call for an initial premium of .5% of the loan amount for 20% coverage.

Example:

   $155,000   sales price
   $139,500   90% loan
   $139,500   loan amount
    x .0050   initial premium
      $698   PMI at closing

The renewal premium for a standard fixed rate, 90% loan averages about .34% of the loan amount annually. The annual fee is divided by 12 and added to the buyer's monthly payment.

Example:

$139,500   loan amount
x .0034   (.34%)
 $474   annual premium

$474 ÷ 12 = $39.50 monthly premium

Figure 9-4 is a mortgage insurance rate chart for primary residences published by a national mortgage insurance company. Although the focus of this discussion has been on insuring fixed rate mortgages, private mortgage insurance companies also insure adjustable rate mortgages (ARMs). Today, rates vary somewhat between companies for different types and amounts of coverage. **The chart is intended to serve only as a general example and not as a current price guide.**

2. One Time PMI Premium

Some private mortgage insurance companies offer one-time premium programs as an alternative to the traditional program of an initial premium plus renewal premiums. Under this alternative, the initial premium and renewal premiums are combined into a single, one-time premium. The one-time premium is financed over the loan term rather than paid as a lump sum; the premium amount is simply added to the mortgage amount before calculating the monthly payment. The one-time premium has two advantages for borrowers: there is no cash requirement at closing and the monthly payments, including a share of the amortized one-time premium, are usually smaller than the monthly payments including a share of the renewal premium required under the traditional program.

3. Cancellation

Lenders require mortgage insurance on high loan-to-value, low down payment loans as protection against borrower default.

Once the increased risk of borrower default is eliminated, usually when the loan balance has been reduced to 80% or less of the

Figure 9-4

FIXED PAYMENT MORTGAGES [1] [7]

| MGIC Coverage | LTV | SINGLE Term to 80% [8] | | ANNUAL | RENEWAL PREMIUMS | Constant [4] | |
		No Refund	Refund [9]	1st-Year Premiums	Declining [3]	Yrs. 2-10	Yrs. 11-Term
25%	90.01 - 95%	3.60%	4.40%	1.10%	.50%	.49%	.25%
	85.01 - 90%	2.50	3.10	.65	.35	.34	.25
	85% & under	2.15	2.45	.50	.35	.34	.25
22%	90.01 - 95%	3.25	4.30	1.00	.50	.49	.25
	85.01 - 90%	2.35	3.00	.55	.35	.34	.25
	85% & under	2.05	2.40	.45	.35	.34	.25
20%	90.01 - 95%	3.05	4.15	.90	.50	.49	.25
	85.01 - 90%	2.20	2.95	.50	.35	.34	.25
	85% & under	1.95	2.35	.40	.35	.34	.25
17%	85.01 - 90%	2.00	2.85	.40	.35	.34	.25
	85% & under	1.75	2.30	.35	.35	.34	.25
12%	85.01 - 90%	1.70	2.80	.35	.35	.34	.25
	85% & under [5]	1.50	2.00	.30	.30	.29	.25

NONFIXED PAYMENT MORTGAGES [2] [7]

| MGIC Coverage | LTV | SINGLE Term to 80% [8] | | ANNUAL | RENEWAL PREMIUMS | Constant [4] [6] | |
		No Refund	Refund [9]	1st-Year Premiums	Declining [3]	Yrs. 2-10	Yrs. 11-Term
25%	90.01 - 95%	4.20%	5.20%	1.35%	.55%	.54%	.25%
	85.01 - 90%	3.15	3.90	.75	.45	.44	.25
	85% & under	2.50	3.15	.60	.45	.44	.25
22%	90.01 - 95%	3.85	5.05	1.20	.55	.54	.25
	85.01 - 90%	2.90	3.80	.65	.45	.44	.25
	85% & under	2.35	3.10	.55	.45	.44	.25
20%	90.01 - 95%	3.60	4.90	1.10	.55	.54	.25
	85.01 - 90%	2.75	3.75	.60	.45	.44	.25
	85% & under	2.20	3.05	.50	.45	.44	.25
17%	85.01 - 90% [5]	2.50	3.65	.50	.45	.44	.25
	85% & under	2.00	2.65	.40	.40	.39	.25
12%	85.01 - 90%	2.05	3.20	.40	.40	.39	.25
	85% & under [5]	1.65	2.30	.35	.35	.34	.25

*An ARM will only be insured by many mortgage insurance companies if the only negative amortization that occurs is a result of payment caps; scheduled negative amortization is not allowed.

home's present value, the mortgage insurance has fulfilled its purpose. Originally, a lender was not required to cancel the insurance policy, even once the risk was reduced.

The mortgage insurance policy is a contract between the insurer and the lender—not the borrower—so only the lender can cancel it.

In many cases, the lender either did not cancel the policy, or cancelled it without passing the savings on to the borrower.

Example: Sometimes insurance premiums are written into the interest rate charged on the loan. If the lender's interest rate is 7% and the cost of the mortgage insurance is .5%, the total interest rate on the mortgage will be 7.5%. In the past, when the lender cancelled the insurance policy, it might have kept the interest rate at 7.5% instead of lowering it back to 7%. This practice is called **loaded couponing**.

FHLMC revised its mortgage insurance cancellation rule in 1985 to prevent this and other practices. Under FHLMC's rule, when the insurance is canceled the lender must modify the mortgage interest rate to reflect the cancellation. However, cancellation is not automatic; the borrower must request the cancellation and often must pay the costs of a new appraisal.

"Loaded Couponing" is the practice of retaining a higher interest rate that includes the premiums for PMI after the insurance has been cancelled.

FHLMC now requires lenders to drop coverage, at the request of borrowers, under certain conditions.

1. The insurance must be cancelled if the loan is at least seven years old and has been paid down to 80% or less of the home's current value.

2. If the mortgage is less than seven years old, lenders must cancel the policy only if the loan has been paid down to 80% of the home's value and the borrower meets established payment history criteria.

FHLMC MORTGAGE INSURANCE CANCELLATION RULES

IF:	REQUIREMENT:
1. Insurance is cancelled	Lender must reduce interest to reflect cancellation
2. Loan is at least seven years old and has been paid down to 80%	Insurance must be cancelled and rate reduced
3. **Fixed rate** loan is less than seven years old but paid down to 80% of home's current value*	Insurance must be cancelled and rate reduced, provided no mortgage payments have been more than 30 days past due during the preceding **12 months**
4. **Adjustable rate** loan is less than seven years old but paid down to 80% of home's current value*	Same as above, except no mortgage payments have been more than 30 days past due during the preceding **24 months**

***Buyer must obtain appraisal at own expense**

3. If the borrower has a fixed payment mortgage, payments must not have been more than 30 days past due in the immediately preceding 12 months.

4. If the loan is an adjustable rate mortgage, there must have been no payment over 30 days past due for the preceding 24 months.

FNMA also requires lenders to cancel PMI under certain conditions. In 1987, FNMA implemented a rule which requires all lenders who sell their mortgages to FNMA to cancel PMI if a new appraisal shows that the loan has been paid down to 80% of the property's current value (no matter how old the loan is).

The borrower must pay for a lender-approved appraisal, and if the appraisal shows the loan balance to be 80% or less of current value, the borrower then makes a formal request to terminate the

PMI. The lender must cancel the policy and reduce the monthly mortgage payment by the amount of the PMI premium.

Cancelling mortgage insurance, but failing to pass on the savings to the borrower, is a violation of the Real Estate Settlement Procedures Act (RESPA), according to the Department of Housing and Urban Development (HUD).

The practice of collecting premiums on cancelled insurance, referred to as **SELF-INSURANCE**, is thought to be common, although no accurate figures are available. The RESPA ruling is similar to the HUD policy on FHA loans, which considers self-insurance a fraudulent practice.

4. Rising Mortgage Delinquency

In the early 1980s, and again in the early 1990s, the amount of past-due mortgages and foreclosures began to rise dramatically. Indeed, in the early 1990s the rate reached historic levels not seen since the Great Depression. These increases in loan delinquencies and foreclosures prompted the mortgage insurance industry to raise its premiums and to institute new underwriting guidelines. Although the rate of delinquencies has now declined to ordinary levels, private mortgage insurance companies continue to apply strict standards to the mortgages they insure.

Most loan defaults occur between the third and fifth year of the life of the loan.

The losses experienced in 1984 and 1985 and again in 1991-1993 were largely due to loans originated in 1980-1982 and 1987-1990. The defaults occurred at a time of high unemployment and high interest rates which depressed home values and the housing market. Those who lost their jobs lost their homes as well, because they could not sell at a price equal to or greater than the mortgage balance.

The lesson that has (hopefully) been learned is that homebuyers can no longer expect inflation alone to bail them out of problem loans, as was the case during the 1970s.

Previous high inflation rates in the 1975 to 1985 period almost always ensured that the selling price of the home would exceed the original mortgage balance, so that a hard-pressed homeowner could sell the home for a profit, or at least enough to pay off the mortgage. When inflation levels lowered and the economy became depressed, the values of the homes declined drastically, and homeowners were unable, in many cases, to sell their homes for enough money to cover the amount that had been loaned on them.

As a result of this experience, mortgage insurance companies began to exert considerable effort to increase the quality of the loans they insure in an attempt to avoid future losses. These efforts resulted in both new policies, procedures, and new products.

A major change in the private mortgage insurance process is the active role that mortgage insurance companies are taking with their own underwriting procedures.

No longer are these companies simply reviewing loans made by lenders and then accepting them with few questions. Mortgage insurance companies now have their own comprehensive set of underwriting guidelines. For example, one national insurance company has its own list of documentation requirements, including lender loan application, credit report, verification of employment and income, verification of deposit, sales agreement, appraisal, and borrower payment history. The mortgage insurance company also requires a comprehensive borrower analysis, involving his or her personal history, employment history, an income ratio analysis, a review of assets, credit ratings, and credit reports. There are certain acceptable sources of equity (cash, gift letters, lot equity, sweat equity, etc.) and a set policy for property appraisals.

In another effort to improve quality control in underwriting, one national mortgage insurance company provides in its master policy that the insurance will not cover losses suffered from misrepresentation, negligence, or fraud. Representations made by lender, borrower, or any other party are considered to be the lender's own representation. It's hoped that these provisions encourage more care in the underwriting process because lenders will bear the burden of any misrepresentation or fraud that escapes their attention. The effect of these types of policy provisions may be somewhat modified by state law. Many states have passed laws providing that fraudulent statements in applications and attached documents for mortgage insurance will block a claim to recover. In some of these laws, if the application contains incorrect information that's not fraudulent, the legislation provides that the misrepresentation shall not prevent a recovery unless it was material to the acceptance of the risk, or the insurer in good faith would not have issued the policy if the true facts had been known. At least 30 states have passed similar legislation.

Another step taken by mortgage insurers, in an effort to control losses, includes employing spot-check appraisers to reevaluate the value of loan properties. Both lenders and insurers are becoming increasingly careful of those with whom they do business. Lenders are examining the financial health of the mortgage insurance company to ensure that they are able to pay all claims. Mortgage insurance companies are rechecking the underwriting standards of the lender to make sure that the loans being made are sound and less likely to default. Many insurance companies have refused to do business with those lenders who have made a large number of defaulted loans. Usually, a very small number of lenders are responsible for most of the loans that default.

One mortgage insurance company concluded that 90% of its defaults had come from only 10% of its lenders.

H. 90% CONVENTIONAL LOAN

Ninety percent loans became increasingly popular with the advent of private mortgage insurance.

The qualifying standards for such loans tend to be more stringent and lenders adhere to those standards more strictly (even though the loan is insured). Marginal buyers and properties are more likely to be rejected if the loan amount requested exceeds 80% of the value or purchase price, whichever is less.

When seeking a 90% loan, the buyer must make at least a 5% down payment out of his or her own cash reserves. The rest of the down payment may be a gift from a family member, equity in other property traded to the seller, or credit for rent already paid under a lease/purchase.

Ninety percent loans usually call for larger loan origination fees and higher interest rates than 80% loans do. This is a generalization and there are certainly exceptions. When thinking in terms of 90% financing, it's a good idea to expect a more expensive loan.

I. 95% CONVENTIONAL LOAN

The success of the 90% loan in the 1960s and early 1970s encouraged lenders and private mortgage insurers to experiment with even higher loan-to-value ratios. With the 95% loan, made primarily by savings banks and mortgage companies, it's possible to obtain conventional financing with as little as 5% cash down.

Applying the generalization "the smaller the down payment the greater the risk of default" (which represents the view of most lenders), it's easy to understand why in most cases the 95% conventional loan is more costly than 80% and 90% loans. Both interest rates and loan fees are generally increased for 95% loans. In fact, private mortgage insurance companies may charge up to a 1.10% premium at closing for 95% loans, as opposed to the .65% for 90% loans (at 25% coverage). Also, the borrower's renewal premium on 95% loans is usually higher than on 90% loans. Depending on the type of coverage requested, the renewal premium will be around .49%.

Figure 9-5 shows a comparison of the mortgage insurance rates for loans with different loan-to-value ratios.

No secondary financing is allowed for 95% conventional loans. The buyer must make the down payment on his or her own, without resorting to secondary financing or gifts.

Ninety-five percent conventional loans are becoming more and more difficult to obtain.

Figure 9-5	PMI COMPARISON CHART

PMI COMPARISON CHART
(for $95,000 loan at 20% coverage)

LTV	1st Year	Annual Renewal Premium
80%	(Mortgage Insurance not required)	
90%	$475.00 (.50%)	$323.00 (.34%)
95%	$855.00 (.90%)	$465.50 (.49%)

Underwriting guidelines are extremely strict for 95% loans, more so than they have been in the past, due to the high foreclosure rate of high loan-to-value loans. A marginal buyer will rarely qualify for a 95% loan. Underwriters "ride the credit line" when evaluating risk with just 5% down. A borrower's application is weak in certain areas, it's probably advisable that some alternate form of financing be considered, such as government-insured or seller financing.

Owner occupancy is required for a 95% loan.

1. FNMA Guidelines for 95% Loans

As an example of stricter underwriting requirements for 95% loans, FNMA guidelines state that the borrower should fall into one of the following three sets of circumstances:

1. The borrower has a good mortgage payment history, good credit, sufficient financial assets, and a credit history indicating the borrower is willing and able to devote a substantial portion of his or her income to a mortgage payment.

2. The borrower has no mortgage payment history (first-time buyer), good credit, sufficient financial assets, and the borrower's total monthly debt service-to-income ratio is **30% or less**.

3. The borrower has no mortgage payment history, but has good credit, sufficient financial assets and financial reserves to carry the mortgage payment. The borrower must normally have on deposit sufficient cash, or other very liquid assets, to

cover **two months' mortgage payments** (principal, interest, taxes, insurance, and mortgage insurance) after the down payment and closing costs.

Private mortgage insurers usually require three months' mortgage payments in reserve, an even stricter standard than FNMA's.

J. 100% OR MORE CONVENTIONAL LOAN

In the late 1990s, some lenders were advertising loans of from 100% to 125%. These loans were made on two assumptions. The first was that borrowers who had a good credit history were unlikely to default. The second assumption was that rapidly increasing property values would soon make up the gap between the property's actual value at the time of the loan and the overall loan amount. As we've seen from past experience, these are very dangerous assumptions to make. Such a loan creates a situation in which a borrower is more likely to default in a severe economic downturn when property values decrease. Indeed, it might be very advantageous for the borrower to default rather than remain "buried" under such a loan.

K. EASY DOCUMENTATION LOANS

In accordance with the general rule that lower down payment loans are more expensive and subject to stricter underwriting scrutiny, higher down payment loans are generally less expensive for the borrower and underwriting standards have been less stringently applied. For example, many lenders have been willing to waive verification of employment or documentation of income if the borrower is willing to make a larger than normal down payment, usually at least 25%-30%, and has good credit. These loans are often referred to as "easy qualifier," "time saver," "low documentation," or "no documentation" loans. They are particularly attractive for high-income borrowers whose income is from self-employment or from a variety of sources, and for whom documentation may be more burdensome than for borrowers whose income is solely from wages or salary.

In addition to the simplified, faster qualifying procedure, these low loan-to-value ratio loans are often less expensive because the lender may impose lower loan fees or slightly lower interest rates. Also, because the down payment is well over 20%, mortgage insurance is not required.

In times of rising delinquency rates, lenders become skeptical about low documentation loans and often refuse to do them. Currently, while difficult to obtain, they are once again acceptable to the market as long as the borrower has an extremely strong credit background.

L. ASSUMING CONVENTIONAL LOANS

Agents should not take chances when writing sales that call for assumption of existing conventional loans. Don't give buyers and sellers advice on whether a loan is assumable, unless it is a certainty.

When there is some question about what will happen if an assumption is attempted, consult the lender, an attorney, or other individual who is particularly qualified to advise you. When a buyer attempts to assume a loan, one of three things will happen:

1. The lender will accept the assumption and the loan terms will be left intact.

2. The lender will accept the assumption but will insist on an assumption fee and/or will increase the loan's interest rate, possibly to present market levels. This frequently defeats the purpose of the assumption, which was to take advantage of the loan's lower-than-market interest rate. Assumption fees vary from lender to lender, some are inconsequential, others are prohibitive (up to 3% of the loan balance or more). The charges are usually spelled out in the mortgage instrument.

3. The lender will refuse to allow the assumption and will call the note, which means demanding full payment of the loan at once. The right to do this must be spelled out in the promissory note or mortgage. If the buyer is an investor, the lender will usually require that the loan be paid down to a 75% loan-to-value ratio.

Don't discover after the sale what the lender plans or is entitled to do. Find out before creating the sale's contract, even if it means not making the sale at all.

M. CONVENTIONAL PREPAYMENT PENALTIES

Historically, most conventional lenders have penalized borrowers who paid off their loans sooner than agreed. Some still do. But because of the volatility of interest rates today, lenders are inclined to make short-term loans. They like the idea of being able to invest their money in real estate at today's rates, to recover it after a relatively short period (3 to 15 years for real estate loans), and to reinvest the funds at whatever rates prevail at the time.

Prepayment penalties discourage early payment of a loan, and this runs counter to most lenders' objectives in today's real estate market. FNMA and FHLMC don't have prepayment penalties in their standard promissory notes and mortgages or trust deeds. In many states, lenders are prohibited from charging prepayment penalties beyond the first five years of the life of the loan for loans on owner-occupied, one-to-four unit dwellings.

II. SUMMARY

The majority of conventional loans are fixed rate, fully amortized 30-year loans. However, 15-year loans have been gaining in popularity because of the significant savings in interest payments. Also, loans may be fully amortized, partially amortized, or interest-only with a balloon payment. Today, virtually all conventional loans are conforming loans, meaning they conform to FNMA/FHLMC standards.

1. Different standards apply to loans of different loan-to-value ratios: loans of not more than 80% LTV, loans of more than 80% LTV, and loans of more than 90% LTV. Generally speaking, the smaller the down payment, the stricter the underwriting standards applied. The loan fees also tend to be higher for loans with higher loan-to-value ratios.

2. Secondary financing is allowed on many conventional loans, but there are specific restrictions that must be followed. For example, a borrower may borrow part of the down payment from another source but must pay at least 10% out of his/her own resources. Also, no prepayment penalties are allowed on the second loan.

3. For loans over 80% LTV, private mortgage insurance is required to insure the lender for part of the loan amount. The borrower pays an initial fee and then an annual renewal premium for the mortgage insurance. Requirements of private mortgage insurers impose another set of standards in addition to the FNMA/FHLMC guidelines for underwriting loans.

4. Before trying to assume a conventional loan, study the original loan papers carefully. Lenders often have the option of charging an assumption fee, raising the interest rate, or refusing the assumption altogether. Conventional loans may or may not include prepayment charges and/or alienation clauses.

III. CHAPTER TERMS

Amortization	Loan Origination Fee
Call Provision	LTV (Loan-to-Value)
Conventional Loan	MIP (Mortgage Insurance Payment)
Fixed Rate Mortgage	PMI (Private Mortgage Insurance)
Jumbo Loan	Self Insurance
Loaded Couponing	

IV. CHAPTER 9 QUIZ

1. A mortgage that remains at the same rate for the life of the loan is called a:

   a. single rate mortgage.
   b. fixed rate mortgage.
   c. closed rate mortgage.
   d. non-assumable mortgage.

2. A loan that exceeds the maximum amount that FHMA or FHLMC will lend is called a:

   a. variable rate mortgage.
   b. maximum loan.
   c. jumbo loan.
   d. none of the above.

3. The current maximum amount for the type of loan in Question 2 is:

   a. $203,000.
   b. $359,650.
   c. $325,000.
   d. none of the above.

4. Jumbo loans:

   a. may be sold into the secondary market.
   b. are no longer offered by lenders.
   c. must be held in the lender's portfolio.
   d. none of the above.

5. A loan origination fee:

   a. is the commission paid to salespersons.
   b. is paid to the borrower by the lender for the privilege of processing the loan.
   c. is a fee to cover administrative costs.
   d. is prohibited by FNMA and FHLMC.

6. The standard loan-to-value (LTV) ratio has historically been:

   a. 95%
   b. 90%
   c. 80%
   d. 75%

7. In a loan with negative amortization, the balance owed:

   a. decreases over time.
   b. remains the same.
   c. increases over time.
   d. none of the above.

8. The practice of continuing to charge interest for PMI that was included within the interest charges on a loan after the insurance has been cancelled is called:

   a. fraud.
   b. a mortgage insurance premium.
   c. a non-cancellation policy.
   d. loaded couponing.

9. The practice of collecting mortgage insurance premiums on a policy that has been cancelled is called:

   a. self insurance.
   b. RESPA.
   c. default.
   d. none of the above.

10. The greatest risk of default is caused by:

    a. large down payments.
    b. small or no down payments.
    c. overpriced housing.
    d. high interest rates.

ANSWERS: 1. b; 2. c; 3. b; 4. c; 5. c; 6. c; 7. c; 8. d; 9. a; 10. b

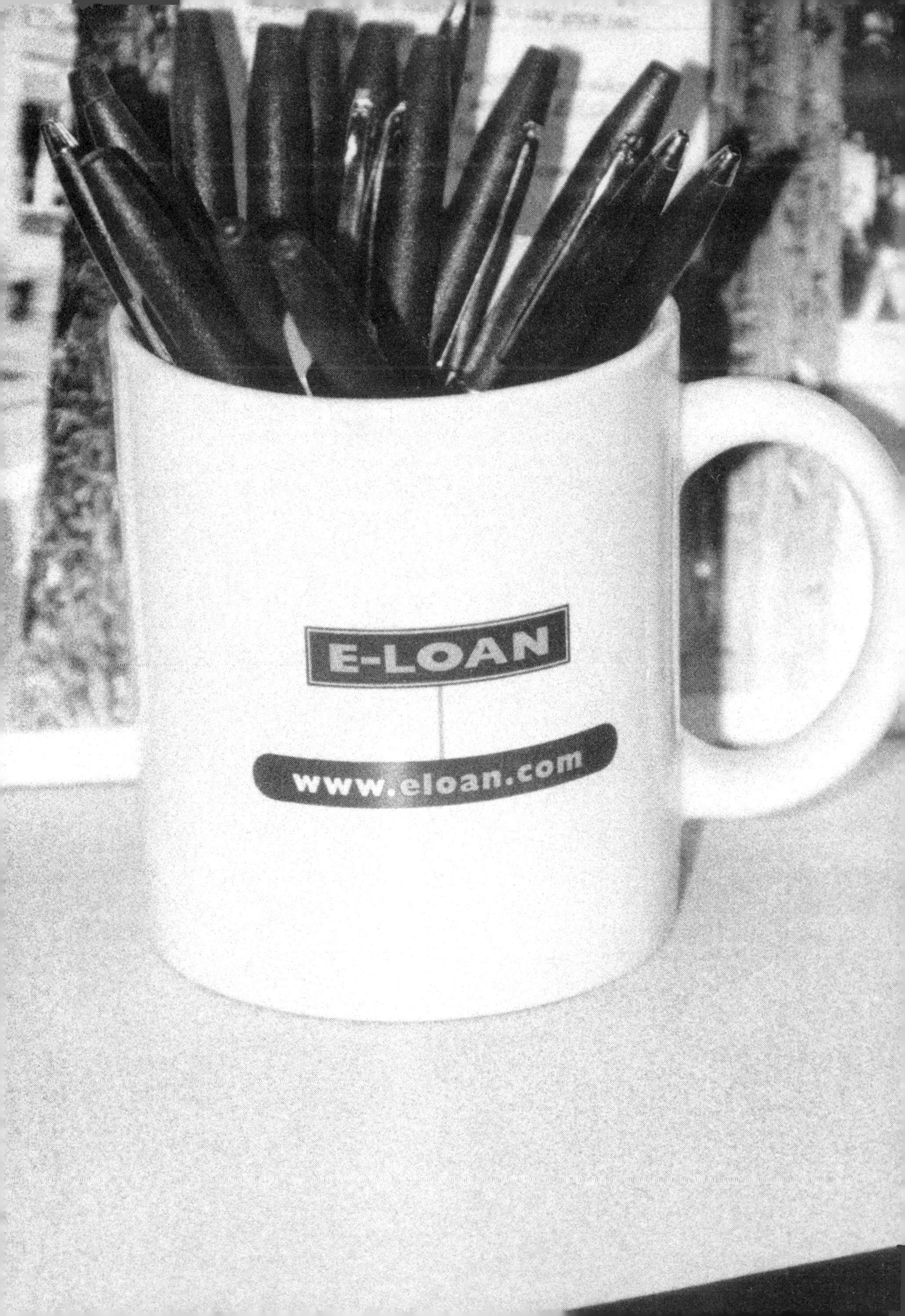
E-LOAN
www.eloan.com

—PART IV—
CHAPTERS 10, 11, AND 12
OTHER TYPES OF FINANCING

CHAPTER 10 - ALTERNATIVE FINANCING

Alternate financing programs were originally developed in the 1980s to meet the dual challenges of higher home prices and higher interest rates. In order to make it easier for borrowers, many of these alternate financial plans involve the payment of discount points, temporary buy-downs, or permanent buy-downs to reduce the borrower's interest or lower the payments.

CHAPTER 11 - GOVERNMENT PROGRAMS: FHA AND VA LOANS

The FHA and VA loan programs are huge federal insurance programs that are backed by the full faith and credit of the U.S. Government. Both programs have found ready acceptance by lenders and borrowers alike. The FHA has been a boon to the lending, construction, and real estate markets since its beginning. The VA programs are designed to provide veterans returning to civilian life an opportunity to enjoy the benefits of home ownership.

CHAPTER 12 - SELLER FINANCING

Seller financing provides an almost limitless variety of creative alternatives to institutional financing and is particularly attractive in tight money markets when loans from institutional lenders often have prohibitive interest rates.

CHAPTER 10

ALTERNATIVE FINANCING

The last two decades have presented the real estate and lending industries with a unique assortment of challenges. The paramount challenge has been to reconcile the investor's need for a high rate of return with the borrower's need for an affordable loan. The search for a solution to this problem spawned many innovative plans, such as buy-downs, adjustable rate mortgages (ARMs), graduated payment mortgages (GPMs), and growth equity mortgages (GEMs).

As interest rates declined from the high point reached in the early 1980s, interest in most alternative financing plans quickly evaporated. The return of affordable fixed rate conventional financing relegated many of the alternate financing plans to the dust-bin (with the sole exception of ARMs). However, today's lower interest rates are not guaranteed to continue, and rising rates can easily rekindle interest in alternative financing programs.

In this chapter, we will examine some of the most popular and successful of the alternative financing methods: buy-downs, ARMs, and GEMs.

CHAPTER 10 OUTLINE

Alternative financing plans are popular in times of high interest rates.

I. Discount Points

Before discussing specific alternative financing programs, it is important to explain **discount points**, often referred to simply as "points." The term "point" is short for "percentage point." A *POINT is one percentage point (one percent) of the loan amount.* For example, with a $100,000 loan, one point would be $1000; six points would be $6,000.

Lenders charge two different types of points in real estate loan transactions. One type, called a loan origination fee, loan fee, service fee, or administrative charge, is designed to pay the administrative costs the lender incurs in processing the loan. For example, a borrower might be required to pay a loan origination fee of 2% of the loan amount (two points).

The other type of point is a discount point. *DISCOUNT POINTS are used to increase the lender's yield from the loan without raising the interest rate.* If the loan is discounted (that is, if discount points are paid), the lender can charge the borrower a lower interest rate than it would otherwise have to charge in order to meet its minimum yield requirements. *The interest rate stated in the promissory note, called the NOMINAL RATE or the COUPON RATE, is less than the EFFECTIVE RATE, which is the lender's effective yield from the loan.*

Discount points were traditionally associated with FHA and VA financing, but they have become increasingly common in conventional loans.

Points may be paid by either the buyer or the seller, but they are most often paid by the seller in a sales transaction. Keep in mind that discounts are computed based on the loan amount, not the sales price. The borrower would, of course, pay the discount points in a refinance transaction.

Example:

$222,000 sales price
$177,600 loan amount
     6% discount
$177,600 loan amount
    x.06
$10,656 discount

Discount points are paid at closing by deducting the amount of the points from the amount of the loan to be advanced.

For instance, if the loan were for $145,000 and the lender required four discount points, 4% of the loan ($5,800) would be deducted from the amount actually advanced to the borrower (the loan would be discounted 4%) and the remainder, $139,200, would be delivered to the borrower to finance the purchase. The borrower would sign a promissory note and mortgage agreeing to repay the entire $145,000 at the stipulated rate of interest. The lender would advance only $139,200, but would be repaid $145,000. The buyer would transfer the loan proceeds ($139,200) to the seller without making up the difference. In effect, the seller would have paid the lender $5,800 to induce the lender to make the loan with a lower-than-market interest rate. The $5,800 would have compensated the lender for the lower yielding loan.

A. POINTS IN VA TRANSACTIONS

Payment of discount points has long been a part of most VA loans.

The interest rates on VA loans are usually somewhat lower than prevailing market rates. This means that a lender making a VA loan does not charge the borrower as much interest as it would for a conventional loan. Lenders, then, have traditionally required the seller to pay enough points to increase the lender's yield on VA loans to a rate that is competitive with conventional loans.

Under VA regulations, the buyer is prohibited from paying any discount points. Any points required by the lender must be paid by the seller or a third party, such as a builder.

B. POINTS IN CONVENTIONAL LOANS

The purpose of points in conventional loan transactions is usually to increase the lender's yield from the rate the borrower is willing or able to pay to the rate the lender requires as a yield on its loans. While the buyer is not prohibited from paying discount points on conventional or FHA loans, in most instances the seller is the one who pays the points as a way of reducing the interest rate to be paid by the buyer. In effect, this makes the property more marketable. *When the seller (or a third party) pays points to reduce the buyer's interest rate, it is called a* **BUY-DOWN**. It is far easier to sell property if the buyer's interest rate is relatively low and affordable.

C. HOW MANY POINTS?

The question of how many points must be paid can only be answered with up-to-the-minute information concerning yields required by lenders, which are affected to a large degree by existing market conditions.

The number of points required to increase the lender's yield by 1% is affected by many factors, including prevailing interest rates, the average time that loans are outstanding before being paid off, and to some degree, the terms of the loan documents themselves. The number of points to be paid is often computed on the assumption that it takes six points to increase the lender's yield on a 30-year loan by 1%. This is a "rule of thumb" approach to computing yields and should be confirmed with the lender before a final quote is made.

Example:

$90,000 proposed 30-year loan
   11% required yield
   10% interest rate preferred by borrower

$90,000
  x.06
 $5,400 discount (usually paid by seller)

$90,000
- 5,400
$84,600 advanced by lender after discount

$90,000 note
  x.10 nominal rate paid by borrower
 $9,000 interest paid by borrower

$9,000 ÷ $84,600 = .11 yield to lender

II. Buy-Down Plans

One of the easiest and most agreeable ways to make expensive loans less expensive is the "buy-down."

A buy-down is a way to lower a purchaser's initial monthly mortgage payments as an aid to qualifying for a loan. The seller, builder, or any other person, including the buyer, makes a lump sum payment to the lender at the time the loan is made. The money that has been paid to the lender is used to reduce the borrower's monthly payments either early in or throughout the life of the loan. The following examples will utilize high interest rates, as these are precisely the sort of market conditions under which buy-downs become popular.

Example:

$65,000   30-year, 15% loan
$3,900   buy-down (6 points)

$822   quoted 15% loan payment
- 770   buyer's payment at 14%
$52   savings resulting from buy-down

In the above example, the quoted rate is 15%, but the borrower's interest rate has been bought down by 1%, reducing the interest rate to 14%, for a savings of $52 per month.

A. TWO ADVANTAGES TO A BUY-DOWN

There are two fairly obvious advantages to a buy-down plan:

1. The buyer's monthly payment is lower than normal.
2. The lender evaluates the buyer on the basis of the reduced payment, thereby making it easier to qualify for the loan.

B. PERMANENT BUY-DOWNS

A buy-down can be permanent or temporary. If a portion of a buyer's interest rate is permanently bought down (e.g., for 30 years), the lender's nominal rate (the rate stated in the promissory note) will be reduced by that amount.

Example: Lender quotes 15% for a 30-year loan of $65,000. Builder agrees to buy-down the note rate to 14%. Lender agrees to make the loan at this rate if Builder makes a lump sum payment to Lender of $3,900 to buy down the interest rate by 1%.

1. How to Compute Permanent Buy-Downs

There are two ways to be completely accurate when determining a permanent interest rate buy-down. One way is to obtain a discount/yield table booklet from a lender or title company and learn to use it; the other way is to call your lender for a quote. If you just want a rough estimate of the buy-down amount, the six points per 1% interest formula referred to earlier is reasonably accurate.

C. TEMPORARY BUY-DOWNS

When interest rates are high, temporary buy-downs are very popular as a means of reducing a buyer's payments—sometimes substantially—in the early months or years of the loan.

Many buyers feel they can grow into a larger payment but need time to get established. Temporary buy-down plans take two forms: level payment and graduated payment

1. Level Payment Buy-Down Plan

A *LEVEL PAYMENT BUY-DOWN PLAN calls for an interest reduction that is constant throughout the buy down period.*

Example: Lender makes a 30-year loan for $65,000 at 15% interest. The seller agrees to buy-down the purchaser's interest rate to 13% for three years. (**See Figure 10-1.**)

Figure 10-1

Year	Note Interest Rate	Buydown %	Effective Interest Rate	Monthly Payment at 15%	Actual Monthly Payment	Monthly Subsidy	Annual Subsidy
1.	15%	2%	13%	$822	$719	$103	$1,236
2.	15%	2%	13%	$822	$719	$103	$1,236
3.	15%	2%	13%	$822	$719	$103	$1,236
4.	15%	-0-	15%	$822	$822	-0-	-0-
					TOTAL BUYDOWN		**$3,708**

2. Graduated Payment Buy-Down Plan

A *GRADUATED BUY-DOWN PLAN calls for the largest subsidies in the first year or two of the loan, with progressively smaller subsidies in each of the remaining years of the buy-down period.*

Example: Lender makes a 30-year loan for $70,000 at 14.75% interest. Builder agrees to buy-down purchaser's interest rate by

3% the first year, 2% the second year, and 1% the third year. (**See Figure 10-2.**)

Figure 10-2

Year	Note Interest Rate	Buydown %	Effective Interest Rate	Monthly Payment at 14¾%	Actual Monthly Payment	Monthly Subsidy	Annual Subsidy
1.	14¾%	3%	11¾%	$871	$707	$164	$1,968
2.	14¾%	2%	12¾%	$871	$761	$110	$1,320
3.	14¾%	1%	13¾%	$871	$816	$55	$660
4.	14¾%	-0-	14¾%	$871	$871	-0-	-0-
					TOTAL BUYDOWN		**$3,948**

3. How to Compute Temporary Buy-Downs

To be 100% accurate, use the yield/discount tables previously mentioned or obtain a quote from your lender. As an alternative, temporary buy-downs can be computed with considerable accuracy with the use of the interest rate factors in **Chapter 15** of this book, or a hand calculator programmed to calculate amortized loan payments. The subsidy computation by this method is simple:

1. Compute the buyer's monthly principal and interest payment without the subsidy.

2. Determine the buyer's monthly payment with the subsidy.

3. Subtract the subsidized payment from the actual payment and multiply by twelve for the annual subsidy.

4. Multiply the annual subsidy by the number of years in the buy-down plan.

Example: Level Payment Buy-Down

$76,000 loan amount
16.25% coupon (note) rate
14.25% subsidized rate (five years)

1. Determine monthly principal and interest without subsidy.

$76,000
x .0136494   16.25%, 30-year interest factor
$1,037.35   monthly payment without subsidy

2. Determine payment with subsidy.

$76,000
x .0120469   14.25%, 30-year interest factor
$915.56   monthly payment with subsidy

3. Subtract subsidy payment from actual payment and multiply by 12 (months).

$1,037.35   actual payment
- 915.56   subsidized payment
$121.79   monthly subsidy
x 12
$1,461.48   annual subsidy

4. With a level payment plan, the annual subsidy is constant for the entire buy-down period (in the case of this example, five years). So the final step is to multiply the annual subsidy by the number of years in the buy-down plan.

$1,461.48   annual subsidy
x 5   years in buy-down plan
$7,307.40   total buy-down (subsidy)

III. FNMA/FHLMC Limits on Buy-Downs

FNMA and FHLMC guidelines impose limits on discounts, buy-downs, and other forms of contributions by sellers, or other interested parties, for the purpose of paying for financing costs, including prepaid interest and impounds for property taxes, hazard insurance, and mortgage insurance. Contributions are limited to a percentage of the sales price or appraised value, whichever is less.

If the contributions exceed FNMA and FHLMC guidelines, the contribution amount must be deducted from the value or sales price before determining the maximum loan amount (with the exception of contributions by an employer or immediate family member, which are not subject to these limits). (**See Figure 10-3.**)

Figure 10-3

LTV Ratio	Maximum Contribution
2%	Investment property
3%	Principal residence and greater than 90% LTV
6%	Principal residence and 76% - 90% LTV
9%	Principal residence or second home and 75% or less

Example:

$100,000 sales price (principal residence)
105,000 appraised value
90,000 90% loan
6,000 maximum contribution

Any contribution in excess of $6,000 would be deducted from the sales price (or appraised value, if it were less), with a corresponding reduction in the loan amount.

IV. Adjustable Rate Mortgages (ARMs)

Perhaps the most popular and widely accepted form of alternate financing is the adjustable rate mortgage, universally referred to as an ARM.

Because the ARM shifts the risk of interest rate fluctuations to the borrower, lenders normally charge a lower rate for an ARM than for a fixed rate loan. Although the majority of borrowers prefer the security of a fixed rate (provided the rate is not too high), ARMs have maintained a place in the market despite comparatively low mortgage rates.

Generally, as interest rates rise and fall, so does the popularity of adjustable rate mortgages.

A. WHAT IS AN ADJUSTABLE RATE MORTGAGE?

*An **ADJUSTABLE RATE MORTGAGE (ARM)** is a mortgage that permits the lender to periodically adjust the interest rate so it will accurately reflect fluctuations in the cost of money.* ARMs are made primarily by banks and mortgage companies.

The ARM passes the risk of fluctuating interest levels on to borrowers, where many lenders feel it belongs.

With an ARM, it is the borrower who is affected by interest movements. If rates climb, the borrower's payments go up; if they decline, the payments go down.

B. HOW DOES AN ARM WORK?

The borrower's interest rate is determined initially by the cost of money at the time the loan is made. Once the rate has been set, it is tied to one of several widely recognized and published indexes, and future interest adjustments are based on the upward and downward movements of the index. *An **INDEX** is a statistical report that is a generally reliable indicator of the approximate change in the cost of money.* There are several acceptable indexes published periodically that are easily available to lenders and borrowers alike. Examples include:

1. the indexes for the monthly average yield on three-year Treasury securities;

2. the monthly average of the weekly auction rate on Treasury Bills;

3. the national average mortgage contract rate for major lenders on purchases of previously occupied homes; and

4. the cost of funds (based on the lenders' cost of funds).

At the time a loan is made, the index preferred by the lender is selected, and thereafter the loan interest rate will rise and fall with the rates reported by the index. Since the index is a reflection of the lender's cost of money, it is necessary to add a *MARGIN to the index to ensure sufficient income for administrative expenses and profit. In fact,*

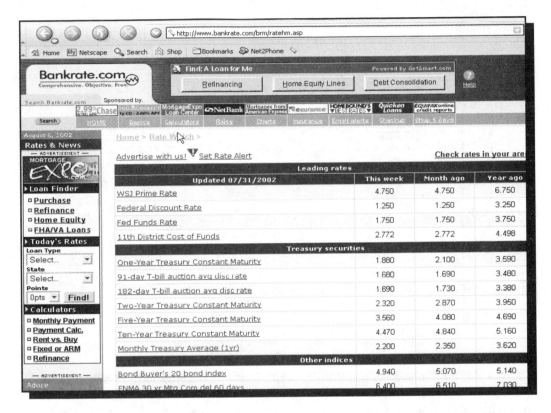

between lenders who use the same index, it is the size of the margin that makes the difference in interest charges. Margins will usually vary from 2% to 3%. The index plus the margin equals the adjustable interest rate.

It is the index rate that fluctuates during the term of the loan and causes the borrower's interest rate to increase and decrease; the lender's margin remains constant.

It should be noted that the lender has the option of increasing or leaving unchanged the borrower's interest rate when the selected index rises. But if the index falls, a reduction in the borrower's rate is mandatory.

Example: The lender has selected the one-year Treasury securities index. The lender's margin is 2%. When the index rate is raised, the ARM's interest rate is raised, and when the index rate falls, the ARM's rate falls. The margin stays the same. (**See Figure 10-4**).

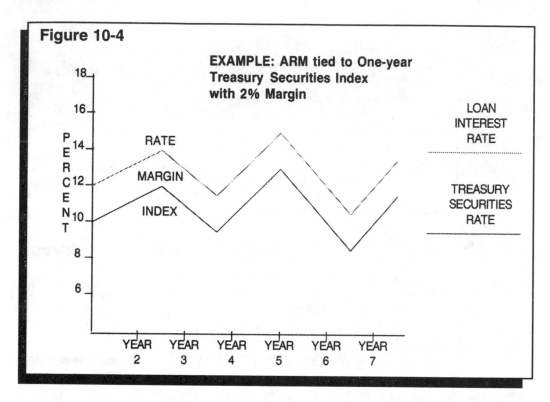

Figure 10-4

EXAMPLE: ARM tied to One-year
Treasury Securities Index
with 2% Margin

LOAN
INTEREST
RATE

TREASURY
SECURITIES
RATE

Terms, rate changes, and other aspects of ARMs are regulated by the
government agencies that oversee lending institutions (principally
the Office of Thrift Supervision and the Federal Reserve). Any
applicable guidelines or requirements of FNMA, FHLMC, FHA,
and/or private mortgage insurers must be followed as well.

C. ELEMENTS OF AN ARM LOAN

There are several elements that give form to an adjustable rate
mortgage. They include:

1. the index;
2. the margin;
3. the rate adjustment period;
4. the interest rate cap (if any);
5. the mortgage payment adjustment period;
6. the mortgage payment cap (if any);
7. the negative amortization cap (if any); and
8. a conversion option (if any).

1. The Index

Most lenders try to use an index that is very responsive to economic fluctuations. Thus, most ARMs have either a Treasury rate (usually one-year) or the cost of funds as an index. The *COST OF FUNDS INDEX (COF) is an average of the interest rates savings and loan associations pay for deposits and other borrowings with a certain range of maturities.*

The cost of funds index is more stable than the Treasury index rate.

The cost of funds index doesn't rise as much as the Treasury index over the long term, but neither does it fall as much. The Treasury index is more volatile, going both lower and higher than the cost of funds index.

2. Margin

The margin is the difference between the index value and the interest charged to the borrower. It remains constant throughout the loan term.

Example:

9.25%	current index value
2.00%	margin
11.25%	mortgage interest rate (note rate)

3. Rate Adjustment Period

The *RATE ADJUSTMENT PERIOD refers to the intervals at which a borrower's interest rate is adjusted,* e.g., six months, one year, or three years. After referring to the rate movement in the selected index, the lender will notify the borrower in writing of any rate increase or decrease. Annual rate adjustments are most common.

4. Interest Rate Cap

Lenders use two different mechanisms to limit the magnitude of payment changes that occur with interest rate adjustments: interest rate caps and payment caps. *If a limit is placed on the*

number of percentage points an interest rate can be increased during the term of a loan, it is said to be CAPPED. Today, most ARMs have caps of some kind.

Lenders, consumers, and congressional leaders alike are concerned with a phenomenon called payment shock. *PAYMENT SHOCK results from increases in a borrower's monthly payments which, depending upon the amount and frequency of payment increases, as well as the borrower's income, may eliminate the borrower's ability to continue making mortgage payments.*

5. Teaser Rates

When lenders discovered the residential adjustable rate mortgage instrument in late 1979, they recognized an opportunity to increase earnings and to insulate themselves from the staggering losses caused by too many fixed rate mortgages that were yielding less than the prevailing cost of money. As public acceptance of ARMs grew, so did the prevailing cost of money. As public acceptance of ARMs grew, so did the competition for adjustable rate mortgage loans.

To compete, lenders lowered the first-year interest rates on the loans they offered and introduced borrowers to discounts and buy-downs. *The low initial rates have subsequently been dubbed TEASER RATES.* Many lenders offered attractive teaser rates merely to enlarge their portfolio of ARMs. But since most ARMs were without interest rate caps prior to 1984, there were many instances where initial interest rates were increased by five to six percent. Clearly a crisis was developing. Consumers were losing confidence in the ARM and lenders were afraid they might experience unprecedented defaults, a phenomenon appropriately referred to as portfolio shock.

Industry leaders (especially the secondary market investors) began demanding more uniform ARM lending practices and a period of self-regulation began. To protect borrowers from payment shock and themselves from portfolio shock, lenders began imposing caps on their ARMS.

6. FNMA and FHLMC Caps

Both FNMA and FHLMC have guidelines relating to ARM interest rate caps. There are many different ARM plans, but as a general guideline, most ARMs purchased by FNMA are limited to rate increases of no more than 2% per year and 5% over the life of the loan. FHLMC rate adjustment guidelines limit rate increases to 2% per year and 5% over the life of the loan.

While FNMA and FHLMC guidelines do not take the form of government regulations, most lenders include these or stricter caps in their loans.

The Federal Home Loan Mortgage Corporation (FHLMC) has developed a set of ARM guidelines that, in its opinion, sets parameters acceptable for "investment quality" ARM loans. Guidelines for periodic interest rate caps are illustrated below. The column titled, "Illustrative Maximum Payment Increase," shows how a monthly payment would increase on a 30-year, $50,000 loan at a 12% interest rate with initial payments of $514.31. (See Figure 10-5.)

Figure 10-5

FEDERAL HOME LOAN MORTGAGE CORPORATION
Guidelines for Periodic Interest Rate Caps

Rate Adjustment Period	Per Rate Adjustment Period	
	Maximum Rate Adjustment	Illustrative Maximum Payment Increase*
Less than six months	0.167%	$ 6.43
Six months or more, but less than one year	1.0%	$ 38.79
One year or more, but less than two years	2.0%	$ 78.13
Two years or more, but less than three years	3.0%	$117.91
Three years or more	5.0%	$198.53

* $50,000 loan, 30 years at 12% interest

7. Mortgage Payment Adjustment Period

The *MORTGAGE PAYMENT ADJUSTMENT PERIOD defines the intervals at which a borrower's actual principal and interest payments are changed.* It is possible they will not coincide with the interest rate adjustments. There are two ways the rate and payment adjustments can be handled:

1. The lender can adjust the rate periodically as called for in the loan agreement and then adjust the mortgage payment to reflect the rate change.

2. The lender can adjust the rate more frequently than the mortgage payment is adjusted. For example, the loan agreement may call for interest rate adjustments every six months but changes in mortgage payments every three years.

If a borrower's principal and interest payment remains constant over a three-year period but the loan's interest rate has steadily increased or decreased during that time, then too little or too much interest will have been paid in the interim. When this happens, the difference is subtracted from or added to the loan balance. *When unpaid interest is added to a loan balance, it is called NEGATIVE AMORTIZATION.*

In an earlier illustration it was shown how a borrower's ARM payments would parallel a chosen index; but this is not always the case. If the loan agreement calls for regular rate changes, but only occasional payment adjustments, the payments will not parallel the index at all, as indicated by **Figure 10-6**.

> **Example:** A borrower's interest payment is set at 12.5%, which includes a 2.5% margin and a beginning index value of 10%. The lender will use the six-month Treasury Bill index for bi-annual rate adjustments, and the borrower's mortgage payment will be adjusted every three years.

You will notice that throughout the loan's first level payment period (years 1-3), rates were increased four times and decreased twice. Though it is impossible to say by looking at the graph, it would appear that the rate increases during this period were more

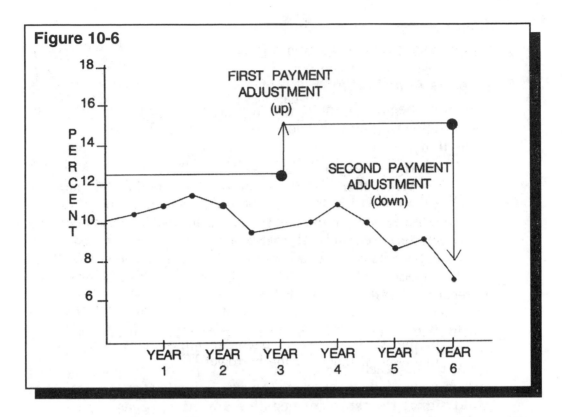

Figure 10-6

FIRST PAYMENT
ADJUSTMENT
(up)

SECOND PAYMENT
ADJUSTMENT
(down)

sustained and, in at least one instance, sharper than the rate declines. There is a good likelihood that during this period there was more interest due than paid, resulting in negative amortization. In the second three years, with only two moderate and relatively brief exceptions, the index value declined. Any negative amortization that occurred during the first three years was probably more than offset by the surplus interest paid by the borrower during the second three years.

8. Mortgage Payment Cap

When there are no limits on the amount mortgage payments can be increased, borrowers are vulnerable to extreme changes in the cost of money. Inevitably, unrestricted increases would create hardships for many borrowers. Some lenders incorporate payment caps into their ARMs, usually in the area of 7.5% annually. Other lenders only impose annual interest rate caps that work to limit payment increases. Still other lenders impose both rate and payment caps. Regardless of which policy a lender

embraces, the objective is the same: to keep payment adjustments within a manageable range for the borrower.

9. Negative Amortization

There has been a dramatic movement away from plans that can result in negative amortization. This is probably because mortgage plans that provide for, or at least have a possibility of, negative amortization are not as attractive to borrowers as plans that do not permit negative amortization. In general, today's borrowers are better informed with respect to adjustable rate loans.

Many lenders see annual interest and payment hikes, with acceptable limitations, as a means of avoiding interest shortfalls and the need for negative amortization. Interest rate fluctuations in recent times have been minor compared to the fluctuations between 1981 and 1982. By establishing rate and payment caps (during 1984), lenders began sharing more of the risk of increased interest rates than they did in the preceding three years. But if interest rates reach the high pre-1983 levels, the rate and payment caps in use today might prove too expensive for lenders, and that could signal the return of negative amortization as a means of keeping borrower's payments at manageable levels.

10. Negative Amortization Cap

Negative amortization has to be watched carefully or it could become an unmanageable problem for both the homeowner and the lender.

Various lenders handle the problem in different ways. Negative amortization becomes more critical at higher initial loan-to-value ratios. The current industry practice is to set a limit between 110%-125% of the initial loan balance. Another approach is to set the limit at 100% of the initial appraised value. This allows households that make larger down payments to have lower payments for a longer period of time. If negative amortization reaches the ceiling, the loan must be recast and further negative amortization is prohibited.

Bear in mind that negative amortization ceilings can be reached only if the interest rate increases several percentage points a year,

224

for a number of years, without relief. The payment caps previously mentioned allow payment increases that are substantial enough to prevent negative amortization in most cases. Negative amortization is most likely to occur when there are frequent rate changes (e.g., every six months) and infrequent payment adjustments (e.g., every three years).

11. Periodic Re-Amortization

As mentioned just above, many ARM loans with a possibility of negative amortization have a maximum cap for the amount of negative amortization. If the cap is reached, the loan payments are re-amortized to a level sufficient to pay off the loan over the remaining term, without regard to any payment cap that might otherwise apply. Some ARMs provide for periodic re-amortization of the loan, instead of or in addition to setting maximum caps for negative amortization. For example, the loan agreement might provide that every fifth year the monthly payments will be adjusted, with no payment cap, so that the new payments fully amortize the loan balance over its remaining term. These re-amortizations are in addition to the normal re-amortization and new payment levels made in connection with the regularly scheduled rate and/or payment adjustments.

Example: Original loan of $65,000 at 12.75% (10% index value + 2.75% margin). During the first five years overall rate increases have exceeded payment adjustments, resulting in negative amortization of $2,250. The loan balance is $67,250. Index value at the fifth year is 12.25%; the margin remains constant at 2.75% for an adjusted rate of 15%.

$67,250   adjusted loan balance
   15%   adjusted interest rate
25 years   remaining term on original 30-year loan

To determine the re-amortized payment, refer to the principal and interest factors in Chapter 15.

$67,250   adjusted loan balance
x .0128084   factor for 15%, 25-year loan
$861.36   re-amortized payment

225

This periodic re-amortization reduces the possibility of a large buildup in the homeowner's debt, which would otherwise have to be paid in the form of a balloon payment when the house is sold or the loan becomes due.

D. CONVERTIBLE ARMs

One of the most popular innovations in ARM loans is the conversion option. A *CONVERTIBLE ARM is one in which the borrower has the right to convert from an adjustable rate loan to a fixed rate loan.* ARMs with a conversion option normally include the following:

1. Higher interest rate (often both the initial rate and the converted rate are higher);

2. Limited time to convert (e.g., between the first and fifth year); and

3. Conversion fee (typically about 1%).

For example, in one convertible ARM program, the loan may be converted between the 13th and 60th month for a $250 conversion fee paid to the lender. The initial rate on the ARM loan is the same as for other ARMs, but if converted, the fixed rate is 1/8% higher than the standard fixed rate at the time of conversion.

E. ARM LOAN-TO-VALUE (LTV) RATIOS

ARMs with loan-to-value ratios of 80%, 90%, and 95% are available. However, higher LTV loans are often subject to some restrictions. For example, many lenders refuse to make 90% or 95% ARM loans if there is a possibility of negative amortization. In most cases, borrowers seeking 90% or 95% ARMs will be required to occupy the property being purchased. FNMA and FHLMC require owner-occupancy for all ARMs. Owner-occupants are considered better risks than non-occupant borrowers.

F. FHLMC AND FNMA LTV GUIDELINES FOR ARMs

FNMA and FHLMC have stricter guidelines for adjustable rate mortgages than the guidelines established for fixed rate mortgages.

Loan-to-value ratios may not exceed 90% for ARMs. The lower loan-to-value requirements are due to the potential risk involved from payment increases when the interest rate is adjusted.

G. DISCOUNTS AND SUBSIDY BUY-DOWNS ON ARMs

Some ARMs have initial interest rate discounts or subsidy buy-downs. A discounted rate, in this context, means the borrower pays less than the *NOTE RATE (index rate plus margin)* prior to the first interest rate adjustment. The discounted rate is frequently referred to as a teaser rate. Loans with a subsidy buy-down reduce the borrower's initial rate by payment of funds in advance. The subsidy buy-down is usually paid by the seller. The probability that payment shock will occur is increased, because a payment increase after the first adjustment period is almost inevitable, even if there has been no increase in the value of the index in the interim. Of course, an increase in the index during this same period would make the payment shock even greater.

Moreover, initial rate discounts and subsidy buy-downs have been used to make ARMs more attractive to borrowers who have trouble qualifying for financing at higher rates. Thus, these loans are inherently more risky than most other types of loans, and lenders now underwrite them conservatively.

For ARMs with a 2% annual interest rate adjustment cap and an LTV over 80%, FHLMC requires the borrower to be qualified on the basis of payments made on the mortgage at the initial rate plus 2% (the maximum second-year mortgage rate increase). For example, a borrower seeking an ARM loan with an initial interest rate of 9% would have to qualify at an 11% interest rate (initial rate plus 2%).

Similarly, when an ARM involves a buy-down, FNMA requires the borrower to be qualified on the basis of the original interest rate without the buy-down. FNMA limits seller contributions to 2% if the loan-to-value ratio is over 90%, and to 9% if the loan-to-value ratio is 90% or less.

H. HOUSING EXPENSE-TO-INCOME RATIOS ON ARMs

Certain ARMs contain features that increase the likelihood that housing expense-to-income ratios will increase to dangerous levels

after the first rate adjustment. (Expense-to-income ratios are covered in *Qualifying the Buyer*, Chapter 13.) ARMs with no rate or payment caps have the potential for large increases in the ratios. Likewise, loans with rate discounts or subsidy buy-downs that exceed 2% add to the chances of significant payment shock. When ARMs are made with these features, secondary market investors, and many private mortgage insurance companies, are insisting that the traditional housing expense-to-gross income and total monthly debt payment-to-income ratios of 28% and 36% be disregarded in favor of lower, more conservative ratios.

The FHLMC recommends a 25% housing expense-to-income ratio, and a 33% total monthly debt service-to-income ratio, for ARM loans with any of the following features:

1. rate or payment cap outside FHLMC guidelines, or no caps;

2. discount or subsidy buy-down exceeds 2%;

3. rate cap over 1% or payment cap over 7.5%; or

4. difference between rate and payment adjustment periods exceeds three years, and the payment cap does not meet FHLMC guidelines.

I. APPRAISALS ON PROPERTIES SECURED BY ARMs

Because ARMs introduce additional elements of risk to mortgage lending, many lenders adhere more strictly to their underwriting guidelines when evaluating an application for an ARM. A lender is particularly likely to review the appraisal for an ARM with special care.

Nowadays lenders insist that appraisal reports accurately reflect property values influenced by buy-downs or other financing concessions. If a comparable property was sold with special financing arrangements, the buyers may have paid more for it than they would have without those arrangements. The appraiser must take the effect of the financing arrangements into account when using the comparable's selling price as an indication of the subject property's value.

When underwriting an ARM, the underwriter will review the appraisal report very closely to determine if the appraiser has performed this analysis satisfactorily. If not, the appraisal will be considered deficient.

J. ARM STANDARDIZATION

The widespread acceptance of ARMs represents a major evolutionary phase in the housing industry.

Initially, the estimated 200-plus adjustable rate plans fueled sharp criticism. Customers were understandably confused by the proliferation of ARM programs. The threat of government regulation, increased dangers of foreclosure, and the refusal of the secondary market to buy ARMs caused lenders to standardize many of their ARM programs.

Uniform ARM underwriting standards have since been adopted and the secondary market agencies are now purchasing ARMs on a large-scale basis. Originally, lenders were underwriting ARMs on the basis of their own standards and were largely keeping them in portfolio.

With standardization, lenders follow secondary market guidelines and resell ARMs just as they do fixed rate loans.

K. ARM DISCLOSURE

Lenders offering adjustable rate mortgages must comply with the Federal Reserve's guidelines under Regulation Z of the Truth in Lending Act requiring certain disclosures to be made to ARM borrowers.

These rules require a **general brochure** to be given borrowers and **certain specific disclosures** to be made if relevant to the particular ARM program. They also establish guidelines for calculating and disclosing the annual percentage rate (APR). Disclosures must be provided to the borrower when the loan application is made or before payment of any nonrefundable fee, whichever occurs first.

A lender may comply with the requirement to provide a general informational brochure on adjustable rate loans by giving the loan applicant the *Consumer Handbook on Adjustable Rate Mortgages*, which has been prepared by the Federal Reserve and the Federal Home Loan Bank Board. The following disclosures must be made, if appropriate, to the individual loan program applied for:

229

1. The index used to determine the interest rate.

2. Where the borrower may find the index.

3. An explanation of how the interest rate and payment will be determined.

4. A suggestion that the borrower ask the lender about the current margin and interest rate.

5. If the initial rate is discounted, a disclosure of that fact and a suggestion that the borrower inquire as to the amount of the discount.

6. The interest and payment adjustment periods.

7. Any rules regarding changes in the index, interest rate, payment amount, or loan balance (including an explanation of any caps, a conversion option, or the possibility of negative amortization).

8. An explanation of how to calculate the payments for the loan.

9. A statement that the loan has a demand feature (that is, a "call" provision or acceleration clause).

10. A description of the information that will be included in the adjustment notices and when those notices will be provided.

11. A statement that disclosure forms are available for the lender's other ARM programs.

The lender must also give the borrower a historical example illustrating how the payments on a $10,000 loan would have been affected by rate changes over the past 15 years, and an example of how the maximum interest rate and payment would be calculated for a $10,000 loan.

The lender must give the borrower advance notice of any change in the payment, interest rate, index, or loan balance. These disclosures must be provided at least 25 days, but no more than 120 days, before a new payment level goes into effect, and at least once in each year in which the interest rate changes without a corresponding payment adjustment.

When calculating the annual percentage rate for an adjustable rate mortgage, a lender is allowed to base the APR on the loan's initial interest rate.

At closing, this is usually the only interest rate for the loan that the lender can be sure of. The rates that will apply later on are uncertain, because they depend on changes in the index to which the loan is tied. However, the lender is required to state that the APR may increase ("10.41% APR, subject to increase after closing").

If the loan has a teaser rate (a special low initial interest rate) and the interest rate is scheduled to rise by a specific amount, the APR, must be a composite figure taking into account every interest rate that the lender knows at closing will apply to the loan. The APR can't be based on the teaser rate alone.

The guidelines are an effort to ensure that when mortgage rates are adjusted, borrowers, whose disclosure forms are based only on a discounted initial rate, are not faced with unexpectedly large increases in their payments.

L. WHAT YOU NEED TO KNOW ABOUT ARMs

As an agent, you must always be prepared to answer buyers' and sellers' questions. You are expected to be knowledgeable. When it comes to ARM financing, it would be reasonable to expect the following questions:

1. What will my interest rate be?

It is usually not necessary to break the rate down into index and margin. The buyer is concerned only with the total. Monitor local rates; they change regularly.

2. How often will my interest rate change?

The rate adjustments will be spelled out in the loan agreement. Depending on lender preference (index used), they will occur every six months, annually, every three years, or every five years. The six-month and one-year intervals are most common. In order to be specific, you have to know your lenders and their policies.

3. How often will my payment change?

Again, in order to give an accurate answer, you have to be familiar with the policies of the local lenders. The majority of lenders have

shown a preference for simultaneous rate and payment changes, but there are many exceptions.

4. Is there any limit to how much my interest rate can be increased?

Most ARMs have payment caps. The most common life-of-the-loan caps are 5% and 6% caps imposed by FHLMC and FNMA. Annual interest rate caps are usually between 1% and 2%.

5. Is there any limit to how much my payment can be increased at any one time?

Some ARMs have payment caps while others keep payment hikes under control with interest rate caps. Where payment caps exist, they are usually limited to 7.5%-15% of the payment amount or the equivalent of a 1%-2% interest rate change.

6. What is the probability of runaway negative amortization?

The answer is: remote to nonexistent. Interest rate caps, negative amortization caps, and re-amortization requirements protect borrower and lender in this regard. But the best protection is undoubtedly the changing nature of the money market itself. Interest rates rise and fall; they always have. A borrower's rate will be increased at one interval and reduced at another. If, at one point, there is negative amortization because the interest due exceeded interest paid, there is an excellent chance that not long afterwards index declines will result in the opposite: accelerated amortization. This up and down pattern, though always unpredictable, continues throughout the life of the loan.

7. Can my ARM be converted to a fixed rate loan?

Many ARMs now contain a conversion option which permits the borrower to convert to a fixed rate loan for a fee at certain periods or points in the loan term. ARMs with a conversion option often have higher interest rates than those without.

V. The Growth Equity Mortgage (GEM)

Sometimes called a building equity mortgage (BEM) or rapidly amortizing mortgage (RAM), the GEM solves many of the problems that have limited the appeal of ARMs. Still, today it enjoys only limited public acceptance.

Though there are numerous variations of the growth equity mortgage, all of them share the following characteristics:

1. The interest rate is fixed over the life of the loan.
2. First year payments of principal and interest are based on a 30-year term.
3. The borrower's payments are increased at specified intervals (usually annually) for all, or a portion of, the life of the loan.
4. Because the interest rate is fixed, 100% of the annual payment increases are used to reduce the principal balance.

A. DETERMINING ANNUAL PAYMENT ADJUSTMENTS

There are any number of annual payment adjustment plans, but by far the most popular method is to increase the payments by a fixed percentage—typically 3% or 5%.

Example: $86,000 loan at 10.25% (fixed rate) based on a 30-year term. Payments to be increased 3% annually.

$86,000
x .0089610   10.25%, 30-year factor
$770.65   initial monthly payment

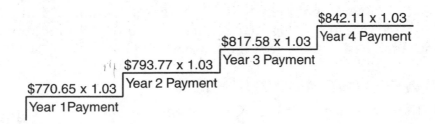

$842.11 x 1.03 | Year 4 Payment
$817.58 x 1.03 | Year 3 Payment
$793.77 x 1.03 | Year 2 Payment
$770.65 x 1.03 | Year 1 Payment

In the example above, the borrower's payments are increased by 3% each year, and the entire increase is always applied to the loan balance.

B. EQUITY BUILDS UP QUICKLY

Because payment increases are used to reduce the mortgage debt, a borrower will pay off a GEM much sooner than a 30-year fixed rate mortgage. If payments are increased 3% per year on a 15% loan, the entire debt will be retired in 13 years and 7 months; with 5% annual increases, the same loan will pay off in just 11 years and 4 months. A GEM's repayment term is dependent on the interest rate and the magnitude of the annual payment increases. Most GEMs pay off in 11 to 17 years. **Figure 10-7** demonstrates the difference between the repayment patterns of a GEM and a 30-year fixed rate mortgage.

It is clearly illustrated by the Comparison of Repayment Pattern graph that GEM payments become substantially higher than the level fixed rate payments. In the past, this annual rate of increase was well below the inflationary trends and GEM payment increases did not rise as fast as borrowers' incomes. Borrowers had few difficulties adjusting to payment hikes, and furthermore, to many borrowers the payment increase drawback was insignificant when weighed against the remarkable advantage of accelerated equity accumulation. A 30-year, fixed rate mortgage shows a balance of $65,620.93 after 13 years and 4½ months. At the end of the same period, the GEM loan is paid in full. At current low rates of inflation, the GEM payment increases do not look so attractive. The primary advantages of GEMs, fast amortization and predictable payments, are also available with the more popular level payment 15-year, fixed rate loans discussed in the previous chapter.

C. PAYMENTS ARE PREDICTABLE

The borrower's payments will increase annually, but unlike adjustable rate mortgages that are tied to an index, the amount of the annual increase is known at the outset of the loan.

D. NO NEGATIVE AMORTIZATION

To the contrary, with a GEM, there is accelerated positive amortization.

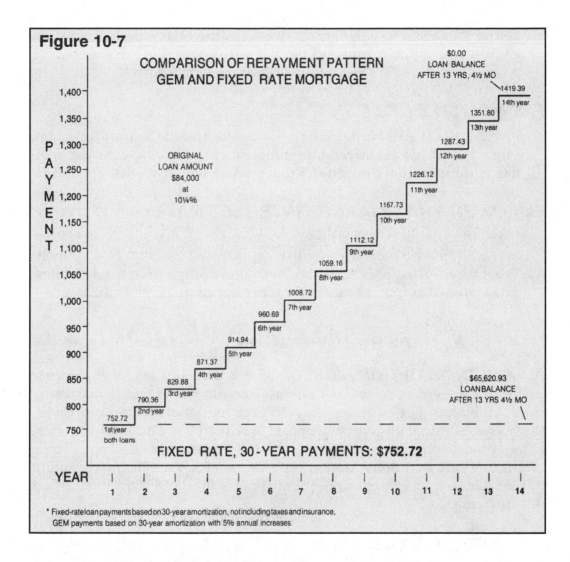

Figure 10-7

COMPARISON OF REPAYMENT PATTERN
GEM AND FIXED RATE MORTGAGE

$0.00
LOAN BALANCE
AFTER 13 YRS, 4½ MO

ORIGINAL
LOAN AMOUNT
$84,000
at
10¼%

$65,620.93
LOAN BALANCE
AFTER 13 YRS 4½ MO

FIXED RATE, 30-YEAR PAYMENTS: $752.72

* Fixed-rate loan payments based on 30-year amortization, not including taxes and insurance.
  GEM payments based on 30-year amortization with 5% annual increases.

E. REDUCED INTEREST COSTS

A GEM borrower will pay less than half the interest he or she would pay with a traditional 30-year, fixed rate mortgage.

By referring back to the "Comparison of Repayment Pattern" chart (Figure 10-7), you can see that after 13 years and 4½ months the borrower will have paid only $18,379.07 in principal on the 30-year, fixed rate mortgage. The balance of the $120,811.56 in payments will have been applied to interest, with much more interest to be paid

before the loan's 30-year term is over. On the other hand, interest on a GEM loan is much less and the interest portion of each succeeding payment will decline as rapidly as the loan balance itself.

F. SIMPLICITY OF LOAN

In contrast to ARMs, the GEM is easy to understand and explain. There is little doubt buyers are reluctant to commit to a major debt, like a home loan, if they do not understand how it works.

G. LOWER-THAN-MARKET INTEREST RATE

Very often lenders are willing to make GEM loans at lower-than-market rates because they will recapture the principal so quickly. Recaptured principal can be reinvested at competitive market rates. The lower-than-market rate makes it easier to qualify for the loan.

VI. Reduction Option Mortgage

A **REDUCTION OPTION MORTGAGE** *is a fixed rate loan that gives the borrower a limited opportunity to reduce the interest rate without paying refinancing costs.* For example, on a 30-year reduction option mortgage, the borrower might be given the option of reducing the interest rate once, at any time during the second through fifth years of the loan term. There might be some additional limitations; for example, the borrower might not be allowed to exercise the option unless market interest rates had declined at least 2%.

If the borrower chose to exercise the option, the lender would charge a processing fee, usually in the neighborhood of a few hundred dollars. This is substantially less than the fees typically charged for refinancing, which are ordinarily between 1% and 2% of the loan amount. Other costs of refinancing, such as an appraisal fee, are also avoided with a reduction option mortgage. Interest rates for reduction option mortgages tend to be slightly higher than for fixed rate loans without the reduction option.

VII. Bi-Weekly Loans

A **BI-WEEKLY LOAN** *is a fixed rate mortgage set up in a fashion similar to a standard 30-year conventional loan. Both interest rate and payments are fixed.*

However, payments are made every two weeks instead of every month. Each payment is equal to half of what the monthly payment would be for a fully amortized 30-year, fixed rate loan of the same amount at the same interest rate.

Bi-weekly loans offer significant savings over the life of a loan. For example, if a $70,000 loan at an interest rate of 10.5% is paid on a bi-weekly schedule, instead of a monthly payment plan, the borrower would save approximately $60,000 in interest. Because payments are made every two weeks (not twice a month), 26 payments are made each year (i.e., the equivalent of an extra monthly payment is made each year). As interest is calculated on the remaining balance, this provides a rather large interest savings. Bi-weekly loans are generally paid off in approximately 20 to 21 years, instead of 30 years.

Example: A $70,000 loan with a 10.5% fixed rate and a 30-year amortization schedule would have the following results:

Schedule of Payments	Payment	# of payments	Total Amount Paid
Monthly	$640.32	360	$230,515.20
Bi-weekly	$320.21	532	$170,352.39

The bi-weekly loan would pay off in about 20½ years, with total interest payments of approximately $60,189.81 less than the monthly payment schedule.

NOTE: In this example, bi-weekly payments are slightly more than one-half the monthly payment in order to avoid a partial final payment.

Although bi-weekly loans have been available for some time, especially in the Northeast and Midwest, they have not been widely promoted by lenders because of the increased servicing costs associated with handling 26 payments instead of 12 payments per year. However, FNMA began purchasing bi-weekly loans in February 1988. With FNMA available as a purchaser for the loans, lenders are relieved of the burden of packaging bi-weekly mortgages for private investors, which may lead to some growth in their popularity. Loans with a payment schedule that coincides with the way many people are paid would seem to have some natural appeal.

VIII. Home Equity Conversion Mortgages (Reverse Mortgages)

The **HOME EQUITY CONVERSION MORTGAGE** *is commonly known as the "reverse mortgage." Reverse mortgages are designed to help elderly homeowners achieve financial security by converting their home equity into cash.*

> *A reverse mortgage borrower generally must be over age 62 and own a home with little or no outstanding mortgage balance.*

Typically, the homeowner mortgages his or her home to a bank or savings bank and, in return, receives a monthly check from the lender. The amount of the monthly payment depends on the appraised value of the home, the age of the homeowner, the length of the loan, when the loan must be repaid, and the amount of interest charged.

The most basic reverse mortgage is the **TERM LOAN**, *which provides monthly advances for a fixed period of time (generally three to 12 years).* At the end of the period, all principal advances, plus interest, are due.

> *Term loans have had limited success because borrowers fear having to sell their home at the end of the term.*

The **SPLIT TERM LOAN** *is similar to the basic term loan, except that it does not have to be repaid until the borrower moves, dies, or sells the house.* This type of reverse mortgage provides more peace of mind for the borrower.

Under a **TENURE LOAN**, *the lender makes monthly payments only as long as the borrower occupies the house as a principal residence.* Tenure payments are generally lower than other types of reverse mortgages because of the uncertainty as to when the mortgage will be repaid.

The **LINE OF CREDIT LOAN** *is slightly different from the other reverse mortgages in that payments are not made on a regular basis.* The borrower withdraws funds whenever necessary, up to a maximum number of times. Repayment is deferred until the borrower dies, sells, or moves. In the past decade, the equity line of credit has also become popular. This loan is based on the owner's equity in the home and may be withdrawn in a similar manner as the line of credit. However, repayments begin with the first withdrawal.

IX. SUMMARY

Alternative financing programs were originally developed in the 1980s to meet the dual challenges of higher home prices and higher interest rates. The combination of these two factors made it extremely difficult for buyers to qualify for a home loan. In order to make it easier for borrowers, many of these alternate financial plans involve the payment of discount points, temporary buy-downs, or permanent buy-downs to reduce the borrower's interest or lower the payments.

Out of the many programs introduced, only a few have achieved continued acceptance and popularity with consumers. These consist primarily of the various ARM programs offered by lenders. Borrowers contemplating applying for an ARM should be made aware of the following important elements: the lender's index for adjusting the interest rate, the lender's margin above the index rate, rate and payment adjustment periods, the possibility of negative amortization, whether there is an option to convert to a fixed rate loan, and whether there are any periodic or lifetime caps on the interest rate.

X. CHAPTER TERMS

AML	Index
APR	Line of Credit
ARM (Adjustable Rate Mortgage)	Margin
Buy-Down	Negative Amortization
CAP	SAM (Shared Appreciation
Certain Specific Disclosures	Mortgage)
Cost of Funds Index (COF)	Split Term Loan
Discount Points	Teaser Rate
GEM (Growth Equity Mortgage)	Tenure Loan
GPM (Graduated Payment Mortgage)	Term Loan

XI. CHAPTER 10 QUIZ

1. A loan balance that grows rather than decreases due to unpaid interest being added back into the loan is said to have:

   a. a split term.
   b. a margin.
   c. negative amortization.
   d. positive amortization.

2. Alternate financing plans are popular:

   a. during times of low interest rates.
   b. during times of high interest rates.
   c. with older borrowers.
   d. with younger borrowers.

3. The payment of points to reduce the amount of interest on a loan is called:

   a. meeting margin.
   b. an index loan.
   c. a cap.
   d. a buy-down.

4. An amount added to cover administrative costs and profit is called:

   a. an index.
   b. cost of funds.
   c. margin.
   d. a cap.

5. Mortgage payment caps are generally limited by lenders to an annual increase of:

   a. 1%.
   b. 2%.
   c. 5%.
   d. 7.5%.

6. A borrower who has a 90% loan, at 6.5% interest with a 2% annual interest rate must qualify at:

    a. 7%.
    b. 7.5%.
    c. 8%.
    d. 8.5%.

7. Lenders offering adjustable rate mortgages must:

    a. comply with Regulation Z.
    b. provide the borrower with a general brochure.
    c. make certain specific disclosures.
    d. all the above.

8. In a Growth Equity Mortgage (GEM):

    a. payments increase annually.
    b. payments decrease annually.
    c. interest increases annually.
    d. interest decreases annually.

9. "One Point" is:

    a. $1,000.
    b. 1% of the sales price.
    c. 1% of the loan amount.
    d. none of the above.

10. What age must a reverse mortgage borrower be?

    a. Under 60
    b. Over 62
    c. Over 64
    d. Over 65

ANSWERS: 1. *c*; 2. *b*; 3. *d*; 4. *c*; 5. *d*; 6. *d*; 7. *d*; 8. *a*; 9. *c*; 10. *b*

Real Estate Español.com

Real Estate for Hispanic-Americans

Sel

Refina

Purc

GOVERNMENT PROGRAMS: FHA AND VA LOANS

This chapter will examine the function of two government agency programs misleadingly labeled "loan" programs: Federal Housing Administration (FHA) and Veterans Administration (VA) loans.

Neither FHA nor VA makes loans directly to the public.

The FHA and VA are also not part of the secondary market—they do not buy loans or sell loan-backed securities. Instead, they act as giant federal insurance agencies and insure approved lenders against losses caused by borrower default. Each agency has a number of separate programs which have made home ownership possible for millions of Americans who otherwise might not have been eligible for conventional loans.

Lenders are extremely comfortable with the insurance programs of each agency as they are backed by the full faith and credit of the United States government.

Chapter 11

CHAPTER 11 OUTLINE

Government Programs: FHA and VA Loans

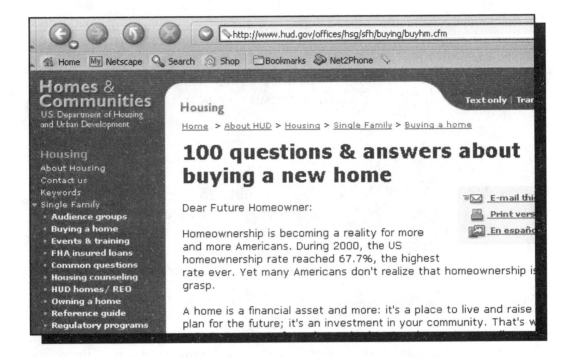

I. Federal Housing Administration (FHA)

The Federal Housing Administration (FHA) was created by Congress in 1934 as part of the *NATIONAL HOUSING ACT*. *The purpose of the act, and of the FHA, was to generate new jobs through increased construction activity, to exert a stabilizing influence on the mortgage market, and to promote the financing, repair, and sale of real estate nationwide.* Today, the FHA is part of the Department of Housing and Urban Development (HUD).

The FHA's primary function is to insure loans. FHA approved lenders are insured against losses caused by borrower default.

The FHA insurance program is called the **Mutual Mortgage Insurance Plan (MMI)**. Under the plan, lenders who have been approved by the FHA to make insured loans either submit applications from prospective borrowers to the local FHA office for approval, or, if authorized by the FHA to do so, perform the underwriting functions themselves (review of appraisal, mortgage credit examinations, etc.). *Lenders who are authorized*

247

by the FHA to fully underwrite their own FHA loan applications are called **DIRECT ENDORSEMENT LENDERS (DE LENDERS).** A direct endorsement lender is responsible for the entire mortgage process, from application through closing. When a DE lender has approved and closed a loan, the application for mortgage insurance is submitted to the FHA.

> *Most FHA loans are closed under the direct endorsement program.*

As the insurer, the FHA incurs full liability for losses resulting from default and property foreclosure. In turn, the FHA regulates many of the terms and conditions of the loan. FHA regulations have the force and effect of law. These FHA regulations, practices, and procedures have done much to shape the present face of the real estate lending industry.

A. FHA LOAN FEATURES

Any loan intended for submission for FHA insurance has a number of features that distinguishes it from a conventional loan. The most significant of these features are:

1. **Less stringent qualifying standards.** For example: FHA will allow re-establishment of credit within two years after a discharge of bankruptcy, when any judgments have been fully paid, any tax liens have been repaid, or a repayment plan has been established by the IRS, and within three years after a foreclosure has been resolved.

2. **Low down payment.** The 3% cash down payment is generally less than for a similar conventional loan.

3. **No secondary financing is allowed for the down payment.** The FHA minimum down payment for a loan must be paid by the borrower in cash. The borrower is not allowed to resort to secondary financing from the seller or from any lender to make up any part of the down payment. The FHA permits the use of either a non-repayable gift of money, credit from a portion of rents from a rent/purchase contract between a buyer and seller, or some home repairs made by the purchaser ("sweat equity") to be used to satisfy the statutory 3% down payment costs. This is ordinarily not permitted with conventional loans.

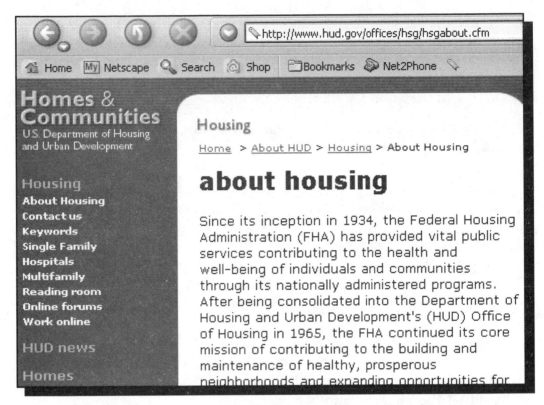

Housing

Home > About HUD > Housing > About Housing

about housing

Since its inception in 1934, the Federal Housing Administration (FHA) has provided vital public services contributing to the health and well-being of individuals and communities through its nationally administered programs. After being consolidated into the Department of Housing and Urban Development's (HUD) Office of Housing in 1965, the FHA continued its core mission of contributing to the building and maintenance of healthy, prosperous neighborhoods and expanding opportunities for

4. **Some closing costs may cover down payment.** While a borrower may not finance any of the closing costs along with the sales price, FHA permits the use of some closing costs to satisfy the 3% statutory down payment requirement.

5. **FHA mortgage insurance is required** for the loan regardless of the amount of the down payment. In contrast, conventional loans usually do not require mortgage insurance unless the loan-to-value ratio exceeds 80%.

6. **No prepayment penalties are allowed.** Some conventional loans have substantial prepayment penalties for the first few years of the mortgage term. An FHA loan may be paid off in full at any time with no additional charges. A lender is allowed to require that any such payment be made on a regular installment due date. Loans that were made before August 1985 require a 30-day notice of the intention to prepay the loan.

7. **The property must be owner-occupied.** The FHA used to insure investor properties but they have virtually eliminated all such

Chapter 11

programs. Two-to-four unit properties qualify if they are owner occupied.

B. OTHER CHARACTERISTICS OF FHA LOANS

The typical FHA loan has a thirty-year term. However, FHA offers loan terms as short as fifteen years. They also offer adjustable loans and home repair loans, which will be discussed in the section on FHA programs.

The FHA requires their loans to have a first lien position.

The FHA used to set the maximum interest rates, but now the rate is freely negotiable between the borrower and the lender. They still tend to be lower than conventional rates because the lender's risk is lessened by the FHA mortgage insurance.

A lender may only charge a 1% origination fee on an FHA loan, but is allowed to charge discount points. Typically, discount points allow a lender to recover any interest loss up front. These points may be paid by either the buyer or another party.

Although discount points may be paid by the buyer in an FHA transaction, they are almost always paid by the seller.

The lender is required to obtain an appraisal of the property from an FHA approved appraiser. *The appraiser will note any health and safety deficiencies and necessary repairs needed on a VALUATION CONDITIONS FORM* (**Figure 11-1**). The lender is required to provide the buyer with a **HOMEBUYER SUMMARY** *of all the deficiencies noted by the appraiser* (**Figure 11-2**). All problems with health and safety conditions, as well as necessary repairs, must be completed before the FHA will issue insurance on the property.

Unlike many conventional loans, FHA loans are fully assumable without any increase in interest rates. A lender is also prohibited from exercising any "due on sale" clause on an FHA transfer. As of 1989,

Figure 11-1

Department of Housing
and Urban Development
Office of Housing-Federal Housing Commissioner

OMB Approval No. 2502-0538
(exp. 04/30/03)

NOTICE TO THE LENDER

Case Number: _____

All required repairs must be completed in a professional manner, in compliance with HUD's guidelines and satisfied prior to closing. The lender is responsible for coordinating repairs. A professionally licensed, bonded, registered engineer, licensed home inspector or appropriately registered/licensed trades person, as applicable, must provide documentation that all deficiencies have been acceptably corrected upon completion of repairs.

SITE CONSIDERATIONS

VC-1 SITE HAZARDS AND NUISANCES
Check the appropriate response for *readily observable* evidence of hazards. Hazards, as defined below, are conditions that endanger the health and safety of the occupants and/or the marketability of the property. Use these criteria to determine the extent of the hazard. Please refer to HUD Handbook 4150.2 Section 2-2 for unacceptable locations and the protocol in Appendix D of the Handbook for further guidance. If the required component is not visible during the site visit, provide a detailed comment.

Provide a description of yes responses on Page 4:
a. Surface evidence of subsidence/sink holes
( ) yes
b. Operating oil or gas wells within 300 feet of existing construction
( ) yes
c. Operating oil or gas wells within 75 feet of new construction
( ) yes
d. Abandoned oil or gas well within 10 feet of new/existing
( ) yes
e. Readily observable evidence of slush pits
( ) yes
f. Excessive noise or hazard from heavy traffic area
( ) yes
g. New/proposed construction in airport clear zone
( ) yes
h. High-pressure gas or petroleum lines within 10 feet of property
( ) yes
i. Overhead high voltage transmission lines within engineering (designed) fall distance
( ) yes
j. Excessive hazard from smoke, fumes, offensive noises or odors
( ) yes
k. New/proposed construction in Special Flood Hazard Areas without LOMA or LOMR
( ) yes
l. Stationary storage tanks with more than 1000 gallons of flammable or explosive material.
( ) yes

PROPERTY CONSIDERATIONS
Mark "YES" for any *readily observable* deficiency noted below. Each "YES" constitutes a limiting condition on the appraisal. Each condition requires repair or further inspection. These conditions must be satisfied prior to closing for the mortgage to be eligible for FHA mortgage insurance. Please refer to HUD Handbook 4150.2, Section3-6 for guidance on HUD's General Acceptability Criteria. Also, refer to the protocol in Appendix D of the Handbook for repair and inspection requirement parameters.

VC-2 SOIL CONTAMINATION
Check the appropriate response for evidence of environmental contamination
Provide a description of yes responses on Page 4:
a. On-site septic shows observable evidence of system failure

( ) yes ( ) no
b. Surface evidence of an Underground Storage Tank (UST)
( ) yes ( ) no
c. Proximity to dumps, landfills, industrial sites or other locations that could contain hazardous materials
( ) yes ( ) no
d. Presence of pools of liquid, pits, ponds, lagoons, stressed vegetation, stained soils or pavement, drums or odors
( ) yes ( ) no

VC-3 GRADING AND DRAINAGE
Check the appropriate response for evidence of topographical problems.
Provide a description of yes responses on Page 4:
a. Grading does not provide positive drainage from structure
( ) yes ( ) no
b. Standing water proximate to structure
( ) yes ( ) no

VC-4 WELL, INDIVIDUAL WATER SUPPLY AND SEPTIC
Check the appropriate response with regard to individual wells and septic system.
Provide a description of yes responses on Page 4:
a. Property lacks connection to public water*
( ) yes ( ) no
b. Property lacks connection to a public/community sewer system
( ) yes ( ) no
*Lender will require water testing for "yes" response.
NOTE: Connection should be made to public or community water/sewage disposal system. Estimate distance to sewer or water hook-up and whether hook-up is practical.

VC-5 WOOD DESTROYING INSECTS
Check the appropriate response for evidence of wood infestation
Provide a description of yes responses on Page 4:
a. Structure and accessory buildings are ground level and/or wood is touching ground
( ) yes ( ) no
b. The house and/or other structures within the legal boundaries of the property show obvious evidence of active termite infestation
( ) yes ( ) no

Form **HUD-92564-VC (8/99)**

Part 2: Comprehensive Valuation Package
Valuation Conditions

Department of Housing
and Urban Development
Office of Housing-Federal Housing Commissioner

OMB Approval No. 2502-0538
(exp. 04/30/03)

VC-6 Private Road Access And Maintenance
Check the appropriate response for evidence of Private Road Access and maintenance problems.
Provide a description of yes responses on Page 4:
a. Property inaccessible by foot or vehicle
   ( ) yes ( ) no
b. Property accessible only by a private road or drive*
   ( ) yes ( ) no
c. Property is not provided with an all-weather surface (gravel is acceptable).
   ( ) yes ( ) no

*In all cases where a private road exists, submit evidence that _____
                    (name of road)
is protected by a permanent recorded easement (non-exclusive, non-revocable roadway, driveway easement without trespass from the property to a public street/road) and that there is an acceptable maintenance agreement recorded on the property.

Provide a detailed description of the road's condition:

_____

_____

_____

VC-7 STRUCTURAL CONDITIONS
Check the appropriate response for evidence of structural condition problems.
Provide a description of yes responses on Page 4:
Floor Support Systems
a. Significant cracks
   ( ) yes ( ) no
b. Evidence of water/leakage or damage
   ( ) yes ( ) no
c. Rodent Infestation
   ( ) yes ( ) no
Framing/Walls/Ceiling
d. Significant cracks
   ( ) yes ( ) no
e. Visible holes in exposed areas that could effect structure
   ( ) yes ( ) no
f. Significant water damage
   ( ) yes ( ) no
Attic
g. Evidence of holes
   ( ) yes ( ) no
h. Support structure not intact or damaged
   ( ) yes ( ) no
i. Significant water damage visible from interior
   ( ) yes ( ) no
j. No ventilation by vent, fan or window
   ( ) yes ( ) no

VC-8 FOUNDATION
(Appraiser must have full access to these areas)
Check the appropriate response for evidence of foundation/basement or crawl space problems.
Provide a description of yes responses on Page 4:
Foundation/Basement
a. Inadequate access
   ( ) yes ( ) no
b. Evidence of significant water damage
   ( ) yes ( ) no
c. Significant cracks or erosion in exposed areas that could effect structural soundness
   ( ) yes ( ) no

Crawl Space
d. Inadequate Access
   ( ) yes ( ) no
e. Space inadequate for maintenance and repair (<18 inches)
   ( ) yes ( ) no
f. Support beams not intact
   ( ) yes ( ) no
g. Excessive dampness or ponding of water
   ( ) yes ( ) no

VC-9 ROOFING
Check the appropriate response for evidence of all roofing problems
Provide a description of yes responses on Page 4:
a. Does not cover entire house
   ( ) yes ( ) no
b. Evidence of deterioration of roofing materials
   ( ) yes ( ) no
c. Roof life less than two years*
   ( ) yes ( ) no
d. Holes
   ( ) yes ( ) no
e. Signs of leakage observable from ground (i.e., missing tiles)
   ( ) yes ( ) no
f. Flat Roof**
   ( ) yes ( ) no

*HUD/FHA requires that the roof have at least 2 years remaining life. If the roof has less than 2 years remaining life, then the appraiser must call for re-roofing or repair. The condition must clearly state whether the subject is to be repaired or re-roofed. FHA will accept a maximum of 3 layers of existing roofing. If more than 2 layers exist and repair is necessary, then all old roofing must be removed as part of the re-roofing.

**All flat roofs require inspection.

VC-10 MECHANICAL SYSTEMS
(All utilities must be turned on at time of appraisal, if possible)
Check the appropriate response for evidence of mechanical system problems.
Provide a description of yes responses on Page 4:
Furnace/Heating System
a. Unit does not turn 'On'
   ( ) yes ( ) no
b. Warm air is not emitted
   ( ) yes ( ) no
c. Unusual or irregular noises are heard
   ( ) yes ( ) no
d. Smoke or irregular smell is emitted
   ( ) yes ( ) no
e. Unit shuts down prior to reaching desired temperature
   ( ) yes ( ) no
f. Significant holes or deterioration on the unit(s)
   ( ) yes ( ) no
Air Conditioning (central)
g. Unit does not turn 'On'
   ( ) yes ( ) no
h. Cold air is not emitted
   ( ) yes ( ) no
i. Irregular noises are heard
   ( ) yes ( ) no
j. Smoke or irregular smell is emitted
   ( ) yes ( ) no
k. Unit shuts down prior to reaching desired temperature
   ( ) yes ( ) no
l. Significant holes or deterioration on the unit(s)
   ( ) yes ( ) no

Part 2: Comprehensive Valuation Package
Valuation Conditions

Department of Housing
and Urban Development
Office of Housing-Federal Housing Commissioner

OMB Approval No. 2502-0538
(exp. 04/30/03)

Electrical System

m. Electrical switches do not turn 'on' or 'off'
   (check representative sample)
   ( ) yes ( ) no

n. Outlets do not function (check representative
   sample)
   ( ) yes ( ) no

o. Presence of sparks or smoke from outlet(s)
   ( ) yes no

p. Exposed wiring visible in living areas
   ( ) yes ( ) no

q. Frayed wiring
   ( ) yes ( ) no

Plumbing System

Toilet

r. Toilets do not function
   ( ) yes ( ) no

s. Presence of leak(s)
   ( ) yes ( ) no

Leaks

t. Structural damage under fixtures
   ( ) yes ( ) no

u. Puddles present
   ( ) yes ( ) no

Sewer System

v. Observable surface evidence of malfunction
   ( ) yes ( ) no

Sinks

w. Basin or pipes leak
   ( ) yes ( ) no

x. Water does not run
   ( ) yes ( ) no

Water

y. Significant drop or limitation in pressure
   ( ) yes ( ) no

z. No hot water
   ( ) yes ( ) no

VC-11 OTHER HEALTH AND SAFETY DEFICIENCIES
*Check the appropriate response for evidence of
health and safety deficiencies.*
Provide a description of yes responses on Page 4:

a. Multiple Broken windows
   ( ) yes ( ) no

b. Broken or missing exterior stairs
   ( ) yes ( ) no

c. Broken or missing exterior doors
   ( ) yes ( ) no

d. Inadequate/blocked entrances or exits
   ( ) yes ( ) no

e. Steps without handrails
   ( ) yes ( ) no

f. The mechanical garage door does not reverse
   or stop when meeting reasonable resistance
   during closing
   ( ) yes ( ) no

g. Please identify location of all health and/or
   safety deficiencies, and note others not
   included in this or any other VC on the
   comment page

VC-12 LEAD BASED PAINT HAZARD
For any home built prior to 1978, check for
evidence of defective paint surfaces, including:
peeling, scaling or chipping paint.

Provide a description of yes responses on Page 4:

a. Evidence on interior
   ( ) yes ( ) no

b. Evidence on exterior
   ( ) yes ( ) no
   Year built _____

If the home was built before 1978, this may indicate a
lead paint hazard. For all FHA insured properties, the
seller is required to correct all defective paint in or on
dwelling units built before January 1, 1978 in accordance
with 24 CFR Part 35.

VC-13 CONDOMINIUMS AND PLANNED UNIT
DEVELOPMENTS (PUD)
Provide a description of yes responses on Page 4:

a. This project is not on FHA's approval list
   ( ) yes ( ) no
   The property does not meet owner-occupancy
standards
   ( ) yes ( ) no
   This property does not meet completion
standards
   ( ) yes ( ) no

ADDENDA

**A. Provide the current full/market assessed
value:**

$_____

**B. Provide a summary of estimated repair
costs:**

$_____

Please attach any additional information/reports
and give number of attached pages.

Public reporting burden for the collection of
information is estimated to average 30 minutes to
complete the Comprehensive Valuation Package.
This includes the time for reviewing the associated
Handbook and reporting the data. This does not
include the requisite market research or the
appraisal process. This agency may not collect this
information, and you are not required to complete
this form unless it displays a currently valid OMB
control number.

Privacy Act Notice: This information is required
for the U.S. Department of Housing and Urban
Development to endorse a single family mortgage
and is used for underwriting purposes. The
collection of this information is necessary to comply
with HUD's Home Buyer Protection Plan. The
information may be made available to a federal
agency for review. This information is not
confidential and will be made available to the public.

Part 2: Comprehensive Valuation Package
Valuation Conditions

Department of Housing
and Urban Development
Office of Housing-Federal Housing Commissioner

OMB Approval No. 2502-0538
(exp. 04/30/03)

Description of Responses and Related Comments

VC#	Section (a,b,c..)	Comments _____

Figure 11-2

Part 3: Comprehensive Valuation Package **Homebuyer Summary**	**Department of Housing and Urban Development** Office of Housing Federal Housing Commissioner	OMB Approval No. 2502-0538 (exp. 04/30/03) Case Number: _____

Property Address: _____
_____
_____

Important	**NOTICE TO THE HOMEBUYER**	**Read Carefully**

As part of our job insuring the mortgage for the lender, the FHA requires the lender to conduct an appraisal to:
  *estimate the value of your potential new home
  *make sure it meets *minimal* FHA standards
  *ensure that it will be marketable

Appraisals are different from home inspections. Home inspections give more detailed information about your potential new home.

This report is a summary of the observations of an appraiser who visited the property. If there was a problem, the appraiser answered "YES" under "Problem".

If any condition is marked [yes], this means that the property you want to buy does not currently meet FHA's Minimum Property Standards. Until this condition is resolved, your lender may not provide you with an FHA insured loan consistent with FHA procedures.

You should speak to your lender about how this situation needs to be handled. You should also make sure that you are confident that the physical condition of this property meets all of your expectations.

For a copy of the full appraisal, contact your lender.

If you have any questions, call us at **1-800-569-4287.**

Physical Condition	**Problem (Y)**	**Comments**
Site Hazards		
Soil Contamination		
Grading and Drainage Problems		
Well, Individual Water Supply and Septic Problems		
Wood Destroying Insects		
Private Road Access and Maintenance Problems		
Structural Deficiencies		
Foundation Deficiencies		
Roofing Deficiencies		
Mechanical Systems Problems		
General Health and Safety Deficiencies		
Deteriorated Paint		

The conditions listed above are reflected on the Valuation Conditions Form (Part 2 of the Comprensive Valuation Package) of this appraisal. **The lender is required to transmit this Notice to the Homebuyer form to the buyer at least five business days prior to loan closing.**

X _____   _____   _____
  FHA Roster Appraiser Signature   ID Number   Valuation Date

Homebuyer acknowledges receipt of Part 3: Summary:

X _____   _____

X _____   _____
  Homebuyer(s) Signature(s):   Date Received

Form HUD-92564-HS (8/99)

AC APPRAISALS

https://entp.hud.gov/idapp/html/hicostlook.cfm

Home   My Netscape   Search   Shop   Bookmarks   Net2Phone

hud home pag

homes and communities   U.S. DEPARTMENT OF HOUSING AND URBAN DEVELOPMENT

fha mortgage limits

Welcome to the FHA Maximum Mortgage Limits page. This page allows you to lo
limits for your area or several areas, and then list them by state, county, or Metrop
Detailed **help** is available. If you have additional questions or comments, please

Sorted By: State

State: All States

County:

County Code:

MSA Name:

MSA Code:

Last Updated: / /

Send   Reset

sellers are released from all liability under an assumption, however buyers must qualify under the standard FHA 203b income rules.

FHA loans are not assumable by investors.

C. INCOME QUALIFICATIONS AND MAXIMUM LOAN AMOUNTS

There is no minimum income requirement for an FHA loan. Borrowers must show two years of steady employment and demonstrate that they have consistently paid their bills on time. The FHA has a ratio of 29% and 41%. This means that the payments for a home loan may not exceed 29% of the borrower's gross monthly income and all installment debt, including the home loan payment, may not exceed 41%. These figures are more liberal than the conventional limits underwritten by FNMA and FHLMC.

The FHA sets maximum mortgage loan amounts. These amounts, which vary by state as well as location within a state, are adjusted yearly. On January 1, 2005, the maximum amount for low cost areas, such as Wyoming, was $172,632. The maximum for high cost areas, such as Los Angeles, California, was $312,895. Section 214 of the National Housing Act provides that Hawaii, Guam, Alaska, and the Virgin Islands may have a maximum of $469,342.

D. MUTUAL MORTGAGE INSURANCE (MMI)

All FHA loans require a mortgage insurance premium.

The mortgage insurance is referred to as **MUTUAL MORTGAGE INSURANCE (MMI)**. FHA charges an up front premium of 1.5% of the loan amount. In addition, FHA charges a monthly premium equal to .05% of the loan amount annually. If the property is sold within the first 84 months of the loan term, any unused portion of the up front MMI will be returned to the borrower. When the loan balance drops below 78% of the original purchase price, the monthly payment will automatically be cancelled, provided the borrower has made monthly payments for five years on a thirty-year mortgage.

II. FHA Programs

A. FHA 203b FIXED RATE PROGRAM

With a *203b FIXED RATE PROGRAM, a down payment of 3% of the sales price is required.* Gifts from family members are allowed, as are payments from government or non-profit agencies that are designed to help first time or low income buyers. FHA does not require the borrower to have cash reserves. As noted earlier, only two years of employment prior to application is required. Lenders may only charge closing fees that are found on an FHA approved list. Fees for document preparation, processing fees, underwriting fees, and lender's tax services are not allowed. All owner occupied one-to-four

unit family residences are eligible. Homes located in planned unit developments (PUDs) must be HUD approved projects.

B. FHA 251 ADJUSTABLE PROGRAM

The *FHA 251 ADJUSTABLE PROGRAM is a thirty-year adjustable rate mortgage.* It is indexed to the one-year Treasury Bill rate and is adjusted annually. The adjusted rate may not move higher or lower than 1% per year. The rate is capped at 5%. This means that the rate may not go higher than 5% over the life of the loan. To qualify for the 251 Adjustable Program, a borrower must qualify at 1% above the initial rate. Eligible property types, mortgage insurance premiums, closing costs rules, down payment requirements, and qualifying ratios are the same as for the 203b program.

C. FHA 203k PURCHASE AND REHABILITATION PROGRAM

The *FHA 203k PURCHASE AND REHABILITATION PROGRAM was developed to help revitalize communities and neighborhoods*. It was developed by HUD and is administered by the FHA. Many areas have older housing stock that is basically sound, but in need of extensive repairs. Normally, in conventional practice, a homebuyer must first purchase the home and then obtain construction financing to rehabilitate the home. This often creates multiple short-term mortgages at high interest rates. In most cases, conventional lenders will not make a mortgage loan until all repairs are completed. As a result, many basically sound properties in need of repair were left vacant, and at risk of further deterioration and vandalism, simply because prospective homebuyers were unable to afford the purchase price without a loan.

The 203k program permits a borrower to obtain a property in need of rehabilitation with just one loan. Available loans may be either at a fixed rate or adjustable rate. The maximum amount of the loan, including acquisition and rehabilitation, is eligible for FHA insurance when the mortgage proceeds are disbursed and a rehabilitation account is established. Thus, the lender can have a fully insured FHA loan, acceptable to the secondary market.

A 203k loan combines acquisition cost and rehabilitation cost in one mortgage loan.

The program allows loans on one-to-four unit family dwellings that are at least one-year old. Loans may also be made on properties that have been demolished, as long as the foundation remains. The program allows conversion of single-family dwellings into two-to-four unit dwellings and conversion of larger than four unit dwellings into one-to-four unit dwellings. It also permits a dwelling to be transported from one site to another. The 203k program also allows loans on mixed use properties. A *MIXED USE PROPERTY combines a*

single-family residence with a commercial building. The loans are limited to no more than 25% commercial use on a one-story property, 49% on a two-story property, and 33% on a three-story property.

Condominium units are also eligible for 203k mortgages, as long as they are owner-occupied and the borrower is not an investor. The rehabilitation of the unit is restricted to the interior of the building only. In addition, the rules dictate that after rehabilitation, individual buildings within the project may not contain more than four units.

A 203k loan has a minimum requirement of $5,000 in needed repairs. Eligible repairs are those that cover the health and safety of the occupants. These would include, but are not limited to, repair of structural damage, elimination of lead-based paint, room additions, replacement of roofing, flooring, energy efficient improvements, electrical systems, plumbing systems, and heating and air conditioning systems. Improvements that provide handicapped accessibility are fully covered. Repairs that are not eligible for loans include such luxury items as new swimming pools, gazebos, and tennis courts. The maximum mortgage amount is either the "as-is" value of the property plus the cost of repairs, or 110% of the expected market value of the property after the completion of all repairs.

1. Steps in the 203k Program

The steps in the process are slightly different than in a regular purchase. First, after locating a prospective property, the buyer and his or her real estate agent make a preliminary analysis of the extent of repairs necessary and a rough estimate of the cost of the work to be carried out. Then a sales contract is executed, including provisions that the borrower has applied for 203k financing and that the contract is contingent upon approval of this financing. The buyer then contacts an approved FHA lender. The lender will, at this stage, recommend an FHA-approved 203k consultant (generally a contractor) to help the buyer draw up the necessary work write-ups and cost estimates. Upon receipt of these documents, the lender will ask the FHA to issue a case number and assign an FHA-approved plan reviewer, appraiser, and inspector. The plan reviewer will meet with the buyer and the consultant (contractor) at the property to insure that the repairs are acceptable.

The appraiser will then carry out an appraisal of the property. The lender will review the application and issue a conditional commitment and statement of appraised value. After the buyer has completed the necessary documentation for an FHA loan, the lender will issue a firm commitment. This document will detail the maximum amount that can be loaned. The mortgage will then close and the lender will submit the closing documents to FHA. FHA then issues a mortgage insurance certificate to the lender. Repair work may begin at the time of closing and must be completed within six months. The repair funds are disbursed as each stage of rehabilitation is completed. Upon overall completion, a final inspection is carried out by the FHA-approved inspector.

D. FHA TITLE I PROGRAM

The *FHA TITLE I PROGRAM is designed to allow homeowners to finance light repairs or permanent improvements to their homes*. Loans of up to $25,000.00 will be insured for a maximum of twenty-five years. Interest rates are set at market by the lender. The borrower also pays a mortgage insurance premium for a Title I loan. Title I loans are only available through FHA approved Title I lenders.

III. VA Loan Guaranties

In 1944, a grateful U.S. Congress passed the Serviceman's Readjustment Act to provide returning World War II veterans with education, medical, and home loan benefits to help them readjust to civilian life. *This law is often referred to as the G.I. BILL*. The original act has been amended many times over the years. These amendments have served to broaden and extend the earned benefits for veterans of conflicts that our nation has been involved in, as well as the original WWII veterans. *Veteran's benefits are managed by the U.S. DEPARTMENT OF VETERANS AFFAIRS (VA)*. One very important benefit is the VA home loan guaranty. This guaranty is extended to eligible veterans to assist them in the purchase of owner-occupied residential property of up to four units. No investor loans of any type are guaranteed by the VA.

The G.I. Bill is the legislation that provides for VA loan guaranties.

A. VA LOAN GUARANTY CHARACTERISTICS

The VA program has a number of features that are attractive to borrowers who qualify:

1. A VA loan may not have prepayment penalties.

2. A VA loan may be assumed by anyone; the new buyer does not have to be a veteran.

3. No mortgage insurance is required.

4. Funding fees may be financed.

5. Builder warranty is required on new homes.

6. Closing costs may be paid by seller.

While no mortgage insurance is required, the VA charges a funding fee that is currently set at 2% on non-down payment loans. For second time users with eligibility, the fee is 3%. With a down payment of 5%, the fee for both first and second time users is 1.5%. For a 10% down payment, the fee drops to 1.25%. The fee may be financed in the loan.

Closing costs are not permitted to be financed in the loan. However, the VA sets maximum fees for these items. These fees are changed from time to time by the VA. Current closing cost items include:

1. A maximum 1% origination fee.
2. Appraisal fees are set by Regional VA offices. The fee may not be more than is reasonable and customary for the area.
3. Credit report fees may not exceed the cost charged to the lender. Credit research fees of $50.00 charged by Loan Prospector® are allowed.
4. The veteran may pay for hazard and flood insurance, if required.
5. The veteran may pay for title insurance.
6. The veteran must pay the VA funding fee.
7. The veteran may pay for recording fees.
8. The veteran is responsible for prorated interest and property taxes.

Aside from the veteran borrower, the seller, or any other party, may pay closing cost fees.

1. Sale by Assumption

Veterans who obtain loans guaranteed by the VA are legally obligated to indemnify (pay back) the United States government for any claim paid out by the VA under the loan guaranty.

This is the case for the life of the loan, regardless of whether the property has been sold, foreclosed, or transferred to another. It is important that the veteran who sells or transfers a home, where the VA loan will not be paid off in full, be made aware of this fact. A veteran may be released from liability on that loan only if the following three conditions are met:

1. The loan must be current.

2. The purchaser must be an acceptable credit risk.

3. The purchaser must assume the obligations and liabilities of the veteran on the loan, including the indemnity obligation. The *INDEMNITY OBLIGATION means that the veteran must reimburse the U.S. Government for any loss on the loan.* The assumption of the obligations must be evidenced by a written agreement as specified by the VA.

To facilitate a veteran's release from liability on a loan a new buyer intends to assume, it is best to include in the sales contract a provision to that effect. The sales agreement should provide that the buyer will assume all the seller's loan obligations, including the liability for indemnity on the VA loan, and that the sale will not be closed unless and until the VA approves the credit and income of the purchaser. The seller must apply to the VA for a formal release of liability.

Unfortunately, this procedure is often neglected and sales are consummated without submitting the application for release of liability to the VA, and in many cases, without the new buyer formally agreeing to assume payment of the loan. If the sale closes without first obtaining the release from the VA, the veteran will find that he or she is fully liable in the case of a default.

2. Restoration of Entitlement

A veteran who has paid off his or her loan, and sold the house on which the loan was secured, may have all his or her entitlement restored. *ENTITLEMENT is the maximum insurance amount that the VA will provide for the veteran's home loan. By act of Congress, the veteran is entitled to the amount by virtue of his or her service in the armed forces.* Entitlement may also be restored if the property is sold to another veteran who substitutes his or her entitlement for the seller's. To restore entitlement, the veteran must apply to the VA and fill out the necessary forms.

3. Eligibility

Eligibility requirements for a VA loan vary depending on when and where a veteran served and the length of the service. In general, the periods for active wartime service are:

WWII	09/16/40 - 07/25/47
Korean Conflict	06/27/50 - 01/31/55
Vietnam Era	08/05/64 - 05/07/75

The veteran must have had a minimum of **90 days** of active service and have been discharged under conditions other than dishonorable.

Persian Gulf War 08/02/90-TBD

Gulf War veterans must have completed 24 months of active duty or the full period (at least 90 days) for which they were called up to active war duty. A veteran who was discharged for a service-connected disability, for hardship, or at the convenience of the government, is also eligible.

Peacetime veterans are also eligible for the periods:

07/26/47 to 06/26/50
02/01/55 to 08/04/64
05/08/75 to 09/07/80 (enlisted) 10/16/81 (officer)

Veterans must have had at least **181 days of continuous active duty** and a discharge under other than dishonorable conditions. Peacetime veterans after 09/07/80 to 08/01/90 must have had 24 months of active duty service and similar discharge requirements. Current active duty personnel are eligible after 181 days of continuous service. Selected reserves and National Guard are eligible after six years of service and having attended weekend drills and two-week active duty for training, or if they have been honorably discharged, retired, or transferred to Standby Reserve or Ready Reserve. They may be eligible before six years for a service-connected disability. Eligibility for Selected Reservists expires on 09/30/2007.

The spouse of a serviceperson who died while in service from a service connected disability, became missing in action, or became a prisoner of war may also be eligible for VA home loan benefits. In addition, certain U.S. citizens who served in the armed forces of the allied nations during WWII are also eligible. Lastly, Public Health Service officers, cadets at the service academies, some merchant seamen of WWII, and officers of the National Oceanic and Atmospheric Administration may be eligible as well.

4. VA Loan Guaranty Amounts

The VA does not guarantee the entire amount of a loan. What is guaranteed is the top portion of a loan. This is the area where a lender is most at risk in the event of a default. The maximum entitlement amount has been adjusted upwards several times by Congress from the original $4,000 that was in effect for WWII veterans. A veteran may use the maximum entitlement in effect at the time of purchase. A veteran's maximum entitlement is currently $36,000. This may be adjusted upwards to $89,912 on certain loans of over $144,000. While the VA itself does not have a maximum loan amount, GNMA will not buy VA loans in excess of $359,650.

The current program works as follows:

1. Loan amount of up to $45,000 = 50% of the loan amount.
2. Loan amount of $45,001 - $56,250 = $22,500.
3. Loan amount of $56,251 - $144,000 = 40% of the loan with a maximum of $36,000.
4. Loan amount greater than $144,000 = 25% of the loan amount with a maximum of $89,912 (on loans for purchase or construction of a home or condominium unit).

5. Partial Entitlement

A veteran who used his entitlement to purchase a home in the past may use that portion of his remaining entitlement to purchase a second home.

Example: A veteran used the maximum entitlement of $25,000 that was available in 1978 to purchase a home. Today, he wishes to purchase a second vacation home. The home is priced at $100,000. The veteran has $11,000 remaining in entitlement ($36,000 - $25,000 = $11,000).

B. THE VA LOAN PROCESS

The first step in the process is to determine if the veteran has a Certificate of Eligibility. A *CERTIFICATE OF ELIGIBILITY notifies the lender that the veteran is eligible for a VA loan and what his or her entitlement will be.* Presently, veterans receive this form as part of their discharge papers. If the veteran does not have this form, he or she will have to apply to the VA for a Certificate of Eligibility. This is done by submitting a **Request for a Certificate of Eligibility (VA Form 26-1880 - Figure 11-3)** along with a copy of his or her DD-214 (discharge paper). This form needs to be submitted before any other part of the loan goes forward because only the VA may determine the veteran's eligibility for a loan, and it is likely that this process will take some time.

The VA allows the use of uniform loan application forms and encourages the use of electronic loan underwriting utilizing FHLMC's Loan Prospector®, FNMA's Desktop Underwriter®, and Countrywide's CLUES® system (Countrywide loan submissions only). All lenders are responsible for conforming in full to VA requirements. This includes the use of VA-approved appraisers and underwriters. All VA loans require the following additional documents from the lender:

1. VA Form 26-0286 Loan Summary Sheet
2. VA Form 26-8320 Certificate of Eligibility
3. VA Form 26-8998 Acknowledgement of Receipt of Funding Fee
4. VA Form 26-1843 Certificate of Reasonable Value (provided with appraisal)
5. VA Form 26-1820 Report and Certification of Loan Disbursement.
6. A HUD-1 Settlement Statement
7. Name and mailing address to be used in requesting file for audit
8. E-mail address to be used in lieu of mailings

Figure 11-3

OMB Approved No. 2900-0086
Respondent Burden: 15 minutes

VA Department of Veterans Affairs	TO	Department of Veterans Affairs Attn: Loan Guaranty Division
REQUEST FOR A CERTIFICATE OF ELIGIBILITY FOR VA HOME LOAN BENEFITS		

NOTE: Please read information on reverse before completing this form. If additional space is required, attach a separate sheet.

1. FIRST-MIDDLE-LAST NAME OF VETERAN	2. DATE OF BIRTH	3. VETERAN'S DAYTIME TELEPHONE NO. ( )

4. ADDRESS OF VETERAN (No., street or rural route, city or P.O., State and ZIP Code)	5. MAIL CERTIFICATE OF ELIGIBILITY TO: (Complete ONLY if the Certificate is to be mailed to an address different from the one listed in Item 4)

6. MILITARY SERVICE DATA (ATTACH PROOF OF SERVICE - SEE PARAGRAPH "D" ON REVERSE)

A. ITEM	B. PERIODS OF ACTIVE SERVICE		C. NAME (Show your name exactly as it appears on your separation papers or Statement of Service)	D. SOCIAL SECURITY NUMBER	E. SERVICE NUMBER (If different from Social Security No.)	F. BRANCH OF SERVICE
	DATE FROM	DATE TO				
1.						
2.						
3.						
4.						

7A. WERE YOU DISCHARGED, RETIRED OR SEPARATED FROM SERVICE BECAUSE OF DISABILITY OR DO YOU NOW HAVE ANY SERVICE-CONNECTED DISABILITIES? ☐ YES ☐ NO (If "Yes," complete Item 7B)	7B. VA CLAIM FILE NUMBER C-

8. PREVIOUS VA LOANS (Must answer N/A if no previous VA home loan. DO NOT LEAVE BLANK)

A. ITEM	B. TYPE (Home, Refinance, Manufactured Home, or Direct)	C. ADDRESS OF PROPERTY	D. DATE OF LOAN	E. DO YOU STILL OWN THE PROPERTY? (YES/NO)	F. DATE PROPERTY WAS SOLD (Submit a copy of HUD-1, Settlement Statement, if available)	G. VA LOAN NUMBER (If known)
1.						
2.						
3.						
4.						
5.						
6.						

I CERTIFY THAT the statements herein are true to the best of my knowledge and belief.

9. SIGNATURE OF VETERAN (Do NOT print)	10. DATE SIGNED

FEDERAL STATUTES PROVIDE SEVERE PENALTIES FOR FRAUD, INTENTIONAL MISREPRESENTATION, CRIMINAL CONNIVANCE OR CONSPIRACY PURPOSED TO INFLUENCE THE ISSUANCE OF ANY GUARANTY OR INSURANCE BY THE SECRETARY OF VETERANS AFFAIRS.

FOR VA USE ONLY

11A. DATE CERTIFICATE ISSUED	11B. SIGNATURE OF VA AGENT

VA FORM **26-1880**
MAR 2004

EXISTING STOCKS OF VA FORM 26-1880, MAY 2002, WILL BE USED.

Government Programs: FHA and VA Loans

INSTRUCTIONS FOR VA FORM 26-1880

PRIVACY ACT INFORMATION: No Certificate of Eligibility may be issued unless VA receives sufficient information to determine that you are eligible (38 U.S.C. 3702). You are not required to furnish the information, including the Social Security Number, but are urged to do so, since it is vital to proper action by VA in your case. Specifically, your Social Security Number is requested under authority of 38 U.S.C. 3702 and is requested only if the service department used your Social Security Number as a service number. Failure to provide a completed application will deprive VA of information needed in reaching decisions which could affect you. Responses may be disclosed outside VA only if the disclosure is authorized under the Privacy Act, including the routine uses identified in the VA system of records, 55VA26, Loan Guaranty Home, Condominium and Manufactured Home Loan Applicant Records, Specially Adapted Housing Applicant Records, and Vendee Loan Applicant Records - VA, published in the Federal Register.

RESPONDENT BURDEN: VA may not conduct or sponsor, and respondent is not required to respond to this collection of information unless it displays a valid OMB Control Number. Public reporting burden for this collection of information is estimated to average 15 minutes per response, including the time for reviewing instructions, searching existing data sources, gathering and maintaining the data needed, and completing and reviewing the collection of information. If you have comments regarding this burden estimate or any other aspect of this collection of information, call 1-800-827-1000 for mailing information on where to send your comments.

A. Mail this completed form, along with proof of service, to the Eligibility Center at P.O. Box 20729, Winston-Salem, NC 27120 (for veterans located in the eastern half of the country) or P.O. Box 240097, Los Angeles, CA 90024 (for veterans located in the western half of the country). Veterans stationed overseas may use either address.

B. Military Service Requirements for VA Loan Eligibility: (NOTE: Cases involving other than honorable discharges will usually require further development by VA. This is necessary to determine if the service was under other than dishonorable conditions.)

1. Wartime Service. If you served anytime during World War II (September 16, 1940 to July 25, 1947), Korean Conflict (June 27, 1950 to January 31, 1955), or Vietnam Era (August 5, 1964 to May 7, 1975) you must have served at least 90 days on active duty and have been discharged or released under other than dishonorable conditions. If you served less than 90 days, you may be eligible if discharged because of service-connected disability.

2. Peacetime Service. If your service fell entirely within one of the following periods: July 26, 1947 to June 26, 1950, or February 1, 1955 to August 4, 1964, you must have served at least 181 days of continuous active duty and have been discharged or released under conditions other than dishonorable. If you entered service after May 7, 1975 but prior to September 8, 1980 (enlisted) or October 17, 1981 (officer) and completed your service before August 2, 1990, 181 days service is also required. If you served less than 181 days, you may be eligible if discharged for a service-connected disability.

3. Service after September 7, 1980 (enlisted) or October 16, 1981 (officer) and prior to August 2, 1990. If you were separated from service which began after these dates, you must have: (a) Completed 24 months of continuous active duty for the full period (at least 181 days) for which you were called or ordered to active duty, and been discharged or released under conditions other than dishonorable; or (b) Completed at least 181 days of active duty and been discharged under the specific authority of 10 U.S.C. 1173 (hardship discharge) or 10 U.S.C. 1171 (early out discharge), or have been determined to have a compensable service-connected disability; or (c) Been discharged with less than 181 days of service for a service-connected disability. Individuals may also be eligible if they were released from active duty due to an involuntary reduction in force, certain medical conditions, or, in some instances for the convenience of the Government.

4. Gulf War. If you served on active duty during the Gulf War (August 2, 1990 to a date yet to be determined), you must have: (a) Completed 24 months of continuous active duty or the full period (at least 90 days) for which you were called or ordered to active duty, and been discharged or released under conditions other than dishonorable; or (b) Completed at least 90 days of active duty and been discharged under the specific authority of 10 U.S.C. 1173 (hardship discharge), or 10 U.S.C. 1171 (early out discharge), or have been determined to have a compensable service-connected disability; or (c) Been discharged with less than 90 days of service for a service-connected disability. Individuals may also be eligible if they were released from active duty due to an involuntary reduction in force, certain medical conditions, or, in some instances, for the convenience of the Government.

5. Active Duty Service Personnel. If you are now on active duty, you are eligible after having served on continuous active duty for at least 181 days (90 days during the Persian Gulf War) unless discharged or separated from a previous qualifying period of active duty service.

6. Selected Reserve Requirements for VA Loan Eligibility. If you are not otherwise eligible and you have completed a total of 6 years in the Selected Reserves or National Guard (member of an active unit, attended required weekend drills and 2-week active duty training) and (a) Were discharged with an honorable discharge; or (b) Were placed on the retired list or (c) Were transferred to the Standby Reserve or an element of the Ready Reserve other than the Selected Reserve after service characterized as honorable service; or (d) Continue to serve in the Selected Reserve. Individuals who completed less than 6 years may be eligible if discharged for a service-connected disability.

C. Unmarried surviving spouses of eligible veterans seeking determination of basic eligibility for VA Loan Guaranty benefits are NOT required to complete this form, but are required to complete VA Form 26-1817, Request for Determination of Loan Guaranty Eligibility-Unmarried Surviving Spouse.

D. Proof of Military Service

1. "Regular" Veterans. Attach to this request your most recent discharge or separation papers from active military duty since September 16, 1940, which show active duty dates and type of discharge. If you were separated after January 1, 1950, DD Form 214 must be submitted. If you were separated after October 1, 1979, and you received DD Form 214, Certificate of Release or Discharge From Active Duty, 1 July edition, VA must be furnished Copy 4 of the form. You may submit either original papers or legible copies. In addition, if you are now on active duty submit a statement of service signed by, or by direction of, the adjutant, personnel officer, or commander of your unit or higher headquarters showing date of entry on your current active duty period and the duration of any time lost. Any Veterans Services Representative in the nearest Department of Veterans Affairs office or center will assist you in securing necessary proof of military service.

2. Selected Reserves/National Guard. If you are a discharged member of the Army or Air Force National Guard you may submit a NGB Form 22, Report of Separation and Record of Service, or NGB Form 23, Retirement Points Accounting, or it's equivalent (this is similar to a retirement points summary). If you are a discharged member of the Selected Reserve you may submit a copy of your latest annual point statement and evidence of honorable service. You may submit either your original papers or legible copies. Since there is no single form used by the Reserves or National Guard similar to the DD Form 214, it is your responsibility to furnish adequate documentation of at least 6 years of honorable service. In addition, if you are currently serving in the Selected Reserve you must submit a statement of service signed by, or by the direction of, the adjutant, personnel officer or commander of your unit or higher headquarters showing the length of time that you have been a member of the unit.

IV. SUMMARY

The FHA and VA loan programs are huge federal insurance programs that are backed by the full faith and credit of the U.S. Government. Both programs have found ready acceptance by lenders and borrowers alike. The FHA has been a boon to the lending, construction, and real estate markets since its beginning. The insurance provided by the FHA is called the Mutual Mortgage Insurance Plan (MMI). An FHA insured mortgage has less stringent down payment and qualifying requirements and is readily assumable. The FHA has several programs, the most notable of these are the 203b fixed rate program, which is the most frequently used, and the 203k program, which allows a sale and major rehabilitation construction costs to be combined into one loan. The FHA also has a Title I home repair loan program which allows homeowners to carry out minor repairs to their homes without having to resort to refinancing their original loan.

The VA programs are designed to provide veterans returning to civilian life an opportunity to enjoy the benefits of home ownership. This program, which was instituted following WWII, has been periodically updated by the U.S. Congress to keep pace with the rise in the price of housing over the past five decades. A VA loan may have no prepayment penalties and may be assumed by anyone. No mortgage insurance is required. However, the veteran is directly liable to the U.S. government until the loan is either paid off in full, or has been assumed by someone else who also assumes this "indemnity" obligation to the government. In the case of a property loan assumption, it is important that both real estate and lending professionals inform their clients about the indemnity obligation and the adverse consequences that will occur in the event of a default. A veteran may have his or her entitlement restored once his or her loan is paid in full and the house is sold. A veteran may also use any partial entitlement remaining from the purchase of his or her first home to use in the purchase of a second home. Both wartime and peacetime veterans are eligible for VA loans.

The Veterans Benefits Act of 2004 (affecting the Loan Guaranty Program) was signed by the President on December 10, 2004. A Public Law number has not yet been assigned. This law changed the maximum guaranty amount to $89,912, and expanded eligibility for Specially Adapted Housing (SAH) grants. It also gives the VA authority to guarantee Adjustable Rate Mortgages (ARMs), which it has not had since 1995. (For more information, see www.homeloans.va.gov)

V. CHAPTER TERMS

Certificate of Eligibility	Indemnity Obligation
Certificate of Reasonable Value	Mixed Use Property
DD 214	Mutual Mortgage Insurance Plan
Direct Endorsement Lender	203b Program
Discount Points	203k Program
Entitlement	VA Form 26-1880 (Request for a
G.I. Bill	Certificate of Eligibility)
Homebuyer's Summary	Valuations Condition Form

VI. CHAPTER 11 QUIZ

1. The statutory FHA down payment is:

    a. 2%.
    b. 3%.
    c. 4%.
    d. 5%.

2. The FHA maximum debt ratios are:

    a. 29% & 41%.
    b. 25% & 29%.
    c. 39% & 41%.
    d. None of the above.

3. The current basic maximum entitlement for a VA loan guaranty is:

    a. $240,000.
    b. $144,000.
    c. $36,000.
    d. $261,000.

4. The maximum FHA mortgage loan amount in high cost states is:

    a. $144,000.
    b. $312,895.
    c. $459,650.
    d. $500,000.

5. After an appraisal inspection, an FHA lender must give the borrower a:

    a. Certificate of Eligibility.
    b. Valuation Conditions Form.
    c. Certificate of Reasonable Value.
    d. Homebuyer's Survey.

6. The program that permits rehabilitation costs to be included with acquisition costs is:

    a. Title I.
    b. FHA 203b.
    c. FHA 203k.
    d. FHA 251.

7. On a "mixed use" property, the commercial usage for a single-story building must not be more than:

   a. 33%.

   b. 25%.

   c. 49%.

   d. 23%.

8. What amount in needed property repairs qualifies for a 203K loan?

   a. $20,000

   b. $5,000

   c. $10,000

   d. None of the above

9. The maximum origination fee for both FHA and VA loans is:

   a. 1%.

   b. 1.5%.

   c. 2%.

   d. None of the above.

10. Mutual Mortgage Insurance (MMI) may be cancelled when the loan balance:

    a. drops to 78% of the original purchase price and loan payments for 5 years.

    b. drops to 80% of the original purchase price and loan payments for 5 years.

    c. payments have been made for ten years.

    d. is fully paid off.

ANSWERS: 1. b; 2. a; 3. c; 4. b; 5. d; 6. c; 7. b; 8. b; 9. a; 10. a

CHAPTER 12

SELLER FINANCING

In tight money markets, it's not uncommon for a seller to make a deal to finance part of the purchase price. Mortgage money from traditional lenders may be too costly in terms of interest rates, or simply unavailable. Buyers may be unable to come up with the necessary cash for the down payment required by a conventional mortgage, or simply wish to take advantage of the low interest rate on the seller's existing mortgage. In any case, sellers can often enhance the salability of their properties by offering financing in the form of purchase money mortgages or land contracts.

I. Purchase Money Mortgage/Trust Deed

A *PURCHASE MONEY MORTGAGE is given by a buyer to a seller to finance the purchase. The seller is the mortgagee or beneficiary.* Institutions such as banks and savings banks are not the only ones who make loans secured by mortgages or deeds of trust. An individual seller can just as easily be a mortgagee or beneficiary. The central advantage of this arrangement is that sellers are not bound by institutional policies regarding loan ratios, interest rates, or qualifying standards. To make the sale, a seller may

275

Chapter 12

finance the entire purchase price for the buyer (relying on a mortgage as security), charge below market interest, and/or offer financing to a buyer who is considered a credit risk by institutional lenders.

> *The seller is taking a risk with a purchase money mortgage, but it may be justified if it allows the sale to proceed or enables the seller to get a higher price for his or her home.*

As with any other form of seller financing, purchase money financing can be advantageous if the seller does not need immediate cash from the sale. Because the profit from the sale is spread over several years, the seller may benefit from a lower rate of income taxation.

> *Taking the full profit at the time of sale could push the seller into a higher tax bracket. But when the profit is paid on an installment basis, only the amount actually received in a given year is considered taxable income for that year.*

A. UNENCUMBERED PROPERTY

The simplest form of purchase money financing is where the seller has clear title to the property, free of any mortgages or other liens. The buyer and seller simply negotiate the amount and terms of their financing arrangement and draw up the appropriate documents. Purchase money financing may take any of the many forms discussed in earlier chapters, such as variable interest rates, graduated payments, or partial amortization with balloon payment. Virtually the only limit is the imagination of the parties.

Example: Grandma Perkins decides to move to her sister's farm in the country and wants to sell her townhouse. The mortgage on the townhouse has long since been paid. Mr. and Mrs. Jenkins want to buy the townhouse, but cannot qualify for conventional financing. However, Grandma believes they are honest and reliable people who can be trusted to pay off a loan, so she offers them the following deal: sales price of $90,000, with $8,000 down and the balance in the form of a purchase money loan, secured by deed of trust with Grandma as the beneficiary. Interest will accrue at the

277

rate of 6% for the first year, and increase ½ of 1% per year until it reaches 7.5%, where it will stay for the balance of the 30-year loan term. Payments are to be interest only for the first six years, and the principal then fully amortized over the balance of the term.

B. ENCUMBERED PROPERTY

Because many residential properties are encumbered by existing mortgages or deeds of trust, seller financing often involves assumption or refinancing of existing debt. There are several ways to deal with an existing mortgage. Perhaps the most simple method is to allow the buyer to assume liability for the existing note.

1. Assumption

If the seller's existing mortgage does not contain an alienation clause (due-on-sale clause), it is assumable.

The buyer can simply agree to take over payment of the seller's debt with the terms of the note unchanged. The property still serves as the basic security for the loan, but the buyer becomes primarily liable for repayment of the debt. If there is a foreclosure and the proceeds are insufficient to satisfy the debt, the lender may sue the buyer for the deficiency.

2. Assumption and Release

An assumption can take two forms. In the first case, it is an agreement strictly between the buyer and seller. The buyer assumes liability for the loan, but the seller is not completely released from responsibility; he or she remains **secondarily liable**. If the lender cannot recover the loan amount from the buyer or through foreclosure, it may still sue the seller for the deficiency. In order for the seller to be relieved of this responsibility, he or she must obtain a **release** from the lender. In this instance, the lender agrees to accept the buyer as the new mortgagor and to release the seller from all obligations on the mortgage. The lender will normally charge a loan assumption fee on assumable loans, renegotiate the loan assumption fee on assumable loans, or renegotiate the interest rate if the mortgage contains an alienation clause. A lender and/or an attorney who is familiar with real estate finance should always be consulted to determine if a loan is assumable.

A seller must obtain a release of liability from a lender or he or she may still be liable for the loan if the buyer defaults.

> **Example:** Ned Taylor sells a rental house to Sam Jones, who assumes Ned's existing $90,000 mortgage. Ned does not get a release from the lender. A year later, with $88,000 still owing on the mortgage, Sam encounters financial difficulties and decides to bail out. He leaves his obligations behind, but does not leave a forwarding address. The mortgage payments are not made, so the lender forecloses, obtaining only $70,000 at the foreclosure sale, due to the dilapidated condition in which Sam's tenants left the property. By the time of the sale, the total amount owed, including delinquent interest and the costs of foreclosure and sale, reaches $93,500, leaving a deficiency of $23,500 ($93,500 debt - $70,000 sale proceeds = $23,500 deficiency). The lender cannot locate Sam to collect the deficiency, so it sues Ned. Ned may be held responsible for the deficiency because he was never released from liability on the mortgage when it was assumed by Sam.

3. Alienation Clause

The seller's existing mortgage may contain an *ALIENATION CLAUSE, which is designed to restrict the seller's right to transfer the property.* The clause may be triggered by the transfer of title or by the transfer of significant interest in the property (e.g., a long-term lease). The alienation clause may give the lender the right to declare the entire loan balance immediately due and payable, the right to raise the interest rate on the loan, or the right to do either at its option.

C. PURCHASE MONEY SECOND MORTGAGE

Even in cases where there is an assumable loan, or where the buyer can obtain financing from an institutional lender, it may be beneficial

for the seller to provide additional financing in the form of a second mortgage or second deed of trust. If the buyer does not have sufficient cash to cover the difference between the sales price and the institutional financing, a purchase money second mortgage can be the key to closing the sale.

Example: George Hatfield owns property with an existing $45,000 mortgage. The mortgage is assumable, and has 120 payments of $582.30 remaining. Ray McCarthy is interested in buying the property, but does not have the $55,000 cash needed to meet the sales price of $100,000. Ray offers to buy the house with a $20,000 down payment if George will take back a second deed of trust for the remaining $35,000. George agrees and the sale is finalized.

Seller-sponsored second mortgages are subject to the same lien priority rules as institutional mortgages.

In the event of default and foreclosure, the first mortgage is paid in full from the proceeds of sale before any proceeds are allocated to the second mortgage. Sellers who take back second mortgages should keep this in mind when negotiating the amount of seller financing. This is especially true if there is a possibility of declining property values, or if the financing is set up to result in negative amortization over the early years of the loan.

D. SELLER-SPONSORED WRAP-AROUND FINANCING

The wrap-around mortgage or all-inclusive trust deed is a device sometimes used in place of an assumption. By using a wrap-around installment mortgage sales contract, the seller can pass on the benefit of an existing loan at lower-than-market interest rates, even if the buyer is unwilling to directly assume the loan. The "wrap" is sometimes used to get around the provisions of an alienation clause (which limits the ability to assume a loan). If the lender becomes aware of the subterfuge, the transaction can be foreclosed under the terms of the alienation clause.

Example: Mary Cudahy wants to sell her house for $91,000. There is an existing $32,000, 8% deed of trust on the property. Jeff Cochran offers to buy with $20,000 down and a seller-financed second deed of trust for the balance of $71,000. Under the terms of the agreement, a portion of Jeff's monthly payments will be used to make the payment on Mary's loan, which remains a lien on the property.

The attractiveness of the wrap-around is that it enables the buyer to obtain financing at below market interest rates while still providing a market rate of return for the seller. An example will illustrate this apparent contradiction.

Example: Seller Johnson has a $51,000, 10% trust deed against his property. He sells to Abernathy for $69,000, with $8,000 down and the $61,000 balance secured by a wrap-around deed of trust at 12% interest based on 30-year amortization with a balloon payment for the entire balance in 15 years. Seller Johnson will receive 12% interest on the $61,000 wrap-around, but has actually extended only $10,000 in credit.

> $69,000 sales price
> - 8,000 down payment
> - 51,000 underlying trust deed
> $10,000 credit extended—net owed to seller

To determine the seller's yield in the first year:

1. Calculate the interest the seller will receive in the first year on the wrap-around trust deed.

> $61,000
>   x .12
> $7,320

2. Calculate the interest the seller will pay the same year on the underlying trust deed.

> $51,000
>   x .10
> $5,100

3. Determine the net interest to the seller.

$7,320
-5,100
$2,220

4. Divide the net interest to the seller by the amount of credit actually extended.

2,220 ÷ 10,000 = 22%

Stated more simply, the seller is paying out $5,100 a year in interest on the original deed of trust and is receiving $7,320 in interest on the wrap from the buyer. This leaves the seller with a net gain of $2,220. The amount of credit actually extended by the seller under the wrap is $10,000, so the seller is receiving $2,220 in interest payments on $10,000 of credit. The yield on the credit extended is thus 22%. If the market interest rates are at 12.5%, the seller is receiving 9.5% over the market rate while the buyer is paying .5% below the market rate. Even if the rate charged by the seller on the wrap is not below the market rate, the arrangement may still be attractive to the buyer because of the greater flexibility of seller financing. The example shows the excellent return that is available to the seller when the amount of credit actually extended by the seller is relatively small.

The more credit extended by the seller, the lower the return.

E. WRAP-AROUND VS. ASSUMPTION PLUS SELLER SECOND

In an assumption, the buyer receives the benefit of an existing low interest rate loan. If the transaction is structured with a wrap-around loan at market rates, the seller receives the benefit of the existing low interest rate loan and is able to receive a very attractive rate of return on the portion of the financing that is actually extended by the seller.

Example: A sale is made for a price of $100,000, with the buyer making a $20,000 down payment. The seller's existing loan with a balance of $60,000 carries an interest rate of 9%. Prevailing market interest rates at the time of sale are approximately 12%. (**See Figure 12-1.**)

Figure 12-1

	WRAP-AROUND	ASSUME + 2ND
Sales price	$100,00	$100,000
Down payment	$20,000	$20,000
Balance financed	$80,000@12% wrap	$60,000@9% assumed $20,000@12% 2nd
Credit extended by seller	$20,000	$20,000
Approximate yield to seller on credit extended	21%	12%
Approximate overall interest to buyer on $80,000 financed	12%	9.75%

As you can see from the above example, if a wrap-around loan is made at market rates, the seller enjoys a high yield on the portion of credit extended by the seller. If the transaction is structured with an assumption and a second mortgage to the seller at market rates, the buyer enjoys financing at a very low overall rate.

A wrap-around transaction can also be structured so that the seller receives above market rates on the credit actually extended and, at the same time, the buyer pays below market rates on the total amount financed. It can appear as if both of them are getting a good deal. If in the example given in Figure 12-1 the wrap-around loan was made at an interest rate of 10.5%, the buyer would be paying an overall rate 1.5% less than the prevailing market rates of 12%. At the same time, the seller would be receiving a rate of approximately 15% on the $20,000 of credit extended by the seller.

F. RESALE OF PURCHASE MONEY SECURITIES

If a seller wants the option of cashing out at some time in the future, he or she can do so without giving up the ability to offer purchase

money financing. Since 1980, FNMA has been willing to buy purchase money securities on the secondary market. The catch is that the securities must conform to FNMA underwriting standards, which defeats some of the advantages of seller financing, such as freedom from loan-to-value ratios, and other institutional limitations. If the seller desires to resell his or her loan immediately or in the future, the seller should use standard FNMA forms for writing the financing agreement with the buyer. This will ensure that the loan meets FNMA standards. The only other requirement is that the loan be serviced by a FNMA approved lender. The seller then has the option, at any time, of ordering the lender to pass the loan through to FNMA, thereby cashing out the seller. By choosing the proper time to resell (when market interest rates are low), the seller can pass the loan through with a minimum discount.

II. Land Contract

In some areas, a popular form of purchase money financing is the land contract. This type of financing has many of the same advantages as purchase money mortgages and trust deeds, such as freedom from institutional loan qualifying standards, deferral of income taxation, and flexibility of terms. Its main disadvantage, when compared to purchase money mortgages, is that land contracts cannot be resold to FNMA, although a few private secondary market investors may be willing to buy contracts.

The distinguishing feature of a land contract is that the seller retains legal title to the property until the buyer has made all of the payments on the contract.

In its simplest form, the land contract is made by a seller who owns the property free and clear. Such a seller need only negotiate the term and interest rate of the contract, along with the amount of down payment, if any.

Example: Assume a ten-year, fully amortized contract at 12%.

Real Estate Contract

Buyer agrees to pay $15,000 as down payment, including deposit. The balance shall be paid as follows: $85,000 in the form of a real estate contract, payable at $1,219.50 or more per month, including principal and interest at the rate of 12% per year for 120 months until the balance is paid in full.

Example: Assume a five-year, partially amortized contract at 14%.

Real Estate Contract

Buyer agrees to pay $15,000 as down payment, including deposit. The balance shall be paid as follows: $85,000 in the form of a real estate contract, payable at $1,007.14 or more per month, including principal and interest at the rate of 14% per year, computed on the basis of a 30-year amortization, for 60 months, at which time the balance shall be due and payable in full.

In a partially amortized contract, a portion of the principal balance remains unpaid at the conclusion of the contract term. The buyer will have to pay this balance ("balloon" payment) in cash at that time, or else refinance the property.

A. CONTRACT SUBJECT TO EXISTING MORTGAGE

It is rare to find a seller whose property is not encumbered by some form of mortgage lien. When this is the case, the existing mortgage(s) must be taken into account. The simplest way to do this is to make the contract subject to the existing mortgage. The contract is written for the full purchase price, but the buyer's property rights under the contract are subject to the rights of the seller's mortgagee. The seller remains liable to make the payments on the loan and the property may be foreclosed if the seller defaults.

The obvious problem with this arrangement, from the buyer's point of view, is how to make sure the seller does not default on the loan payments. If this should occur, the buyer may lose everything; the seller will no longer have title to convey after a foreclosure (**remember that the buyer doesn't get a deed until the contract is paid in full**) and the buyer will be forced to resort to a lawsuit to try to recover his or her payments on the contract. The solution is to include in the contract a provision requiring the seller to make timely payments on his or her loan and allowing the buyer to make such payments directly to the lender if the seller fails to do so.

Example: Seller shall maintain the existing mortgage in good standing; in the event that seller fails to make any payment when due, or in any other way causes or allows the loan to go into default, buyer shall be entitled to cure such default, and deduct all costs from the amounts next falling due to seller on this contract.

In order for a provision like the one above to be effective in preventing foreclosure, there must be some way for the buyer to receive notice when the seller falls into arrears. This may be the true crux of the problem, as the only sure way to obtain such notice is to request it from the seller's lender. This is a routine procedure, unless the seller's mortgage contains an enforceable **alienation (due-on-sale) clause**. There is always the possibility that when the lender learns of the proposed sale, it will elect to enforce the alienation provision in the existing mortgage, thus frustrating the sale.

1. Contract Escrow

One approach that is sometimes used, to ensure the seller makes the payments on the existing mortgage, is to set up an escrow account or servicing agreement for the contract payments. This is fairly simple to do, especially since a deed is usually placed in escrow pending completion of the contract anyway. In a *CONTRACT ESCROW, the buyer makes payments into the escrow account, and the escrow agent pays the seller's loan payments out of the account.* The balance in the account (after the loan payments are made) is disbursed to the seller. In this fashion, the buyer is protected from the consequences of a default by the seller.

Sample Escrow Instructions

1. Seller shall place a deed to the property in escrow, to be conveyed to buyer upon full payment of the contract debt.

2. Buyer shall make all payments into an escrow account to be maintained by the escrow agent.

3. Upon receipt of each monthly payment, the escrow agent shall immediately make all payments due on seller's mortgage.

4. The escrow agent shall maintain a balance in the account equal to two monthly mortgage payments; all funds in excess of this minimum balance shall be disbursed to seller after compliance with provision three of these instructions.

---

2. Estoppel Letter

It is always good practice, in any transaction where an existing mortgage is to be left in place, to obtain the lender's written consent to the proposed transaction.

This is not essential where there is no alienation clause in the seller's promissory note or mortgage. Where alienation clauses do exist, most lenders will insist on renegotiation of the loan to reflect current interest rates, or demand that the loan be paid off entirely. But occasionally a lender will consent to a sale without any change in the existing mortgage. *The lender's consent is given in the form of a letter, called an ESTOPPEL LETTER*, acknowledging the transfer and waiving the lender's right to accelerate the loan on account of the transfer. By writing the letter, the lender is **ESTOPPED** *(legally prevented)* from later trying to accelerate the loan on the basis of the sale.

An estoppel letter is often requested even in transactions where the underlying financing does not contain an alienation clause. The holder of the underlying mortgage or contract is asked to state in the estoppel letter the amount of the outstanding principal balance and to acknowledge that the loan is not in default. The buyer then has written confirmation from the lien holder as to the

amount of the obligation the buyer is planning to assume or take subject to and is also assured that the seller is current on the payments and other obligations.

B. CONTRACT WITH ASSUMPTION OF EXISTING MORTGAGE

In the previous section, we saw how a seller could enter into a land contract while still maintaining his or her existing mortgage. If the seller does not wish to remain liable for the mortgage payments, but the buyer cannot (or will not) refinance the debt, the buyer may be able to assume (take over) the seller's mortgage and pay the balance of the purchase price under a contract. In this arrangement, the buyer becomes personally liable for payment of the mortgage debt; the buyer makes one payment to the mortgagee and another payment to the seller.

Example: Jim Dalton wishes to sell his home for $70,000. The property is encumbered by an assumable 9.5% mortgage with a balance of $34,000 and monthly payments of $336.35 (204 payments remain to be made). Andy Smith agrees to buy the property at the proposed price, with $10,000 down, assumption of the mortgage and the balance to be paid over ten years on a contract at 12.75%.

  $70,000 purchase price
  - 10,000 down payment
  <u>- 34,000</u> assumed loan
  $26,000 balance due on contract

   $26,000 contract balance
  <u>x .0147840</u> 10 yr. 12.75% amortization factor
   $384.38 monthly contract payment

Thus, Andy will pay:

1. $10,000 down payment to seller
2. $336.35/mo. for 204 months to seller's mortgagee
3. $384.38/mo. for 120 months to seller

The advantage of an assumption for the buyer is the ability to get financing at lower-than-market interest rates. Of course, if the seller's loan bore a higher interest rate than the buyer could obtain elsewhere, there would be no point in assuming the loan. The advantage for the seller is that his or her property is more attractive when it can be financed at the lower rate, and he or she is also relieved of responsibility for making the monthly payments to the lender.

C. CONTRACT PLUS ASSUMPTION PLUS INSTITUTIONAL SECOND

In some transactions, the seller will be willing to let the buyer assume the existing mortgage and also be willing to finance part of the price on a land contract, but he or she will desire at least a partial cash-out of his or her equity, perhaps to use as a down payment on another purchase. This is no problem if the buyer can provide a sufficient down payment to cover the seller's cash requirements. But even if the buyer cannot come up with the cash from his or her own assets, there is still an alternative: an institutional second mortgage.

Example: Arthur Dodge has listed his property with a sales price of $160,000. He has an assumable first mortgage in the amount of $95,000, and is willing to finance a portion of the balance on a land contract, but he needs at least $50,000 in cash from the sale. Olga Turner would like to buy Art's property, but has only $20,000 towards a down payment. Olga asks Art whether he would agree to a second mortgage from an institutional lender, which would take priority over the land contract. Art says yes, and the deal is closed on the following terms:

$20,000	cash from Olga
+ $30,000	cash from 2nd mortgage
$50,000	cash to seller
$50,000	cash to seller
+ $95,000	assumed 1st mortgage
+ $15,000	land contract
$160,000	total purchase price

Olga applies to Sam's Mortgage Company, which loans her $30,000 secured by a second mortgage on the property. The original (assumed) mortgage remains first in priority, and both mortgages have priority over the land contract.

Note that the buyer may have difficulty obtaining an institutional second because most lenders would hesitate to loan money on property where the title remains with the seller (as with a land contract).

1. Lien Priority

The significance of lien priority becomes apparent only when the borrower defaults. If the property must be sold through foreclosure to satisfy a debt, then each lender is paid from the proceeds of the sale according to its priority. If there is only enough money to pay the first lender, then the other (secondary) lenders are out of luck because their security has been exhausted.

> **Example:** Using the facts from the previous example, assume that Olga defaults and the property is sold under foreclosure, the proceeds of the sale (after taxes, costs, etc.) amounting to $120,000. The first mortgage is paid first, in the amount of $95,000, leaving $25,000 in proceeds. The remaining $25,000 is paid to the second mortgagee, which takes a $5,000 loss because its loan was for $30,000. Art gets nothing at all, because he is last in priority and there are no more proceeds.

2. Deeds and Security

In the preceding example, Olga did not receive a deed to the property because part of the purchase price was secured by a land contract; Art still holds the deed as security for the repayment of the contract debt. If Olga did not have legal title to the property, how could she get a second mortgage? There are two possible answers. The most likely is that Art, the legal title holder, consented to the mortgage. Art could agree to let the property stand as security for the loan without assuming personal responsibility for its repayment, meaning that the second mortgagee could recover the property if Olga defaulted, but could not sue Art for any deficiency.

The other alternative would have been for Olga to mortgage her equitable interest in the property, that is, her right to acquire title by making timely payments on the land contract. Such an equitable interest may be used as security, but most lenders do not prefer it. In foreclosure of such an interest, the lender would merely acquire Olga's contract rights, not the property itself. In order to obtain title, the lender would still have to pay off the contract. Under this second arrangement, the so-called "second" mortgage is really third in priority because it can never result in a sale of the property until after the contract has been paid off.

> **Example:** Using the same circumstances as in the foregoing example, assume that Art did not consent to a second mortgage, but that Olga was still able to borrow $30,000 with her equitable interest (contract rights) as security. If Olga defaults on the loan, Sam's Mortgage Company can take over her rights under the contract. Sam's can acquire title by paying off the contract, and then attempt to sell the property in order to recover its loan. Note that the property is still encumbered by the original $95,000 mortgage.

III. Other Forms of Creative Financing

As mentioned at the beginning of this chapter, imagination is the only limit to the types of seller financing that are possible. In the final section of this chapter, we will review some of the less conventional arrangements that are being used today.

A. LEASE/OPTIONS

The lease/option plan is comprised of two elements: a lease, and an option to purchase the leased property within a specific time period (usually within the term of the lease).

Obviously the lease/option is not the equivalent of a sale, but there is at least a strong possibility that a sale will eventually take place under the terms of the lease/option.

An **OPTION** *is an agreement to keep open, for a predetermined period of time, an offer to purchase or sell property. The prospective purchaser is referred to as the **OPTIONEE**; the property owner is the **OPTIONOR**.* For the most part, the option contract is designed to assure the optionee the right to purchase the property at an agreed upon price and within a specified period of time. Usually, the optionee is keenly interested in the property, but will not exercise the right to complete the purchase unless certain problems are resolved or questions answered beforehand. Some of the instances in which an option might be used are:

1. **Speculation.** The prospective purchaser believes that the property will increase in value. For example, it is soon to be rezoned. However, the purchaser wants to wait until the change in zoning actually occurs before purchasing the property.

2. **Investment.** The prospective purchaser thinks the property will be a good investment but wants to wait until he or she can find other investors willing to contribute capital and share the risk before actually purchasing the property.

3. **Comparison.** The prospective purchaser thinks the property is a good buy but wants to investigate other properties before coming to a final decision.

4. **Profit.** The purchaser plans on selling the option (if the option is assignable) for a profit.

5. **Time to acquire cash to close.** The prospective purchaser needs additional time to save for the down payment, to sell other property, to obtain the down payment, or otherwise obtain the cash needed to close the transaction.

6. **Qualifying.** The buyer is unable to qualify for a loan at present, but has reason to believe that circumstances will change shortly and that he or she will be able to qualify for a loan within the next year. For example, perhaps the buyer is expecting a raise, will soon pay off another debt and thereby reduce his or her monthly obligations, will be able to save or otherwise obtain a larger down payment, or perhaps simply hopes that the property will increase in value enough over the next year so that he or she can obtain a larger loan than is now possible and be able to pay the seller the purchase price.

7. **Rent credit.** The buyer and seller may agree to credit part or all of the lease payments to the down payment, loan amount, or sales price (which would reduce both the down payment and the necessary loan amount), making it easier for the buyer to make the purchase in another six months or year.

1. Consideration for an Option

To be enforceable, an option must be supported by consideration. The *CONSIDERATION is something of value given by the optionee to the optionor in return for a commitment to sell the property to the optionee at some time in the future. The consideration is usually a sum of money, but it can be anything of value. It is sometimes called the OPTION MONEY.*

In most cases, the consideration must pass to the optionor for the option contract to be binding. In other words, if the purchaser simply promised to pay the property owner $5,000 in return for the owner's promise to sell him the property but had not actually delivered the option money to the owner, the option contract would not be enforceable.

Once paid, the option money is not refundable, regardless of whether the optionee proceeds with the purchase.

In many instances, purchasers and sellers agree that the option money will be credited to the purchase price, much like a good faith deposit in an ordinary purchase and sale agreement.

Example:

```
$73,000   purchase price
- 5,000   option money
$68,000   balance due if sale is consummated
```

This is not always the case, however, so such an arrangement should be clearly spelled out in the option contract. If the buyer and seller have not clearly agreed in the written option contract to credit the option money against the purchase price, the presumption is that the balance due would be the entire price recited in the option.

Example:

    $73,000 purchase price
     $5,000 option money
    $73,000 balance due if sale is consummated

2. Other Option Essentials

An option is required to include all of the terms of the underlying contract of sale.

This means that a binding contract is formed at the moment the optionee exercises his or her option to purchase. Required information includes, but is not necessarily limited to, the following:

    a. names and addresses of the optionor and the optionee;
    b. date of the option;
    c. nature and amount of consideration;
    d. words indicating that an option is being given;
    e. date option expires; and
    f. purchase price and essential terms.

3. How Does a Lease/Option Work?

The seller/landlord leases the property to the buyer/tenant for a specific term (six months, one year, etc.), with the provision that part of the rental payments may be applied to the purchase price if the tenant decides to buy before the lease expires.

> **Example:** Mavis Rutland is selling her house for $75,000. Huey Anderson is interested in the property, but will not be able to qualify for a loan until he receives a raise, which he expects in two months. Huey and Mavis agree that Huey will rent the property for six months at $500.00/month, with half the rental payments being applicable to the sales price if Huey buys within six months. Huey also gets an option, which means that Mavis agrees not to sell to anyone else within the six-month lease period. If Huey decides to buy after six months, he will pay $73,500, the amount still due after deducting half the rental payments. However, failure to exercise the option will not entitle Huey to a

refund of the portion that would have been applied to the purchase price had the property been purchased.

The essential terms of a lease/option, in addition to the option requirements recited previously, include:

a. rental amount;
b. rent credit, if any;
c. reference to security deposit, if any;
d. a statement that a default by the optionee/lessee in connection with the lease agreement will result in a forfeiture of option rights; and
e. type of acceptable financing.

4. Advantages and Disadvantages of the Lease/Option

The main advantage of the lease/option is keeping a sale alive until the parties are in a position to close.

Although this could be done with a simple option agreement, the lease/option also allows the "buyer" to reduce the selling price over a period of time, making it easier to come up with a down payment or to qualify for a loan when the option is exercised. Also, the "seller" is receiving some income from the property, which can be used to make payments on a new house until the old house is sold, or to cover payments on existing financing on the old house.

The primary disadvantage of the lease/option is that the "seller" cannot sell the property to anyone other than the tenant during the term of the option.

Thus the lease/option is used only when it seems unlikely that other offers will be forthcoming in the near future. In addition, the "seller" cannot occupy the property during the term of the lease, so this plan normally involves sellers who have already purchased a new home or who have been holding the subject property for income production rather than as a personal residence.

5. Ways to Structure a Lease/Option

The crediting of rental payments may be done in a variety of ways, depending on the needs of the buyer. Rental payments may be credited towards the amount needed for a down payment if the buyer is short on cash, or they may be used to reduce the amount of financing required if the buyer cannot qualify for an appropriate loan. If desired, part of the credit may be applied to the purchase price, reducing both the down payment and the loan balance.

B. LEASE CONTRACT SEPARATE FROM OPTION CONTRACT

A problem with the lease/option agreement is that too often the optionee/tenant does not exercise the right to purchase. The result is wasted effort, with no sale and no commission.

Why the lease/option has such a high mortality rate is arguable, but there are at least two characteristics inherent in every lease/option agreement that promise trouble:

1. The prospective buyer's minimal cash investment—sometimes as little as a first and last lease payment.

2. The prospective buyer's extended occupancy of the property before a commitment is made.

Every property, especially a resale property, is flawed to some extent, and frequently optionees who have not yet committed themselves to a purchase will point to every minor imperfection when the time for a decision arrives. They will either refuse to exercise their right to buy or they will try to use the problems with the property, however inconsequential they might be, to negotiate further concessions on the part of the owner. A more forceful, and consistently more successful, method of structuring lease/option arrangements is to treat the lease and the option as two separate contracts. Generally, the transaction would be formed as follows:

1. The lease agreement would be written as a **TRIPLE-NET LEASE** *(in addition to rent, buyer is responsible for payment of property taxes, insurance and utilities).* If possible, rental payments would be set at

above market rates. The above normal rental commits the buyer to the property and acts as an incentive to exercise the option to buy at the earliest possible date.

2. Secure the option with substantial cash consideration. Because it is not refundable, the consideration immediately passes to the seller. Because of the substantial nature of the option money, it is usually applied to the purchase price when the option to buy is exercised.

The agent's commission can be paid from the option money immediately, thereby emphasizing to the prospective buyer that a lease/option is a viable form of seller financing.

Experience shows that once a purchaser is financially committed to a property, he or she is not likely to walk away from it. Minor imperfections seem less important to someone who has already made a substantial investment in a property.

Of course, the amount of consideration to be paid by the optionee is negotiable.

The general rule is simple: the more option money paid, the more secure the transaction.

To make the effort worth while for an agent, the option money should, at a minimum, equal the amount of the commission.

C. LEASE/PURCHASE OR LEASE/SALE

A lease/purchase or lease/sale is quite similar to a lease/option. The primary difference is that, along with a lease, the buyer and seller sign a purchase and sale agreement instead of an option. The purchase contract is normally written with a substantial nonrefundable deposit and with a closing date set six months or a year in the future.

Most agents believe that a lease/purchase arrangement is more likely to result in a successful sale than a lease/option.

The fact that the buyer is willing to sign a purchase agreement is an indication that he or she has already decided to buy the property and

will do so, instead of delaying that decision for another six months or year, as would be the case with an option.

Although the buyer's willingness to sign a written contract to buy the property may certainly be an indication of the buyer's intent, the differences between a lease/purchase and a lease/option may be more psychological than financial. The practical consequences of a lease/purchase are pretty much the same as a lease/option. Lease/purchase agreements are usually written so that the seller is entitled to the deposit if the buyer does not close the transaction as agreed in the purchase and sale agreement. This means that the buyer forfeits the deposit if he or she fails to go through with the purchase, which is little different from paying the option money.

As with a lease/option, the most reliable indicator of a successful lease/purchase is usually the amount of money put up by the buyer.

However, even though the economic realities of lease/purchase and lease/option transactions may be essentially the same, many sellers prefer a lease/purchase (lease/sale). Therefore, structuring a transaction as a "sale" with a closing one year later, instead of as a one-year option, may be acceptable to some sellers who would be reluctant to agree to an option.

D. EQUITY EXCHANGES

When a buyer cannot come up with sufficient cash for a sale, the difference can be made up with other assets, such as land, another house, cars, boats, or any other property in which the buyer has an equity interest and that the seller would be willing to accept as part of the down payment. If the transaction involves an exchange of real estate that is used in a trade or business, or is held for the production of income or investment, some or all of the capital gain can be deferred in a "tax-free" exchange.

The tax-free exchange is not available for the parties' residences or for property held for sale by a dealer.

If the transaction does qualify for tax-free exchange treatment, any gain that is purely a result of the exchange is deferred. However, any property or money that does not qualify (i.e., is not "like-kind" property held for income business or investment) is treated as "boot" and is taxable.

Example: Ben Hummel owns a rental house which he would like to sell. He lists the house for $174,000, including an assumable mortgage of $127,000. Cathy Collier is interested in the property, but has only $15,000 cash for a down payment. Bill Broker suggests an exchange of Cathy's triplex, valued at $115,000 with an assumable mortgage of $80,000, for Ben's house, with Cathy to assume Ben's loan. Ben will receive $35,000 in the form of Cathy's equity in the triplex, and $12,000 cash. He will assume Cathy's loan, which will result in "mortgage relief" of $47,000. He owed $127,000 on the loan which is to be assumed by Cathy and will owe only $80,000 on the loan which he is to assume (a difference of $47,000).

In the above example, Cathy will pay no income tax on the sale of her triplex. She will receive only qualifying property in return for her property. Ben will owe taxes on the $12,000 in cash received and also on the $47,000 of mortgage relief. Both are treated as taxable boot.

E. PARTICIPATION LOAN

In a *PARTICIPATION LOAN or shared equity loan, the buyer enters into a form of partnership with an investor who provides cash for the sale.* The investor may be the seller, a bank, or any private investor. Instead of charging interest, the investor in a participation plan receives a percentage of the equity (the difference between the property's value and the indebtedness secured by the property). Different investors will have varying requirements as to the percentage of equity to be shared, and as to the method of repayment of the investment. These issues are a matter of institutional policy or negotiation between buyer and investor. The important points to consider when arranging a participation loan are listed below.

1. **How will the loan be applied?** An investor may simply put up cash for the down payment, or the primary lender may reduce the interest rate in exchange for a share of the equity. In the first case,

the participation loan is essentially a form of secondary financing, with "interest" paid in the form of a share of the equity instead of a percentage of the loan amount.

Example:

$100,000   sales price
<u>- 20,000</u>   participation loan
  80,000   conventional loan

In the second instance, the participation loan is a variation of the permanent buy-down, except that the buyer must repay the buy-down when the equity is divided.

Example:

$100,000 sales price; the lender quotes 15% interest rate for the $80,000, 30-year conventional loan. The lender agrees to 13% interest rate in exchange for a share of the equity. The buyer makes a $20,000 down payment.

2. **How will the equity be calculated? EQUITY** *is the difference between the value of the property and the outstanding indebtedness secured by the property.* For the purposes of a participation loan, the buyer and investor must agree at the outset as to how the property is to be valued. Any method acceptable to both parties may be used. The value of the property at the time of purchase may be periodically adjusted according to an agreed upon index, or the parties many choose a particular appraiser whose opinion of value they will accept.

The parties should also determine whether the participation loan is to be considered part of the indebtedness on the property. A critical factor here is whether the participation loan is secured by a lien against the property. If it is, then it reduces the equity.

Example:

$110,000   value of property
<u>- 72,000</u>   balance on participation loan
$38,000   equity to be shared

3. **What percentage of the equity will the investor receive?** This amount is negotiable, but should be large enough to provide at least a market rate of return to the investor. Factors of influence in this regard are:

   a. the amount of the participation loan in proportion to the value of the property;
   b. the projected rate of increase in the value of the property;
   c. the rate at which any conventional financing will be paid off (that is, the rate of equity growth if the value of the property remains constant); and
   d. the term of the participation.

4. **When will the investor be repaid?** The investor may cash out his or her share of equity at a pre-agreed time (e.g., after five years), or else at the time the property is sold. Notice that if the investor is cashed out before the property is sold, the buyer will most likely have to refinance at that time. If the investor is to be repaid when the property is sold, provision should be made for establishing an acceptable resale price for the property.

5. **How will improvements be handled?** The agreement should specify whether the investor will share in any changes in equity resulting from improvements made on the property. If the buyer invests $5,000 of her own funds in an addition that adds $7,000 to the value of the property, does the investor get a share of the $2,000 equity created by the addition? Conversely, if a $5,000 remodeling project only adds $3,000 to the overall value of the property, does the investor share in the $2,000 reduction of equity? Questions such as these should be addressed in the original loan agreement.

6. **Who will be responsible for payment of taxes and insurance?** Usually the buyer will pay the property taxes and homeowner's insurance premiums, but this point may be negotiable in the case of some private investors.

You will note from the foregoing discussion that participation plans can be fairly complex in comparison to other creative financing

methods. Agreements such as these should be clearly spelled out, with provisions for all possible contingencies.

The services of an experienced real estate attorney should always be obtained when preparing participation plan financing.

IV. Broker's Responsibilities

Several creative financing arrangements have been explained in this chapter, but this is by no means an exhaustive survey of the possibilities for imaginative buyers and sellers. The old saying "where there's a will, there's a way" is particularly true of creative finance. The advantages of open-minded negotiation among buyer, seller, lender, and agent cannot be overemphasized. However, when using an arrangement that has not been tried and proven by others in the past, the greatest care should be taken to protect the rights of all parties through detailed specification of all terms of the agreement, preferably with the advice and assistance of legal counsel.

As you have seen, the variety of creative financing plans is almost without limit. The variety of plans and the associated wide variety of rights and obligations of all parties—the buyer, the seller, the lender (if any), and the real estate agent—require that professional real estate agents involved in negotiating creative transactions be especially well informed and take particular care to properly represent their clients and to make proper disclosures. In many cases, it will be advisable to seek the counsel of real estate attorneys and/or certified public accountants.

The area of law which governs such creative financing transactions is as yet unsettled, but one California case should serve as notice to real estate agents and brokers working in this field. In *Peirce v. Hom*, the real estate broker arranged two mortgage loans for the purchaser, who was an elderly widow. When she ultimately was unable to make the payments and lost the property through foreclosure, she sued the broker. The California Court of Appeal held that real estate agents, holding themselves out as having professional knowledge in the area of real estate finance, have an obligation to give expert advice to their clients regarding the economic consequences of a transaction. In this particular case, the widow, after making both mortgage payments, had scarcely enough money to pay for the necessities of life. The court held that the broker should have inquired into the buyer's ability to repay the loans and possibly advised her of a more prudent way to obtain the money.

V. CHAPTER SUMMARY

Seller financing provides an almost limitless variety of creative alternatives to institutional financing and is particularly attractive in tight money markets when loans from institutional lenders often have prohibitive interest rates. Seller financing is also attractive to borrowers who cannot qualify for an institutional loan. However, for seller financing to be a feasible alternative, the seller must not have an immediate need for cash from the sale.

The same financial instruments are used for seller financing that are used by institutional lenders, such as promissory notes and mortgages. The simplest form of seller financing is when the seller owns the property free and clear. However, most seller-financed sales are of properties that are encumbered by previous financing. In this case, the buyer must take the property subject to the prior financing. There are various ways to structure such a transaction, and they include:

1. Assumption
2. Wrap-around Financing
3. Land Contract Subject to Existing Financing
4. Contract with Assumption of Existing Mortgage
5. Contract Plus Assumption Plus Institutional Second Mortgage
6. Lease Option
7. Lease Contract Separate from Option Contract
8. Lease/Purchase
9. Equity Exchange
10. Participation Plan

Finally, professional brokers and agents who are involved in creative financing need to exercise caution, enlisting the services of a qualified real estate attorney. The agent/broker has a professional obligation to determine the best financial course for the buyer to adopt and the ability of the participants in the transaction to understand the transaction before proceeding.

VI. CHAPTER TERMS

Alienation Clause	Optionor
Estoppel Letter	Release
Optionee	Secondarily Liable
Option Money	

VII. CHAPTER 12 QUIZ

1. An estoppel letter is used to:

   a. prevent a lender from participating in a mortgage.
   b. protect an agent entering into a creative financing transaction.
   c. prevent a lender from exercising the "due-on-sale" clause.
   d. prevent the state from forbidding a seller-financed transaction.

2. The simplest form of purchase money financing is:

   a. when the property is encumbered.
   b. when the property is unencumbered.
   c. when the property is estopped.
   d. when the property is in foreclosure.

3. An alienation clause:

   a. allows the lender to estoppel the property.
   b. allows the lender to exercise foreclosure rights.
   c. allows the lender to encumber the property.
   d. allows the lender to make its loan due and payable at time of sale.

4. A purchaser of an option is called the:

   a. optionor.
   b. optionee.
   c. lessee.
   d. lessor.

5. To prevent secondary liability, a seller must obtain a(n):

   a. release from the lender.
   b. estoppel letter.
   c. option.
   d. none of the above.

6. A wrap-around mortgage can:

   a. provide a market rate of return to the seller.
   b. allow the buyer to have a below market interest rate.
   c. be used in place of an assumption.
   d. all the above.

7. A form of purchase money financing where the seller retains legal title to the property until the buyer has made all the payments on the contract is called a(n):

    a. assumption.
    b. wrap-around mortgage.
    c. land contract.
    d. none of the above.

8. The order in which lenders are paid in the event of a default is called:

    a. equitable foreclosure.
    b. option exercise.
    c. default priority.
    d. lien priority.

9. A lease/option is used to:

    a. keep a sale alive.
    b. reduce the selling price over time.
    c. provide income to the seller while awaiting the close of the sale.
    d. all the above.

10. Those who participate in creative financing should:

    a. consult a real estate attorney.
    b. exercise caution.
    c. both a and b.
    d. none of the above.

ANSWERS: 1. c; 2. b; 3. d; 4. b; 5. a; 6. d; 7. c; 8. d; 9. d; 10. c

— PART V —
CHAPTERS 13, 14, AND 15
QUALIFYING BY THE NUMBERS

CHAPTER 13 - QUALIFYING THE BORROWER

The loan underwriting process evaluates both the property and the borrower's willingness and ability to pay off the loan. This analysis will be made by applying the guidelines of the agency that will be involved in the loan.

CHAPTER 14 - QUALIFYING THE PROPERTY

Lenders demand professional appraisals because they want an entirely objective opinion of the true market values of the properties upon which they loan. The appraisers utilized by lenders are Licensed or Certified. The appraiser's client is the lender, not anyone else associated with the transaction.

CHAPTER 15 - REAL ESTATE FINANCE MATHEMATICS

Agents, brokers, and loan officers need to be able to solve basic real estate math problems in order to provide professional service to their clients. It is of particular importance to be able to answer a client's questions regarding interest rates, appreciation in value, and proration of closing costs.

CHAPTER 13

QUALIFYING THE BORROWER

Before agreeing to make a real estate loan, a lender will evaluate both the borrower's ability and willingness to repay the loan, and whether or not the property is of sufficient value to serve as collateral for the loan. This evaluation process is called **LOAN UNDERWRITING.** *The individual who conducts this process is called an* **UNDERWRITER.**

The primary concern of the underwriter is to limit the amount of the lender's risk.

The degree of risk in any individual loan is determined by answering two fundamental questions:

1. Does the borrower's overall financial situation, which is comprised of income, assets, and credit history, indicate that he or she can reasonably be expected to make the proposed monthly loan payments in a timely manner?

2. Is there sufficient value in the property pledged as collateral to assure recovery of the loan amount in the event of a default?

CHAPTER 13 OUTLINE

The Federal Home Loan Mortgage Corporation (Freddie Mac) refers to loans which have met these questions in an affirmative manner as **INVESTMENT QUALITY LOANS**.

Until the 1980s, it was not uncommon for lenders to have their own individual underwriting guidelines. Loans were quite often made from funds obtained from local deposits. The lending guidelines of many local institutions were often liberal. The lenders made their own rules because it was their money. Any loan that did not meet the requirements of the secondary market was simply kept in the lender's portfolio. However, in the 1980s, lenders experienced a massive loss of deposits by depositors who were attracted to other higher paying investments. This situation is called **disintermediation**. To continue to make loans, the lenders who did not fail during this period were required to sell their loans into the secondary market. This meant that they had to play by the rules of the secondary market.

Because most lenders now underwrite to the FNMA and the FHLMC conventional underwriting standards, which for all practical purposes are nearly the same, it is important that real estate agents and loan brokers be familiar with those standards in order to expertly pre-qualify their clients. FHA and VA have some slight differences that will also be addressed. Property collateral issues will be addressed in the following chapter.

I. FHLMC/FNMA Underwriting Standards

According to the FHLMC, *"underwriting mortgage loans is an art, not a science. It cannot be reduced to mathematical formulas, but requires sensitive weighing of the many aspects of the loan."* There are many factors related to the borrower's loan application that an underwriter will consider; they will all relate to income, net worth, and credit history. (**See Figures 13-1 and 13-2.**)

A. INCOME

Conventional lenders consider a borrower's income adequate for a loan if the proposed payment of principal, interest, taxes, and insurance does not exceed 28% of his or her stable monthly income.

Figure 13-1

Uniform Underwriting and Transmittal Summary

I. Borrower and Property Information

Borrower Name _____ SSN _____

Co-Borrower Name _____ SSN _____

Property Address _____

Property Type
- ☐ 1 unit
- ☐ 2–4 units
- ☐ Condominium
- ☐ PUD ☐ Co-op
- ☐ Manufactured Housing
    - ☐ Single Wide ☐ Multiwide

Project Classification
- ☐ A/III Condo ☐ E PUD ☐ 1 Co-op
- ☐ B/II Condo ☐ F PUD ☐ 2 Co-op
- ☐ C/I Condo

Project Name _____

Occupancy Status
- ☐ Primary Residence
- ☐ Second Home
- ☐ Investment Property

Additional Property Information

Number of Units _____

Sales Price $ _____

Appraised Value $ _____

Property Rights
- ☐ Fee Simple
- ☐ Leasehold

II. Mortgage Information

Loan Type
- ☐ Conventional
- ☐ FHA
- ☐ VA
- ☐ USDA/RHS

Amortization Type
- ☐ Fixed-Rate—Monthly Payments
- ☐ Fixed-Rate—Biweekly Payments
- ☐ Balloon
- ☐ ARM (type) _____
- ☐ Other (specify) _____

Loan Purpose
- ☐ Purchase
- ☐ Cash-Out Refinance
- ☐ Limited Cash-Out Refinance (Fannie)
- ☐ No Cash-Out Refinance (Freddie)
- ☐ Home Improvement
- ☐ Construction to Permanent

Lien Position
- ☐ First Mortgage

Amount of Subordinate Financing

$ _____

(If HELOC, include balance and credit limit)
- ☐ Second Mortgage

Note Information

Original Loan Amount $ _____

Initial P&I Payment $ _____

Initial Note Rate _____ %

Loan Term (in months) _____

Mortgage Originator
- ☐ Seller
- ☐ Broker
- ☐ Correspondent

Broker/Correspondent Name and Company Name:

Buydown
- ☐ Yes
- ☐ No

Terms _____

If Second Mortgage

Owner of First Mortgage
- ☐ Fannie Mae ☐ Freddie Mac
- ☐ Seller/Other

Original Loan Amount of First Mortgage

$ _____

III. Underwriting Information

Underwriter's Name _____

Appraiser's Name/License # _____

Appraisal Company Name _____

Stable Monthly Income

	Borrower	Co-Borrower	Total
Base Income	$	$	$
Other Income	$	$	$
Positive Cash Flow (subject property)	$	$	$
Total Income	$	$	$

Qualifying Ratios

Primary Housing Expense/Income _____ %

Total Obligations/Income _____ %

Debt-to-Housing Gap Ratio (Freddie) _____ %

Qualifying Rate
- ☐ Note Rate _____ %
- ☐ _____ % Above Note Rate _____ %
- ☐ _____ % Below Note Rate _____ %
- ☐ Bought-Down Rate _____ %
- ☐ Other _____ %

Risk Assessment
- ☐ Manual Underwriting
- ☐ AUS
    - ☐ DU ☐ LP ☐ Other _____

AUS Recommendation _____

DU Case ID/LP AUS Key# _____

LP Doc Class (Freddie) _____

Representative Credit/Indicator Score _____

Loan-to-Value Ratios

LTV _____ %

CLTV/TLTV _____ %

HCLTV/HTLTV _____ %

Level of Property Review
- ☐ Exterior/Interior
- ☐ Exterior Only
- ☐ No Appraisal

Form Number: _____

Escrow (T&I)
- ☐ Yes ☐ No

Present Housing Payment: $ _____

Proposed Monthly Payments

Borrower's Primary Residence

First Mortgage P&I	$
Second Mortgage P&I	$
Hazard Insurance	$
Taxes	$
Mortgage Insurance	
HOA Fees	$
Lease/Ground Rent	$
Other	$
Total Primary Housing Expense	$

Other Obligations

Negative Cash Flow (subject property)	$
All Other Monthly Payments	$
Total All Monthly Payments	$

Borrower Funds to Close

Required	$
Verified Assets	$

Source of Funds _____

No. of Months Reserves _____

Interested Party Contributions _____ %

Community Lending/Affordable Housing Initiative ☐ Yes ☐ No

Home Buyers/Homeownership Education Certificate in file ☐ Yes ☐ No

Underwriter Comments

_____

_____

_____

_____

_____

_____

_____

IV. Seller, Contract, and Contact Information

Seller Name _____

Seller Address _____

Seller No. _____ Investor Loan No. _____

Seller Loan No. _____

Master Commitment No. _____

Contract No. _____

Contact Name _____

Contact Title _____

Contact Phone Number _____ ext. _____

Contact Signature _____

Date _____

Freddie Mac Form 1077 01/04   Page 1 of 1   Fannie Mae Form 1008 01/04

Figure 13-2

Calyx Software
MORTGAGE LOAN DISCLOSURE STATEMENT/GOOD FAITH ESTIMATE

Borrower's Name(s): _____

Real Property Collateral: the intended security for this proposed loan will be a Deed of Trust on (street address or legal description)

_____

This joint Mortgage Loan Disclosure Statement/Good Faith Estimate is being provided by _____ a real estate broker acting as a mortgage broker, pursuant to the Federal Real Estate Settlement Procedures Act (RESPA) and similar California law. In a transaction subject to RESPA, a lender will provide you with an additional Good Faith Estimate within three business days of the receipt of your loan application. You will also be informed of material changes before settlement/close of escrow. The name of the intended lender to whom your loan application will be delivered is:

☐ Unknown   ☐ _____ (Name of lender, if known)

GOOD FAITH ESTIMATE OF CLOSING COSTS

The information provided below reflects estimates of the charges you are likely to incur at the settlement of your loan. The fees, commissions, costs and expenses listed are estimates; the actual charges may be more or less. Your transaction may not involve a charge for every item listed and any additional items charged will be listed. The numbers listed beside the estimate generally correspond to the numbered lines contained in the HUD-1 Settlement Statement which you will receive at settlement if this transaction is subject to RESPA. The HUD-1 Settlement Statement contains the actual costs for the items paid at settlement. When this transaction is subject to RESPA, by signing page two of this form you are also acknowledging receipt of the HUD Guide to Settlement Costs.

HUD-1	Item	Paid to Others	Paid to Broker
800	**Items Payable in Connection with Loan**		
801	Lender's Loan Origination Fee	$	$
802	Lender's Loan Discount Fee	$	$
803	Appraisal Fee	$	$
804	Credit Report	$	$
805	Lender's Inspection Fee	$	$
808	Mtg Broker Commission/Fee	$	$
809	Tax Service Fee	$	$
810	Processing Fee	$	$
811	Underwriting Fee	$	$
812	Wire Transfer Fee	$	$
		$	$
		$	$
		$	$
		$	$
900	**Items Required by Lender to be Paid in Advance**		
901	Interest for ____ days at $ _____ per day	$	$
902	Mortgage Insurance Premiums	$	$
903	Hazard Insurance Premiums	$	$
904	County Property Taxes	$	$
905	VA Funding Fee	$	$
		$	$
1000	**Reserves Deposited with Lender**		
1001	Hazard Insurance: ____ months at $ _____ /mo.	$	$
1002	Mortgage Insurance: ____ months at $ _____ /mo.	$	$
1004	Co. Property Taxes: ____ months at $ _____ /mo.	$	$
		$	$
1100	**Title Charges**		
1101	Settlement or Closing/Escrow Fee:	$	$
1105	Document Preparation Fee	$	$
1106	Notary Fee	$	$
1108	Title Insurance:	$	$
		$	$
		$	$
1200	**Government Recording and Transfer Charges**		
1201	Recording Fees:	$	$
1202	City/County Tax/Stamps:	$	$
		$	$
1300	**Additional Settlement Charges**		
1302	Pest Inspection	$	$
		$	$
		$	$
		$	$
Subtotal of Initial Fees, Commissions, Costs and Expenses		$	$

Total of Initial Fees, Commissions, Costs and Expenses $ _____

Compensation to Broker (Not Paid Out of Loan Proceeds):
Mortgage Broker Commission/Fee: $ _____
Any Additional Compensation from Lender ☐ No ☐ Yes $ _____ (If known)

CALYX Form Mlds1.frm 6/98   Page 1 of 2   MLDS 554071293C

ADDITIONAL REQUIRED CALIFORNIA DISCLOSURES

I. Proposed Loan Amount: $_____

           Initial Commissions, Fees, Costs and
              Expenses Summarized on Page 1: $_____
           Payment of Other Obligations (List):
              Credit Life and/or Disability Insurance (see VI below) $_____
              Purchase Price / Payoff $_____
           _____ $_____

Subtotal of All Deductions: $_____
Estimated Cash at Closing ☐ **To You**   ☐ **That you must pay** $_____

II. Proposed Interest Rate: _____ %   ☐ Fixed Rate   ☐ Initial Variable Rate

III. Proposed Loan Term: _____   ☐ Years   ☐ Months

IV. Proposed Loan Payments: Payments of $_____ will be made ☐ Monthly ☐Quarterly ☐Annually for _____ (number of months, quarters or years). If proposed loan is a variable interest rate loan, this payment will vary (see loan documents for details).

The loan is subject to a balloon payment: ☐ No ☐ Yes If Yes, the following paragraph applies and a final balloon payment of $ _____ will be due on _____ [estimated date (month/day/year)].

Notice to Borrower: If you do not have the funds to pay the balloon payment when it comes due, you may have to obtain a new loan against your property to make the balloon payment. In that case, you may again have to pay commissions, fees, and expenses for the arranging of the new loan. In addition, if you are unable to make the monthly payments or the balloon payment, you may lose the property and all of your equity through foreclosure. Keep this in mind in deciding upon the amount and terms of this loan.

V. Prepayments: The proposed loan has the following prepayment provisions.
     ☐ No prepayment penalty.
     ☐ Other (see loan documents for details).
     ☐ Any payment of principal in any calendar year in excess of 20% of the ☐ original balance ☐ unpaid balance will include a penalty not to exceed_____ months advance interest at the note rate, but not more than the interest that would be charged if the loan were paid to maturity (see loan documents for details).

VI. Credit Life and/or Disability Insurance: The purchase of credit life and/or disability insurance by a borrower is NOT required as a condition of making this proposed loan.

VII. Other Liens: Are there liens currently on this property for which the borrower is obligated? ☐No ☐Yes
If Yes, describe below:

     Lienholder's Name   Amount Owing   Priority

_____

_____

Liens that will remain or are anticipated on this property after the proposed loan for which you are applying is made or arranged (including the proposed loan for which you are applying).

     Lienholder's Name   Amount Owing   Priority

_____

_____

NOTICE TO BORROWER: Be sure that you state the amount of all liens as accurately as possible. If you contract with the broker to arrange this loan, but it cannot be arranged because you did not state these liens correctly, you may be liable to pay commissions, costs, fees, and expenses even though you do not obtain the loan.

VIII. Article 7 Compliance: If this proposed loan is secured by a first deed of trust in a principal amount of less than $30,000 or secured by a junior lien in a principal amount of less than $20,000, the undersigned licensee certifies that the loan will be made in compliance with Article 7 of Chapter 3 of the Real Estate Law.

A. This loan ☐may ☐will ☐will not be made wholly or in part from broker controlled funds as defined in Section 10241(j) of the Business and Professions Code.

B. If the broker indicates in the above statement that the loan "may" be out of broker-controlled funds, the broker must inform the borrower prior to the close of escrow if the funds to be received by the borrower are in fact broker-controlled funds.
DRE license information telephone number : 916-227-0931

_____   _____
Name of Broker   License #   Broker's Representative   License #

_____
Broker's Address

_____   OR   _____
Signature of Broker   Date   Signature of Representative   Date

IX. NOTICE TO BORROWER: THIS IS NOT A LOAN COMMITMENT. Do not sign this statement until you have read and understood all of the information in it. All parts of this form must be completed before you sign. Borrower hereby acknowledges the receipt of a copy of this statement.

_____   _____
Borrower   Date   Borrower   Date

Review completed on _____ by _____
                 Date   Broker or Designated Representative   Dept. of Real Estate License #

STABLE MONTHLY INCOME is the borrower's gross monthly income from primary base employment and any secondary income that is considered reliable and likely to endure. We will take a closer look at acceptable income sources shortly.

Example:

> $2,900   stable monthly income
> $700   proposed mortgage payment*
>
>   700 ÷ 2,900 = .24

> * Includes principal, interest, taxes, insurance (PITI), and private mortgage insurance (PMI), if applicable.

A second but equally important concern is that the total of the borrower's housing expenses (as explained above), plus any installment debts with more than ten (10) remaining payments, as well as alimony, child support or maintenance payments, if any, not exceed 36% of his or her stable monthly income.

Example:

> $2,900   stable monthly income
>
> $700   proposed mortgage payment
> $225   auto payment (18 installments remain)
> + 100   child support
> $1,025
>
>   1,025 ÷ 2,900 = .35 total expense-to-income ratio

The total expense-to-income ratio, called a **TOTAL DEBT SERVICE RATIO**, frequently is a more realistic measure of the borrower's ability to support the loan payments because it takes into account the borrower's other recurring financial obligations.

Using these ratios, it is a simple matter to determine the maximum mortgage payment for which a borrower will qualify. First, take the borrower's stable monthly income and multiply that by the maximum housing expense-to-income ratio (0.28). The answer is the maximum

mortgage payment allowable under the first ratio. Then, take the stable monthly income and multiply that by the maximum total debt service ratio (0.36). The answer is the amount of total monthly long-term debts the borrower is permitted to have. Take this total amount and subtract the monthly long-term obligations (not including mortgage payments), and the resulting figure is the largest mortgage payment allowed under the total debt service ratio. The mortgage payment determined through calculating the total debt service ratio is more than likely to be smaller than the housing expense-to-income figure. This is because other monthly debts are taken into consideration. Because the borrower must qualify under both ratios, the smaller of the two is the maximum allowable mortgage payment.

Example: Mary Smith has a stable monthly income of $3,200. She has three long-term monthly debt obligations: a $220 car payment, a $75 personal loan payment, and a $50 revolving charge card payment. What is the maximum monthly mortgage payment she can qualify for?

Housing expense-to-income ratio: 28%

$3,200.00	monthly income
x .28	income ratio
$896.00	maximum mortgage payment under housing expense-to-income ratio

Total debt service ratio: 36%

$3,200.00	monthly income
x .36	income ratio
$1,152.00	maximum total debt service

$1,152.00	maximum total debt service
- 220.00	car payment
- 75.00	personal loan
- 50.00	revolving charge card payment
$807.00	maximum mortgage payment under total debt service ratio

The maximum monthly mortgage payment Mary would qualify for would be $807. Remember, Mary must qualify under both ratios, so the lower figure is the most Mary can get. Of course, if she could pay off some of her debts and reduce her total long-term monthly obligations, she would be able to qualify for a larger mortgage payment.

For loans which exceed 90% loan-to-value ratios (95% loans), the total expense-to-monthly income ratio is 33%. The housing expense ratio may not exceed 25%.

FNMA/FHLMC RATIOS		
Loan-to-Value	Housing Expense	Total Debt Service/ Fixed Payments
90% or less (down payment 10% or more)	28%	36%
FNMA more than 90% (down payment 5%)	25%	33%

1. Stable Monthly Income

STABLE MONTHLY INCOME is the base income of the borrower (both husband and wife), plus earnings from acceptable secondary sources. SECONDARY EARNINGS take the form of, but are not limited to, bonuses, commissions (over and above base salary), part-time employment, social security payments, military disability and retirement payments, interest on savings or other investments, and the like.

Analyzing a borrower's income is a three-dimensional procedure. Before concluding there is a sufficient quantity of income, the underwriter must decide what portion of the total verified earnings are acceptable as a part of his or her stable monthly income. This is accomplished by studying the quality (dependability) of the income source(s) and the durability (probability of continuance) of the income.

Quality. A *QUALITY SECONDARY SOURCE is one that is reasonably reliable, such as an established employer, government agency, interest-yielding investment account, etc.*

Durability. *DURABLE INCOME is that income which can be expected to continue for a sustained period.* Permanent disability, retirement earnings and interest on established investments clearly are enduring types of income.

Bonuses, Commissions, and Part-Time Earnings. These sources are considered durable if they can be shown to have been a consistent part of the borrower's overall earnings pattern for at least one, but preferably two, years. Proof of such consistency can be obtained by submitting copies of the borrower's W-2 forms or federal income tax statements from the previous year, or a verification of employment and earnings from the employer.

Overtime. Overtime earnings are technically eligible for inclusion in a borrower's stable monthly income, but underwriters are most reluctant to rely on such earnings because their durability is so uncertain.

It is recommended that you not count on overtime earnings when qualifying your buyers, unless they are clearly a consistent part of his or her earnings pattern.

Unemployment and Welfare. These earnings are almost never treated as stable monthly income because they are viewed as temporary.

Alimony, Child Support, or Maintenance. These sources of income can be considered part of the borrower's stable monthly income if it is determined they are likely to be consistently made. Such a determination is dependent on whether the payments are required by written agreement or court decree, the length of time the payments have been received, the age of the child (child support payments generally stop at age 18), the overall financial and credit status of the payer, and the ability of the borrower to compel payment if necessary.

A copy of the divorce decree is generally sufficient to establish the amount and the enforceability of the required payments. In some instances, where the underwriter is not satisfied that the full payments are received regularly, the borrower may be asked to submit proof of receipt.

The closer a child gets to age 18, the less durable child support income paid for he or she appears. There is no official cut-off date used by underwriters, but it is safe to say that once the child is between 16 and 17 years of age, most underwriters will see the support payments as terminal and will not include them in the stable monthly income.

Income from Other Family Members. Generally, only the earnings of the head(s) of household will be considered when calculating the stable monthly income. Support income from teenage children or other family members could stop without notice; income of this sort lacks both quality and durability.

Self-Employment Income. Self-employed borrower's should be prepared to provide, if possible, audited profit and loss statements and balance sheets for the two years prior to the loan application; additionally, the underwriter will require copies of the borrower's federal income tax statements for the same two years.

If a borrower has been self-employed for less than two years it will be difficult to qualify him or her for a loan; if the borrower has been in business for less than one year it will be more difficult still.

Underwriters are wary of new businesses and are generally unswerving in their insistence that the self-employed borrower must have operated the business profitably for at least two years.

The requirement for documentation of income may be waived in some cases. Some lenders offer "easy qualifier" or "no documentation" loans for borrowers meeting certain requirements. A borrower with sufficient assets, good credit, and who is able to make a large down payment (usually at least 30%) may be able to obtain a

loan without providing documentation of income and income tax returns for the preceding two years. Recently, these types of loans have suffered a high default rate and are currently in disfavor.

Co-Mortgagor. Frequently, a co-mortgagor is used to aid a primary borrower in qualifying for a loan. Today, parents often lend their established earnings pattern and financial status to their children who otherwise would be unable to purchase a home. A *CO-MORTGAGOR is simply a co-borrower, an individual who, along with the primary borrower, accepts responsibility for repayment of the loan by signing the promissory note and mortgage.* Like the primary borrower, the co-mortgagor must have earnings, assets, and a credit history that are acceptable to the underwriter.

Keep in mind that if a co-mortgagor is used, he or she must be able to support both his or her own housing expense and a proportionate share, if not all, of the proposed housing expense. Marginal co-mortgagors should not be relied on very heavily; they may do more harm than good to a loan application.

Rental Income. Income from rental properties can be counted as stable monthly income if a stable pattern of rental income can be verified. Authenticated copies of the owner's books showing gross earnings and operating expenses for the previous two years should be submitted along with the borrower's application for loan approval.

Verifying Income. Until early 1987, lenders were required to verify income by sending an income verification form directly to the applicant's employer. The employer filled out the form and then sent it directly back to the lender. The borrower was not allowed to have any contact with the verification forms. However, FNMA and FHLMC have changed income verification procedures and income may now be verified by the borrower. The borrower can substantiate his or her own employment and income by providing W-2 forms for the previous two years and payroll stubs or vouchers for the previous 30-day period. The pay stubs must identify the borrower, employer, and the borrower's gross earnings for both the current pay period and year-to-date.

Lenders then confirm the employment and earnings by a phone call to the employer.

2. Computing Monthly Earnings

When converting hourly wages to monthly earnings, multiply the hourly wage by 40 (hours in a work week), then multiply by 52 (weeks in a year) and divide by 12 (months in a year).

Example:

Hourly Wage: $20.00
Weekly Income: $20.00 x 40 = $800
Annual Income: $800 x 52 = $41,600
Monthly Income: $41,600 ÷ 12 = $3,466.67

3. Employment History

When evaluating the elements of a borrower's income (quantity, quality, and durability), the underwriter will analyze the individual's employment stability. A borrower with a history of steady, full employment will be given more favorable consideration than one who has changed employers frequently, unless the changes are properly explained.

As a general rule, a borrower should have continuous employment for at least two years in the same field.

However, every borrower is unique and if there is not an established two-year work history, there may be explainable circumstances which would warrant loan approval, such as having recently finished college or been discharged from the service.

4. Advancement

If the borrower has changed employers for the sake of advancement within the same line of work, the underwriter will likely view the change favorably. On the other hand, persistent job hopping without advancement usually signifies a problem of some kind and an underwriter will tend to regard the individual's earnings as unstable.

5. Education and Training

Special education or training that prepares an individual for a specific kind of work can strengthen a loan application. Such education or training can offset minor weaknesses with respect to earnings or job tenure if the underwriter is convinced there is a continuing demand for individuals in this line of work. The type of work should promote job stability and opportunities for advancement.

B. NET WORTH

According to the Federal National Mortgage Association (FNMA), *"accumulation of net worth is a strong indication of credit worthiness."* A borrower who has built up a significant net worth from earnings, savings, and other investment activities clearly has the ability to manage financial affairs and accumulate wealth. An individual's **NET WORTH** *is determined by subtracting personal liabilities from total assets.*

If a borrower has a marginal debt service-to-income ratio, an above normal net worth can offset the deficiency. Underwriters know that net worth in liquid form can be used to pay unexpected bills or to support a borrower when there has been a temporary interruption in income.

1. Required Reserves After Closing

As a safeguard against unexpected bills or temporary loss of income, and as a general indicator of financial ability, FNMA requires the borrower to have sufficient cash on deposit, or in the form of highly liquid assets, to cover two months' payments (principal, interest, taxes, insurance, and if applicable, mortgage insurance) after making the down payment and paying all closing costs. FHLMC guidelines require a minimum of two months' payments for all owner-occupant loans, without regard to loan-to-value ratio, and three to six months for non-owner-occupant loans.

2. Verification of Assets

Included in every loan application is a section devoted to assets. The underwriter will take whatever steps are necessary to verify the nature and value of assets held by the borrower. The purpose of the asset verification process is twofold:

a. It must be determined that the borrower has sufficient liquid assets to make the cash down payment and pay the closing costs and other expenses incidental to the purchase of the property. *LIQUID ASSETS include cash and any other assets that can be quickly converted to cash.*

b. The underwriter wants to know that the borrower has sufficient reserves to handle typical household emergencies, whatever they might be and whenever they might arise.

3. Verification of Deposit

The underwriter will use the Request for Verification of Deposit form (**Figure 13-3**) to prove the borrower has the necessary funds in his or her bank account(s). This form is sent directly to the bank and returned to the underwriter without passing through the borrower's hands. When the underwriter receives the completed verification of deposit, there are four things he or she will look for:

a. Does the verified information conform to the statements in the loan application?

b. Does the borrower have enough money in the bank to meet the expenses of purchase?

c. Has the bank account been opened only recently (within the last couple of months)?

d. Is the present balance notably higher than the average balance?

Recently opened accounts or higher than normal balances must be explained, as these are strong indications that the buyer has resorted to borrowed funds to pay the down payment and closing costs.

4. Alternative Verification Method

When FNMA changed its rules regarding verification of income (early 1987), it also changed its rules on verification of deposits. Lenders may now use an alternative method of verifying deposits: the borrower may submit the original bank statements for the previous three months to verify sufficient cash for closing.

Figure 13-3

REQUEST FOR VERIFICATION OF DEPOSIT

INSTRUCTIONS: LENDER - Complete Items 1 thru 8 Have applicant(s) complete Item 9. Forward directly to depository named in Item 1.
DEPOSITORY - Please complete Items 10 thru 15 and return DIRECTLY to lender named in Item 2

PART I - REQUEST

1. TO (Name and address of depository)	2. FROM (Name and address of lender)
You Betcha Bank 1919 2nd St. Anytown, USA	

3. SIGNATURE OF LENDER	4. TITLE	5. DATE	6. LENDER'S NUMBER (Optional)
	loan officer		

7. INFORMATION TO BE VERIFIED

TYPE OF ACCOUNT	ACCOUNT IN NAME OF	ACCOUNT NUMBER	BALANCE
checking	Carl B. Able	11616-6	$ 482
savings	Carl B. Able	61161-1	$ 3,100
			$
			$

TO DEPOSITORY: *I have applied for a mortgage loan and stated in my financial statement that the balance on deposit with you is as shown above. You are authorized to verify this information and to supply the lender identified above with the information requested in Items 10 thru 12. Your response is solely a matter of courtesy for which no responsibility is attached to your institution or any of your officers.*

8. NAME AND ADDRESS OF APPLICANT(s)	9. SIGNATURE OF APPLICANT(s)
Carl B. Able 1800 3rd Avenue Anytown, USA	

PART II - VERIFICATION OF DEPOSITORY

10. DEPOSIT ACCOUNTS OF APPLICANT(s)

TYPE OF ACCOUNT	ACCOUNT NUMBER	CURRENT BALANCE	AVERAGE BALANCE FOR PREVIOUS TWO MONTHS	DATE OPENED
checking	11616-6	$ 200	$ 200	
savings	61161-1	$ 3,600	$ 1,000	
		$	$	
		$	$	

11 LOANS OUTSTANDING TO APPLICANT(s)

LOAN NUMBER	DATE OF LOAN	ORIGINAL AMOUNT	CURRENT BALANCE	INSTALLMENTS (Monthly/Quarterly)	SECURED BY	NUMBER OF LATE PAYMENTS
	none	$	$	$ per		
		$	$	$ per		
		$	$	$ per		

12. ADDITIONAL INFORMATION WHICH MAY BE OF ASSISTANCE IN DETERMINATION OF CREDIT WORTHINESS:
(Please include information on loans paid-in-full as in Item 11 above)

None

13. SIGNATURE OF DEPOSITORY	14. TITLE	15. DATE
	assistant vice president	

The confidentiality of the information you have furnished will be preserved except where disclosure of this information is required by applicable law. The form is to be transmitted directly to the lender and is not to be transmitted through the applicant or any other party.

RE 016 (Rev 3-80)

FNMA Form 1006
Rev. June 78

5. Financial Statement

If a borrower's assets are substantial and diverse, an audited financial statement may be the best way to explain the borrower's creditworthiness to the underwriter. A *FINANCIAL STATEMENT is a summary of facts showing the individual's financial condition; it contains an itemized list of assets and liabilities which serves to disclose net worth.* (**See Figure 13-4.**)

6. Real Estate for Sale

If a borrower is selling a property to raise cash to buy the subject property, the equity may be counted as a legitimate asset. *EQUITY is the difference between the market value of the property and the sum of the selling expenses, mortgages and other liens against the property.* Equity is what the buyer should receive from the sale of the property. In cases where the equity is the primary or exclusive source of money for the purchase of the subject property, the underwriter might require, before making the new loan, evidence that the former property has been sold and the proceeds from that sale have been received by the borrower.

If the purpose of the loan is to finance the construction of a home on a lot owned by the borrower, the underwriter will treat the borrower's equity in that lot as cash or its equivalent.

Example:

```
  $75,000  estimated construction costs
 + 10,000  lot value
  $85,000  total property value

  $85,000  total property value
    x .80  loan-to-value ratio (80%
  $68,000  maximum loan amount

  $85,000  total property value
 - 68,000  maximum loan amount
  $17,000  required down payment
  $10,000  lot value
  - 4,000  liens against lot (mortgage)
   $6,000  borrower's equity
```

Figure 13-4

INDIVIDUAL FINANCIAL STATEMENT

_____ Office As of _____ 19 ___

LAST NAME	FIRST	MIDDLE	AGE	SOCIAL SECURITY NUMBER
Parks,	Dorothy	M.	54	111-00-1111

ADDRESS	NUMBER AND STREET	CITY, STATE, ZIP CODE
1000 East 10th St.		Metro City, Kansas

HOME PHONE	BUS.PHONE	AGES OF DEPENDENT CHILDREN	EMPLOYER OR SELF-EMPLOYED	NUMBER OF YEARS	POSITION OR OCCUPATION
777-8010	777-9000	NONE	SELF-EMPLOYED	10	

Do not complete this marital status section or information below concerning your PRESENT spouse if you reside in Alaska, Oregon or another non-community property state and are applying for individual unsecured credit.

☐ Married   ☒ Unmarried (Single, widowed, divorced)
☐ Separated

ASSETS	(Omit Cents)	LIABILITIES	(Omit Cents)
Cash on hand and in banks	$ 50,000	Open accounts payable — Schedule G	$ 2,500
Accounts receivable — Schedule A			
Notes receivable — Schedule B		Notes payable — Schedule H	
		Accrued expenses	
		Federal income tax payable	
Listed stocks and bonds — Schedule D	50,000	Due relatives and related concerns; describe:	
		Installment obligations — Schedule I	
TOTAL CURRENT ASSETS	**$ 100,000**	**TOTAL CURRENT LIABILITIES**	**$ 2,500**
Real Estate — Schedule F	5,210,000	Real Estate Mortgage and Contracts – Schedules C & F	3,440,000
Automobiles and trucks	25,000		
Machinery and tools		Other liabilities; describe	
Contracts and Mortgages Receivable — Schedule C	80,000		
Unlisted stocks and bonds — Schedule E	25,000		
Due from relatives and related concerns; describe:		Amount borrowed on life insurance	
		TOTAL LIABILITIES	**$ 3,465,000**
Household goods	15,000		
Other assets; describe Art & Jewelry	30,000	**NET WORTH**	**$ 2,040,000**
Cash Surrender value of life insurance	20,000		
TOTAL ASSETS	**$ 5,505,000**	**TOTAL LIABILITIES AND NET WORTH**	**$ 5,505,000**
INCOME FOR YEAR:		CONTINGENT LIABILITY:	$
Salary or wages		Guaranteed or cosigned loans or paper	
Proprietorship/partnership draws	45,000	Surety bonds	
Commissions and bonus		Other	
Dividends and interest	20,000	INSURANCE	
Rentals	140,000	Buildings	4,800,000
Other (See Item 2 below)		Liability (auto, etc.)	2,000,000
TOTAL NET INCOME	**$ 205,000**	Life insurance — face value	500,000

Payable to: Loretta Parks

Are any of the above assets pledged to secure indebtedness other than liabilities listed? Describe _____

Last filing IRS return? 19 _84_   Have you made your will? ☒ YES NO ☐   Have you ever taken bankruptcy?   ☐ YES NO ☒

Income taxes paid $_30,000_   Has your spouse made a will? ☐ YES NO ☐   Judgments, suits or litigation?   ☐ YES NO ☒

COMPLETE EACH SCHEDULE BY WRITING "NONE" IN THOSE THAT DO NOT APPLY

Schedule A. ACCOUNTS RECEIVABLE

Name	Amount	Due Date
None		
TOTAL	$	

Schedule B. NOTES RECEIVABLE

Name	Amount	Due Date
None		
TOTAL	$	

Schedule C. CONTRACTS AND MORTGAGES RECEIVABLE

Name of Debtor	Security and To Whom	Receivable		Owing on This Property	
		Balance	Mo.Payment	Balance	Mo.Payment
M. D. Nelson	3 Bdrm. Residence	80,000	903	— —	— —
	1920 South River Drive				
	Metro City				
	TOTAL	$ 80,000	$ 903	$	$

Schedule D. LISTED STOCKS AND BONDS

Name of Company	Registered Name	Number of Shares	Market Per Share	Total Mkt. Value
Blue Chip	Blue Corp.	1,000	$ 50	$ 50,000
	TOTAL			$ 50,000

Schedule E. UNLISTED STOCKS AND BONDS

Name of Company	Registered Name	Number of Shares	Market Per Share	Total Mkt. Value
Metro City Bonds Due 1995		25	1,000	$ 25,000
	TOTAL			$ 25,000

Schedule F. REAL ESTATE

Unless otherwise noted, title stands in name of: Dorothy M. Parks

Location, Size, Description	Year Acquired	Current Value Land	Buildings	Total	Payable To	Mortgages or Contracts Balance	Mo.Payment
50 Unit Apartment Complex		$ 300,000	$2,000,000	2,300,000	1st Bank	$1,500,000	$ 14,475
1500 N. 50th , Metro City							
2 Story Office Bldg.		200,000	2,500,000	2,700,000	N. B. Sailors	1,500,000	19,850
506 Main, Metro City							
Residence		60,000	150,000	210,000	1st Federal St. L.	140,000	1,540
1000 East 10th, Metro City							
			TOTAL	$ 5,210,000	**TOTAL**	$ 3,440,000	$ 35,865

Schedule G. OPEN ACCOUNTS PAYABLE

Payable To	Amount	Due Date
VISA	1,000	
Sara Interiors	1,500	
TOTAL	$ 2,500	

Schedule H. NOTES PAYABLE TO OTHERS

Payable To	Amount	Due Date
NONE		
TOTAL	$	

Schedule I. INSTALLMENT OBLIGATIONS

Payable To	Collateral	Balance	Final Due Date	Monthly Pmt.
NONE				
TOTAL	$			$

The borrower shows $6,000 equity in the lot, which is included in the list of assets necessary to satisfy the down payment and settlement cost requirements.

7. Other Assets

Any assets held by the borrower will help the loan application. Assets, other than cash and real estate, typically listed in a loan application include automobiles, furniture, jewelry, stocks and bonds, and cash value in a life insurance policy.

Keep in mind that the assets which will most favorably influence the underwriter's decision are the liquid assets; those that can be quickly converted to cash.

8. Gift Letter

If an applicant lacks the necessary funds to close a transaction, a gift of the required amount from relatives is usually acceptable to the underwriter. The gift should be confirmed by means of a (gift) letter signed by the donor. The letter should clearly state that the money represents a gift and does not have to be repaid.

The gift usually must be from an immediate family member.

Even if the gift letter requirements are satisfied, the borrower will normally have to make some cash payment out of his or her own cash resources. FNMA requires that the borrower make at least a 5% down payment in addition to the gift, unless the gift is 20% or more of the purchase price. If the gift equals 20% or more, then the borrower is not required to make the additional 5% down payment.

C. CREDIT HISTORY

As a part of the loan evaluation, the underwriter will analyze the credit history of the borrower; this is accomplished by obtaining a credit report from a responsible credit rating bureau. (**See Figure 13-5.**)

CREDIT SCORING is the automated practice used by credit agencies to quantify a borrower's entire credit history into a single score or number so

Figure 13-5

STANDARD FACTUAL DATA REPORT

ACCOUNT NO. _____ 8572F _____
ACCOUNT NAME _____
REPORT ORDERED BY _____
DATE ORDERED _____ March 3, 199x
DATE COMPLETED _____ March 17, 199x
INDIVIDUAL OR JOINT REPORT _JOINT_
TYPE REPORT (CASE OR FILE NO.) _____
REPORT PREPARED BY _____
PRICE _____

| | BASE | NON-LOCAL | ADDITIONAL | TAX | TOTAL |

REPOSITORY INFORMATION
OBTAINED FROM: JOHN J. JONES   JOAN J. JONES
(BORROWER)   (CO-BORROWER)

ALL INQUIRIES WITHIN THE LAST 6 MONTHS HAVE BEEN CHECKED AND ANY OPENED ACCOUNTS ARE REFLECTED BELOW.

This standard factual data report meets all underwriting requirements set by FHA, VA, FNMA and FHLMC.

GENERAL INFORMATION

1. BORROWER'S NAME AND AGE / CO-BORROWER'S NAME AND AGE	JOHN J. JONES, 37; JOAN J. JONES, 35
2. CURRENT ADDRESS	101 1ST AVE., ANYTOWN, USA 00000
3. LENGTH OF TIME AT PRESENT ADDRESS / OWN?	6 MONTHS/NO
4. PREVIOUS ADDRESS	275 14TH STREET, ANYTOWN, USA 00000
5. BORROWER SS # / CO-BORROWER SS #	001-01-1111; 100-10-2222
6. MARITAL STATUS / YEARS / DEPENDENTS	MARRIED/4/3

BORROWER'S EMPLOYMENT

7. NAME OF EMPLOYER / ADDRESS	LUCKY LARRY'S USED AUTO; 121 MAIN STREET, ANYTOWN
8. POSITION HELD / LENGTH OF EMPLOYMENT	SALESPERSON/ 8 MONTHS
9. EMPLOYMENT VERIFIED BY	LARRY JONES
10. PREVIOUS EMPLOYMENT / LENGTH OF EMPLOYMENT	TOTEM CAR SALES/18 MONTHS

CO-BORROWER'S EMPLOYMENT

11. NAME OF EMPLOYER / ADDRESS	ABC DEPARTMENT STORE; 421 MAIN STREET, ANYTOWN
12. POSITION HELD / LENGTH OF EMPLOYMENT	DEPARTMENT MANAGER/ 8 YEARS
13. EMPLOYMENT VERIFIED BY	C. BELLOWS
14. PREVIOUS EMPLOYMENT / LENGTH OF EMPLOYMENT	—

THE REPORTING BUREAU CERTIFIES THAT: Public records have been checked for judgments, garnishments, foreclosures, bankruptcies and other legal action involving the BORROWER ☒ CO-BORROWER ☒ (or equivalent results have been obtained through the use of qualified public records reporting services) with the following results:
PUBLIC RECORD ITEMS FOUND BORROWER _DIVORCE_ 8/9x   PUBLIC RECORD ITEMS FOUND CO-BORROWER _N/A_
THE REPORTING BUREAU CERTIFIES THAT: The credit record of the borrower (and co-borrower if any) has been checked as to payment of obligations: a. ☐ through the credit accounts extended by designated credit grantors, if any; and, b. ☒ through accumulated credit records of such credit grantors of the community in which the subject(s) resides, with the results indicated below.

CREDIT HISTORY

BUSINESS	DATE ACCOUNT OPENED	HIGHEST CREDIT	BALANCE OWING	MONTHLY PAYMENT	PAYMENT PATTERN	PAST DUE AMOUNT	30	60	90+	DATE LAST PAST DUE
BOLES INC.	7/9x	$200	-0-	$17	AS AGREED	-0-				---
ACME DRUGS	9/9x	$150	$90	REVOLV. SLOW	SLOW	$26	12	2		CURRENT
PENNEY'S	8/9x	$950	$900	$45	SLOW	$45	2	1		CURRENT
MASTERCARD	9/9x	$500	$429	REVOLV.	AS AGREED	-0-				---
ABC FINANCE	2/9x	$1,500	$1,500	$92	TOO SOON TO RATE	-0-				---
HFC FINANCE	6/9x	$4,800	$1,900	$185	SLOW	$185	4			CURRENT

that an estimate of the risk of making a loan can be determined. Of course, the rule applies: the more a borrower really needs a loan, the less chance credit agencies want to risk lending the money. Here are some helpful hints to increase your credit score:

1. **Pay bills on time.** Late payments, collection, and bankruptcy are negative factors.

2. **Limit outstanding debt.** Amounts owed close to your credit limit are negatives.

3. **Have a long credit history.** Insufficient credit history is a negative.

4. **Restrict your credit.** Applying for too many recent accounts is a negative.

5. **Too much credit.** Too many credit cards is a negative.

If the borrower's credit history reflects a slow payment record or other derogatory credit information, the loan application could be declined. Derogatory credit information, over and above a slow payment record, includes suits, judgments, repossessions, collections, foreclosures, and bankruptcies.

In some instances, derogatory ratings do not prevent a borrower from obtaining a loan. If the credit problems can be satisfactorily explained so the underwriter is satisfied they do not represent the borrower's overall attitude towards credit obligations, and that the circumstances leading to the problems were temporary and no longer exist, the loan application might be approved.

1. Explaining Derogatory Credit

Most people try to meet their credit obligations on time; when they do not, there is usually a reason. A loss of job, hospitalization, illness, death in the family or even divorce can create extraordinary financial pressures and adversely affect a credit report. It may be possible to successfully explain the ratings if the borrower can show that the problems occurred during a specific period of time for an understandable reason, and that prior and subsequent credit ratings have been good.

When explaining credit difficulties to a lender, it is a mistake to blame the problems on misunderstandings or on the creditors themselves. Too frequently, underwriters listen to explanations from borrowers who refuse to accept responsibility for their own acts, insisting instead that the blame lies elsewhere. The reaction to such explanations is very predictable: skepticism, disbelief, and rejection. Underwriters reason that a borrower's reluctance to take responsibility for prior credit problems is an indication of what can be expected from him or her in the future.

If a borrower's credit report is laced with derogatory ratings over a period of years, there is probably little hope for loan approval.

Perpetual credit problems more likely reflect an attitude instead of a circumstance, and it is reasonable to presume that the pattern will continue in the future.

All credit problems are resolved with time, and if a buyer indicates he or she has had some credit problems in the past, it would be a mistake to automatically presume the buyer cannot qualify for a loan. Refer him or her to a competent lender and get an expert's opinion.

2. Bill Consolidation, Refinancing

Even in the absence of derogatory ratings, there are matters that can be revealed by a credit report which might indicate the borrower is a marginal credit risk. If an individual's credit pattern is one of continually increasing liabilities and periodically "bailing out" through refinancing and debt consolidation, he or she may be classified as a marginal risk. The pattern suggests a tendency to live beyond a prudent level. This is a subjective consideration likely to influence the underwriter's decision if the borrower is weak in other critical areas, such as income or assets.

3. Illegal Discrimination

A borrower must be of legal age (usually age 18 or older) before he or she can qualify for a loan; after that, an applicant's age is not a valid reason for rejecting a loan.

In addition to age, a lender cannot use as a basis for denying a loan the race, color, creed, national origin, religion, handicap, familial status (children), marital status, or sex of the borrower. **(See Figure 13-6.)**

Figure 13-6

Equal Housing Lender

We Do Business In Accordance With The Federal Fair Housing Law

(Title VIII of the Civil Rights Act of 1968, as Amended by the Housing and Community Development Act of 1974)

IT IS ILLEGAL TO DISCRIMINATE AGAINST ANY PERSON BECAUSE OF RACE, RELIGION, CREED, COLOR, NATIONAL ORIGIN, ANCESTRY, PHYSICAL HANDICAP, MEDICAL CONDITION, FAMILIA STATUS, SEX, OR AGE TO:

- Deny a loan for the purpose of purchasing, constructing, improving, repairing or maintaining a dwelling or

- Discriminate in fixing of the amount, interest rate, duration, application procedures or other terms or conditions of such a loan.

IF YOU BELIEVE YOU HAVE BEEN DISCRIMINATED AGAINST, YOU MAY SEND A COMPLAINT TO:

U.S. DEPARTMENT OF HOUSING AND URBAN DEVELOPMENT
Assistant Secretary for Fair Housing and Equal Opportunity Washington, D.C. 20410

or call your local HUD Area or Insuring Office.

II. Summary of Qualifying the Borrower

A buyer's ability to qualify for a real estate loan depends on many factors, all of which relate to income, net worth, and credit history. While there are established guidelines for determining adequacy of income in relation to proposed housing expense, it would be wrong to apply them too rigidly. All aspects of the buyer's financial situation must be considered before deciding on his or her qualification for a loan. Considering the quality, quantity, and durability of a buyer's income and relating it to net worth is substantial enough to indicate an ability to manage financial affairs. Conversely, strong earnings and substantial assets may not be enough to offset the damage caused by poor credit paying habits. A borrower must be both able (income/assets) and willing (credit) to pay the housing expense.

Finally, keep in mind that a good property with a considerable cash equity can offset marginal credit or income because borrowers who make large investments (down payments) in their properties are far less likely to default than borrowers with little or no equity.

III. FHA Underwriting Standards

FHA's qualifying ratios are based on the borrower's gross income.

Once the borrower's gross income has been identified, it must be compared against the proposed housing expense. Included in FHA's estimated housing expense are the principal and interest payments, the monthly property taxes, the monthly homeowner's insurance premium, an estimated monthly maintenance expense, an estimated monthly utilities expense, monthly homeowners' association dues (if any), and monthly property assessments (if any).

Sample Housing Expense:

$538.42	principal and interest
40.00	property taxes
15.00	homeowner's insurance

33.00 maintenance expense
80.00 utilities expense
-0- homeowners' association dues
<u>-0-</u> assessments
$706.42 total housing expense

The FHA will allow a maximum ratio of housing expense-to-gross income of 29%.

$706.42 (housing expense) ÷ .29 = $2,435.93 minimum gross income necessary

In addition to its concern for the borrower's ratio of housing expense-to-income, FHA will want to know the borrower can support the family's fixed monthly payments as well. **FIXED PAYMENTS** *include automobile and personal loans, revolving credit card obligations, and child support or alimony payments.*

The maximum ratio for housing expense plus fixed payments-to-gross income is 41%.

Example:

$706.42 housing expense
fixed monthly payments:
92.65 auto payment
<u>20.00</u> revolving account
$819.07 Total

$819.07 (housing expense and fixed payments) ÷ .41 = $1,997.73 minimum gross income necessary.

IV. VA Qualifying Standards

Prior to 1986, the Veterans Administration used a cash flow qualifying method. In 1986, the VA began using both the cash flow method and an income ratio method. This means that those underwriting VA guaranteed loans will have to determine two separate figures in their analysis, the residual income of the borrower and the income ratio of the borrower.

RESIDUAL INCOME is the amount of income a loan applicant has left after taxes, recurring obligations, and the proposed housing expense has been deducted from his or her gross monthly income.

The amount of the veteran's residual income must meet the VA's minimum requirements. The VA frequently publishes tables of residual income that are defined both by region and by family size.

A. MINIMUM RESIDUAL STANDARDS ARE GUIDELINES

The balance available for family support is an important factor in evaluating a loan application, but is not the only consideration. The VA standards are intended to be guidelines in judging the borrower's relative strength or weakness with regards to residual income, which is only one of the many factors to be considered in underwriting VA loan applications.

B. OTHER FACTORS

In addition to the residual income standards, other important factors considered in underwriting a loan application include:

1. The borrower's demonstrated ability to accumulate cash or other liquid assets.

2. The borrowers demonstrated ability to use credit wisely and to avoid incurring an excessive amount of debt.

3. The relationship between the shelter expense for the property being acquired and the expense that the borrower is accustomed to paying.

4. The number and ages of the borrower's dependents.

5. The locality and general economic level of the neighborhood where the property is located.

6. The likelihood that the borrower's income may increase or decrease.

7. The borrower's employment history and work experience.

8. The borrower's demonstrated ability and willingness to make payments on time.

9. The amount of any down payment made.

10. The borrower's available cash after paying closing costs and other prepaid items.

C. INCOME RATIO ANALYSIS

In addition to residual income, a ratio based on total monthly debt payments (housing expense, installment debts, child support, etc.) to gross monthly income will be considered by a VA underwriter. The ratio is determined by taking the sum of the housing expense (principal, interest, tax and insurance payments) and monthly obligations and dividing that by gross income. If the obligations-to-income ratio is 41% or less, the underwriter may approve the loan. If the ratio is above 41%, the underwriter must present other factors (e.g., sufficient residual income, significant liquid assets, or a substantial down payment) before approving the loan. A VA underwriter may generally approve the loan if the residual income is at least 20% over the required minimum.

The VA has emphasized that these underwriting standards are only guidelines for approval and should not be automatic reasons for approving or rejecting a loan.

When the borrower actually applies for a loan with a lender, he or she will have already entered into a purchase and sale agreement for a particular home at a particular purchase price and will be asking for a certain loan amount. Because the lender knows the requested loan amount and purchase price, he or she can calculate (with fair accuracy) what insurance, taxes, mortgage insurance and maintenance costs will be. When you are pre-qualifying a buyer, however, you will usually not have a particular purchase price in mind, but you will still need to know an approximate figure for these costs. In the qualifying forms, assume that 10% of the total mortgage payment will go towards taxes, insurance, and mortgage insurance. This is only an approximation, but it should be close enough for pre-qualifying purposes. Average figures for these costs will vary from place to place, depending on property tax rates and other factors. If you are pre-qualifying a borrower with a specific loan amount in mind, you should be able to determine approximate figures for these amounts by asking a local lender. See **Figures 13-7** through **13-11**.

Figure 13-7

INCOME QUALIFYING – CONVENTIONAL LOANS
FIXED-RATE, 90% OR LESS LTV

Monthly Gross Income:

Base salary	_____		
Overtime	_____		
Bonuses	_____		
Commissions	_____		
Other	_____		
Total	_____		

Long-Term Monthly Debt:

Car payment	_____	_____
Child support	_____	_____
Credit cards	_____	_____
Other loans	_____	_____
Other debts	_____	_____
Total	_____	_____

(Consider 5% payments on all revolving charges)

Housing Expense-to-Income Ratio:

_____	Stable Monthly Income
x .28	Income Ratio
_____	Maximum Mortgage Payment (PITI)

Total Debt Service Ratio:

_____	Stable Monthly Income
x .36	Income Ratio
_____	Maximum Monthly Obligations

_____	Maximum Monthly Obligations
--	Monthly Obligations
_____	Maximum Mortgage Payment (PITI)

MAXIMUM MORTGAGE PAYMENT (PITI) _____

_____	Maximum PITI
	(less 10% of mortgage payment)
--	(Insurance, taxes, PMI)
_____	Maximum Principal and Interest
	Payment

_____	**MAXIMUM LOAN AMOUNT** (using calculator or interest factor tables)

Figure 13-8   INCOME QUALIFYING – CONVENTIONAL LOANS
FIXED-RATE, MORE THAN 90% LTV

Monthly Gross Income: **Long-Term Monthly Debt:**

Monthly Gross Income		Long-Term Monthly Debt	
Base salary	_____	Car payment	_____
Overtime	_____	Child support	_____
Bonuses	_____	Credit cards	_____
Commissions	_____	Other loans	_____
Other	_____	Other debts	_____
Total	_____	**Total**	_____

(Consider 5% payments on all revolving charges)

Housing Expense-to-Income Ratio:

_____	Stable Monthly Income
x .25	Income Ratio
_____	Maximum Mortgage Payment (PITI)

Total Debt Service Ratio:

_____	Stable Monthly Income
x .33	Income Ratio
_____	Maximum Monthly Obligations

_____	Maximum Monthly Obligations
_____	Monthly Obligations
_____	Maximum Mortgage Payment (PITI)

MAXIMUM MORTGAGE PAYMENT (PITI)_____

_____	Maximum PITI
	(less 10% of mortgage payment)
—	(Insurance, taxes, PMI)
_____	Maximum Principal and Interest
	Payment

_____	**MAXIMUM LOAN AMOUNT** (using calculator or interest factor tables)

Figure 13-9

INCOME QUALIFYING – CONVENTIONAL LOANS
ADJUSTABLE-RATE, 90% OR LESS LTV

Monthly Gross Income:

Base salary _____
Overtime _____
Bonuses _____
Commissions _____
Other _____
Total _____

Long-Term Monthly Debt:

Car payment _____
Child support _____
Credit cards _____
Other loans _____
Other debts _____
Total _____

(Consider 5% payments on all revolving charges)

Housing Expense-to-Income Ratio:

_____ Stable Monthly Income
x .28 Income Ratio
_____ Maximum Mortgage Payment (PITI)

Total Debt Service Ratio:

_____ Stable Monthly Income
x .36 Income Ratio
_____ Maximum Monthly Obligations

_____ Maximum Monthly Obligations
– Monthly Obligations
_____ Maximum Mortgage Payment (PITI)

MAXIMUM MORTGAGE PAYMENT (PITI)_____

_____ Maximum PITI
(less 10% of mortgage payment)
– (Insurance, taxes, PMI)
_____ Maximum Principal and Interest
Payment

_____ **MAXIMUM LOAN AMOUNT** (using
calculator or interest factor tables)

Figure 13-10

INCOME QUALIFYING — FHA-INSURED LOANS
Income Ratio Method

Monthly Gross Income:

		Long-Term Monthly Debt:	
Base salary	_____	Car payment	_____
Overtime	_____	Child support	_____
Bonuses	_____	Credit cards	_____
Commissions	_____	Other loans	_____
Other	_____	Other debts	_____
Total	_____	**Total**	_____

(Consider 5% payments on all revolving charges)

Housing Expense-to-Income Ratio 29%

_____
<u>x .29</u>   Stable Monthly Income
_____   Income Ratio
                      Maximum Mortgage Payment (PITI)

Total Debt Service Ratio 41%

_____
<u>x .41</u>   Stable Monthly Income
_____   Income Ratio
                      Maximum Monthly Obligations

_____   Maximum Monthly Obligations
<u>—</u>   Monthly Obligations
_____   Maximum Mortgage Payment (PITI)

MAXIMUM MORTGAGE PAYMENT (PITI)_____

_____   Maximum PITI
<u>—</u>   (less 10% of mortgage payment)
_____   (Insurance, taxes, MIP)
                      Maximum Principal and Interest Payment

_____   **MAXIMUM LOAN AMOUNT** (not to exceed regional mortgage amount limitations)

Figure 13-11

INCOME QUALIFYING – VA GUARANTEED LOANS
Residual Income Method

Monthly Gross Income:

Base salary _____
Overtime _____
Bonuses _____
Commissions _____
Other _____
Total _____

Long-Term Monthly Debt:

Car payment _____
Child support _____
Credit cards _____
Other loans _____
Other debts _____
Total _____

(consider 5% payments
on all revolving charges)

Less All Taxes:

Federal Income tax _____
Social Security (7.65%) _____
State Income tax _____
Other Tax _____
Total _____

Net Income _____
less:
long-term debts _____
required reserves _____
Total _____

MAXIMUM HOUSING EXPENSE _____

Total Housing Expense _____
less 20% (taxes, _____
insurance, maintenance,
utilities) _____

Maximum Principal and Interest Payment _____

MAXIMUM LOAN AMOUNT (not to exceed lender limitations)

_____

Income Ratio Method

Total Debt Service Ratio: 41%

_____ Stable Monthly Income
____ x .41 ____ Income Ratio
_____ Maximum Monthly Obligations

_____ Maximum Monthly Obligations
____ – ____ Monthly Obligations
_____ Maximum Mortgage Payment (PITI)

MAXIMUM MORTGAGE PAYMENT (PITI) _____

_____ Maximum PITI
(less 10% of mortgage payment)
____ – ____ (Insurance, taxes, PMI)
_____ Maximum Principal and Interest
Payment

_____ **MAXIMUM LOAN AMOUNT** (not to exceed lender limitations)

343

V. CHAPTER SUMMARY

The loan underwriting process evaluates both the property and the borrower's willingness and ability to pay off the loan. An underwriter will make a determination of these factors by analyzing the borrower's current income, debt levels, overall net worth, and credit history. This analysis will be made by applying the guidelines of the agency that will be involved in the loan. For conventional loans, these will be the guidelines of FNMA and FHLMC. FHA and VA programs have slightly different guidelines. Conventional and FHA loans emphasize income-to-debt ratios. VA standards emphasize residual income requirements as well as income-to-total debt ratios. As a result, the VA program is somewhat more lenient. Once the borrower has been qualified, the underwriter will call for a property appraisal to determine if the property qualifies for the particular loan program as well. This process will be covered in the next chapter.

VI. CHAPTER TERMS

Co-Mortgager

Disintermediation

Equity

Investment Quality Loan

Loan Underwriting

Net Worth

Request for Verification of Deposit

Stable Monthly Income

Total Debt Service Ratio

VII. CHAPTER 13 QUIZ

1. The process of qualifying both a borrower's ability to pay and a property's worth is called:

    a. net worth.
    b. loan underwriting.
    c. stabilization of income.
    d. none of the above.

2. A loan that meets the requirements of FHLMC (Freddie Mac) is called a(n):

    a. investment quality loan.
    b. stable loan.
    c. equitable loan.
    d. debt serviced loan.

3. In a conventional loan, the housing expense to stable income ratio must not be more than:

    a. 25%.
    b. 28%.
    c. 33%.
    d. 41%.

4. The total debt service ratio for a VA loan is:

    a. 25%.
    b. 29%.
    c. 33%.
    d. 41%.

5. The value of a property minus the debts owed on it is called the:

    a. debt service ratio.
    b. investment quality.
    c. owner's equity.
    d. all the above.

6. In addition to the income-to-total debt service ratio, the VA uses which of the following to qualify a loan?

   a. Income ratio analysis
   b. Disintermediation
   c. Residual income
   d. Stable monthly income

7. For conventional loans exceeding 90% LTV, the expense ratios must not exceed:

   a. 25% & 29%.
   b. 25% & 33%.
   c. 29% & 41%.
   d. 33% & 41%.

8. In evaluating a borrower, an underwriter looks at:

   a. income.
   b. assets.
   c. credit history.
   d. all the above.

9. Which of the following is not considered stable monthly income?

   a. Overtime
   b. Self-employment income
   c. Alimony
   d. Unemployment benefits

10. As a general rule, a borrower should have how many years of continuous employment to obtain a home loan?

    a. 1 year
    b. 2 years
    c. 3 years
    d. Less than one year.

ANSWERS: 1. b; 2. a; 3. b; 4. d; 5. c; 6. c; 7. b; 8. d; 9. d; 10. b

CHAPTER 14

QUALIFYING THE PROPERTY

Qualifying the property involves an analysis of its many features to determine whether it has sufficient value to serve as collateral for a real estate loan, and whether its value can be expected to remain stable in the months and years to come.

Lenders do not make loans in anticipation of foreclosure. They make loans in anticipation of being repaid in a timely manner. Every underwriting decision is based on this premise. Regardless of whether the borrower has sterling credit or not, the property will serve as security for the debt. A wise lender will make certain before extending a loan that there is enough value in the property to protect its investment.

I. The Lender's Perception of Value

Lenders utilize Licensed and Certified Appraisers to provide a professional opinion of market value for each residence they loan upon.

Chapter 14

By both state and federal law appraisers are required to provide an unbiased and independent analysis of the property. Appraisers are required to adhere to the Uniform Standards of Professional Appraisal Practice (USPAP) in carrying out each appraisal. The USPAP applies to all Licensed and Certified Appraisers as well as the users of appraisals.

The seller, buyer, or their agents are not the appraiser's clients. **The lender is the primary client of the appraiser**. The USPAP makes it very clear that the appraiser is expected to safeguard the primary lender, the investors of the secondary market, and the federal insurance funds. The penalties for not doing so can be quite severe. The appraiser must follow the *APPRAISAL PROCESS, an outline contained in the USPAP of the material that the appraiser must address in carrying out the appraisal.* In addition, the appraiser is required to adhere to all state laws and federal lending regulator guidelines governing appraisals. All appraisals for federally related transactions must be in writing and must be made to market value. *MARKET VALUE is the price paid by a typical buyer; it is based on the analysis of a group of actual sales that occurred in the marketplace.* The exact definition of Market Value that an appraiser must follow is included in the FNMA form shown in **Figure 14-1**.

When the appraiser is retained by the lender to estimate the market value of a residence, he or she is being asked to make a thorough analysis of the property and its surroundings and to issue an objective analysis of its market value. As such, the appraiser's conclusions may not coincide with the price agreed upon by the seller and the buyer. It is not unusual for the deposit receipt to reflect the emotional or subjective considerations that are valuable to both buyer and seller, but are not pertinent to the actual market value of the property.

It is this true market value that a lender seeks, because if a foreclosure is ever necessary, the lender has some assurance that the property can be sold for an amount that can enable them to recover most, if not all, of their investment.

A. LTV AND MAXIMUM LOAN AMOUNT

As we discussed in a previous chapter, loans are generally made at a loan-to-value ratio of from 80% to 90% of the value of the property.

Figure 14-1

Statement of Limiting Conditions

File #:

DEFINITION OF MARKET VALUE: The most probable price which a property should bring in a competitive and open market under all conditions requisite to a fair sale, the buyer and seller, each acting prudently, knowledgeably and assuming the price is not affected by undo stimulus. Implicit in this definition is the consumation of a sale as of a specified date and the passing of title from seller to buyer under conditions whereby: (1) buyer and seller are typically motivated; (2) both parties are well informed or well advised, and each acting in what he considers his own best interest; (3) a reasonable time is allowed for exposure in the open market; (4) payment is made in terms of cash in U.S. dollars or in terms of financial arrangements comparable thereto; and (5) the price represents the normal consideration for the property sold unaffected by special or creative financing or sales concessions* granted by anyone associated with the sale.

* Adjustments to the comparables must be made for special or creative financing or sales concessions. No adjustments are necessary for those costs which are normally paid by sellers as a result of tradition or law in the market area; these costs are readily identifiable since the seller pays these costs in virtually all sales transactions. Special or creative financing adjustments can be made to the comparable property by comparisons to financing terms offered by a third party institutional lender that is not already involved in the property or transaction. Any adjustment should not be calculated on a mechanical dollar cost of the financing or concession but the dollar amount of any adjustment should approximate the market's reaction to the financing or concessions based on the appraiser's judgement.

STATEMENT OF LIMITING CONDITIONS AND APPRAISER'S CERTIFICATION

CONTINGENT AND LIMITING CONDITIONS: The appraiser's certification that appears in the appraisal report is subject to the following conditions:

1. The appraiser will not be responsible for matters of legal nature that affect either the property being appraised or the title to it. The appraiser assumes that the title is good and marketable and, therefore, will not render any opinions about the title. The property is appraised on the basis of it being under responsible ownership.

2. The appraiser has provided a sketch in the appraisal report to show approximate dimensions of the improvements and the sketch is included only to assist the reader of the report in visualizing the property and understanding the appraiser's determination of its size.

3. The appraiser has examined the available flood maps that are provided by the Federal Emergency Management Agency (or other data sources) and has noted in the appraisal report whether the subject site is located in an identified Special Flood Hazard Area. Because the appraiser is not a surveyor, he or she makes no guarantee, express or implied, regarding the determination.

4. The appraiser will not give testimony or appear in court because he or she made an appraisal of the property in question, unless specific arrangements to do so have been made beforehand.

5. The appraiser has estimated the value of the land in the cost approach at its highest and best use and the improvements at their contributory value. These separate valuations of the land and improvements must not be used in conjunction with any other appraisal and are invalid if they are so used.

6. The appraiser has noted in the appraisal report any adverse conditions (such as, needed repairs, depreciation, the presence of hazardous wastes, toxic substances, etc.) observed during the inspection of the subject property or that he or she became aware of during the normal research involved in performing the appraisal. Unless otherwise stated in the appraisal report, the appraiser has no knowledge of any hidden or unapparent conditions of the property or adverse environmental conditions (including the presense of hazardous waste, toxic substances, etc.) that would make the property more or less valuable, and has assumed that there are no such conditions and makes no guarantees or warranties, express or implied, regarding the condition of the property. The appraiser will not be responsible for any such conditions that do exist or for any engineering or testing that might be required to discover whether such conditions exist. Because the appraiser is not an expert in the field of environmental hazards, the appraisal report must not be considered as an environmental assessment of the property.

7. The appraiser obtained the information, estimates, and opinions that were expressed in the appraisal report from sources that he or she considers to be reliable and believes them to be true and correct. The appraiser does not assume responsibility for the accuracy of such items that were furnished by other parties.

8. The appraiser will not disclose the contents of the appraisal report except as provided for in the Uniform Standards of Professional Appraisal Practice.

9. The appraiser has based his or her appraisal report and valuation conclusion for an appraisal that is subject to satisfactory completion, repairs, or alterations on the assumption that completion of the improvements will be performed in a workmanlike manner.

10. The appraiser must provide his or her prior written consent before the lender/client specified in the appraisal report can distribute the appraisal report (including conclusions about the property value, the appraiser's identity and professional designations, and references to any professional appraisal organizations or the firm with which the appraiser is associated) to anyone other than the borrower; the mortgagee or its successors and assigns; the mortgage insurer; consultants; professional appraisal organizations; any state or federally approved financial institution; or any department agency, or instrumentality of the United States or any state or the District of Columbia; except that the lender/client may distribute the property description section of the report only to data collection or reporting service(s) without having to obtain the appraiser's prior written consent. The appraiser's written consent and approval must also be obtained before the appraisal can be conveyed by anyone to the public through advertising, public relations, news, sales, or other media.

Freddie Mac Form 439 6-93   Fannie Mae Form 1004B 6-93

AC APPRAISALS

Thus, if a property was appraised at $100,000 and a lender's maximum LTV ratio is 80%, the maximum loan would be $80,000. Lenders generally make loans based on either the sales price or the appraised value, **whichever is lower**.

Example:

$180,000.00 Sales Price
$150,000.00 Appraised Value

$150,000.00 Appraised Value
     x .80   Loan to Value Ratio
$120,000.00 Maximum Loan

In the example, the maximum loan is predicated on the lower of the two figures, the appraised value. If the lender were to base the loan on the higher of the two figures, it would be loaning an amount that would be 96% of the appraised market value. This is obviously unacceptable.

B. ESTIMATING MARKET VALUE

It is not necessary for agents and loan officers to be able to appraise properties. However, it is helpful to understand the mechanics of the appraisal process and to know something about the reasoning and logic that underlies many of the appraiser's conclusions.

For real estate agents, an understanding of how lenders and their appraisers perceive value will enable them to write and arrange financing for sales that will hold together.

Appraisers use three approaches to determine value in residential appraisal. These are the market approach, the cost approach, and the income approach. While all three approaches are utilized, the market approach is generally given the most weight by residential appraisers.

II. The Market Approach

The market approach to value is the most easily understood by the layman.

The **MARKET APPROACH** *involves a comparison of the property being appraised against other similar properties in the same neighborhood that have recently sold or are currently being offered for sale.* Appraisers know that no informed buyer who is acting free of pressure will pay more for a particular property than he or she would have to pay for an equally desirable substitute property. An informed seller is not likely to sell for less than is necessary, and if he or she is objective, the selling price will be based on the results of recent sales in the neighborhood.

The sales that appraisers actually use are those that have closed escrow. These are considered the best indicators of actual value.

Asking or listing prices are only helpful to the appraiser to the extent that they indicate the general upward or downward trend of the market in the area. Often the asking price of a property is set at a figure that is slightly higher than the seller expects to receive. This practice leaves the seller negotiating room and permits the buyer to claim the victory of a successful downward negotiation in the sales price of the property.

A. IDENTIFYING LEGITIMATE COMPARABLES

When utilizing the market approach, the appraiser must be certain that the sales used as a basis for comparison are, in fact, relevant in the areas that have the most impact on value.

An appraiser will compare the properties and make dollar adjustments for differences between them.

Adjustments are always made to the comparable and never to the subject property.

If a comparable sale has a feature that is superior, its sale price will be adjusted downwards. If the comparable is inferior in some aspect when compared to the subject, it will have its sale price adjusted upwards. Obviously, the most comparable properties will require the least adjustments. When evaluating a sale to see if it qualifies as a legitimate comparable, the appraiser is concerned with the following five issues.

1. Sale Date of the Comparable Sale

The sale should be recent—within the past six months, if possible.

The sale may not be over one year old. Recent sales are used because they most accurately reflect what is occurring in the current market and do not require adjustments for time. Older sales, up to one year in time, may have to be adjusted to reflect any inflationary or deflationary trends that have taken place since the sale. Adjustments for time are tricky and can sometimes be based on faulty or misapplied statistical analysis. An appraiser must be able to both understand and properly apply statistical information.

Example: Prices for homes in Wagner City have risen by 17% within one year. A home that was worth $300,000 eleven months ago is adjusted upwards 17%. There is nothing wrong with that, right? Wrong! First of all, the percentage was for a whole year, not eleven months. The statistical percentage, if correct, would have to be prorated. But the most important detail might be that research of sales of homes in the specific neighborhood shows that prices actually declined in value by 3%. Therefore, the comparable's time adjustment would be overvalued by 20%!

2. Location of the Comparable Sale

Comparables should be selected from the neighborhood of the subject property.

In the absence of any legitimate comparable sales in the neighborhood, the appraiser can select comparables from nearby similar neighborhoods. Care must be taken that the properties and the neighborhoods have similar physical and demographic characteristics.

It is generally conceded that location contributes more to the value of real estate than any other characteristic.

3. Physical Characteristics

To qualify as a comparable, a property should have physical characteristics that are essentially similar to the subject property.

4. Terms of Sale

With the increase of seller participation in financing today, the terms of sale have become much more of a factor when estimating value. Buyers have demonstrated a readiness that often borders on foolishness to pay inflated prices for housing. Often, eager sellers have provided extended payment terms and below market rates while adjusting the price of the house upwards to recover the difference in interest. In these cases, the inflated price paid for the home distorts the actual values in the neighborhood. Where a seller has given extremely favorable terms there is an excellent chance that the price of the home does not represent the true value of homes in the neighborhood. The appraiser is required to research the terms of sale of comparables to determine what influence they had on the sale price.

5. Arm's Length Transaction

Before a sale can be relied upon as an indication of what the subject property is worth, it must be an *ARM'S LENGTH TRANSACTION*. *This means that buyer and seller are both well informed, under no pressure to either buy or sell, and that the property is offered for a reasonable time on the open market.*

"Distress sales," REO (bank) sales, and trust sales are not considered to be arm's length transactions.

III. The Cost Approach

The cost approach is based on the presumption that buyers will not pay more for an older property than the cost of purchasing a newly constructed residence at the site.

Residential appraisers keep abreast of current construction costs in their areas and refer to them when using the cost approach. Cost handbooks utilized by appraisers for each local area are published by major construction cost service firms including **Marshall and Swift** and **Boekh**.

There are three steps in the cost approach:

1. Estimate the cost of replacing the house with a new home that is similar to the existing one utilizing the information from the cost handbook.

2. Estimate and deduct accrued depreciation from all sources.

3. Add the value of the lot to the depreciated value of the house.

The cost handbooks are set up to utilize the square foot method of estimating construction costs.

Once the appraiser has measured the subject property and determined the overall square footage, he or she has only to compare the square

footage of the subject with the tables contained in the cost handbook to determine the cost to construct a new house. The appraiser will then deduct all sources of accrued depreciation from the cost new. This is the most difficult part of the process. It is based on the presumption that a used home is not as valuable as a new home and that it may have suffered a loss in value for one of the following three reasons:

1. *Physical deterioration or deferred maintenance (**PHYSICAL OBSOLESCENCE**).*

2. *Inadequacies caused by poor design (**FUNCTIONAL OBSOLESCENCE**).*

3. *Factors outside the property itself, such as a deteriorating neighborhood. (**ECONOMIC OBSOLESCENCE**).*

Physical obsolescence is determined from age/life charts published in the cost handbooks. Functional obsolescence is determined by comparison of the subject's floor plan, materials used, and compliance with current building codes to newly constructed housing.

In most cases, both physical and functional obsolescence are curable.

The **COST TO CURE** *refers to the amount of money necessary to repair or replace structural components and functional deficiencies in a structure.* If the cost to cure an item is more than the value added by it being replaced , it is said to be incurable.

Economic obsolescence is based on location and is not curable.

Economic Obsolescense results in a permanent loss of value to the property in a residential use.

After depreciation is calculated, the cost of the depreciated structure is added to the land value to determine the overall value by the cost approach. Appraisers have several methods of making this calculation, however, the most desirable determination is made by comparison of actual sales prices of similar building lots.

IV. Income Approach

The majority of single-family residences are not income producing properties (rentals), so traditional income analysis and appraisal techniques do not apply. However, some single-family residences are rented, for which lenders will request an income approach. Generally, this is provided by using a gross rent multiplier. The *GROSS RENT MULTIPLIER is determined by dividing the sales price of a series of at least three recent sales of similar single family rental properties by their monthly rental income.*

> **Example:** Sales price $100,000 ÷ $900 monthly rent = 111 gross rent multiplier.

The appraiser will then select a multiplier from the range that has been developed. Generally, this will be from the property that is most similar to the subject. He or she will then multiply that multiplier by the subjects rent to determine the value by the income approach. As residential properties are generally rented from month to month rather than by multi-year leases, the contract rent is generally the same as the economic or market rent. However, when there is a long-term lease, the possibility exists that the contract rent may be below market. In that case, the appraiser would have to determine what the subject's current market rent should be.

V. Understanding the Appraisal Process

Real estate agents and loan brokers need to understand the basic steps in the appraisal process because it will help them eliminate, or at least minimize, a prevalent problem that has plagued the industry—both agents and loan brokers tend to overvalue properties. This is because both are concerned with getting the maximum amount for their client, whether they are the seller or the borrower. Also, some listings are set at a higher price than the market will support. When an uninformed buyer and/or his or her agent do not negotiate that price downward, the property can sell at an unrealistic price. If the agent, broker, or loan representative has an unrealistic view of the property's value, they can be assured that an appraiser will rain on their parade. The result will be a low appraisal. There are only five possible responses to a low appraisal:

1. Reduce the sales price to the appraised value.

2. Keep the price where it is and have the buyer make up the difference.

3. Strike a compromise between buyer and seller at a new price between the appraised value and the selling price. Again, the buyer has to make up the difference.

4. Ask for a reconsideration of the appraised value in the hope that it will be increased to the selling price.

5. Terminate the sale.

While it is entirely possible to carry out options 1-3, it is entirely likely that all parties to the transaction will find that distasteful. The seller has a sale at the high price; why should he or she budge? The buyer will claim that he or she is unable to come up with the necessary additional payment. The agents and loan representatives will not want to decrease their commission. This leaves alternative number four. This is a viable response if the agent has done his or her homework, and the appraiser is unaware of data that can be used to justify the higher price or has made errors within the report. In all fairness, appraisers, being human, also make mistakes. Most appraisers are perfectly willing to look at and use information that may help all the parties achieve their goals. Unfortunately, many agents and loan officers do not know how to properly go about this and are left with alternative number five.

A. HOW TO SOLVE PROBLEMS CAUSED BY LOW APPRAISALS

Of course the best way to eliminate the problems created by low appraisals is to avoid them in the first place by pricing properties realistically. A seller should not be given an unrealistic estimate of his property's worth. Even if a buyer can be persuaded to pay the unrealistic price, the appraisal will come back low and the real problems of trying to keep the sale together will set in. If the property could not be priced correctly when listed, an attempt to do so should be made at the time of sale. No case can be made for overstating values when properties are listed and sold, because sooner or later every sale that is dependent on financing must yield to the conclusions of a professional appraiser.

1. Request for Reconsideration of Value

Regardless of how objective an appraiser may be, there are some subjective considerations and conclusions in every report.

An appraisal is an opinion of value.

If you are affected by a low appraisal and sincerely believe that the appraiser has made a mistake, you can appeal his or her decision and, with the proper documentation, get the appraisal increased, possibly to the figure originally requested. Please see the Uniform Residential Appraisal Report (URAR) in **Figure 14-2**. The market analysis is the heart of this form. It shows what informed buyers have been willing to pay in the past for similar properties. The lender can only presume that the value indicated by these comparable sales is what informed buyers will be willing to pay for the property if it is foreclosed and resold. Lenders rely heavily on this comparable sale information.

What this means is that if you disagree with the appraisal and plan to ask the lender to reconsider the appraised amount, you will have to support your request by submitting at least three comparable sales that indicate a higher value estimate is in order. If you are to convince the lender to accept your comparables over those used by the appraiser, they must be at least as similar to the subject property as the comparables utilized by the appraiser.

2. Format for Reconsideration Request

Lenders are familiar with the market data analysis format used in the URAR. It therefore makes sense to arrange your reconsideration request in much the same way. Write a cover letter making your request to the lender (**See Figure 14-3**). **Do not** contact the appraiser directly. Both the lender and the appraiser might consider an attempt to contact the appraiser directly as undue pressure. **UNDUE PRESSURE** *is an attempt to illegally coerce an appraiser's opinion.* Be aware that, generally, the appraiser has access to nationwide comparable resources, including FNC, Inc. and First American Real Estate Solutions, as well as, in many cases, the Multiple Listing Service (MLS) for your area. FNC, Inc. provides comparable data of sales from the actual appraisals of those

Figure 14-2

UNIFORM RESIDENTIAL APPRAISAL REPORT

Property Description   File No. _____

Property Address		City		State	Zip Code
Legal Description				County	

Assessor's Parcel No.		Tax Year	R.E. Taxes $	Special Assessments $

Borrower _____ Current Owner _____ Occupant: ☐ Owner ☐ Tenant ☐ Vacant

Property rights appraised ☐ Fee Simple ☐ Leasehold Project Type ☐ PUD ☐ Condominium (HUD/VA only) HOA$ _____ /Mo.

Neighborhood or Project Name _____ Map Reference _____ Census Tract _____

Sale Price $ _____ Date of Sale _____ Description and $ amount of loan charges/concessions to be paid by seller

Lender/Client _____ Address _____,

Appraiser _____ Address _____

Location	☐ Urban	☐ Suburban	☐ Rural	**Predominant**	**Single family housing**		**Present land use %**	**Land use change**
Built up	☐ Over 75%	☐ 25-75%	☐ Under 25%	**occupancy**	PRICE $(000)	AGE (yrs)	One family ___	☐ Not likely ☐ Likely
Growth rate	☐ Rapid	☐ Stable	☐ Slow	☐ Owner	Low ___		2-4 family ___	☐ In process
Property values	☐ Increasing	☐ Stable	☐ Declining	☐ Tenant	High ___		Multi-family ___	To: _____
Demand/supply	☐ Shortage	☐ In balance	☐ Over supply	☐ Vacant (0-5%)	Predominant		Commercial ___	
Marketing time	☐ Under 3 mos.	☐ 3-6 mos.	☐ Over 6 mos.	☐ Vacant (over 5%)				

Note: Race and the racial composition of the neighborhood are not appraisal factors.

Neighborhood boundaries and characteristics: _____

Factors that affect the marketability of the properties in the neighborhood (proximity to employment and amenities, employment stability, appeal to market, etc.): _____

Market conditions in the subject neighborhood (including support for the above conclusions related to the trend of property values, demand/supply, and marketing time - - such as data on competitive properties for sale in the neighborhood, description of the prevalence of sales and financing concessions, etc.): _____

Project Information for PUDs (If applicable) - - Is the developer/builder in control of the Home Owner's Association (HOA)? ☐ Yes ☐ No

Approximate total number of units in the subject project _____ Approximate total number of units for sale in the subject project _____

Describe common elements and recreational facilities: _____

Dimensions _____	Topography _____
Site area _____ Corner Lot ☐ Yes ☐ No	Size _____
Specific zoning classification and description _____	Shape _____
Zoning compliance ☐ Legal ☐ Legal nonconforming (Grandfathered use) ☐ Illegal ☐ No zoning	Drainage _____
Highest & best use as improved: ☐ Present use ☐ Other use (explain) _____	View _____

Utilities	Public	Other	**Off-site Improvements**	Type	Public	Private	Landscaping _____
Electricity	☐		Street		☐	☐	Driveway surface _____
Gas	☐		Curb/gutter		☐	☐	Apparent easements _____
Water	☐		Sidewalk		☐	☐	FEMA Special Flood Hazard Area ☐ Yes ☐ No
Sanitary sewer	☐		Street lights		☐	☐	FEMA Zone _____ Map Date _____
Storm sewer	☐		Alley		☐	☐	FEMA Map No. _____

Comments (apparent adverse easements, encroachments, special assessments, slide areas, illegal or legal nonconforming zoning use, etc.): _____

GENERAL DESCRIPTION	**EXTERIOR DESCRIPTION**	**FOUNDATION**	**BASEMENT**	**INSULATION**
No. of Units ___	Foundation ___	Slab ___	Area Sq. Ft. ___	Roof ☐
No. of Stories ___	Exterior Walls ___	Crawl Space ___	% Finished ___	Ceiling ☐
Type (Det./Att.) ___	Roof Surface ___	Basement ___	Ceiling ___	Walls ☐
Design (Style) ___	Gutters & Dwnspts. ___	Sump Pump ___	Walls ___	Floor ☐
Existing/Proposed ___	Window Type ___	Dampness ___	Floor ___	None ☐
Age (Yrs.) ___	Storm/Screens ___	Settlement ___	Outside Entry ___	Unknown ☐
Effective Age (Yrs.) ___	Manufactured House ___	Infestation ___		

ROOMS	Foyer	Living	Dining	Kitchen	Den	Family Rm.	Rec. Rm.	Bedrooms	# Baths	Laundry	Other	Area Sq. Ft.
Basement												
Level 1												
Level 2												

Finished area **above grade contains:** _____ Rooms; _____ Bedroom(s); _____ Bath(s); _____ Square Feet of Gross Living Area

INTERIOR	Materials/Condition	**HEATING**	**KITCHEN EQUIP.**	**ATTIC**		**AMENITIES**		**CAR STORAGE:**	
Floors	___	Type ___	Refrigerator ___	None	☐	Fireplace(s) # ___		None	☐
Walls	___	Fuel ___	Range/Oven ___	Stairs	☐	Patio ___		Garage	# of cars
Trim/Finish	___	Condition ___	Disposal ___	Drop Stair	☐	Deck ___		Attached	___
Bath Floor	___	COOLING	Dishwasher ___	Scuttle	☐	Porch ___		Detached	___
Bath Wainscot	___	Central ___	Fan/Hood ___	Floor	☐	Fence ___		Built-In	___
Doors	___	Other ___	Microwave ___	Heated	☐	Pool ___		Carport	___
		Condition ___	Washer/Dryer ___	Finished	☐			Driveway	___

Additional features (special energy efficient items, etc.): _____

Condition of the improvements, depreciation (physical, functional and external), repairs needed, quality of construction, remodeling/additions, etc.: _____

Adverse environmental conditions (such as, but not limited to, hazardous wastes, toxic substances, etc.) present in the improvements, on the site, or in the immediate vicinity of the subject property: _____

ESTIMATED SITE VALUE . . . . = $ _____	Comments on Cost Approach (such as, source of cost estimate, site value, square foot calculation and for HUD, VA and FmHA, the estimated remaining economic life of the property):
ESTIMATED REPRODUCTION COST-NEW-OF IMPROVEMENTS:	
Dwelling _____ Sq. Ft. @ _____ = $ _____	
_____ Sq. Ft. @ _____ = _____	
_____ = _____	
Garage/Carport _____ Sq. Ft. @ _____ = _____	
Total Estimated Cost New . . . . = $ _____	
Physical Functional External	
Less	
Depreciation _____ | _____ | _____ = $ _____	
Depreciated Value of Improvements . . . . = $ _____	
"As-is" Value of Site Improvements . . . . = $ _____	
INDICATED VALUE BY COST APPROACH . . . . = $ _____	

ITEM	SUBJECT	COMPARABLE NO. 1		COMPARABLE NO. 2		COMPARABLE NO. 3	
Address							
Proximity to Subject							
Sales Price	$		$		$		$
Price/Gross Liv. Area	$	$		$		$	
Data and/or Verification Source							
VALUE ADJUSTMENTS	DESCRIPTION	DESCRIPTION	+(-) $ Adjustment	DESCRIPTION	+(-) $ Adjustment	DESCRIPTION	+(-) $ Adjustment
Sales or Financing Concessions							
Date of Sale/Time							
Location							
Leasehold/Fee Simple							
Site							
View							
Design and Appeal							
Quality of Construction							
Age							
Condition							
Above Grade Room Count	Total Bdrms Baths	Total Bdrms Baths		Total Bdrms Baths		Total Bdrms Baths	
Gross Living Area	Sq. Ft.	Sq. Ft.		Sq. Ft.		Sq. Ft.	
Basement & Finished Rooms Below Grade							
Functional Utility							
Heating/Cooling							
Energy Efficient Items							
Garage/Carport							
Porch, Patio, Deck, Fireplace(s), etc.							
Fence, Pool, etc.							
Net Adj. (total)		+ | - | $		+ | - | $		+ | - | $	
Adjusted Sales Price of Comparable		% Net % Grs $		% Net % Grs $		% Net % Grs $	

Comments on Sales Comparison (including the subject property's compatibility to the neighborhood, etc.): _____

ITEM	SUBJECT	COMPARABLE NO. 1	COMPARABLE NO. 2	COMPARABLE NO. 3
Date, Price, and Data Source, for prior sales within year of appraisal				

Analysis of any current agreement of sale, option, or listing of the subject property and analysis of any prior sales of subject and comparables within one year of the date of appraisal: _____

INDICATED VALUE BY SALES COMPARISON APPROACH . . . . = $ _____

INDICATED VALUE BY INCOME APPROACH   (If Applicable) Estimated Market Rent $ _____ /Mo. x Gross Rent Multiplier _____ = $ _____

This appraisal is made ☐ "as is" ☐ subject to repairs, alterations, inspections or conditions listed below ☐ subject to completion per plans and specifications.

Conditions of Appraisal: _____

Final Reconciliation: _____

The purpose of this appraisal is to estimate the market value of the real property that is the subject of this report, based on the above conditions and the certification, contingent and limiting conditions, and market value definition that are stated in the attached Freddie Mac Form 439/Fannie Mae Form 1004B (Revised _____).

I (WE) ESTIMATE THE MARKET VALUE, AS DEFINED, OF THE REAL PROPERTY THAT IS THE SUBJECT OF THIS REPORT, AS OF _____

(WHICH IS THE DATE OF INSPECTION AND THE EFFECTIVE DATE OF THIS REPORT) TO BE $ _____

APPRAISER:	SUPERVISORY APPRAISER (ONLY IF REQUIRED):	
Signature	Signature	☐ Did ☐ Did Not
Name LEVIN P. MESSICK	Name	Inspect Property
Date Report Signed	Date Report Signed	
State Certification # State	State Certification # State	
Or State License # State	Or State License # State	

Figure 14-3

REQUEST FOR RECONSIDERATION OF VALUE

Dear Mr. Jewel:

Attached is a market data analysis that supports this request for reconsideration of your value estimate for 412 Acme Drive, dated April 17, 20xx.

I believe the market data presented indicate that an estimate of value in the amount of $138,000 Is justified.

Your earliest consideration of this request will be appreciated.

Sincerely,

Thomas M. Crane

MARKET DATA ANALYSIS
412 Acme Road

Item	Subject Prop.	Comparable 1	Comparable 2	Comparable 3
Address	412 Acme Drive	131 Skip Road	221 Sutter St.	168 Bow Road
Sales price	$135,000	$141,000	$134,500	$129,500
Data source	sales contract	pres. owner	MLS	selling broker
Date of sale	9/1/20xx	6/29/20xx	7/14/20xx	5/17/20xx
Location	high qual. suburb	same	same	same
Site /view	inside lot	corner lot	corner lot	inside lot
Design /appeal	rambler/exc.	same	same	same
Constr. quality	good	good	good	good
Age	7 yrs.	6 yrs.	8 yrs.	8 yrs.
Condition	good	good	good	good
No. of rooms	8	7	7	6
No. of bedrooms	4	4	3	3
No. of baths	2½	2½	2	2
Liv. area (sq. ft.)	2,700	3,300	2,350	2,150
Garage/ carport	2-car attached gar.	same	same	same
Patios, pools, etc.	15' x 21' patio	15' x 26' patio	18' x 16' patio	15' x 17' patio

Additional data	2 fireplaces range, oven D/W, disposal central air	2 fireplaces range, oven D/ W central air	1 fireplace range, oven D/ W central air	1 fireplace range, oven D/ W

Comments	Subject has superior energy efficiency to comps 2 and 3 and is at least equal in this respect to comp 1. Principal difference between comps 1 and 2 is square footage.

properties. It is considered to be a highly reliable source of data by appraisers because it is provided by appraisers. The appraiser will have to confirm the information provided by you through at least two of these sources. All sales that you provide must be sold and closed. Listings are not acceptable. Your best chance of success is that there are several sales that the appraiser did not consider that you feel are more similar to the subject property than those that the appraiser used. Put this information into a market data analysis similar to that shown in Figure 14-3 and provide your reasons why you believe that these sales are actually more representative of the subject. Do your homework, be professional, be courteous and you have a good chance of success. If you are sloppy, you will be facing the dreaded alternative number five.

VI. Key Considerations to a Residential Appraiser

There are many things to consider during the residential appraisal process. Some of them are very important, others are not. The principal method for appraising residential property is the market approach. Since this amounts to a series of comparisons between the subject property and similar properties that have sold recently, it stands to reason that the most critical elements of comparison are the ones that will have the greatest impact on value. If you are also aware of how these add or detract from value, than you will be less likely to be adversely impacted by a low appraisal. When you are confronted with a low appraisal, you will also be better equipped to resolve it. The following is a summary of property features that are considered important by appraisers.

Location. The subject and the comparables should be from the same neighborhood. This is a major consideration for appraisers.

Owner-occupied. Owner-occupied neighborhoods are considered to be better maintained and less susceptible to deterioration than rental neighborhoods.

Vacancies. Vacant homes and lots are symptomatic of either declining values or low buyer interest in the area.

Rental Levels. Do rents compare favorably with other areas?

Construction Activity. New home construction indicates increased interest in an area.

Conformity. Values are protected if there is a reasonable level of social and economic homogeneity in the neighborhood. This includes styles, ages, prices, sizes, and construction quality of the housing.

Strictly enforced zoning and private restrictions do much to promote conformity. This is a major consideration for appraisers.

Changing Land Use. Is the neighborhood in transition from residential to another use? If so, the properties within the area are probably declining in value, even though the eventual change may promise higher values, because of the potential for more productive use in the future. This is a major consideration for appraisers.

Size and Shape of Lots. Rectangular lots are more desirable than irregular lots. There is no premium for corner lots in residential appraisal. Corner lots have traffic on two sides and possible noise detriment from that traffic. Larger lots have additional value. However, if the lot is vastly greater in size than other lots in the neighborhood (say, a 1 acre lot in a neighborhood of 7500 sq. ft. lots), the added value might be minimal.

Contour of the Land. Mildly rolling is preferred over flat or steep lots.

Street Patterns. Cul-de-sac streets are preferable. Next, wide gently curving streets are more appealing. Streets on main traffic arteries are the least desirable.

Utilities. Are electricity, water, sewer, and telephone service readily available?

Nuisances. For example, close proximity to bad odors, industrial plants, and high noise levels from factories, aircraft, freeways, and trains. This is a major consideration for appraisers.

Proximity to Services. Is the property close to schools, employment, public transportation, and shopping? Is it closely served by police and fire departments? This is a major consideration for appraisers.

Zoning. Does the property have residential zoning and is it enforced? This is a major consideration for appraisers.

Site/View. Is the property of sufficient size for the improvements? Does it have the proper setbacks (distance of improvements from lot lines) required by zoning? Is the property under-improved (more land than is necessary to support the improvements—a 600 square foot house on twenty acres)? These are major considerations for appraisers. While views certainly add value, the amount they add is in the eye of the beholder (subjective). Do not expect your appraiser to be unduly impressed by the view.

Design and Appeal. Is the property's appeal to the average buyer good, average, or poor? This is a subjective judgment.

Construction Quality. Is the quality of the materials and craftsmanship excellent, good, average, or fair? This is a major appraisal consideration.

Age/Condition. Are the subject and the comparable properties similar in age and condition? This is a major appraisal consideration.

Functional Utility. Is the floor plan and building orientation functional? This is a major appraisal consideration.

Energy-Efficient Items. Even though these items have assumed more importance in a high energy cost world, they can be viewed as an over-improvement of the property with little or no added value if the systems are redundant. For example, having both solar water heating and a gas fired furnace would provide two systems for heating where only one is needed.

Room Count. This includes the overall total of rooms in the house, the number of bedrooms, and the number of baths. Differences in the number of bedrooms and baths can have a notable effect on value. This is a major appraisal consideration.

Square Footage. The overall square footage can have an appreciable impact on market value. Comparables should have square footage that is not more or less than 20% different than the subject property. The closer in size to the subject the better. This is a major appraisal consideration.

As can be seen from the above, some appraisal considerations are subjective, others are of average importance, and some are major considerations. To successfully challenge an appraisal, it is often necessary to show that a major appraisal consideration has been overlooked or that several comparables that reflect these major appraisal considerations have been overlooked. Another possibility might be that the appraiser is making large downward adjustments in areas that could be considered subjective. In any case, the authors would like to reiterate that the best defense against low appraisals is to list properties at realistic prices.

VII. Rural and Suburban Homes

Properties in outlying areas are eligible for maximum financing by both the primary and secondary market subject to the following conditions.

1. The value of the land is not more than 49% of the overall value of the property.

2. There are adequate public or private utilities in service on the property.

3. The property is accessible by a federal, state, or county highway or an all-weather secondary road.

4. The present or anticipated use of adjacent real estate does not unfavorably affect the value of the property as a residence.

VIII. Atypical Property and Loan Types

ATYPICAL PROPERTIES, which are also called non-conforming properties, include, but are not limited to, manufactured homes, dome homes, and log cabins. These must be appraised by a Certified Level Appraiser only. If there is any atypical or creative financing, the services of a Certified Appraiser must be utilized. Licensed Level Appraisers are only permitted to appraise conforming properties and loans. They are also limited to appraising conforming residential properties that are less than one million dollars in value.

IX. SUMMARY

Lenders demand professional appraisals because they want an entirely objective opinion of the true market values of the properties they loan upon. Loan-to-value ratios are based on the sales price or the appraised value, whichever is lower. The appraisers utilized by lenders are Licensed or Certified. The appraiser's client is the lender, not anyone else associated with the transaction. All appraisers, and those who use their appraisals for federal loan transactions, must adhere to the Uniform Standards of Professional Appraisal Practice (USPAP) as well as state and federal lending and appraisal regulations. The appraiser is required to follow the appraisal process. This is a format that is laid out in the USPAP. For loans, the appraiser is asked to determine the "Market Value" of the property. This is a specifically defined value that may be either higher or lower than the actual selling price of a property.

Appraisers use the market approach, the cost approach, and the income approach when valuing properties.

The market approach is the most useful for residential properties, as it reflects what actually is occurring in the marketplace. Comparables used in this approach should be recent sales in the same general neighborhood or area as the subject and as similar to the subject as possible. They must be real closed sales at "arm's length."

The cost approach is carried out with the use of cost handbooks. Appraisers estimate the overall accrued depreciation of a property by taking into account any physical, functional, or economic obsolescence that it may have incurred.

The income approach is seldom used unless the property is a rental. Then a Gross Rent Multiplier is used to determine value.

It is useful for agents, brokers, and others to understand the appraisal process in order to keep from overvaluing properties and losing sales as a result. While it is possible to successfully challenge a low appraisal, it must be done utilizing established fact that addresses the key considerations that lenders and appraisers consider in an appraisal. It should be presented to the lender in an understandable format. Wishful thinking and hoping on the part of agents, brokers, and others is insufficient reason for either an appraiser or the lender to change an opinion regarding value.

Atypical property and loan types must be carried out by a Certified Appraiser.

X. CHAPTER TERMS

Accrued Depreciation	Gross Rent Multiplier
Appraisal Process	Income Approach
Atypical Property	Licensed Appraiser
Certified Appraiser	Market Approach
Cost Approach	Market Value
Curable	Physical Obsolescence
Economic Obsolescence	Uniform Standards of Professional
Functional Obsolescence	Appraisal Practice (USPAP)

XI. CHAPTER 14 QUIZ

1. Appraisals of atypical properties may be carried out by:

    a. Certified Appraisers only.
    b. Licensed Appraisers only.
    c. both Licensed and Certified Appraisers.
    d. any real estate professional.

2. Appraisers must obey:

    a. USPAP.
    b. federal and state regulations.
    c. lender requirements.
    d. all the above.

3. The outline of the appraisal process is contained in:

    a. FNMA regulations.
    b. USPAP.
    c. state law.
    d. all the above.

4. Determining economic obsolescence is part of the:

    a. Market Approach.
    b. Cost Approach.
    c. Income Approach.
    d. all the above.

5. If a structural item can be readily repaired or replaced, it is said to be:

    a. curable.
    b. incurable.
    c. functionally obsolescent.
    d. physically obsolescent.

6. The best method of dealing with a low appraisal is to:

    a. challenge it.
    b. get the seller to lower the sales price.
    c. get the buyer to make up the difference.
    d. not to have one in the first place.

7. Appraisers are required to use:

    a. listings.
    b. pending sales.
    c. closed sales.
    d. all the above.

8. The appraiser's client is the:

    a. loan broker.
    b. selling and listing agents.
    c. buyer and seller.
    d. lender.

9. Market Value is the:

    a. actual sale price.
    b. price to an individual buyer.
    c. price to a typical buyer.
    d. none of the above.

10. Which of the following is a major appraisal consideration?

    a. Owner-occupied
    b. Conforms to neighborhood
    c. Contour of the land
    d. Design and Appeal

ANSWERS: 1. a; 2. d; 3. b; 4. b; 5. a; 6. d; 7. c; 8. d; 9. c; 10. b

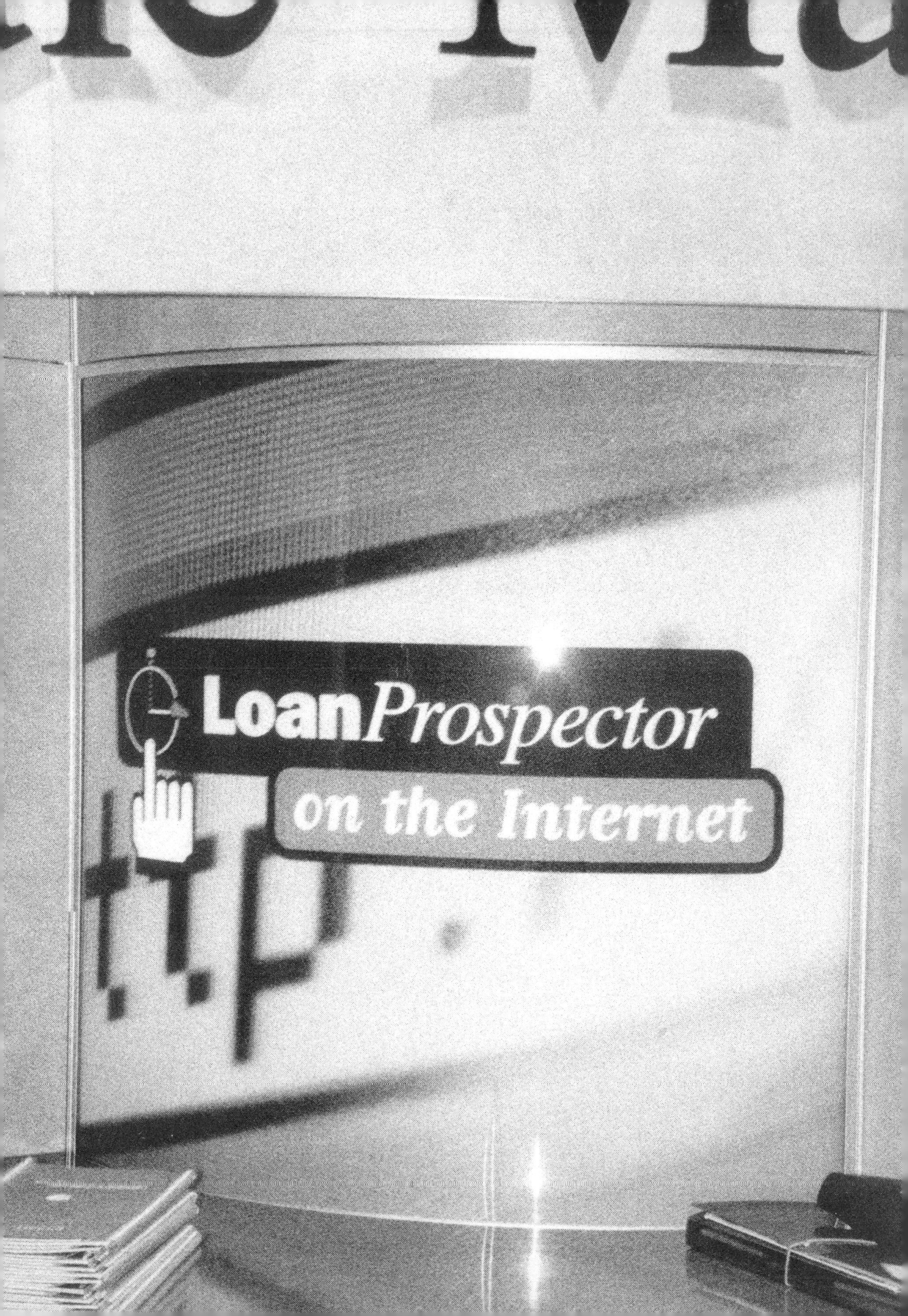
LoanProspector
on the Internet

CHAPTER 15

REAL ESTATE FINANCE MATHEMATICS

Math is a fundamental tool used in the financing process. As you explain the various finance programs, qualify a buyer for a loan, describe discounts and buy-downs, and determine closing costs, you will be using mathematical formulas. While the prospect of mathematical computations arouses fear in the hearts of many of us, the math principles you will need to know are actually very simple. The following is a brief description of those formulas.

I. Approach to Solving Math Problems

Solving math problems is simplified by using a step-by-step approach.

The most important step is to thoroughly understand the problem.

You must know what answer you want before you can successfully work any math problem. Once you have determined what it is you are to find (for example, interest rate, loan-to-value ratio, amount, or profit), you will know what formula to use.

375

CHAPTER 15 OUTLINE

For example, the profit and loss formula is **value after = percent x value before (VA = % x VB)**. The formulas you will most likely be using will be explained in this chapter.

The next step is to substitute the numbers you know into the formula. In many problems you will be able to substitute the numbers into the formula without any additional steps. However, in many other problems it will be necessary to take one or more preliminary steps, for instance, converting fractions to decimals.

Once you have substituted the numbers into the formula you will have to do some computations to find the unknown. Most of the formulas have the same basic form: **A=B x C**. You will need two of the numbers (or the information that enables you to find two of the numbers) and then you will either have to divide or multiply them to find the third number—the answer you are seeking.

Whether you will need to multiply or divide is determined by which quantity (number) in the formula you are trying to discover.

For example, the formula A=B x C may be converted into three different formulas. All three formulas are equivalent, but are put into different forms, depending upon the quantity (number) to be discovered. If the quantity A is unknown, then the following formula is used:

$$A = B \: x \: C$$

The number B is multiplied by C; the product of B times C is A.

If the quantity B is unknown, the following formula is used:

$$B = A \div C$$

The number A is divided by C; the quotient of A divided by C is B.

If the quantity C is unknown, the following formula is used:

$$C = A \div B$$

The number A is divided by B; the quotient of A divided by B is C. Notice that in all these instances, the unknown quantity is always by itself on one side of the "equal" sign.

II. Converting Fractions to Decimals

There will be many times when you will want to convert a fraction into a decimal. Most people find it much easier to work with decimals than fractions. Also, hand calculators can multiply and divide by decimals.

To convert a fraction into a decimal, you simply divide the top number of the fraction (the "numerator") by the bottom number of the fraction (the "denominator").

Example: To change 3/4 into a decimal, you must divide 3 (the top number) by 4 (the bottom number).

$$3.00 \div 4 = .75$$

To change 1/5 into a decimal, divide 1 by 5

$$1 \div 5 = .20$$

If you are using a hand calculator, it will automatically give you the right answer with the decimals in the correct place.

To add or subtract by decimals, **line the decimals up by decimal point** and add or subtract.

Example:

```
     23.77
    746.1
      1.567
     82.6
+ 1134.098
   1988.135
```

To multiply by decimals, do the multiplication. **The answer should have as many decimal places as the total number of decimal places in the**

multiplying numbers. Just add up the decimal places in the numbers you are multiplying and put the decimal point the same number of places to the left.

Example:

> *57.999*
> *x 23.7*
> ---
> *1374.5763*

To divide by decimals, move the decimal point in the outside number all the way to the right and then move the decimal point in the inside number the same number of places to the right.

Example:

> *44.6 ÷ 5.889*
> *44600 ÷ 5889 = 7.57*

Just as with addition and multiplication, the above steps are unnecessary if you use a hand calculator. If the numbers are punched in correctly, the calculator will automatically give you an answer with the decimal in the right place.

III. Percentage Problems

You will often be working with percentages in real estate finance problems. For example, loan-to-value ratios and interest rates are stated as percentages.

> *It is necessary to convert the percentages into decimals and vice versa, so that the arithmetic in a percentage problem can be done in decimals.*

To convert a percentage to a decimal, remove the percentage sign and **move the decimal point two places to the left**. This may require adding zeros.

> *80% becomes .80*
> *9% becomes .09*
> *75.5% becomes .755*
> *8.75% becomes .0875*

To convert a decimal to percentage, do just the opposite. Move the decimal **two places to the right** and add a percentage sign.

Example:

.88 becomes 88%
.015 becomes 1.5%
.09 becomes 9%

Whenever something is expressed as a percent of something, it means multiply. The word "of" means to multiply.

Example: If a lender requires a loan-to-value ratio of 75% and a house is worth $89,000, what will be the maximum loan amount? (What is 75% of $89,000?)

.75 x $89,000 = $66,750 maximum loan amount

Percentage problems are usually similar to the above example. You have to find a part of something, or a percentage of the total.

A general formula is:

A percentage of the total equals the part, or part = percent x total

$$P = \% \ x \ T$$

Example: Smith spends 24% of her monthly salary on her house payment. Her monthly salary is $2,750. What is the amount of her house payment?

1. Find amount of house payment.
2. Write down formula: $P = \% \ x \ T$.
3. Substitute numbers into formula.

$$P = 24\% \ x \ \$2,750$$

Before you can perform the necessary calculations, you must convert the 24% into a decimal. Move the decimal two places to the left: **24% = .24**

$$P = .24 \; x \; \$2{,}750$$

4. Calculate: multiply the percentage by the total.
   .24 x $2,750 = $660

Smith's house payment is $660.

IV. Interest Problems

Interest can be viewed as the "rent" paid by a borrower to a lender for the use of money (the loan amount, or principal). *INTEREST is the cost of borrowing money.* There are two types of interest, simple and compound.

SIMPLE INTEREST is interest paid only on the principal owed. COMPOUND INTEREST is interest paid on accrued interest, as well as on the principal owed.

Simple interest problems are worked in basically the same manner as percentage problems, except that the simple interest formula has four components rather than three: interest, principal, rate, and time.

Interest = Principal x Rate x Time

$$I = P \; x \; R \; x \; T$$

Interest: The cost of borrowing expressed in dollars; money paid for the use of money.

Principal: The amount of the loan in dollars on which the interest is paid.

Rate: The cost of borrowing expressed as a percentage of the principal paid in interest for one year.

Time: The length of time of the loan, usually expressed in years.

One must know the number values of three of the four components in order to compute the fourth (unknown) component.

a. Interest unknown

Interest = Principal x Rate x Time

Example: Find the interest on $3,500 for six years at 11%.

1. $I = P \, x \, R \, x \, T$
2. $I = (\$3,500 \, x \, .11) \, x \, 6$
3. $I = \$385 \, x \, 6$
4. $I = \$2,310$

b. Principal unknown

Principal = Interest ÷ Rate x Time

$P = I \div (R \, x \, T)$

Example: How much money must be loaned to receive $2,310 interest at 11% if the money is loaned for six years?

1. $P = I \div (R \, x \, T)$
2. $P = \$2,310 \div (.11 \, x \, 6)$
3. $P = \$2,310 \div .66$
4. $P = \$3,500$

c. Rate unknown

Rate = Interest ÷ Principal x Time

$R = I \div (P \, x \, T)$

Example: In six years $3,500 earns $2,310 interest. What is the rate of interest?

1. $R = I \div (P \, x \, T)$
2. $R = \$2,310 \div (\$3,500 \, x \, 6)$
3. $R = \$2,310 \div \$21,000$
4. $R = .11 \, or \, 11\%$

d. Time unknown

Time = Interest ÷ Rate x Principal

$T = I \div (R \, x \, P)$

Example: How long will it take $3,500 to return $2,310 at an annual rate of 11%?

1. $T = I \div (R \times P)$
2. $T = \$2,310 \div (\$3,500 \times .11)$
3. $T = \$2,310 \div \$385$
4. $T = 6\ years$

A. COMPOUND INTEREST

Compound interest is more common in advanced real estate subjects, such as appraisal and annuities. Compound interest tables are readily available, but the principle is discussed here to further your understanding.

As previously stated, compound interest is interest on the total of the principal plus its accrued interest. For each time period (called the "conversion period"), interest is added to the principal to make a new principal amount. Therefore, each succeeding time period has an increased principal amount on which to compute interest. Conversion periods may be monthly, quarterly, semi-annual, or annual.

The compound interest rate is usually stated as an annual rate and must be changed to the appropriate "interest rate per conversion period" or "periodic interest rate." To do this, you must divide the annual interest rate by the number of conversion periods per year. **This periodic interest rate is called "i."** The formula used for compound interest problems is interest = principal x periodic interest rate, or

$$I = P \times i$$

Example: A $5,000 investment at 9% interest compounded annually for three years earns how much interest at maturity?

$$I = P \times i$$
$$I = \$5,000 \times (.09 \div 1)$$
$$First\ year's\ I = \$5,000 \times .09\ or\ \$450.$$
$$Add\ to\ \$5,000.$$
$$Second\ year's\ I = \$5,450 \times .09\ or\ 490.50.$$

Add to $5,450.
Third year's I = $5,940.50 x .09 or $534.65.
Add to $5,940.50

At maturity, the borrower will owe $6,475.15. The $5,000 loan has earned interest of $1,475.15 in three years.

Example: How much interest will a $1,000 investment earn over two years at 12% interest compounded semi-annually?

Since the conversion period is semi-annual, the interest is computed every six months. Thus, the periodic interest rate "i" is divided by two conversion periods: i = 6%.

$$I = P \ x \ i$$

1. Original principal amount   = $1,000.00
2. Interest for 1st period ($1,000 x .06)   = $60.00
3. Balance beginning 2nd period   = $1,060.00
4. Interest for 2nd period ($1,060 x .06)   = $63.60
5. Balance beginning 3rd period   = $1,123.60
6. Interest for 3rd period ($1,123.60 x .06) = $67.42
7. Balance beginning 4th period   = $1,191.02
8. Interest for 4th period ($1,191.02 x .06) = $71.46
9. Compound principal balance   = $1,262.48

i for 2 years = $1,262.48 - $1,000 or $262.48

The same problem, using annual simple interest, results in $22.48 less interest for the lender:

$1,000 x .12 x 2 = $240 simple interest

Obviously, no one in actual practice is going to go through the tedious process outlined above to calculate compound interest, especially if it is compounded daily over a 30-year period! Instead, standardized compound interest tables or calculators can be used to find the answer quickly.

B. EFFECTIVE INTEREST RATE

The *NOMINAL or "NAMED" INTEREST RATE is the rate of interest stated in the loan documents.* The *EFFECTIVE INTEREST RATE is the rate the borrower is actually paying.* In other words, the loan papers may say one thing when the end result is another, depending upon how many times a year the actual earnings rate is compounded.

The effective interest rate equals the annual rate, which will produce the same interest in a year as the nominal rate converted a certain number of times.

For example, 6% converted semi-annually produces $6.09 per $100; therefore, 6% is the nominal rate and 6.09% is the effective rate. A rate of 6% converted semi-annually yields the same interest as a rate of 6.09% on an annual basis.

C. DISCOUNTS

As discussed in the chapter on alternative methods of financing, often the loan proceeds disbursed by the lender are less than the face value of the note. This occurs when the borrower (or a third party) pays discount points. The lender deducts the amount of the points from the loan amount up front as compensation for making the loan on the agreed terms. The borrower thus receives less than must be repaid under the contract. When a discount is paid, the interest costs to the borrower (and the yield to the lender) are higher than the contract interest rate.

When more accurate yield and interest tables are unavailable, it is possible to approximate the effective interest cost to the borrower and the yield rate to the lender when discounted loans are involved. The formula for doing so is as follows:

$$i = [r + (d/n)] \div (P - d)$$

i: approximate effective interest rate (expressed as a decimal)

r: contract interest rate (expressed as a decimal)

d: discount rate, or points deducted (expressed as a decimal)

P: principal of loan (expressed as the whole number 1 for all dollar amounts)

n: term (years, periods, or a fraction thereof)

Example: What is the estimated effective interest rate on a $60,000 mortgage loan, with a 20-year term, contract rate, if interest being 10% per annum, discounted 3%, so that only $58,200 is disbursed to the borrower?

$$i = \frac{.10 + (.03/20)}{1 - .03} = \frac{.10 + .0015}{.97} = \frac{.10150}{.97} = .10463 \text{ or } 10.46\%$$

The effective interest rate (or yield) on the loan is 10.46%.

V. Profit and Loss Problems

Every time a homeowner sells a house, a profit or loss is made. If the house is sold for more than was initially paid for it, the owner makes a profit. If it is sold for less, the owner suffers a loss. Many times you will want to be able to calculate the amount of that profit or loss. Profit and loss problems are solved with a formula that is a variation of the percent formula: **value after = percentage x value before**.

$$VA = \% \ x \ VB$$

The **VALUE AFTER** *is the value of the property after the profit or loss is taken.* The **VALUE BEFORE** *is the value of the property before the profit or loss is taken.* The percent is 100% plus the percent of profit or minus the percent of loss. The idea is to express the value of the property after a profit or loss as a percentage of the property's value before the profit or loss. If there is no profit or loss, the value has not changed. If there is a profit, the value after will be greater than 100% of the value before, since the value has increased. If there is a loss, the value after is less than 100% of the value before, since the value has decreased.

Example: Green bought a house ten years ago for $50,000 and sold it last month for 45% more than she paid for it. What was the selling price of the house?

VA = % x VB
VA = 145% x VB *(To get the percent, you must add the percent of profit to or subtract the percent of loss from 100%).*
VA = 1.45 x $50,000
VA = $72,500 *was the selling price*

Example: Now we will use the profit and loss formula to calculate another one of the components.

Green sold her house last week for $117,000. She paid $121,000 for it five years ago. What was the percent of loss?

VA = % x VB
$117,000 = % x $121,000
(Because the percent is the unknown, you must divide the value after by the value before.)
% = $117,000 ÷ $121,000
% = .9669 *or* 97% *(rounded)*
Now subtract 97% *from* 100% *to find the percent of loss.*
% = 100% - 97% = 3% *loss*

Example: Your customer just sold a house for 17% more than was paid for it. The seller's portion of the closing costs came to $4,677. The seller received $72,500 in cash at closing. What did the seller originally pay for the house?

VA = % x VB
$72,500 + 4,677 = 117% x VB
VB = ($72,500 + 4,677) ÷ 117%
(Since the value before is 117% unknown, you must divide the value after [the total of the closing costs and the escrow proceeds] by the percent of profit.)
VB = $77,177 ÷ 1.17
VB = $65,963.25 *was the original price*

VI. Prorations

There are some expenses connected with owning real estate that are often paid for either in advance or in arrears. For example, fire insurance premiums are normally paid for in advance. Landlords usually collect rents in advance, too. On the other hand, mortgage interest accrues in arrears.

Chapter 15

When expenses are paid in advance and the owner then sells the property, part of these expenses have already been used up by the seller and are rightfully the seller's expense. Often, however, a portion of the expenses of ownership still remain unused and when title to the property transfers to the buyer, the benefit of these advances will accrue to the buyer. It is only fair that the buyer, therefore, reimburse the seller for the unused portions of these homeownership expenses. For example, suppose the seller of a home paid $1,400 annual property taxes for the coming year, one month before the property was sold. The seller has only benefited from one month of the tax year, but the buyer will benefit from the next 11 months of the prepaid taxes. Unless the buyer reimburses the seller for 11 months' worth of the taxes, the seller will be stuck with paying the taxes for someone else's property.

These adjustments, or reimbursements, are made by the process of **PRORATION**. *This means apportioning the expenses (or benefits) fairly to each party.*

For example, a seller sells the property six months after paying the annual property taxes for the ensuing year. One half of the tax payment will thus accrue to the benefit of the buyer. In this case, the buyer pays half of the tax amount to the seller. (This example is over-simplified, because in practice, prorations are figured down to the day.)

Prorations are usually calculated at real estate closings, where the costs of such items as taxes and insurance are allocated between the buyer and the seller.

The formula for proration is: **share = daily rate x number of days:**

$$S = R \, x \, D$$

To work a proration problem:

1. Find the annual or monthly amount of the expense.
2. Then find the daily rate of the expense (per diem).
3. Next, determine the number of days for which the person is responsible for the expense.

4. Finally, substitute the daily rate and number of days into the formula and calculate.

Example: The seller paid the June homeowner's insurance premium of $28 on the first of the month. The transaction closes on the 18th of the month. How much of the insurance premium does the buyer owe to the seller?

$$S = R \ x \ D$$

The premium is $28 per month. To find the daily rate of the expense, divide $28 by 30, since there are 30 days in June.

$28 \div 30 = .93$
The rate is $.93 per day.

Next, find out how many days the buyer is responsible for. (The buyer pays for the day of closing.) There are 13 days left in the month that the buyer is responsible for.

$S = R \ x \ D$
$S = .93 \ x \ 13$
$S = 12.09 *is the amount owed to the seller.*

Example: A sale closes on September 14. The annual property taxes of $1,750 have not been paid. How much will the seller owe the buyer at closing?

The property tax year runs from July 1 through June 30. The seller owes for the period from July 1 up to September 14.

The annual amount is $1,750, which must be divided by 365 days to get the daily rate.

$1,750 \div 365 = $4.79 per day$

Next, you must figure the number of days.

July - 31
August - 31
September - 13
        75 days

$S = R \; x \; D$
$S = 4.79 \; x \; 75$
$S = \$359.25 \; owed \; to \; the \; buyer \; at \; closing.$

VII. Mathematical Tables and Their Use

The scope of this book does not permit a full discussion of the use of the various tables relating to real estate finance. Generally speaking, the following tables are most commonly used.

A. AMORTIZATION TABLES

These are commonly available in booklet form from various title companies, escrow companies, and banks. They indicate the monthly payment needed for the periodic repayment of both the principal amount of the loan and the interest due. One form of amortization table has a list of possible loan terms (expressed in years) along one axis. The other axis is the interest rate. There is a separate table for each loan amount. At the intersection of any two axes in the table is the monthly payment in dollars and cents. (**See Figure 15-1.**)

An alternative type of table for figuring loan payments is the Interest Rate Factors Table. (**See Figure 15-2.**) It would be helpful to take a moment to examine this table and follow the instructions set out at the beginning of the table. This table gives you interest rate factors, which, multiplied by the loan amount, give you the amount of the monthly loan payment.

B. PRORATION TABLE

This is simply a table that gives the number of days between various dates. It is used to prorate such items as interest, insurance premiums, or rents. (**See Figure 15-3.**)

C. REMAINING BALANCE TABLES OR LOAN PROGRESS CHARTS

Remaining balance tables show the remaining balance of a loan expressed as a percentage of the original loan amount, using the data: original loan amount, interest rate, age of loan and original term of loan. A loan progress chart also allows you to find the remaining loan balance by giving you the amount still owing for every $1000 borrowed. (**See Figure 15-4**.)

D. MORTGAGE YIELD TABLES

These are used to determine the yield on a mortgage at a specified discount. A point discount table is shown in **Figure 15-5**.

E. BALLOON PAYMENT TABLES

These are used to determine the unpaid balance due and payable on a loan. Loans, especially second trust deed loans, often have terms of four or five years, but are amortized over 12 or 15 years. This will leave a large lump sum payment of principal owing at the end of the loan term.

F. CONSTANT ANNUAL PERCENTAGE TABLES

An annual constant is the sum of 12 monthly payments expressed as a percent of a principal loan amount. When multiplied by the loan amount, the annual loan payment may be determined. The remaining term of a loan, remaining loan balance, and interest rate of a loan may also be determined by use of a constant annual percent table.

Online Mortgage Calculators
(Increasing First-Time Homebuyers Knowledge)

Although online mortgage calculators are rapidly replacing printed amortization tables and handheld electronic amortization calculators, it is doubtful they will ever fully replace the original printed tables. We have provided several examples of printed amortization tables in this text because it is important to understand the concepts behind the shortcuts. Therefore, it is strongly recommended that you study the tables printed in the book to gain a full comprehension of how the formulas work. Then you can use the shortcuts with confidence, and will have the ability to explain the process, if necessary, to new homebuyers.

Online mortgage calculators can accomplish several things, including:

1. calculate a simple monthly payment;
2. figure the effects of prepaying a mortgage; and
3. analyze the composition of monthly payments in the future.

The latter is particularly helpful in projecting mortgage-interest tax write-offs in future years. Many online calculators offer graph and chart conversions to help illustrate how equity builds over time or how interest declines as a percentage of the monthly payment.

There are numerous mortgage calculators available at no charge on the Internet, allowing even novices in the homebuying arena the opportunity to choose a loan by calculating the monthly payments they can afford, as well as figuring how much of each payment goes towards the principal versus the interest. A better prepared customer saves time and paperwork, and can make a professional's job easier in the long run.

Although we do not endorse or guarantee any website, below is a listing of just a few of the more well-known companies that provide online mortgage calculators.

www.countrywide.com
www.bloomberg.com
www.indymacmortgage.com
www.smartmoney.com
www.calcbuilder.com
http://quickenloans.quicken.com
www.bankrate.com

Figure 15-1

LOAN AMORTIZATION
MONTHLY PAYMENT FOR A $1,000 LOAN

YEARS	7%	7½%	8%	8½%	8¾%	9%	9¼%	9½%	9¾%	10%	10¼%	10½%
1.0	86.53	86.76	86.99	87.22	87.34	87.45	87.57	87.68	87.80	87.92	88.03	88.15
1.5	58.69	58.91	59.14	59.37	59.48	59.60	59.71	59.83	59.94	60.06	60.17	60.29
2.0	44.77	45.00	45.23	45.46	45.57	45.68	45.80	45.91	46.03	46.14	46.26	46.38
2.5	36.43	36.66	36.89	37.12	37.23	37.35	37.46	37.58	37.70	37.81	37.93	38.04
3.0	30.88	31.11	31.34	31.57	31.68	31.80	31.92	32.03	32.15	32.27	32.38	32.50
3.5	26.91	27.15	27.38	27.61	27.73	27.84	27.96	28.08	28.20	28.32	28.44	28.55
4.0	23.95	24.18	24.41	24.65	24.77	24.89	25.00	25.12	25.24	25.36	25.48	25.60
4.5	21.64	21.88	22.11	22.35	22.47	22.59	22.71	22.83	22.95	23.07	23.19	23.32
5.0	19.80	20.04	20.28	20.52	20.64	20.76	20.88	21.00	21.12	21.25	21.37	21.49
5.5	18.30	18.54	18.78	19.02	19.14	19.27	19.39	19.51	19.64	19.76	19.88	20.01
6.0	17.05	17.29	17.53	17.78	17.90	18.03	18.15	18.27	18.40	18.53	18.65	18.78
6.5	15.99	16.24	16.48	16.73	16.86	16.98	17.11	17.23	17.36	17.49	17.61	17.74
7.0	15.09	15.34	15.59	15.84	15.96	16.09	16.22	16.34	16.47	16.60	16.73	16.86
7.5	14.31	14.56	14.81	15.06	15.19	15.32	15.45	15.58	15.71	15.84	15.97	16.10
8.0	13.63	13.88	14.14	14.39	14.52	14.65	14.78	14.91	15.04	15.17	15.31	15.44
8.5	13.04	13.29	13.54	13.80	13.93	14.06	14.19	14.33	14.46	14.59	14.73	14.86
9.0	12.51	12.76	13.02	13.28	13.41	13.54	13.68	13.81	13.94	14.08	14.21	14.35
9.5	12.03	12.29	12.55	12.81	12.95	13.08	13.22	13.35	13.49	13.62	13.76	13.90
10.0	11.61	11.87	12.13	12.40	12.53	12.67	12.80	12.94	13.08	13.22	13.36	13.49
10.5	11.23	11.49	11.76	12.02	12.16	12.30	12.43	12.57	12.71	12.85	12.99	13.13
11.0	10.88	11.15	11.42	11.69	11.82	11.96	12.10	12.24	12.38	12.52	12.66	12.80
11.5	10.57	10.84	11.11	11.38	11.52	11.66	11.80	11.94	12.08	12.22	12.37	12.51
12.0	10.28	10.55	10.82	11.10	11.24	11.38	11.52	11.66	11.81	11.95	12.10	12.24
12.5	10.02	10.29	10.57	10.85	10.99	11.13	11.27	11.41	11.56	11.70	11.85	12.00
13.0	9.78	10.05	10.33	10.61	10.75	10.90	11.04	11.19	11.33	11.48	11.63	11.78
13.5	9.56	9.83	10.11	10.40	10.54	10.68	10.83	10.98	11.12	11.27	11.42	11.57
14.0	9.35	9.63	9.91	10.20	10.34	10.49	10.64	10.78	10.93	11.08	11.23	11.38
14.5	9.16	9.44	9.73	10.02	10.16	10.31	10.46	10.61	10.76	10.91	11.06	11.21
15.0	8.99	9.27	9.56	9.85	9.99	10.14	10.29	10.44	10.59	10.75	10.90	11.05
15.5	8.82	9.11	9.40	9.69	9.84	9.99	10.14	10.29	10.44	10.60	10.75	10.91
16.0	8.67	8.96	9.25	9.54	9.69	9.85	10.00	10.15	10.30	10.46	10.62	10.77
16.5	8.53	8.82	9.11	9.41	9.56	9.71	9.87	10.02	10.17	10.33	10.49	10.65
17.0	8.40	8.69	8.98	9.28	9.43	9.59	9.74	9.90	10.05	10.21	10.37	10.53
17.5	8.27	8.56	8.86	9.16	9.32	9.47	9.63	9.78	9.94	10.10	10.26	10.42
18.0	8.16	8.45	8.75	9.05	9.21	9.36	9.52	9.68	9.84	10.00	10.16	10.32
18.5	8.05	8.34	8.64	8.95	9.11	9.26	9.42	9.58	9.74	9.90	10.06	10.23
19.0	7.94	8.24	8.55	8.85	9.01	9.17	9.33	9.49	9.65	9.81	9.98	10.14
19.5	7.84	8.15	8.45	8.76	8.92	9.08	9.24	9.40	9.56	9.73	9.89	10.06
20.0	7.75	8.06	8.36	8.68	8.84	9.00	9.16	9.32	9.49	9.65	9.82	9.98
20.5	7.67	7.97	8.28	8.60	8.76	8.92	9.08	9.25	9.41	9.58	9.74	9.91
21.0	7.58	7.89	8.20	8.52	8.68	8.85	9.01	9.17	9.34	9.51	9.68	9.85
21.5	7.51	7.82	8.13	8.45	8.61	8.78	8.94	9.11	9.27	9.44	9.61	9.78
22.0	7.43	7.75	8.06	8.38	8.55	8.71	8.88	9.04	9.21	9.38	9.55	9.73
22.5	7.36	7.68	8.00	8.32	8.48	8.65	8.82	8.99	9.15	9.33	9.50	9.67
23.0	7.30	7.61	7.93	8.26	8.43	8.59	8.76	8.93	9.10	9.27	9.44	9.62
23.5	7.24	7.55	7.88	8.20	8.37	8.54	8.71	8.88	9.05	9.22	9.40	9.57
24.0	7.18	7.50	7.82	8.15	8.32	8.49	8.66	8.83	9.00	9.17	9.35	9.52
24.5	7.12	7.44	7.77	8.10	8.27	8.44	8.61	8.78	8.95	9.13	9.31	9.48
25.0	7.07	7.39	7.72	8.05	8.22	8.39	8.56	8.74	8.91	9.09	9.26	9.44
25.5	7.02	7.34	7.67	8.01	8.18	8.35	8.52	8.70	8.87	9.05	9.23	9.40
26.0	6.97	7.29	7.63	7.96	8.13	8.31	8.48	8.66	8.83	9.01	9.19	9.37
26.5	6.92	7.25	7.58	7.92	8.09	8.27	8.44	8.62	8.80	8.97	9.15	9.33
27.0	6.88	7.21	7.54	7.88	8.06	8.23	8.41	8.58	8.76	8.94	9.12	9.30
27.5	6.84	7.17	7.50	7.85	8.02	8.20	8.37	8.55	8.73	8.91	9.09	9.27
28.0	6.80	7.13	7.47	7.81	7.99	8.16	8.34	8.52	8.70	8.88	9.06	9.25
28.5	6.76	7.09	7.43	7.78	7.95	8.13	8.31	8.49	8.67	8.85	9.03	9.22
29.0	6.72	7.06	7.40	7.75	7.92	8.10	8.28	8.46	8.64	8.82	9.01	9.19
29.5	6.69	7.02	7.37	7.72	7.89	8.07	8.25	8.43	8.62	8.80	8.98	9.17
29.8	6.67	7.00	7.35	7.70	7.88	8.06	8.24	8.42	8.60	8.79	8.97	9.16
30.0	6.65	6.99	7.34	7.69	7.87	8.05	8.23	8.41	8.59	8.78	8.96	9.15
35.0	6.39	6.74	7.10	7.47	7.65	7.84	8.03	8.22	8.41	8.60	8.79	8.98
40.0	6.21	6.58	6.95	7.33	7.52	7.71	7.91	8.10	8.30	8.49	8.69	8.89

Figure 15-2

INTEREST RATE FACTORS

Example: $50,000 loan @ 12¼% for 30 years

Problem: find monthly payment

Step 1: Find the **column** that corresponds to the interest rate of the proposed loan.

Step 2: Find the **row** that corresponds to the term of the proposed loan. For example, calculations for a loan of 30 years would use the last (bottom) row of the charts.

Step 3: Take the number found at the intersection of the appropriate column and row, and **add a decimal point and a zero at the front** of the number. In our example, the chart shows a figure of 104789, which should be converted to **.0**104789.

Step 4: **Multiply** the proposed **loan amount** by the answer from step 3 to get the monthly loan payment. In our example, multiply $50,000 times .0104789.

YEARS	12%	12¼%
1	888487	889657
1½	609820	610982
2	470734	471903
2½	387481	388661
3	332143	333338
3½	292756	293968
4	263338	264567
4½	240565	241812
5	222444	223709
6	195501	196804
7	176527	177867
8	162528	163905
9	151842	153255
10	143470	144919
12	131341	132859
15	120016	121629
20	110108	111856
21	108869	110641
22	107793	109586
23	106856	108670
24	106038	107871
25	105322	107174
26	104695	106564
27	104144	106030
28	103661	105562
29	103235	105150
30	102861	104789

$$\begin{array}{r} \$50,000 \\ \times\ .0104789 \\ \hline \$523.95 \end{array}$$

Thus, the monthly payment on a $50,000, 30-year loan at 12¼% is $523.95 per month.

YEARS	10½%	10¼%	10%	9¾%	9½%	9¼%	9%	8¾%	8½%	8¼%	8%	YEARS
1	881486	880322	879158	877996	876835	875675	874515	873356	872198	871041	869884	1
1½	602875	601722	600570	599420	598271	597123	595977	594831	593687	592544	591403	1½
2	463760	462603	461449	460296	459144	457995	456847	455701	454557	453414	452273	2
2½	380443	379277	378114	376952	375793	374637	373482	372329	371178	370030	368883	2½
3	325024	323846	322671	321499	320329	319162	317997	316835	315675	314518	313364	3
3½	285547	284356	283168	281982	280800	279621	278445	277272	276102	274934	273770	3½
4	256033	254828	253625	252426	251231	250039	248850	247665	246483	245304	244129	4
4½	233161	231941	230724	229510	228301	227096	225894	224696	223501	222311	221124	4½
5	214939	213702	212470	211242	210018	208779	207584	206372	205165	203963	202764	5
6	187789	186521	185258	184000	182746	181499	180255	179017	177784	176556	175332	6
7	168606	167306	166011	164722	163439	162162	160891	159625	158365	157111	155862	7
8	154400	153067	151741	150422	149108	147802	146502	145208	143921	142641	141367	8
9	143508	142144	140786	139436	138093	136758	135429	134108	132794	131487	130187	9
10	134934	133539	132150	130770	129397	128033	126676	125327	123986	122653	121328	10
12	122414	120956	119507	118068	116637	115216	113803	112400	111006	109621	108245	12
15	110539	108995	107460	105936	104422	102919	101427	099945	098474	097014	095565	15
20	099837	098164	096502	948516	093213	091587	089973	088371	086782	085207	083644	20
21	098459	096763	095078	093404	091743	090094	088458	086835	085224	083627	082043	21
22	097250	095531	093824	092129	090446	088775	087117	085472	083841	082222	080618	22
23	096186	094446	092718	091001	089297	087606	085927	084261	082609	080970	079345	23
24	095248	093487	091738	090002	088277	086566	084866	083181	081508	079850	078205	24
25	094418	092638	090870	089113	087369	085638	083920	082214	080523	078845	077182	25
26	093682	091884	090097	088322	086559	084810	083072	081348	079638	077942	076260	26
27	093030	091214	089409	087616	085836	084068	082313	080570	078842	077128	075428	27
28	092450	090617	088796	086986	085188	083403	081630	079871	078125	076393	074676	28
29	091934	090085	088247	086421	084607	082805	081016	079240	077477	075729	073995	29
30	091473	089610	087757	085915	084085	082268	080462	078670	076891	075127	073376	30

YEARS	10¾%	11%	11¼%	11½%	11¾%	12%	12¼%	12½%	12¾%	13%	13¼%	YEARS
1	882650	883816	884983	886150	887318	888487	889657	890828	892001	893173	894347	1
1½	604029	605185	606342	607500	608659	609820	610982	612145	613311	614476	615643	1½
2	464918	466078	467239	468403	469568	470734	471903	473073	474245	475419	476594	2
2½	381610	382780	383952	385126	386302	387481	388661	389844	391029	392216	393405	2½
3	326045	327387	328572	329760	330950	332143	333338	334536	335737	336940	338145	3
3½	286741	287938	289138	290341	291547	292756	293968	295182	296401	297621	298845	3½
4	257242	258455	259670	260890	262112	263338	264567	265799	267036	268275	269518	4
4½	234386	235614	236846	238082	239322	240565	241812	243063	244319	245577	246839	4½
5	216179	217424	218673	219926	221183	222444	223709	224979	226254	227531	228813	5
6	189062	190340	191623	192911	194204	195501	196804	198111	199425	200742	202063	6
7	169912	171224	172541	173864	175193	176527	177867	179212	180564	181920	183282	7
8	155739	157084	158435	159793	161157	162528	163905	165288	166678	168073	169475	8
9	144880	146258	147644	149036	150436	151842	153255	154675	156103	157536	158977	9
10	136338	137750	139168	140595	142029	143470	144919	146376	147840	149311	150789	10
12	123880	125355	126839	128331	129832	131341	132859	134385	135912	137463	139014	12
15	112094	113659	115234	116818	118413	120016	121629	123252	124884	126525	128174	15
20	101522	103218	104925	106642	108370	110108	111856	113614	115382	117158	118944	20
21	100167	101887	103617	105357	107108	108869	110641	112421	114213	116012	117820	21
22	098980	100722	102474	104237	106010	107793	109586	111389	113202	115023	116853	22
23	097382	099700	101474	103258	105052	106856	108670	110493	112327	114168	116018	23
24	097019	098802	100596	102400	104214	106038	107871	109714	111567	113427	115296	24
25	096209	098011	099823	101646	103479	105322	107174	109035	110906	112784	114671	25
26	095492	097312	099143	100984	102835	104695	106564	108442	110330	112225	114128	26
27	094857	096695	098542	100400	102268	104144	106030	107924	109828	111738	113656	27
28	094293	096147	098012	099885	101769	103661	105562	107471	109389	111314	113246	28
29	093793	095662	097542	099431	101329	103235	105150	107074	109005	110944	112889	29
30	093348	095232	097126	099029	100940	102861	104789	106725	108670	110620	112578	30

YEARS	13½%	13¾%	14%	14¼%	14½%	14¾%	15%	15¼%	15½%	15¾%	16%	YEARS
1	895521	896696	897872	899048	900226	901404	902584	903764	904945	906126	907309	1
1½	616812	617981	619152	620324	621498	622672	623848	625026	626204	627384	628565	1½
2	477771	478949	480129	481311	482495	483680	484867	486056	487246	488438	489632	2
2½	394596	395789	396984	398181	399381	400582	407186	402992	404199	405209	406621	2½
3	339353	340564	341777	342992	344210	345431	346654	347879	349107	350338	351571	3
3½	300071	301301	302533	303768	305006	306247	307491	308738	309988	311240	312496	3½
4	270764	272013	273265	274521	275780	277042	278308	279577	280849	282125	283403	4
4½	248105	249374	250647	251924	253205	254489	255777	257068	258363	259662	260964	4½
5	230099	231389	232683	233981	235283	236590	237900	239214	240532	241855	243181	5
5½	215476	216787	218102	219422	220746	222074	223407	224744	226086	227432	228782	5½
6	203390	204722	206058	207399	208745	210095	211451	212811	214175	215545	216919	6
6½	193254	194606	195964	197326	198694	200066	201444	202827	204215	205607	207005	6½
7	184649	186022	187401	188784	190174	191568	192968	194373	195784	197200	198621	7
8	170882	172296	173716	175141	176573	178011	179455	180904	182360	183821	185288	8
9	160424	161877	163338	164804	166278	167758	169244	170737	172236	173741	175253	9
10	152275	153767	155267	156774	158287	159808	161335	162870	164411	165959	167514	10
12	140572	142139	143713	145295	146885	148483	150088	151701	153321	154948	156583	12
15	129832	131499	133175	134858	136551	138251	139959	141675	143400	145131	146871	15
20	120738	122541	124353	126172	128000	129836	131679	133530	135389	137254	139126	20
21	119637	121463	123297	125139	126989	128847	130712	132585	134464	136351	138244	21
22	118692	120538	122393	124256	126127	128005	129890	131783	133682	135587	137500	22
23	117877	119743	121618	123500	125390	127287	129190	131101	133018	134942	136871	23
24	117173	119058	120951	122851	124758	126673	128593	130521	132454	134394	136340	24
25	116565	118467	120377	122293	124217	126147	128084	130026	131975	133929	135889	25
26	116038	117956	119881	121813	123752	125697	127648	129604	131567	133535	135508	26
27	115582	117514	119454	121400	123352	125310	127274	129244	131219	133199	135184	27
28	115185	117132	119084	121043	123008	124978	126954	128936	130922	132913	134909	28
29	114841	116800	118764	120735	122712	124693	126680	128672	130669	132670	134675	29
29½	114686	116651	118621	120597	122579	124566	126558	128555	130556	132562	134572	29½
30	114542	116512	118488	120469	122456	124448	126445	128446	130452	132462	134476	30

YEARS	16¼%	16½%	16¾%	17%	17¼%	17½%	17¾%	18%	18¼%	18½%	18¾%	YEARS
1	908493	909677	910862	912048	913235	914423	915611	916800	917991	919182	920374	1
1½	629747	639031	632115	633301	634489	635677	636867	638058	639251	640444	641639	1½
2	490827	492024	493223	494423	495625	496829	498034	499242	500450	501661	502873	2
2½	407835	409052	410270	411490	412713	413937	415164	416392	417623	418856	420091	2½
3	352806	354044	355285	356528	357773	359021	360272	361524	362780	364038	365298	3
3½	313754	315015	316279	317546	318816	320089	321365	322643	323924	325209	326496	3½
4	284685	285971	287259	288551	289846	291144	292446	293750	295058	296370	297684	4
4½	262270	263580	264894	266210	267531	268855	270183	271514	272849	274188	275530	4½
5	244511	245846	247184	248526	249872	251223	252577	253935	255297	256663	258032	5
5½	230136	231495	232859	234226	235598	236974	238354	239739	241128	242521	243918	5½
6	218298	219681	221069	222462	223859	225261	226667	228078	229494	230914	232339	6
6½	208408	209816	211228	212646	214068	215496	216928	218365	219807	221254	222705	6½
7	200048	201479	202916	204359	205806	207258	208716	210179	211647	213120	214598	7
8	186761	188240	189725	191215	192711	194213	195720	197233	198751	200275	201804	8
9	176771	178295	179826	181362	182905	184454	186009	187569	189136	190709	192287	9
10	169075	170643	172217	173798	175386	176979	178579	180186	181798	183417	185042	10
12	158225	159874	161530	163193	164863	166539	168223	169912	171609	173312	175021	12
15	148617	150371	152133	153901	155676	157458	159247	161043	162845	164653	166467	15
20	141005	142891	144782	146681	148585	150495	152410	154332	156258	158190	160127	20
21	140143	142049	143961	145879	147802	149732	151666	153606	155551	157501	159455	21
22	139418	141342	143272	145208	147149	149096	151048	153004	154966	156932	158902	22
23	138807	140748	142695	144647	146604	148566	150533	152505	154481	156461	158446	23
24	138291	140247	142209	144176	146147	148123	150104	152089	154078	156072	158069	24
25	137855	139825	141800	143780	145765	147753	149746	151743	153744	155749	157757	25
26	134786	139469	141456	143448	145444	147444	149448	151456	153467	155481	157499	26
27	137173	139167	141166	143167	145175	147185	149198	151216	153236	155259	157286	27
28	136909	138913	140921	142933	144949	146968	148990	151015	153044	155075	157109	28
29	136684	138698	140715	142735	144759	146786	148816	150848	152884	154922	156963	29
29½	136585	138603	140624	142648	144675	146706	148739	150776	152814	154856	156899	29½
30	136494	138515	140540	142568	144599	146633	148670	150709	152751	154795	156841	30

YEARS	19%	19½%	20%	20½%	21%	YEARS
1	921566	923954	926346	928740	931138	1
1½	642835	645231	647633	650039	652450	1½
2	504087	506519	508959	511404	513857	2
2½	421328	423808	426296	428793	431298	2½
3	366561	369094	371636	374189	376751	3
3½	327785	330374	332973	335584	338206	3½
4	299002	301647	304304	306974	309657	4
4½	276875	279577	282293	285024	287768	4½
5	259406	262165	264939	267729	270534	5
5½	245320	248135	250968	253817	256682	5½
6	233768	236639	239529	242436	245360	6
6½	224161	227088	230034	232998	235981	6½
7	216081	219062	222062	225083	228123	7
8	203339	206425	209533	212661	215811	8
9	193871	197057	200266	203496	206749	9
10	186673	189953	193256	196583	199932	10
12	176737	180187	183661	187159	190681	12
15	168288	171948	175630	179335	183062	15
20	162069	165967	169883	173816	177765	20
21	161415	165347	169295	173260	177239	21
22	160877	164839	168816	172808	176814	22
23	160434	164423	168426	172442	176470	23
24	160069	164081	168106	172144	176192	24
25	159769	163801	167846	171901	175967	25
26	159520	163571	167632	171704	175784	26
27	159315	163382	167458	171543	175637	27
28	159146	163226	167315	171412	175517	28
29	159006	163098	167198	171306	175419	29
29½	158945	163043	167148	171260	175378	29½
30	158890	162993	167102	171219	175314	30

Figure 15-3   **Counting Days of the Year***
Numbering from January 1

Day of the month	Jan.	Feb.	March	April	May	June	July	Aug.	Sept.	Oct.	Nov.	Dec.
1	1	32	60	91	121	152	182	213	244	274	305	335
2	2	33	61	92	122	153	183	214	245	275	306	336
3	3	34	62	93	123	154	184	215	246	276	307	337
4	4	35	63	94	124	155	185	216	247	277	308	338
5	5	36	64	95	125	156	186	217	248	278	309	339
6	6	37	65	96	126	157	187	218	249	279	310	340
7	7	38	66	97	127	158	188	219	250	280	311	341
8	8	39	67	98	128	159	189	220	251	281	312	342
9	9	40	68	99	129	160	190	221	252	282	313	343
10	10	41	69	100	130	161	191	222	253	283	314	344
11	11	42	70	101	131	162	192	223	254	284	315	345
12	12	43	71	102	132	163	193	224	255	285	316	346
13	13	44	72	103	133	164	194	225	256	286	317	347
14	14	45	73	104	134	165	195	226	257	287	318	348
15	15	46	74	105	135	166	196	227	258	288	319	349
16	16	47	75	106	136	167	197	228	259	289	320	350
17	17	48	76	107	137	168	198	229	260	290	321	351
18	18	49	77	108	138	169	199	230	261	291	322	352
19	19	50	78	109	139	170	200	231	262	292	323	353
20	20	51	79	110	140	171	201	232	263	293	324	354
21	21	52	80	111	141	172	202	233	264	294	325	355
22	22	53	81	112	142	173	203	234	265	295	326	356
23	23	54	82	113	143	174	204	235	266	296	327	357
24	24	55	83	114	144	175	205	236	267	297	328	358
25	25	56	84	115	145	176	206	237	268	298	329	359
26	26	57	85	116	146	177	207	238	269	299	330	360
27	27	58	86	117	147	178	208	239	270	300	331	361
28	28	59	87	118	148	179	209	240	271	301	332	362
29	29	—	88	119	149	180	210	241	272	302	333	363
30	30	—	89	120	150	181	211	242	273	303	334	364
31	31	—	90	—	151	—	212	243	—	304	—	365

* In a leap year, add one to each number after 59 (February 28)

Figure 15-4

LOAN PROGRESS CHARTS

Example: $50,000 loan @ 12¼% for 30 years

Problem: find balance after three years

Step 1

Choose the **chart** that corresponds to the interest rate of the loan in question.

Step 2

Choose the **column** that corresponds to the original term of the loan. For example, 30-year loans are found in the farthest right hand column of the chart.

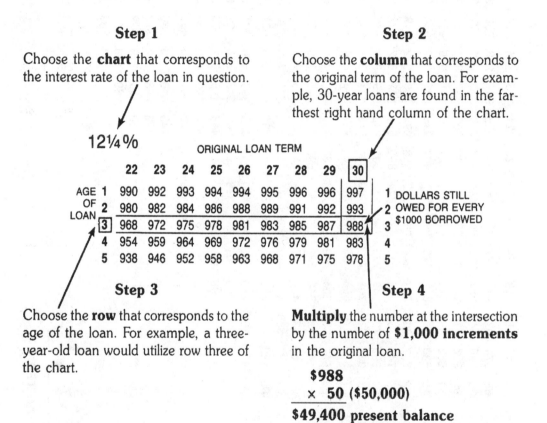

Step 3

Choose the **row** that corresponds to the age of the loan. For example, a three-year-old loan would utilize row three of the chart.

Step 4

Multiply the number at the intersection by the number of **$1,000 increments** in the original loan.

$988
× 50 ($50,000)
$49,400 present balance

If the original loan amount had been **$50,600**,
you would multiply 988 times 50.6.

8%

ORIGINAL LOAN TERM

AGE OF LOAN

Age	5	8	10	12	15	16	17	18	19	20	21	22	23	24	25	26	27	28	29	30
1	831	907	932	948	964	968	971	974	977	979	981	983	984	986	987	988	989	990	991	992
2	647	806	858	892	925	933	940	946	951	956	960	964	967	970	973	975	977	979	981	983
3	448	697	778	831	883	895	906	916	924	931	938	943	949	953	957	961	964	968	970	973
4	233	579	692	766	837	854	869	883	894	904	913	921	929	935	941	946	951	955	959	962
5		451	598	694	788	810	830	847	862	875	887	897	907	915	923	930	936	941	946	951
6		313	497	617	734	762	787	808	827	844	858	872	883	894	903	912	919	926	933	938
7		162	387	534	676	710	740	766	789	810	828	844	858	871	882	892	902	910	918	925
8			268	443	613	654	690	721	749	773	794	813	830	846	859	872	883	893	902	910
9			139	345	545	593	635	672	704	733	758	780	800	818	834	849	862	874	885	894
10				239	471	527	576	619	656	689	719	745	768	789	808	824	840	853	866	877
11				124	391	456	512	561	604	642	676	706	733	757	779	798	815	831	846	859
12					305	379	443	499	548	592	630	664	695	722	747	769	789	807	824	839
13					211	295	368	431	487	537	580	619	654	685	713	738	761	781	800	817
14					110	204	287	358	421	477	526	570	609	645	676	704	730	753	774	793
15						106	199	279	350	412	468	517	561	601	636	668	697	723	746	768
16							103	193	273	343	405	460	509	553	593	628	661	690	716	740
17								100	189	267	336	398	452	502	546	586	622	654	684	710
18									98	185	262	330	391	446	495	539	579	615	648	678
19										96	181	257	325	386	440	489	533	574	610	643
20											94	178	253	320	381	435	484	528	568	605
21												93	175	249	316	376	430	479	523	564
22													91	173	246	312	372	426	475	519
23														90	171	243	309	368	422	471
24															89	168	241	306	365	418
25																88	167	238	303	362
26																	87	165	236	300
27																		86	163	234
28																			85	162
29																				84

8½%

ORIGINAL LOAN TERM

AGE OF LOAN

Age of Loan	5	8	10	12	15	16	17	18	19	20	21	22	23	24	25	26	27	28	29	30
1	832	909	934	950	966	969	973	975	978	980	982	984	985	987	988	989	990	991	992	992
2	650	810	861	895	928	936	943	949	954	958	962	966	969	972	975	977	979	981	983	984
3	451	701	783	836	887	899	910	919	928	935	941	947	952	956	960	964	967	970	973	975
4	235	584	697	771	843	860	875	888	899	909	918	926	933	939	945	950	954	958	962	966
5		456	604	701	794	817	836	853	868	881	893	903	912	921	928	934	940	946	951	955
6		317	503	624	742	770	794	816	834	851	865	878	890	900	909	918	925	932	938	943
7		165	393	541	684	719	749	775	798	818	836	851	865	878	889	899	908	917	924	931
8			273	450	622	663	699	730	758	782	803	822	839	854	867	880	890	900	909	917
9			142	352	554	603	645	682	714	743	768	790	810	828	844	858	871	882	893	902
10				244	480	537	586	629	667	700	729	755	778	799	818	834	849	863	875	886
11				127	399	465	522	572	615	653	687	717	744	768	789	809	826	842	856	868
12					312	387	452	509	559	603	642	676	707	734	759	781	801	818	835	849
13					217	302	377	441	498	548	592	631	666	697	725	750	773	793	812	828
14					113	210	294	367	432	488	538	582	622	657	689	717	743	766	787	806
15						109	204	287	359	423	479	529	574	614	649	681	710	736	760	781
16							106	199	280	352	415	472	522	566	606	642	675	704	730	754
17								104	195	275	346	409	465	515	559	600	636	668	698	725
18									101	191	270	340	403	458	508	553	594	630	663	693
19										99	187	266	335	397	453	503	548	588	625	658
20											98	184	262	331	392	448	498	543	583	620
21												96	182	258	327	388	443	493	538	579
22													95	179	255	323	384	439	489	534
23														93	177	252	320	381	436	485
24															92	175	250	317	378	432
25																91	173	247	314	375
26																	90	172	245	312
27																		89	170	243
28																			89	169
29																				88

9%

ORIGINAL LOAN TERM

AGE OF LOAN	5	8	10	12	15	16	17	18	19	20	21	22	23	24	25	26	27	28	29	30
1	834	911	935	951	967	971	974	977	979	981	983	985	986	988	989	990	991	992	992	993
2	653	813	865	898	931	939	945	951	956	961	965	968	971	974	977	979	981	983	984	986
3	454	706	787	840	891	903	914	923	931	938	945	950	955	959	963	967	970	973	975	978
4	237	589	703	777	848	865	880	893	904	914	923	930	937	943	949	954	958	962	965	969
5		461	610	707	801	823	842	859	874	887	898	909	918	926	933	939	945	950	955	959
6		321	509	631	749	777	802	823	841	858	872	885	896	906	915	923	931	937	943	948
7		167	398	548	692	727	757	783	806	826	843	859	873	885	896	906	915	923	930	936
8			277	457	630	672	708	739	767	791	812	831	847	862	875	887	898	907	916	924
9			145	358	563	612	654	691	724	752	777	799	819	837	852	866	879	890	900	910
10				249	489	546	596	639	677	710	740	765	789	809	827	844	858	872	884	894
11				130	408	474	532	582	626	664	698	728	755	779	800	819	836	851	865	878
12					319	396	462	519	570	614	653	688	718	746	770	792	812	829	845	859
13					222	310	385	451	509	559	604	643	678	710	737	762	785	805	823	839
14					116	215	301	376	442	499	550	595	634	670	702	730	755	778	799	817
15						113	210	294	368	433	491	541	586	627	662	695	723	749	772	793
16							110	205	288	361	426	483	534	579	620	656	688	717	743	767
17								107	201	283	355	420	477	527	573	613	650	682	712	738
18									105	197	278	350	414	471	522	567	608	644	677	707
19										103	194	274	345	409	466	516	562	603	640	673
20											101	191	270	341	404	461	512	557	598	635
21												100	188	267	337	400	457	507	553	594
22													98	186	264	334	396	453	503	549
23														97	184	261	331	393	449	500
24															96	182	259	328	390	446
25																95	180	257	325	388
26																	94	179	255	323
27																		93	177	253
28																			93	176
29																				92

9½%

AGE OF LOAN \ ORIGINAL LOAN TERM	5	8	10	12	15	16	17	18	19	20	21	22	23	24	25	26	27	28	29	30
1	836	912	937	953	968	972	975	978	980	982	984	986	987	989	990	991	992	992	993	994
2	656	816	868	901	934	941	948	954	959	963	967	970	973	976	978	981	982	984	986	987
3	457	710	792	845	895	907	918	927	935	942	948	953	958	962	966	969	972	975	977	980
4	239	593	708	782	853	870	885	898	909	918	927	934	941	947	952	957	961	965	968	971
5		465	616	714	807	829	849	865	880	893	904	914	923	930	937	943	949	954	958	962
6		325	515	638	756	784	809	830	848	864	879	891	902	912	921	929	936	942	947	953
7		170	404	555	700	735	765	791	813	833	851	866	880	892	903	912	921	929	935	942
8			282	464	639	681	717	748	775	799	820	839	855	870	883	894	905	914	922	930
9			148	364	571	621	664	701	733	762	787	809	828	845	861	875	887	898	908	917
10				254	497	555	606	649	687	720	750	775	798	819	837	853	867	880	892	902
11				133	416	483	542	592	636	675	709	739	766	789	810	829	846	861	874	886
12					326	404	471	530	581	625	664	699	730	757	781	803	822	839	855	869
13					227	317	394	461	519	570	615	655	690	721	749	774	796	816	834	850
14					119	221	309	385	452	510	561	607	647	682	714	742	767	790	810	828
15						116	216	302	378	444	502	553	599	639	675	707	736	762	785	805
16							113	211	296	371	437	495	546	592	633	669	701	730	756	780
17								110	207	291	365	431	489	540	586	627	663	696	725	752
18									108	203	286	360	425	483	535	580	622	658	691	721
19										106	200	282	355	420	478	530	576	617	654	687
20											105	197	279	351	416	474	525	571	613	650
21												103	194	276	348	412	470	521	567	609
22													102	192	273	344	409	466	518	564
23														101	190	270	342	406	463	514
24															100	188	268	339	403	460
25																99	187	266	337	400
26																	98	185	264	335
27																		97	184	262
28																			96	183
29																				96

10%

ORIGINAL LOAN TERM

AGE OF LOAN

AGE	5	8	10	12	15	16	17	18	19	20	21	22	23	24	25	26	27	28	29	30
1	838	914	939	955	970	973	976	979	981	983	985	987	988	989	991	992	992	993	994	994
2	658	819	871	904	936	944	950	956	961	965	969	972	975	978	980	982	984	986	987	988
3	460	714	796	849	899	911	922	930	938	945	951	956	961	965	969	972	975	977	979	982
4	242	598	713	788	858	875	890	902	913	923	931	938	945	951	956	960	964	968	971	974
5		470	622	720	813	835	855	871	885	898	909	919	927	935	942	948	953	958	962	966
6		329	521	645	763	791	816	837	855	871	885	897	908	918	926	934	940	946	952	957
7		173	410	562	708	743	773	799	821	841	858	873	886	898	909	918	927	934	941	946
8			286	471	647	689	725	757	784	807	828	847	863	877	890	901	911	920	928	935
9			150	370	580	630	673	710	743	771	796	817	837	854	869	882	894	905	914	923
10				259	506	565	615	659	697	730	759	785	808	828	846	861	876	888	899	909
11				136	424	492	551	602	647	685	719	749	776	799	820	838	855	870	883	894
12					333	412	481	540	591	636	675	710	741	768	792	813	832	849	864	878
13					233	324	403	471	530	581	627	666	702	733	760	785	807	826	844	859
14					122	227	316	394	462	521	573	618	659	694	726	754	779	801	821	839
15						119	221	310	387	454	513	565	611	652	688	720	748	774	796	817
16							116	217	304	380	447	506	559	605	645	682	714	743	769	792
17								114	213	299	375	442	500	553	599	640	677	709	738	765
18									112	209	295	370	436	495	547	594	635	672	705	734
19										110	206	291	366	432	491	543	589	631	668	701
20											108	203	287	362	428	486	539	585	627	664
21												107	201	284	358	424	483	535	582	623
22													105	199	282	355	421	479	532	578
23														104	197	279	353	418	476	529
24															103	195	277	350	415	474
25																102	194	275	348	413
26																	102	192	273	346
27																		101	191	272
28																			100	190
29																				100

10¼%

ORIGINAL LOAN TERM

AGE OF LOAN

Age	5	8	10	12	15	16	17	18	19	20	21	22	23	24	25	26	27	28	29	30
1	839	915	939	955	970	974	977	980	982	984	986	987	989	990	991	992	993	993	994	995
2	660	821	872	906	937	945	952	957	962	966	970	973	976	979	981	983	985	986	988	989
3	462	716	798	851	901	913	923	932	940	947	952	958	962	966	970	973	976	978	980	982
4	243	601	716	790	861	878	892	904	915	925	933	940	947	952	957	962	966	969	972	975
5		473	625	723	816	838	857	874	888	901	912	921	930	937	944	950	955	959	964	967
6		331	524	648	767	795	819	840	858	874	888	900	911	920	929	936	943	949	954	959
7		174	412	566	712	747	777	802	825	844	861	876	890	901	912	921	929	936	943	949
8			289	475	651	693	730	761	788	812	832	850	867	881	893	904	914	923	931	938
9			152	373	584	634	678	715	747	775	800	822	841	858	873	886	898	908	918	926
10				261	510	569	620	664	702	735	764	790	812	832	850	866	880	892	903	913
11				137	428	497	556	607	652	691	725	754	781	804	825	843	859	874	887	898
12					337	417	485	545	596	641	681	715	746	773	797	818	837	854	869	882
13					236	328	407	475	535	587	632	672	707	738	766	790	812	831	849	864
14					124	229	320	399	467	526	578	624	664	700	732	760	785	807	827	844
15						121	224	314	391	459	519	571	617	658	694	726	754	779	802	822
16							118	220	308	385	453	512	565	611	652	688	720	749	775	798
17								115	216	303	380	447	506	559	605	646	683	716	745	771
18									113	212	299	375	442	501	554	600	642	679	711	741
19										112	209	295	371	437	497	549	596	638	675	708
20											110	207	292	367	433	493	545	592	634	671
21												109	204	289	364	430	489	542	589	630
22													107	202	286	361	427	486	538	585
23														106	200	284	358	424	483	536
24															105	199	282	356	422	480
25																104	197	280	354	419
26																	104	196	278	352
27																		103	195	277
28																			102	194
29																				102

10½%

ORIGINAL LOAN TERM

AGE OF LOAN	5	8	10	12	15	16	17	18	19	20	21	22	23	24	25	26	27	28	29	30
1	839	916	940	956	971	975	978	980	982	984	986	988	989	990	991	992	993	994	994	995
2	661	822	874	907	939	946	953	958	963	967	971	974	977	979	982	984	985	987	988	989
3	463	718	800	853	903	915	925	934	941	948	954	959	963	967	971	974	977	979	981	983
4	244	603	719	793	863	880	894	907	917	927	935	942	948	954	959	963	967	971	974	976
5		475	628	726	819	841	860	877	891	903	914	923	932	939	946	951	957	961	965	969
6		333	527	652	770	798	822	843	861	877	891	903	913	923	931	938	945	951	956	960
7		175	415	570	716	751	780	806	828	848	865	880	893	904	915	924	932	939	945	951
8			291	478	656	698	734	765	792	816	836	854	870	884	897	908	917	926	934	941
9			153	377	589	639	682	719	752	780	804	826	845	862	876	890	901	912	921	929
10				264	514	574	625	669	707	740	769	794	817	837	854	870	883	896	907	916
11				139	432	501	561	612	657	696	730	760	786	809	829	848	864	878	891	902
12					340	421	490	550	601	647	686	721	751	778	802	823	842	858	873	886
13					238	331	411	480	540	592	638	678	713	744	771	796	817	836	853	869
14					125	232	324	403	472	532	584	630	670	706	737	765	790	812	832	849
15						122	227	318	396	464	524	577	623	664	700	732	760	785	808	828
16							119	223	312	390	458	518	570	617	658	694	727	755	781	804
17								117	219	307	385	452	512	565	612	653	689	722	751	777
18									115	215	303	380	448	507	560	607	648	685	718	747
19										113	212	299	376	443	503	556	603	644	681	714
20											112	210	296	372	439	499	552	599	641	678
21												110	207	293	369	436	495	548	595	637
22													109	205	290	366	433	492	545	592
23														108	204	288	363	430	490	543
24															107	202	286	361	428	487
25																106	201	284	359	426
26																	106	199	283	357
27																		105	198	281
28																			104	197
29																				104

10¾%

ORIGINAL LOAN TERM

AGE OF LOAN	5	8	10	12	15	16	17	18	19	20	21	22	23	24	25	26	27	28	29	30
1	840	917	941	957	972	975	978	981	983	985	987	988	989	991	992	993	993	994	995	995
2	663	824	875	909	940	947	954	959	964	968	972	975	978	980	982	984	986	987	989	990
3	465	720	802	855	905	917	927	935	943	950	955	960	965	969	972	975	978	980	982	984
4	245	605	721	795	866	882	897	909	920	929	937	944	950	956	960	965	969	972	975	978
5		477	631	729	822	844	863	879	893	906	916	926	934	941	948	953	958	963	967	970
6		335	530	655	774	802	826	846	864	880	894	906	916	925	933	941	947	953	958	962
7		176	418	573	720	754	784	810	832	851	868	883	896	907	918	926	934	941	948	953
8			293	482	660	702	738	769	796	820	840	858	874	888	900	911	920	929	936	943
9			154	380	593	643	687	724	756	784	809	830	849	866	880	893	905	915	924	932
10				266	519	578	629	673	711	745	774	799	821	841	858	874	887	899	910	919
11				140	436	506	566	617	662	701	735	764	791	814	834	852	868	882	894	906
12					344	425	495	555	607	652	691	726	756	783	807	828	846	863	877	890
13					241	335	416	485	545	598	643	683	718	749	777	801	822	841	858	873
14					127	235	328	408	477	537	590	636	676	712	743	771	795	817	837	854
15						124	230	321	401	470	530	583	629	670	706	738	766	791	813	833
16							121	226	316	395	463	524	576	623	664	700	733	761	787	809
17								119	222	311	389	458	518	571	618	659	696	728	757	783
18									117	218	307	385	453	513	566	613	655	692	724	754
19										115	215	303	381	449	509	562	609	651	688	721
20											113	213	300	377	445	505	558	605	647	685
21												112	211	297	374	442	502	555	602	644
22													111	209	295	371	439	499	552	599
23														110	207	293	369	436	496	549
24															109	205	291	367	434	494
25																108	204	289	365	432
26																	107	203	288	363
27																		107	202	286
28																			106	201
29																				106

11%

ORIGINAL LOAN TERM

AGE OF LOAN

Age	5	8	10	12	15	16	17	18	19	20	21	22	23	24	25	26	27	28	29	30
1	841	917	942	957	972	976	979	981	983	985	987	989	990	991	992	993	994	994	995	995
2	664	825	877	910	941	949	955	960	965	969	973	976	979	981	983	985	987	988	989	990
3	466	722	805	857	907	918	928	937	945	951	957	962	966	970	973	976	979	981	983	985
4	246	608	724	798	868	885	899	911	922	931	939	946	952	957	962	966	970	973	976	979
5		480	634	732	825	847	866	882	896	908	919	928	936	943	950	955	960	964	968	972
6		337	533	659	777	805	829	850	867	883	896	908	919	928	936	943	949	955	960	964
7		178	421	577	724	758	788	813	836	855	872	886	899	910	920	929	937	944	950	955
8			296	485	664	706	742	773	800	823	844	862	877	891	903	914	923	931	939	945
9			156	383	597	648	691	728	760	788	813	834	853	869	884	897	908	918	927	935
10				269	523	583	634	678	716	749	778	803	826	845	862	877	891	903	913	923
11				142	440	510	570	622	667	706	740	769	795	818	838	856	872	886	898	909
12					347	429	499	560	612	657	697	731	762	788	812	832	851	867	881	894
13					244	339	420	490	550	603	649	689	724	755	782	806	827	846	863	877
14					129	238	332	412	482	542	595	641	682	717	749	776	801	822	842	859
15						125	233	325	405	475	535	588	635	676	712	743	771	796	818	838
16							123	229	320	399	469	529	582	629	670	706	739	767	792	815
17								121	225	315	394	463	524	577	624	665	702	734	763	789
18									119	221	311	390	459	519	572	619	661	698	731	760
19										117	219	308	386	454	515	568	616	657	694	727
20											115	216	305	382	451	511	565	612	654	691
21												114	214	302	379	448	508	562	609	651
22													113	212	299	377	445	505	559	606
23														112	210	297	374	442	503	556
24															111	209	295	372	440	500
25																110	207	294	370	438
26																	109	206	292	368
27																		109	205	291
28																			108	204
29																				108

410

11 1/4%

ORIGINAL LOAN TERM

AGE OF LOAN	5	8	10	12	15	16	17	18	19	20	21	22	23	24	25	26	27	28	29	30
1	842	918	943	958	973	976	979	982	984	986	988	989	990	991	992	993	994	995	995	996
2	666	827	878	911	942	950	956	961	966	970	974	977	979	982	984	986	987	989	990	991
3	468	725	807	859	909	920	930	939	946	952	958	963	967	971	974	977	980	982	984	986
4	247	610	726	801	871	887	901	913	924	933	941	947	953	959	963	967	971	974	977	980
5		482	636	735	828	850	869	885	899	911	921	930	938	945	951	957	962	966	970	973
6		339	536	662	780	808	832	853	870	886	899	911	921	930	938	945	951	956	961	966
7		179	424	580	727	762	792	817	839	858	875	889	902	913	923	932	939	946	952	957
8			298	488	668	710	746	777	804	827	847	865	881	894	906	917	926	934	941	948
9			157	386	601	652	695	733	765	793	817	838	857	873	887	900	911	921	930	937
10				271	527	587	639	683	721	754	783	808	830	849	866	881	894	906	917	926
11				143	444	514	575	627	672	711	745	774	800	823	843	860	876	890	902	913
12					351	433	504	564	617	662	702	736	767	793	816	837	855	871	885	898
13					247	342	424	495	555	608	654	694	729	760	787	811	832	851	867	882
14					130	241	335	417	487	548	601	647	687	723	754	782	806	827	846	863
15						127	236	329	410	480	541	594	640	681	717	749	777	802	832	843
16							124	231	324	404	474	535	588	635	676	712	744	773	798	820
17								122	228	319	399	469	530	583	630	672	708	740	769	794
18									120	225	315	395	464	525	579	626	667	704	737	766
19										119	222	312	391	460	521	575	622	664	701	734
20											117	219	309	387	456	517	571	619	661	698
21												116	217	306	384	453	514	568	616	658
22													115	215	304	382	451	511	565	613
23														114	214	302	379	448	509	563
24															113	212	300	377	446	507
25																112	211	298	376	444
26																	111	210	297	374
27																		111	209	296
28																			110	208
29																				110

11 1/2 %

ORIGINAL LOAN TERM

AGE OF LOAN	5	8	10	12	15	16	17	18	19	20	21	22	23	24	25	26	27	28	29	30
1	843	919	943	959	973	977	980	982	984	986	988	989	991	992	993	993	994	995	995	996
2	667	828	880	913	944	951	957	962	967	971	974	977	980	982	984	986	988	989	990	991
3	470	727	809	861	910	922	932	940	947	954	959	964	968	972	975	978	980	983	985	986
4	248	612	729	803	873	889	903	915	926	935	942	949	955	960	965	969	972	975	978	981
5		485	639	738	831	853	871	887	901	913	923	932	940	947	953	958	963	967	971	974
6		341	539	665	784	812	835	856	873	889	902	913	924	932	940	947	953	958	963	967
7		180	426	584	731	766	795	821	843	861	878	892	905	916	925	934	941	948	954	959
8			300	492	672	714	750	781	808	831	851	869	884	897	909	919	929	937	944	950
9			159	389	606	656	700	737	769	797	821	842	860	877	891	903	914	924	932	940
10				274	531	592	643	687	725	759	787	812	834	853	870	885	898	909	920	929
11				145	448	519	580	632	677	716	749	779	805	827	847	864	880	893	905	916
12					354	437	508	569	622	667	707	741	772	798	821	841	859	875	889	902
13					249	346	429	499	560	613	659	699	734	765	792	816	837	855	871	886
14					132	244	339	421	492	553	606	653	693	728	759	787	811	832	851	868
15						129	239	333	414	485	546	600	646	687	723	755	782	807	829	848
16							126	234	328	409	479	540	594	641	682	718	750	778	803	825
17								124	231	323	404	474	535	589	636	678	714	746	775	800
18									122	228	319	400	470	531	585	632	674	710	743	772
19										120	225	316	396	466	527	581	628	670	707	740
20											119	223	313	393	462	523	577	625	667	704
21												118	220	311	390	459	520	575	622	664
22													117	219	308	387	457	518	572	620
23														116	217	306	385	454	515	570
24															115	216	304	383	452	513
25																114	214	303	381	450
26																	113	213	302	380
27																		113	212	300
28																			112	211
29																				112

11¾%

AGE OF LOAN / **ORIGINAL LOAN TERM**

Age	5	8	10	12	15	16	17	18	19	20	21	22	23	24	25	26	27	28	29	30
1	844	920	944	960	974	977	980	983	985	987	988	990	991	992	993	994	994	995	996	996
2	668	830	881	914	945	952	958	963	968	972	975	978	981	983	985	987	988	990	991	992
3	471	729	811	863	912	924	933	942	949	955	961	965	969	973	976	979	981	983	985	987
4	249	615	731	806	875	891	905	917	927	936	944	951	957	962	966	970	973	977	979	982
5		487	642	741	834	855	874	890	903	915	925	934	942	949	955	960	965	969	972	975
6		343	542	669	787	815	839	859	876	891	905	916	926	935	942	949	955	960	965	969
7		182	429	587	735	769	799	824	846	865	881	895	908	919	928	936	944	950	956	961
8			302	495	676	718	754	785	812	835	855	872	887	900	912	922	931	939	946	952
9			160	392	610	661	704	741	773	801	825	846	864	880	894	906	917	927	935	942
10				276	535	596	648	692	730	763	792	817	838	857	874	889	901	913	923	931
11				146	452	523	584	636	681	720	754	784	809	832	851	868	884	897	909	919
12					358	442	513	574	627	672	712	746	776	803	826	846	864	879	893	905
13					252	350	433	504	566	619	665	705	740	770	797	821	841	859	875	890
14					133	246	343	425	497	558	611	658	698	734	765	792	816	837	856	872
15						130	242	337	419	490	552	605	652	693	729	760	788	812	834	852
16							128	237	332	413	484	546	600	647	688	724	756	784	809	830
17								126	234	327	409	479	541	595	642	684	720	752	780	805
18									124	231	324	404	475	537	591	638	680	717	749	777
19										122	228	320	401	471	533	587	635	676	713	746
20											121	226	317	398	468	530	584	631	674	711
21												119	224	315	395	465	527	581	629	671
22													118	222	313	392	462	524	578	626
23														117	220	311	390	460	522	576
24															117	219	309	388	458	520
25																116	218	308	387	456
26																	115	217	306	385
27																		115	216	305
28																			114	215
29																				114

12%

ORIGINAL LOAN TERM

AGE OF LOAN	5	8	10	12	15	16	17	18	19	20	21	22	23	24	25	26	27	28	29	30
1	845	921	945	960	975	978	981	983	985	987	989	990	991	992	993	994	995	995	996	996
2	670	831	883	915	946	953	959	964	969	973	976	979	982	984	986	987	989	990	991	992
3	473	731	813	865	914	925	935	943	950	956	962	966	970	974	977	980	982	984	986	988
4	250	617	734	808	877	894	907	919	929	938	946	952	958	963	967	971	975	978	980	982
5		489	645	744	837	858	877	892	906	917	928	936	944	951	957	962	966	970	974	977
6		345	545	672	790	818	842	862	879	894	907	918	928	937	944	951	957	962	966	970
7		183	432	590	738	773	802	828	849	868	884	898	910	921	930	939	946	952	958	963
8			305	499	680	722	758	789	815	838	858	875	890	903	915	925	934	941	948	954
9			161	395	614	665	708	745	777	805	829	850	868	884	897	909	920	929	938	945
10				279	540	600	652	696	735	767	796	821	842	861	878	892	905	916	926	934
11				148	456	528	589	641	686	725	759	788	814	836	855	872	887	900	912	922
12					361	446	518	579	632	677	717	751	781	807	830	850	868	883	897	909
13					255	353	437	509	571	624	670	710	745	775	802	825	846	864	880	894
14					135	249	347	430	501	563	617	663	704	739	770	797	821	842	860	876
15						132	245	341	424	495	557	611	657	698	734	765	793	817	838	857
16							130	240	336	418	489	551	605	652	694	730	761	789	814	835
17								127	237	332	413	485	547	601	648	689	726	758	786	811
18									126	234	328	409	480	542	597	644	686	723	755	783
19										124	231	325	406	477	539	593	641	683	720	752
20											123	229	322	403	473	536	590	638	680	717
21												121	227	319	400	471	533	587	635	677
22													120	225	317	398	468	530	585	633
23														119	224	315	395	466	528	583
24															119	222	314	394	464	526
25																118	221	312	392	462
26																	117	220	311	391
27																		117	219	310
28																			116	219
29																				116

12¼%

AGE OF LOAN	5	8	10	12	15	16	17	18	19	20	21	22	23	24	25	26	27	28	29	30
1	846	922	946	961	975	979	981	984	986	988	989	990	992	993	994	994	995	996	996	997
2	671	833	884	917	947	954	960	965	970	974	977	980	982	984	986	988	989	991	992	993
3	474	733	815	867	915	927	936	945	952	958	963	968	972	975	978	981	983	985	987	988
4	251	620	736	811	880	896	909	921	931	940	947	954	959	964	969	972	976	979	981	983
5		492	648	747	839	861	879	895	908	920	930	938	946	952	958	963	968	971	975	978
6		347	548	675	794	821	845	865	882	897	910	921	930	939	946	953	958	963	968	971
7		184	437	594	742	777	806	831	852	871	887	901	913	924	933	941	948	954	960	964
8			307	502	684	726	762	793	819	842	862	879	893	906	918	928	936	944	950	956
9			163	399	618	669	713	750	782	809	833	853	871	887	901	912	923	932	940	947
10				282	544	605	657	701	739	772	800	825	846	865	881	895	908	919	928	937
11				149	460	532	593	646	691	730	763	793	818	840	859	876	891	904	915	925
12					365	450	522	584	637	682	722	756	786	812	835	854	872	887	900	912
13					258	357	441	514	576	629	675	715	750	780	807	830	850	868	884	897
14					138	252	350	434	506	568	622	669	709	744	775	802	826	846	865	880
15						134	247	345	428	500	562	616	663	704	740	771	798	822	843	862
16							131	243	340	423	495	557	611	658	699	735	767	795	819	840
17								129	240	336	418	490	552	606	654	695	732	763	791	816
18									127	237	332	414	486	548	603	650	692	728	761	789
19										126	234	329	411	482	545	599	647	689	726	758
20											124	232	326	408	479	541	596	644	686	723
21												123	230	324	405	476	539	593	642	684
22													122	229	322	403	474	536	591	639
23														121	227	320	401	472	534	589
24															120	226	318	399	470	532
25																120	225	317	397	468
26																	119	224	315	396
27																		119	223	314
28																			118	222
29																				118

ORIGINAL LOAN TERM

415

12½%

ORIGINAL LOAN TERM

AGE OF LOAN	5	8	10	12	15	16	17	18	19	20	21	22	23	24	25	26	27	28	29	30
1	846	922	946	962	976	979	982	984	986	988	990	991	992	993	994	995	995	996	996	997
2	673	834	886	918	948	955	961	966	971	974	978	980	983	985	987	988	990	991	992	993
3	476	735	817	869	917	928	938	946	953	959	964	969	973	976	979	981	984	986	987	989
4	253	622	739	813	882	898	911	923	933	942	949	955	961	966	970	974	977	980	982	984
5		494	651	750	842	863	882	897	910	922	932	940	948	954	960	965	969	973	976	979
6		349	551	678	797	824	848	868	885	899	912	923	933	941	948	954	960	965	969	973
7		186	438	597	746	780	809	834	856	874	890	904	916	926	935	943	950	956	961	966
8			309	506	688	730	766	797	823	845	865	882	896	909	920	930	939	946	952	958
9			164	402	622	673	717	754	786	813	837	857	875	890	904	915	926	935	942	949
10				284	548	609	661	705	743	776	804	829	850	869	885	899	911	922	931	939
11				151	464	536	598	651	696	735	768	797	822	844	869	880	894	907	918	928
12					368	454	527	589	642	687	727	761	791	816	839	858	876	891	904	915
13					261	361	446	518	580	634	680	720	755	785	811	834	854	872	887	901
14					138	255	354	439	511	573	627	674	714	750	780	807	830	851	869	884
15						135	250	349	433	505	567	622	668	709	745	776	803	827	848	866
16							133	246	344	427	500	562	617	664	705	741	772	800	824	845
17								131	243	340	423	495	558	612	660	701	737	769	797	821
18									129	240	336	419	491	554	608	656	698	734	766	794
19										128	238	333	416	488	550	605	653	695	731	764
20											126	235	330	413	485	547	602	650	692	729
21												125	234	328	410	482	545	600	648	690
22													124	232	326	408	480	542	597	646
23														123	230	324	406	478	540	596
24															122	229	323	404	476	539
25																122	228	321	403	474
26																	121	227	320	402
27																		121	226	319
28																			120	226
29																				120

12¾%

ORIGINAL LOAN TERM

AGE OF LOAN

Age	5	8	10	12	15	16	17	18	19	20	21	22	23	24	25	26	27	28	29	30
1	847	923	947	962	976	980	982	985	987	988	990	991	992	993	994	995	995	996	996	997
2	678	836	887	919	949	956	962	967	972	975	978	981	983	986	987	989	990	991	993	993
3	477	737	819	871	919	930	939	947	954	960	965	970	974	977	980	982	984	986	988	989
4	254	624	741	815	884	900	913	925	935	943	950	957	962	967	971	975	978	980	983	985
5		496	653	753	845	866	884	899	913	924	934	942	949	956	961	966	970	974	977	980
6		351	554	682	800	827	851	870	887	902	915	925	935	943	950	956	962	966	970	974
7		187	440	601	749	784	813	838	859	877	893	906	918	928	937	945	952	958	963	967
8			312	509	692	734	770	800	826	849	868	885	899	912	923	932	941	948	954	960
9			166	405	626	677	721	758	790	817	840	861	878	893	907	918	928	937	945	951
10				287	552	613	665	710	748	780	809	833	854	872	888	902	914	925	934	942
11				152	468	541	603	655	700	739	773	801	826	848	867	883	898	910	921	931
12					372	458	531	593	647	692	732	766	795	821	843	863	879	894	907	918
13					263	364	450	523	585	639	685	725	760	790	816	839	859	876	891	904
14					140	258	358	443	516	579	633	679	720	755	785	812	835	855	873	888
15						137	253	352	437	510	573	627	674	715	750	781	808	832	852	870
16							135	249	348	432	505	568	622	669	710	746	778	805	829	850
17								133	246	344	428	500	563	618	665	707	743	774	802	826
18									131	243	340	424	496	559	614	662	704	740	772	800
19										129	241	337	421	493	556	611	659	701	737	769
20											128	239	335	418	490	553	608	656	698	735
21												127	237	332	415	488	551	606	654	696
22													126	235	330	413	485	549	604	652
23														125	234	329	411	483	547	602
24															124	233	327	410	482	545
25																124	232	326	408	480
26																	123	231	325	407
27																		123	230	324
28																			122	229
29																				122

13%

ORIGINAL LOAN TERM

AGE OF LOAN

Age	5	8	10	12	15	16	17	18	19	20	21	22	23	24	25	26	27	28	29	30
1	848	924	948	963	977	980	983	985	987	989	990	991	993	994	994	995	996	996	997	997
2	675	837	888	921	950	957	963	968	972	976	979	982	984	986	988	989	991	992	993	994
3	479	739	821	873	920	931	941	949	956	961	966	971	974	978	981	983	985	987	989	990
4	255	626	744	818	886	902	915	927	936	945	952	958	964	968	972	976	979	981	984	986
5		499	656	756	847	869	887	902	915	926	936	944	951	957	963	967	971	975	978	981
6		354	557	685	803	830	854	873	890	905	917	928	937	945	952	958	963	968	972	975
7		188	443	604	753	787	816	841	862	880	896	909	921	931	940	947	954	960	965	969
8			314	512	695	738	774	804	830	852	871	888	902	915	926	935	943	950	956	962
9			167	408	630	682	725	762	794	821	844	864	881	896	910	921	931	939	947	954
10				289	556	618	670	714	752	785	813	837	858	876	891	905	917	927	936	944
11				154	472	545	607	660	705	744	777	806	831	852	871	887	901	913	924	934
12					376	462	536	598	651	697	736	770	800	825	847	866	883	898	910	922
13					266	368	454	528	590	644	690	730	765	795	820	843	863	880	895	908
14					142	261	362	447	521	584	638	684	725	760	790	816	839	859	877	892
15						139	256	356	442	515	578	632	679	720	755	786	813	836	857	874
16							136	253	352	437	510	573	628	675	716	752	783	810	833	854
17								134	249	348	432	506	569	623	671	712	748	780	807	831
18									133	246	344	429	502	565	620	668	709	746	777	805
19										131	244	341	426	499	562	617	665	707	743	775
20											130	242	339	423	496	559	614	662	704	741
21												129	240	337	420	493	557	612	660	702
22													128	239	335	418	491	555	610	658
23														127	237	333	417	489	553	606
24															126	236	332	415	488	551
25																126	235	330	414	486
26																	125	234	329	412
27																		125	233	328
28																			124	233
29																				124

13½%

ORIGINAL LOAN TERM

AGE OF LOAN	5	8	10	12	15	16	17	18	19	20	21	22	23	24	25	26	27	28	29	30
1	850	925	949	964	978	981	984	986	988	989	991	992	993	994	995	995	996	997	997	997
2	678	840	891	923	953	959	965	970	974	977	980	983	985	987	989	990	992	993	994	994
3	482	743	825	876	924	934	944	951	958	964	969	973	976	979	982	982	986	988	990	991
4	257	631	749	823	890	906	919	930	940	948	955	961	966	970	974	978	981	983	985	987
5		504	662	761	853	874	891	906	919	930	939	947	954	960	965	970	974	977	980	983
6		358	562	691	809	836	859	879	895	909	921	932	941	949	955	961	966	970	974	978
7		191	449	611	760	794	823	847	868	886	901	914	925	935	944	951	957	963	968	972
8			319	519	703	745	781	811	837	859	878	894	908	920	930	939	947	954	960	965
9			170	414	638	690	733	770	801	828	851	871	888	902	915	926	936	944	951	957
10				294	564	626	679	723	761	793	821	844	865	883	898	911	923	932	941	949
11				157	480	554	616	669	714	753	786	814	839	860	878	894	907	919	930	939
12					383	470	544	607	661	707	746	779	808	834	855	874	890	904	917	927
13					272	375	463	537	600	654	700	740	774	804	829	851	871	887	902	914
14					145	267	369	456	530	594	648	695	735	769	799	825	848	868	885	899
15						142	262	364	451	525	588	643	690	730	765	796	822	845	865	882
16							140	259	360	446	520	584	638	686	727	762	793	819	843	863
17								138	255	356	442	516	580	635	682	723	759	790	817	840
18									136	253	353	438	512	576	631	679	720	756	788	815
19										135	250	350	435	509	573	628	676	718	754	786
20											134	248	347	433	507	571	626	674	716	752
21												133	247	345	431	504	568	624	672	714
22													132	245	343	429	502	566	622	670
23														131	244	342	427	501	565	620
24															130	243	341	425	499	563
25																130	242	339	424	498
26																	129	241	338	423
27																		129	240	338
28																			128	240
29																				128

14%

ORIGINAL LOAN TERM

AGE OF LOAN	5	8	10	12	15	16	17	18	19	20	21	22	23	24	25	26	27	28	29	30
1	851	927	951	965	979	982	985	987	989	990	992	993	994	995	995	996	996	997	997	998
2	681	843	894	926	955	961	967	971	975	979	982	984	986	988	990	991	992	993	994	995
3	485	747	829	880	927	937	946	954	960	966	971	975	978	981	984	986	988	989	991	992
4	259	636	754	827	895	910	923	934	943	951	958	963	968	973	976	979	982	985	987	988
5		508	667	767	858	878	896	911	923	934	943	951	957	963	968	972	976	979	982	984
6		362	568	697	815	842	865	884	900	914	926	936	945	952	959	964	969	973	977	980
7		193	454	618	767	801	829	853	874	891	906	919	930	939	948	955	961	966	970	974
8			323	526	711	753	788	818	844	865	884	900	913	925	935	944	951	958	963	968
9			173	420	646	698	741	778	809	835	858	877	894	908	921	931	940	948	955	961
10				299	572	635	687	731	769	801	828	852	872	889	904	917	928	937	946	953
11				160	487	562	625	678	723	761	794	822	846	867	885	900	913	925	935	943
12					390	479	553	617	670	716	755	788	817	842	863	881	897	911	922	933
13					277	383	471	546	609	664	710	749	783	812	838	859	878	894	908	920
14					148	272	377	465	540	603	658	705	745	779	809	834	856	875	892	906
15						146	268	372	460	534	598	653	700	740	775	805	831	854	873	890
16							143	265	367	455	530	594	649	696	737	772	802	829	851	871
17								141	262	364	451	526	590	645	693	734	769	800	826	849
18									140	259	361	448	523	587	642	690	731	767	798	824
19										138	257	358	445	520	584	640	688	729	765	796
20											137	255	356	443	517	582	637	686	727	763
21												136	253	354	441	515	580	635	684	725
22													135	252	352	439	513	578	634	682
23														135	251	351	437	512	576	632
24															134	250	350	436	510	575
25																134	249	348	435	509
26																	133	248	347	434
27																		133	247	347
28																			132	247
29																				132

15%

ORIGINAL LOAN TERM

AGE OF LOAN	5	8	10	12	15	16	17	18	19	20	21	22	23	24	25	26	27	28	29	30
1	855	930	953	968	981	984	986	988	990	991	993	994	995	995	996	997	997	997	998	998
2	686	849	899	930	958	965	970	975	978	981	984	986	988	990	991	993	994	995	995	996
3	491	754	836	887	933	943	951	959	965	970	974	978	981	984	986	988	990	991	992	993
4	264	645	763	836	902	917	930	940	949	956	963	968	973	977	980	983	985	987	989	991
5		518	678	778	868	888	905	919	931	941	949	957	963	968	973	977	980	983	985	987
6		370	580	710	827	853	875	894	910	923	934	943	952	958	964	969	974	977	981	983
7		199	465	631	780	813	842	865	885	902	916	928	938	947	955	961	967	971	975	979
8			333	539	725	767	802	832	856	877	895	910	923	934	943	951	958	964	969	973
9			179	433	662	713	757	793	823	849	871	889	905	919	930	940	949	956	962	967
10				310	588	651	704	748	785	816	843	865	885	901	915	927	937	946	954	960
11				166	503	579	642	695	740	778	810	838	861	881	898	912	924	935	944	952
12					404	495	571	635	688	734	772	805	833	857	877	894	909	922	933	942
13					289	397	488	564	628	682	728	767	801	829	853	874	892	907	920	931
14					155	284	392	482	558	623	677	724	763	797	826	850	872	890	905	918
15						153	280	387	477	554	618	673	720	760	794	823	848	869	888	903
16							150	277	383	473	549	614	669	717	757	791	821	846	867	886
17								149	274	380	470	546	611	666	714	754	789	819	844	866
18									147	272	377	467	543	608	664	711	752	787	817	842
19										146	270	375	464	541	606	661	709	750	785	815
20											145	268	373	462	538	604	660	707	749	784
21												144	266	371	460	537	602	658	706	747
22													143	265	369	459	535	600	656	705
23														142	264	368	457	534	599	655
24															142	263	367	456	532	598
25																141	262	366	455	532
26																	141	262	365	454
27																		141	261	365
28																			140	261
29																				140

Figure 15-5

POINTS DISCOUNT TABLES

Example: $50,000 loan@12.25% for 30 years
Problem: Find lender's yield if two points are charged

Step 1	**Step 2**
Choose the **chart** that corresponds to the stated interest rate.	Choose the **column** that corresponds to the term of the loan. For a 30-year loan, use the third column from the right.

INTEREST RATE	NET %	LOAN TERM IN YEARS							
		5	10	15	20	25	30	35	40
	95	14.54	13.55	13.23	13.08	13.00	12.96	12.93	12.92
	96	14.07	13.28	13.03	12.91	12.85	12.81	12.79	12.78
12.25%	97	13.60	13.02	12.83	12.74	12.69	12.67	12.65	12.64
	98	13.15	12.76	12.63	12.57	12.54	12.53	12.52	12.51
	99	12.69	12.50	12.44	12.41	12.40	12.39	12.38	12.38

Step 3	**Step 4**
Choose the **row** that corresponds to the discount. For a two-point discount, the net % of the loan (the amount the borrower actually receives) is 98 (100% - 2% = 98%).	Locate the **number** at the intersection of the appropriate column and row. This is the lender's yield. For a 30-year, 12.25% loan with two points charged, the yield is **12.53%**.

If the discount had been **four** points, the net % would be **96** (100 - 4 = 96) and the lender's yield would be **12.81%**.

INTEREST RATE	NET %	LOAN TERM IN YEARS							
		5	10	15	20	25	30	35	40
8%	95	10.20	9.19	8.86	8.70	8.61	8.55	8.51	8.48
	96	9.74	8.95	8.68	8.55	8.48	8.44	8.40	8.38
	97	9.30	8.70	8.51	8.41	8.36	8.32	8.30	8.29
	98	8.86	8.47	8.34	8.27	8.24	8.21	8.20	8.19
	99	8.43	8.23	8.17	8.14	8.12	8.11	8.10	8.09
8¼%	95	10.45	9.45	9.12	8.96	8.86	8.81	8.77	8.74
	96	10.00	9.20	8.94	8.81	8.74	8.69	8.66	8.64
	97	9.55	8.96	8.76	8.67	8.61	8.58	8.56	8.54
	98	9.11	8.72	8.59	8.53	8.49	8.47	8.45	8.44
	99	8.68	8.48	8.42	8.39	8.37	8.36	8.35	8.35
8½	95	10.71	9.70	9.37	9.21	9.12	9.07	9.03	9.00
	96	10.25	9.46	9.19	9.07	8.99	8.95	8.92	8.90
	97	9.80	9.21	9.02	8.92	8.87	8.83	8.81	8.80
	98	9.36	8.97	8.84	8.78	8.74	8.72	8.71	8.70
	99	8.39	8.73	8.67	8.64	8.62	8.61	8.60	8.60
8¾%	95	10.96	9.96	9.63	9.47	9.38	9.32	9.29	9.26
	96	10.51	9.71	9.45	9.32	9.25	9.21	9.18	9.16
	97	10.06	9.46	9.27	9.18	9.12	9.09	9.07	9.05
	98	9.62	9.22	9.09	9.03	9.00	8.97	8.96	8.95
	99	9.18	8.98	8.92	8.89	8.87	8.86	8.85	8.85
9%	95	11.12	10.11	9.78	9.63	9.54	9.48	9.44	9.42
	96	10.66	9.86	9.60	9.48	9.40	9.36	9.33	9.31
	97	10.21	9.62	9.42	9.33	9.27	9.24	9.22	9.21
	98	9.77	9.37	9.25	9.18	9.15	9.13	9.11	9.10
	99	9.33	9.14	9.07	9.04	9.02	9.01	9.01	9.00
9¼%	95	11.47	10.47	10.14	9.99	9.90	9.84	9.81	9.78
	96	11.01	10.22	9.96	9.83	9.76	9.72	9.69	9.67
	97	10.56	9.97	9.78	9.68	9.63	9.60	9.58	9.56
	98	10.12	9.73	9.60	9.54	9.50	9.48	9.47	9.46
	99	9.68	9.49	9.42	9.39	9.38	9.36	9.36	9.35

INTEREST RATE	NET %	LOAN TERM IN YEARS							
		5	10	15	20	25	30	35	40
9½%	95	11.73	10.73	10.40	10.24	10.16	10.10	10.07	10.05
	96	11.27	10.47	10.21	10.09	10.02	9.98	9.95	9.93
	97	10.82	10.22	10.03	9.94	9.89	9.85	9.83	9.82
	98	10.37	9.98	9.85	9.79	9.76	9.73	9.72	9.71
	99	9.93	9.74	9.67	9.64	9.63	9.62	9.61	9.61
9¾%	95	11.98	10.98	10.66	10.50	10.41	10.36	10.33	10.31
	96	11.52	10.73	10.47	10.35	10.28	10.23	10.21	10.19
	97	11.07	10.48	10.29	10.19	10.14	10.11	10.09	10.08
	98	10.62	10.23	10.10	10.04	10.01	9.99	9.97	9.97
	99	10.18	9.99	9.93	9.90	9.88	9.87	9.86	9.86
10%	95	12.24	11.34	10.91	10.76	10.67	10.62	10.59	10.57
	96	11.78	10.98	10.72	10.60	10.53	10.49	10.47	10.45
	97	11.32	10.73	10.54	10.45	10.40	10.37	10.35	10.33
	98	10.88	10.48	10.36	10.30	10.26	10.24	10.23	10.22
	99	10.43	10.24	10.18	10.15	10.13	10.12	10.11	10.11
10¼%	95	12.49	11.50	11.17	11.02	10.93	10.88	10.85	10.83
	96	12.03	11.24	10.98	10.86	10.79	10.75	10.72	10.71
	97	11.58	10.99	10.79	10.70	10.65	10.62	10.60	10.59
	98	11.13	10.74	10.61	10.55	10.52	10.50	10.48	10.47
	99	10.69	10.49	10.43	10.40	10.38	10.37	10.37	10.36
10½%	95	12.75	11.75	11.43	11.27	11.19	11.14	11.11	11.09
	96	12.29	11.49	11.24	11.11	11.05	11.01	10.98	10.97
	97	11.83	11.24	11.05	10.96	10.91	10.88	10.86	10.85
	98	11.38	10.99	10.86	10.80	10.77	10.75	10.74	10.73
	99	10.94	10.74	10.68	10.65	10.63	10.62	10.62	10.61
10¾%	95	13.01	12.01	11.68	11.53	11.45	11.40	11.37	11.35
	96	12.54	11.75	11.49	11.37	11.30	11.26	11.24	11.22
	97	12.08	11.49	11.30	11.21	11.16	11.13	11.11	11.10
	98	11.63	11.24	11.11	11.06	11.02	11.00	10.99	10.98
	99	11.19	10.99	10.93	10.90	10.89	10.88	10.87	10.87
11%	95	13.26	12.26	11.94	11.79	11.71	11.66	11.63	11.61
	96	12.80	12.00	11.75	11.63	11.56	11.52	11.50	11.48
	97	12.34	11.75	11.56	11.47	11.42	11.39	11.37	11.36
	98	11.88	11.49	11.37	11.31	11.28	11.26	11.24	11.24
	99	11.44	11.25	11.18	11.15	11.14	11.13	11.12	11.12

INTEREST RATE	NET %	LOAN TERM IN YEARS							
		5	10	15	20	25	30	35	40
11¼%	95	13.52	12.52	12.20	12.05	11.97	11.92	11.89	11.87
	96	13.05	12.26	12.00	11.88	11.82	11.78	11.76	11.74
	97	12.59	12.00	11.81	11.72	11.67	11.64	11.63	11.62
	98	12.14	11.75	11.62	11.56	11.53	11.51	11.50	11.49
	99	11.69	11.50	11.43	11.40	11.39	11.38	11.37	11.37
11½%	95	13.77	12.78	12.46	12.31	12.23	12.18	12.15	12.13
	96	13.30	12.51	12.26	12.14	12.08	12.04	12.02	12.00
	97	12.84	12.25	12.06	11.98	11.93	11.90	11.88	11.87
	98	12.39	12.00	11.87	11.81	11.78	11.76	11.75	11.75
	99	11.94	11.75	11.69	11.66	11.64	11.63	11.63	11.62
11¾%	95	14.03	13.03	12.71	12.57	12.49	12.44	12.41	12.39
	96	13.56	12.77	12.51	12.40	12.33	12.30	12.27	12.26
	97	13.10	12.51	12.32	12.23	12.18	12.16	12.14	12.13
	98	12.64	12.25	12.13	12.07	12.04	12.02	12.01	12.00
	99	12.19	12.00	11.94	11.91	11.89	11.88	11.88	11.87
12%	95	14.28	13.29	12.97	12.82	12.74	12.70	12.67	12.66
	96	13.81	13.02	12.77	12.65	12.59	12.55	12.53	12.52
	97	13.35	12.76	12.57	12.49	12.44	12.41	12.40	12.39
	98	12.89	12.50	12.38	12.32	12.29	12.27	12.26	12.25
	99	12.44	12.25	12.19	12.16	12.14	12.13	12.13	12.13
12¼%	95	14.54	13.55	13.23	13.08	13.00	12.96	12.93	12.92
	96	14.07	13.28	13.03	12.91	12.85	12.81	12.79	12.78
	97	13.60	13.02	12.83	12.74	12.69	12.67	12.65	12.64
	98	13.15	12.76	12.63	12.57	12.54	12.53	12.52	12.51
	99	12.69	12.50	12.44	12.41	12.40	12.39	12.38	12.38
12½%	95	14.79	13.80	13.49	13.34	13.26	13.22	13.19	13.18
	96	14.32	13.53	13.28	13.17	13.11	13.07	13.05	13.04
	97	13.86	13.27	13.08	13.00	12.95	12.92	12.91	12.90
	98	13.40	13.01	12.88	12.83	12.80	12.78	12.77	12.76
	99	12.95	12.75	12.69	12.66	12.65	12.64	12.63	12.63
12¾%	95	15.05	14.06	13.74	13.60	13.52	13.48	13.46	13.44
	96	14.58	13.79	13.54	13.42	13.36	13.33	13.31	13.30
	97	14.11	13.52	13.34	13.25	13.21	13.18	13.17	13.16
	98	13.65	13.26	13.14	13.08	13.05	13.03	13.02	13.02
	99	13.20	13.00	12.94	12.91	12.90	12.89	12.89	12.88

INTEREST RATE	NET %	LOAN TERM IN YEARS							
		5	10	15	20	25	30	35	40
13%	95	15.31	14.32	14.00	13.86	13.78	13.74	13.72	13.70
	96	14.83	14.04	13.79	13.68	13.62	13.59	13.57	13.56
	97	14.36	13.78	13.59	13.51	13.46	13.44	13.42	13.41
	98	13.90	13.51	13.39	13.33	13.30	13.29	13.28	13.27
	99	13.45	13.26	13.19	13.17	13.15	13.14	13.14	13.14
13¼%	95	15.56	14.57	14.26	14.12	14.04	14.00	13.98	13.97
	96	15.09	14.30	14.05	13.94	13.88	13.85	13.83	13.82
	97	14.62	14.03	13.85	13.76	13.72	13.69	13.68	13.67
	98	14.15	13.77	13.64	13.59	13.56	13.54	13.53	13.53
	99	13.70	13.51	13.45	13.42	13.40	13.39	13.39	13.39
13½	95	15.82	14.83	14.52	14.38	14.30	14.26	14.24	14.23
	96	15.34	14.55	14.31	14.19	14.14	14.10	14.09	14.08
	97	14.87	14.28	14.10	14.02	13.97	13.95	13.94	13.93
	98	14.41	14.02	13.90	13.84	13.81	13.80	13.79	13.78
	99	13.95	13.76	13.70	13.67	13.65	13.65	13.64	13.64
13¾%	95	16.07	15.09	14.77	14.63	14.56	14.52	14.50	14.49
	96	15.59	14.81	14.56	14.45	14.39	14.36	14.35	14.34
	97	15.12	14.54	14.35	14.27	14.23	14.21	14.19	14.18
	98	14.66	14.27	14.15	14.09	14.07	14.05	14.04	14.04
	99	14.20	14.01	13.95	13.92	13.91	13.90	13.89	13.89
14%	95	16.33	15.34	15.03	14.89	14.82	14.78	14.76	14.75
	96	15.85	15.07	14.82	14.71	14.65	14.62	14.60	14.60
	97	15.38	14.79	14.61	14.53	14.48	14.46	14.45	14.44
	98	14.91	14.52	14.40	14.35	14.32	14.30	14.30	14.29
	99	14.45	14.26	14.20	14.17	14.16	14.15	14.15	14.14
14¼%	95	16.58	15.60	15.29	15.15	15.08	15.05	15.02	15.01
	96	16.10	15.32	15.08	14.97	14.91	14.88	14.86	14.85
	97	15.63	15.05	14.86	14.78	14.74	14.72	14.71	14.70
	98	15.16	14.78	14.66	14.60	14.57	14.56	14.55	14.55
	99	14.70	14.51	14.45	14.42	14.41	14.40	14.40	14.40
14½%	95	16.84	15.86	15.55	15.41	15.34	15.31	15.29	15.28
	96	16.36	15.58	15.33	15.22	15.17	15.14	15.12	15.11
	97	15.88	15.30	15.12	15.04	15.00	14.97	14.96	14.96
	98	15.42	15.03	14.91	14.86	14.83	14.81	14.81	14.80
	99	14.95	14.76	14.70	14.68	14.66	14.66	14.65	14.65

INTEREST RATE	NET %	LOAN TERM IN YEARS							
		5	10	15	20	25	30	35	40
14¾%	95	17.10	16.11	15.81	15.67	15.60	15.57	15.55	15.54
	96	16.61	15.83	15.59	15.48	15.43	15.40	15.38	15.37
	97	16.14	15.55	15.37	15.29	15.25	15.23	15.22	15.21
	98	15.67	15.28	15.16	15.11	15.08	15.07	15.06	15.06
	99	15.21	15.01	14.95	14.93	14.91	14.91	14.90	14.90
15%	95	17.35	16.37	16.07	15.93	15.86	15.83	15.81	15.80
	96	16.87	16.09	15.84	15.74	15.68	15.66	15.64	15.63
	97	16.39	15.81	15.63	15.55	15.51	15.49	15.48	15.47
	98	15.92	15.54	15.42	15.36	15.34	15.32	15.31	15.31
	99	15.46	15.27	15.21	15.18	15.17	15.16	15.16	15.15
15¼%	95	17.61	16.63	16.32	16.19	16.12	16.09	16.07	16.06
	96	17.12	16.34	16.10	16.00	15.94	15.92	15.90	15.89
	97	16.64	16.06	15.88	15.80	15.77	15.74	15.73	15.73
	98	16.17	15.79	15.67	15.62	15.59	15.58	15.57	15.57
	99	15.71	15.52	15.46	15.43	15.42	15.41	15.41	15.41
15½%	95	17.86	16.88	16.58	16.45	16.39	16.35	16.33	16.33
	96	17.38	16.60	16.36	16.25	16.20	16.17	16.16	16.15
	97	16.90	16.32	16.14	16.06	16.02	16.00	15.99	15.99
	98	16.42	16.04	15.92	15.87	15.84	15.83	15.82	15.82
	99	15.96	15.77	15.71	15.68	15.67	15.66	15.66	15.66
15¾%	95	18.12	17.14	16.84	16.71	16.65	16.61	16.60	16.59
	96	17.63	16.85	16.61	16.51	16.46	16.43	16.42	16.41
	97	17.15	16.57	16.39	16.32	16.28	16.26	16.25	16.24
	98	16.68	16.29	16.18	16.12	16.10	16.09	16.08	16.08
	99	16.21	16.20	15.96	15.94	15.92	15.92	15.91	15.91
16%	95	18.38	17.40	17.10	16.97	16.91	16.88	16.86	16.85
	96	17.89	17.11	16.87	16.77	16.72	16.69	16.68	16.67
	97	17.40	16.83	16.65	16.57	16.53	16.51	16.51	16.50
	98	16.93	16.55	16.43	16.38	16.35	16.34	16.33	16.33
	99	16.46	16.27	16.21	16.19	16.17	16.17	16.17	16.16
16¼%	95	18.63	17.66	17.36	17.23	17.17	17.14	17.12	17.11
	96	18.14	17.37	17.13	17.03	16.98	16.95	16.94	16.93
	97	17.66	17.08	16.90	16.83	16.79	16.77	16.76	16.76
	98	17.18	16.80	16.68	16.63	16.61	16.59	16.59	16.58
	99	16.71	16.52	16.46	16.44	16.43	16.42	16.42	16.42

INTEREST	NET	LOAN TERM IN YEARS							
RATE	%	5	10	15	20	25	30	35	40
16½%	95	18.89	17.91	17.62	17.49	17.43	17.40	17.38	17.38
	96	18.40	17.62	17.38	17.28	17.24	17.21	17.20	17.19
	97	17.91	17.33	17.16	17.08	17.05	17.03	17.02	17.01
	98	17.43	17.05	16.93	16.89	16.86	16.85	16.84	16.84
	99	16.96	16.77	16.72	16.69	16.68	16.67	16.67	16.67
16¾%	95	19.14	18.17	17.87	17.75	17.69	17.66	17.65	17.64
	96	18.65	17.88	17.64	17.54	17.49	17.47	17.46	17.45
	97	18.16	17.59	17.41	17.34	17.30	17.29	17.28	17.27
	98	17.69	17.30	17.19	17.14	17.12	17.10	17.10	17.09
	99	17.21	17.03	16.97	16.94	16.93	16.93	16.92	16.92
17%	95	19.40	18.43	18.13	18.01	17.95	17.92	17.91	17.90
	96	18.90	18.13	17.90	17.80	17.75	17.73	17.72	17.71
	97	18.42	17.84	17.67	17.59	17.56	17.54	17.53	17.53
	98	17.94	17.56	17.44	17.39	17.37	17.36	17.35	17.35
	99	17.47	17.28	17.22	17.19	17.18	17.18	17.17	17.17
17¼%	95	19.66	18.68	18.39	18.27	18.21	18.18	18.17	18.16
	96	19.16	18.39	18.16	18.06	18.01	17.99	17.98	17.97
	97	18.67	18.10	17.92	17.85	17.82	17.80	17.79	17.79
	98	18.19	17.81	17.70	17.65	17.62	17.61	17.61	17.60
	99	17.72	17.53	17.47	17.45	17.44	17.43	17.43	17.43
17½%	95	19.91	18.94	18.65	18.53	18.47	18.45	18.43	18.43
	96	19.41	18.64	18.41	18.32	18.27	18.25	18.24	18.23
	97	18.92	18.35	18.18	18.11	18.07	18.06	18.05	18.04
	98	18.44	18.06	17.95	17.90	17.88	17.87	17.86	17.86
	99	17.97	17.78	17.72	17.70	17.69	17.68	17.68	17.68
17¾%	95	20.17	19.20	18.91	18.79	18.73	18.71	18.70	18.69
	96	19.67	18.90	18.67	18.57	18.53	18.51	18.50	18.49
	97	19.18	18.61	18.43	18.36	18.33	18.31	18.31	18.30
	98	18.70	18.32	18.20	18.15	18.13	18.12	18.12	18.11
	99	18.22	18.03	17.97	17.95	17.94	17.93	17.93	17.93
18%	95	20.42	19.46	19.17	19.05	19.00	18.97	18.96	18.95
	96	19.92	19.16	18.96	18.83	18.79	18.77	18.76	18.75
	97	19.43	18.86	18.69	18.62	18.59	18.57	18.56	18.56
	98	18.95	18.57	18.46	18.41	18.39	18.38	18.37	18.37
	99	18.47	18.28	18.23	18.20	18.19	18.19	18.18	18.18

VIII. CHAPTER SUMMARY

Agents, brokers, and loan officers need to be able to solve basic real estate math problems in order to provide professional service to their clients. It is of particular importance to be able to answer a client's questions regarding interest rates, appreciation in value, and proration of closing costs. The development of financial tables, and particularly of financial calculators, not only has made the process easier but has resulted in time savings for the real estate professional as well.

IX. CHAPTER TERMS

Compound Interest	Numerator
Denominator	Proration
Effective Interest Rate	Simple Interest
Nominal Interest Rate	

X. CHAPTER 15 QUIZ

1. A stated interest rate of 6% is an example of:

    a. simple interest.
    b. compound interest.
    c. an effective rate.
    d. a nominal rate.

2. If a borrower is actually paying more than the stated rate due to a quarterly conversion, the rate is an example of:

    a. simple interest.
    b. an effective rate.
    c. a nominal rate.
    d. proration.

3. The bottom number of a fraction is the:

    a. denominator.
    b. numerator.
    c. decimal.
    d. formulator.

4. 56.337 x 21.77 =

    a. 122.645
    b. 1,226.456
    c. 12.264
    d. 1,226.000

5. 12.24 + (3.36 -2.08) x 1.23 =

    a. 18.93
    b. 13.81
    c. 16.63
    d. none of the above

6. The profit and loss formula is:

    a. P = % x T
    b. I = P x R x T
    c. VA = % x VB
    d. none of the above

7. If the interest is unknown the formula should be:

   a. $R = I \div P \times T$
   b. $I = P \times R \times T$
   c. $I = P \div R \times T$
   d. none of the above

8. If the principal is unknown the formula should be:

   a. $P = I \div (R \times T)$
   b. $P = I \times R \times T$
   c. $P = T \div (I \times R)$
   d. none of the above.

9. Dividing pre-paid property expenses fairly between buyer and seller is known as:

   a. discounting.
   b. proration.
   c. conversion.
   d. compounding.

10. Interest paid on accrued interest as well as principal is known as:

    a. compound.
    b. simple.
    c. prorated.
    d. all the above.

ANSWERS: 1. d; 2. b; 3. a; 4. b; 5. b; 6. c; 7. b; 8. a; 9. b; 10. a

Chapter 15

— PART VI —
CHAPTERS 16, 17, AND 18
APPENDIX (STATE-SPECIFIC CONCEPTS)

CHAPTER 16 - STATE-SPONSORED HOME LOAN PROGRAMS

Many states offer low interest home loan programs for veterans, first-time homeowners, and low-to-middle income borrowers. Several are listed here, with suggestions as to how to look up a particular state's program on the Internet.

CHAPTER 17 - CAL-VET LOANS (CALIFORNIA EXAMPLE)

Since 1921, an additional type of government-sponsored financing is available to California veterans and veterans who move to California. Funding for the program has been provided since the program's inception through the sale of General Obligation Bonds and Revenue Bonds. The bonds have always been repaid by the veterans who participated in the program and thus there has never been any direct cost to California taxpayers.

CHAPTER 18 - ESCROW PROCEDURES

The typical escrow involves many more participants than just the buyer and seller. It includes the broker, lender, and escrow agent. Important functions are also performed by title companies, notaries public, local county officials (recording office and inspectors), and structural pest inspectors.

CHAPTER 16

STATE-SPONSORED HOME LOAN PROGRAMS

Many state and local governments provide low and moderate mortgage loan programs, as well as other benefits, to qualified borrowers. Many of these programs train participating banks, mortgage companies, credit unions, and real estate professionals in the use of their particular programs, enabling them to match the right loan with the right borrower. Programs include financing, down payment assistance, closing cost assistance, and other programs for first-time homebuyers.

In New York, for example, The State of New York Mortgage Agency (SONYMA) has a Low Interest Rate Mortgage Program which provides qualified low and moderate income first-time homebuyers with low down payment mortgage financing on one-to-four unit dwellings, including condominiums and cooperative apartments, as well as manufactured homes permanently attached to real property. These loans are at fixed interest rates, which are below prevailing conventional rates. The program is financed by SONYMA through the sale of tax-exempt bonds.

The various state programs are too numerous and too diversified to list here, but a simple search of the Internet will provide each state's home loan opportunities. For a list of state housing agencies, go to:

 www.trackproservices.com/links/statelnk.html

The Veterans Administration (VA) also sponsors state-run programs, such as that offered by the Texas Veterans Housing Assistance Program (VHAP), which provides financing up to $200,000 toward the purchase of a home to qualified Texas veterans. Any amount in excess of the maximum must be provided by the veteran, or through a commercial lending institution. As Texas veterans' loan programs are not directly associated with the federal VA loan programs, veterans who have used their VA benefits may still be eligible for state loan programs. (See Chapter 17 for details on California's CAL-VET program.)

For information on federal home loan programs call 1-800-827-1000 or visit their web page at:

 www.homeloans.va.gov.

You can also look up county and city governments for information at:

 www.statelocalgov.net.

The following is just a partial list of state programs available to first-time homeowners, low to moderate income borrowers, and/or qualified veterans.

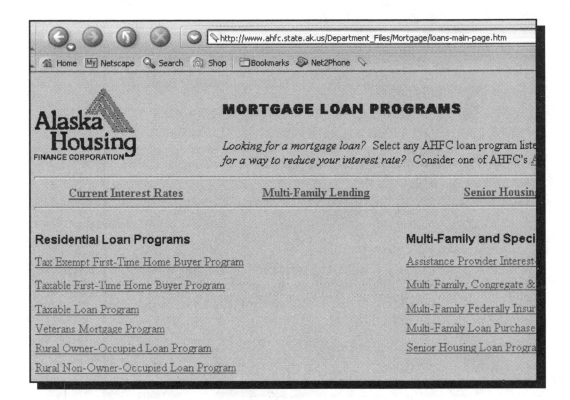

Alaska

(AHFC) Alaska Housing Finance Corporation
Veterans Mortgage Program (VMP)
P.O. Box 101020
Anchorage, AK 99510-1020
(800)478-AHFC(2432) or (907) 338-6100
www.ahfc.state.ak.us/Department_Files/Mortgage/loans-main-page.htm

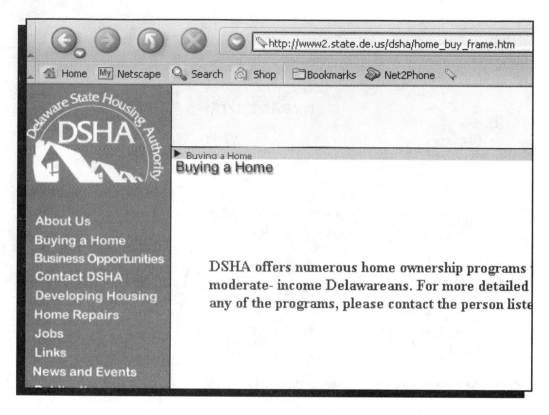

http://www2.state.de.us/dsha/home_buy_frame.htm

Home | My Netscape | Search | Shop | Bookmarks | Net2Phone

▶ Buying a Home

Buying a Home

About Us
Buying a Home
Business Opportunities
Contact DSHA
Developing Housing
Home Repairs
Jobs
Links
News and Events

DSHA offers numerous home ownership programs
moderate- income Delawareans. For more detailed
any of the programs, please contact the person liste

Delaware

Delaware State Housing Authority (DSHA) (Numerous loan programs available)
820 N. French Street
Wilmington, DE 19801
(302) 739-4263 or (302) 577-5001
www2.state.de.us/dsha/home_buy_frame.htm

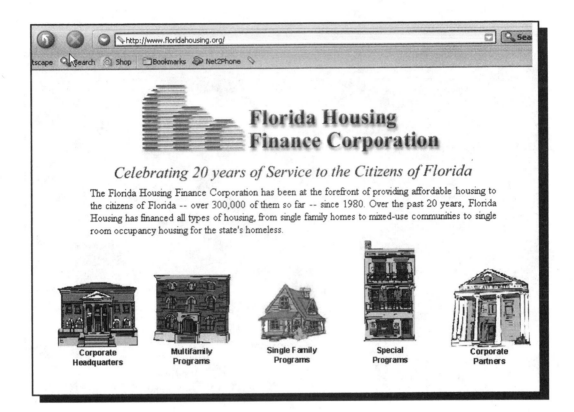

Florida

Florida Housing Finance Corporation (FHFC)
227 North Bronough Street
Suite 5000
Tallahassee, Florida 32301-1329
(850) 488-4197 or Fax: (850) 488-9809
www.floridahousing.org

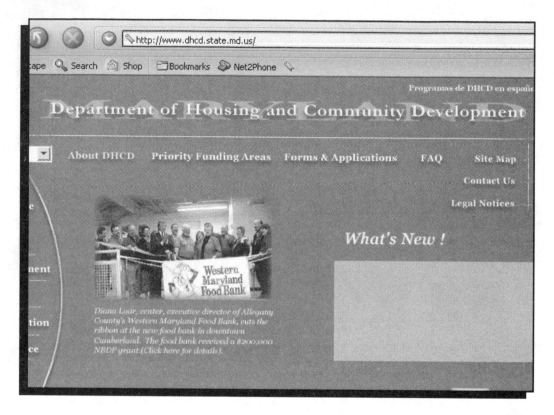

Diana Loar, center, executive director of Allegany County's Western Maryland Food Bank, cuts the ribbon at the new food bank in downtown Cumberland. The food bank received a $200,000 NBDP grant.(Click here for details).

Maryland

Department of Housing and Community Development (DHCD)
Maryland Mortgage Program (MMOP) also known as CDA Mortgage Loans
100 Community Place
Crownsville, MD 21032-2023
(800) 756-0119 or (410) 514-7000
www.dhcd.state.md.us

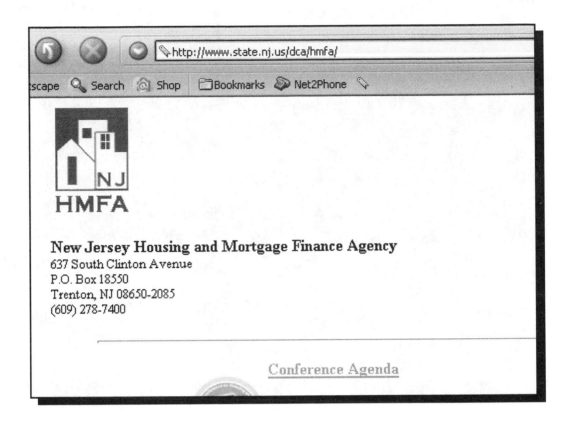

http://www.state.nj.us/dca/hmfa/

tscape   Search   Shop   Bookmarks   Net2Phone

HMFA

New Jersey Housing and Mortgage Finance Agency
637 South Clinton Avenue
P.O. Box 18550
Trenton, NJ 08650-2085
(609) 278-7400

Conference Agenda

New Jersey

New Jersey Housing and Mortgage Finance Agency
Mortgage Opportunity Program (MOP)
637 South Clinton Avenue
PO Box 18550
Trenton NJ 08650-2085
(800) NJ-HOUSE or (609) 278-7400
www.state.nj.us/dca/hmfa/
E-mail: **webmaster@njhmfa.state.nj.us**

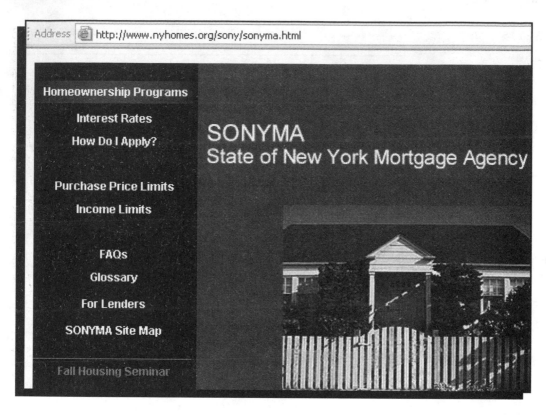

New York

State of New York Mortgage Agency (SONYMA)
641 Lexington Avenue (New York City Office)
New York, NY 10022
1-800-382-HOME (4663) or 212-688-4000
www.nyhomes.org/sony/sonyma.html
E-mail: **CathyO@nyhomes.org**

Oregon

Oregon Department of Veterans' Affairs (ODVA) - Veterans' Home Loan Program
700 Summer Street NE
Salem, OR 97301-1285
(888) 673-8387 or (503) 373-2070
www.odva.state.or.us
E-mail: **orvetshomeloans@odva.state.or.usl**

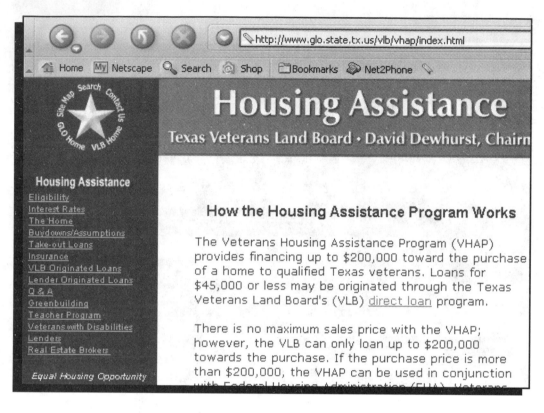

http://www.glo.state.tx.us/vlb/vhap/index.html

Home | My Netscape | Search | Shop | Bookmarks | Net2Phone

Housing Assistance
Texas Veterans Land Board · David Dewhurst, Chairn

Housing Assistance
Eligibility
Interest Rates
The Home
Buydowns/Assumptions
Take-out Loans
Insurance
VLB Originated Loans
Lender Originated Loans
Q & A
Greenbuilding
Teacher Program
Veterans with Disabilities
Lenders
Real Estate Brokers

Equal Housing Opportunity

How the Housing Assistance Program Works

The Veterans Housing Assistance Program (VHAP) provides financing up to $200,000 toward the purchase of a home to qualified Texas veterans. Loans for $45,000 or less may be originated through the Texas Veterans Land Board's (VLB) direct loan program.

There is no maximum sales price with the VHAP; however, the VLB can only loan up to $200,000 towards the purchase. If the purchase price is more than $200,000, the VHAP can be used in conjunction

Texas

Texas Veterans Land Board (VLB) - Veterans' Housing Assistance Program (VHAP)
P.O. Box 12873
Austin, Texas 78711-2873
1-800-252-VETS (8387) or 512/463-9592
www.glo.state.tx.us/vlb/vhap/index.html
E-mail: **vlbinfo@glo.state.tx.us**

http://dva.state.wi.us/

Shop | Bookmarks | Net2Phone

wisconsin.gov   state agencies   subject directory

The **Wisconsin** Department of Veterans Affair:

"Making a difference in the lives o:
Wisconsin veterans and their families."

Eligibility * Benefits * Employment * Museum * News * Links * Forms & Publications
(click here to minimize displayed grap

Wisconsin

Wisconsin Department of Veteran Affairs (WDVA)
Veterans' home mortgage loan program
30 W. Mifflin St.
PO Box 7843
(800) 947-8387 or (608) 266-1311
http://dva.state.wi.us/
E-mail: **wdvaweb@dva.state.wi.us**

Chapter 16

CAL-VET LOANS (CALIFORNIA EXAMPLE)

An additional type of government sponsored financing is available to California veterans. In 1921, the California legislature enacted the California Veteran Farm and Home Purchase Program, which enabled the California Department of Veterans Affairs to provide eligible veterans with affordable financing to purchase home or farm property.

Funding for the program has been provided since the program's inception through the sale of General Obligation Bonds and Revenue Bonds. The bonds have always been repaid by the veterans who participated in the program and thus there has never been any direct cost to California taxpayers. Originally the program was restricted to veterans who were born in California. Due to recent changes the program has been vastly broadened.

I. Eligibility for Cal-Vet Program

The most important change to the new Cal-Vet program is that all veterans who either live in California or who plan to live in California are eligible.

1. No prior residency requirement. Any veteran who moves to California may qualify for a Cal-Vet Loan.

2. Both wartime and peacetime veterans are eligible.

3. Veterans who previously used a Cal-Vet loan may obtain another subject to current eligibility and funding requirements.

4. Loans may be obtained for outright purchase, rehabilitation, or construction.

II. Qualifying and Fees

Cal-Vet now uses the VA underwriting and packaging requirements. Qualifying now follows the VA requirements. Mortgage Insurance is required for loans in which the down-payment is less than 20%. The fee for the mortgage insurance is charged in escrow and may be paid either by the buyer or the seller. There is **no** fee for monthly mortgage insurance. There is no mortgage insurance fee if the down payment is 20% or more or if the veteran has a 10% or more VA Disability rating. The veteran will also have to provide a VA Certificate of Eligibility.

Currently, the maximum loan amount is $359,650 and loans are for a term of thirty years.

Cal-Vet Loans (California Example)

Cal-Vet interest rates tend to be stable with infrequent upward or downward changes. The interest rate is subject to a .5% one-time upward increase at any time during the length of the loan. This feature allows Cal-Vet to enhance the desirability of their bonds to investors. The interest rate was lowered to 4.95% for first time home buyers on January 1, 2005. Veterans who served before 1977 and who apply before thirty years from release from the service qualify for the same rate. All other veterans will be charged 5.5%. Down payments are as low as 2%, if VA mortgage insurance is utilized. If VA mortgage insurance is utilized, the maximum loan amount is $359,650. Private mortgage insurance (PMI) is available with only 3% down. Currently the cost of the insurance is from 1.25 to 3% of the loan amount.

Down payment funds may come from any source other than the seller.

If the veteran needs help in raising down payment funds, Cal-Vet participates with community housing loan agencies to provide loans for this purpose.

III. Broker Origination

Effective March 1, 2001, veterans were allowed to originate their loans through a Certified Cal-Vet Brokerage Firm. Cal-Vet allows certified mortgage brokers to receive a 1% loan origination fee. Brokers who wish to participate in the program must comply with the following requirements:

1. Brokers and loan officers must attend a Cal-Vet lending seminar conducted by Cal-Vet personnel.

2. Cal-Vet will only certify mortgage brokerage companies, not individual loan officers.

3. The company must sign a Cal-Vet Mortgage Broker Agreement and send all their loan officer personnel to Cal-Vet training.

4. Certification is "conditional" until the company has originated at least three Cal-Vet loans within 24 months. At that time certification becomes finalized.

5. Only loan officers who work for a certified mortgage brokerage and have attended Cal-Vet training are eligible to receive the 1% origination fee for a Cal-Vet loan.

6. Previous individual certification obtained before March 1, 2001, is now invalid.

Cal-Vet instituted this new program to insure that participants better understand the program and to insure optimum performance and accountability standards from their brokers.

Further information regarding the Cal-Vet Loan program may be obtained at their website.

Figure 17-1

CALVET BASIC HOME LOAN PACKAGE

This package contains forms and instructions for obtaining a CalVet loan to purchase a home. If you are planning on purchasing an existing home, you will need these forms, plus you will need to download the <u>CalVet Loan Application Forms Package</u> and the <u>CalVet Loan Life and Disability Coverage Package</u>. If you are planning to build a new home, you will also need to download the <u>Construction Loan Supplemental Package</u> of forms and instructions. This supplemental package also contains instructions on which forms from which package you will need.

Before you begin:

Choose the home you wish to purchase. Carefully read the material on the CalVet Home Loan Program on our web site. If you have questions, feel free to send us e-mail at loanserv@cdva.ca.gov or contact the nearest CalVet District Office. A list of CalVet District Offices and the areas they cover is available on CDVA's WWW site at www.cdva.ca.gov/calvet/offices.htm.

<u>Optional, but highly recommended</u>: Download and fill out our Prequalification Form, a FREE service of CalVet. This information will allow us to estimate whether you meet the eligibility qualifications for a loan. Send the completed form to the CalVet District Office for the area where you plan to buy your home.

Please read all of the forms and instructions before submitting your application.

Contents of this package (starred documents must submitted with your CalVet Home Loan application) :

- Form C-13: Thank You for Choosing CalVet

  This pamphlet summarizes the features of the CalVet Home Loan Program.

- Loan Terms

  This document contains the current loan terms, fees and rate.

CalVet Basic Home Loan Package Cover Sheet, page 1 of 3

(5/2004)

CALVET BASIC HOME LOAN PACKAGE

Contents of this package (continued):

- Form A-1T: CalVet Home Loan Application Instruction Sheet

  These instructions explain how to submit the application forms in this package, and what other information you will need to send to CalVet.

- Form A-2: CalVet Home Loan Processing Cycle

  This chart explains how CalVet processes a home loan application. You should read and understand this chart before applying for a CalVet Home Loan.

- Form C-4: Important Notice

  This document provides information about recent changes in the CalVet Home Loan program concerning Loan Guaranties and Loan Processing.

- Form L-10: CalVet Home Loan Funding Sources on front, Safe Harbor Limitations on back

  State and federal law place restrictions on the use of tax exempt bonds. This form explains how these restrictions affect CalVet's ability to make home loans to veterans. This form should be read before you apply for a CalVet Home Loan.

- Form L-8: Special Notice Regarding your CalVet Home Loan Application

  This notice explains Internal Revenue Service limitations placed on funds used for CalVet loans for refinancing a home loan. It also contains the notice required by the California Information Practices Act of 1977 concerning how CalVet may use the information that you supply to us. This notice should be read before you apply for a CalVet Home Loan.

- Address List

  This document contains a list of CalVet offices throughout the state, along address and phone numbers.

CalVet Basic Home Loan Package Cover Sheet, page 2 of 3

(5/2004)

CALVET BASIC HOME LOAN PACKAGE

Contents of this package (continued):

- Form C-14: CalVet Loan Origination Fee/Funding Fee

  This form allows the applicant to notify CalVet concerning their choices for payment of the Loan Origination Fee and CDVA/USDVA Funding Fee.

- Form V-11: Verification of Borrower(s) Name(s)

  This form is used to verify the exact legal name(s) of the loan applicant or applicants.

- Form C-11-3: Borrower's Authorization

  This form is used to authorize CalVet to verify the financial information provided by the borrower.

- Form L-9: Fair Lending Notice

  This notice explains your rights under the Housing Finacial Discrimination Act of 1977. You will asked to sign this form to show that you have read and understood it and return it with your loan application.

- Buyer's Information

  Basic information about yourself, your loan and the property you are purchasing.

- Form A-3: Designation of Agent and General Release

  You may designate another person to act as your agent in connection with the processing of your CalVet Home Loan application. The use of this form is completely optional.

- Form AP-2: Purchaser's Affidavit

  This form contains information that you must provide CalVet as the purchaser of a home. (Includes separate instructions page)

- Form AP-3: Seller's Affidavit

  This form contains information that you must provide CalVet from the person(s) selling a home to you. (Includes separate instructions page)

CalVet Basic Loan Package Cover Sheet, page 3 of 3

(5/2004)

HOME LOANS

THANK YOU FOR CHOOSING CAL-VET

You will be pleased with your selection of CalVet financing for the purchase of your home. CalVet has many features and benefits that will save you money and provide protections for you and your investment. The CalVet district offices, listed on the reverse side of this letter, are ready to assist you in the processing of your loan. If you have a real estate agent, we encourage you to have them be active in the processing of your loan. A form is enclosed to designate them to act on your behalf, however this is optional. The loan may also be processed through a mortgage broker. If you have any questions, please discuss them with your real estate agent or mortgage broker. Of course, you may always call us at the district office.

The CalVet Loan

CalVet is an authorized VA lender and can provide a VA guaranteed loan to eligible veterans. CalVet currently obtains VA guarantees on loans on existing and new homes with a maximum loan amount of $240,000.00. You must be eligible for the full VA loan guarantee entitlement. For applicants or properties that are not eligible for VA loans, the Department obtains private mortgage protection at a cost equivalent to the VA loan guarantee funding fee. All loans are retained for servicing by CalVet. Other features of your CalVet Home Loan include the following:

☞ **A competitive, below market interest rate.**

☞ Maximum loans up to **$333,700** for houses, condominiums and manufactured homes on land, and up to **$125,000** for manufactured homes in rental parks.

☞ A **1%** loan origination fee (collected in escrow)

☞ A **one-time** loan guarantee fee for all loans with down payments of less than 20% which may be paid by the seller or buyer. If the loan is a VA guaranteed loan the funding fee may be financed with the loan. If the loan is guaranteed by the Department's private mortgage protection, the guarantee fee can be financed if you if you make a minimum down payment of 5%of the purchase price.

☞ No down payment for VA guaranteed loans (CalVet/VA), and **3%** for loans using the private mortgage protection program (CalVet97). The loan term is 30 years with shorter terms available upon request.

☞ All CalVet properties are covered by the Department's Disaster Indemnity program which provides **low cost** protection against loss due to floods and earthquakes.

☞ All applicants under age 62 are required to apply for mandatory life insurance, which provides 1 to 5 years (as determined by the insurance carrier) of principal and interest installments in the event of the death of the insured. Supplemental life insurance, disability coverage, and spousal life insurance are available if desired.

C-13 (6/2004-I)   Page 1 of 1

Eligibility

Recent changes in the Military & Veterans Code have made most veterans eligible under state law, including those whose entire active service was during peacetime. Federal law places restrictions on the bond funds used to make CalVet Home Loans. This means that funding may not be available for all veterans who meet the CalVet eligibility criteria. Please review the information sheet *CalVet Funding Sources* (L-10).

Applicants who were released or discharged from active duty under honorable conditions are eligible, as are applicants currently serving on active duty. (Active duty solely for training does not qualify). Applicants must have served at least 90 days on active duty, unless:

- discharged sooner due to service-connected disability, **or**
- eligible to receive a U.S. campaign or expeditionary medal, **or**
- called to active duty from the Reserve or National Guard due to Presidential Order.

Current members of the California National Guard or the US Military Reserves who have served a minimum of one year of a six year obligation are also eligible provided they qualify for Qualified Mortgage Bond (QMB) funding which means they must be first time home buyers or purchase in a Targeted area (see Form L-10).

If your loan will be guaranteed by the USDVA you will be required to submit your VA Certificate of Eligibility (Form 26-8320). If you do not have the Certificate our District Offices can assist you in obtaining one.

For purposes of qualifying for funding with General Obligation bonds or Unrestricted funds, active service during a "war period" is defined as serving at least one day of your active service during one of the following "war periods" (actual service in the area of operations is not required except in the case of the Campaign/Expeditionary Medal).

➢ Gulf War:	August 2, 1990 through a date yet to be determined. (This period includes the Iraq War.)
➢ Vietnam Era:	August 5, 1964 through May 7, 1975.
➢ Korean Period:	June 27, 1950 through January 31, 1955.
➢ World War II:	December 7, 1941 through December 31, 1946.
➢ Campaign/Expeditionary Medal:	Receipt of a campaign or expeditionary medal authorized by the government of the United States

Peacetime veterans must qualify for funding with Revenue Bond funds (see L-10)

For all eligibility questions, please call your local district office:

Bakersfield:	866.653.2507	**Fairfield:**	866.653.2506
Fresno:	866.653.2511	**Redding:**	866.653.2508
Riverside:	800.700.2127	**Sacramento:**	866.653.2510
San Diego:	866.653.2504	**Ventura:**	866.653.2509

You may also reach the California Department of Veterans Affairs at:

Toll Free Automated Information Number: 800.952.5626

Internet Web Site: http://www.cdva.ca.gov

C-13 (6/2004-I)   Page 2 of 2

Chapter 17

Current Loan Terms, Fees & Rates and Funding Source Restrictions (*Effective 6/1/2004*)

Current Rate	Bond Funds Source	Subject to Income & Purchase Price Limits & Federal Recapture	Wartime Service Required	Loan Programs available for
5.10%	Qualified Mortgage Bonds (Revenue Bonds)	Yes (see CDVA FORM L-10)	No	CalVet / VA CalVet 97 CalVet 80/20
4.95%	Qualified Veterans Mortgage Bonds (General Obligation Bonds)[1]	No	Yes	
5.50%	Unrestricted Funds	No	Yes	

Interest rates and loan terms are subject to change. Contact your local CalVet District Office, check our website at *www.cdva.ca.gov,* or call 800-952-5626.

Loan Programs

Loan Program ►	CalVet / VA	CalVet 97	CalVet 80/20
Maximum Loan	$240,000 (including funding fee)	$333,700	$333,700
Property / Program Type	New & Existing Homes (including VA approved Condominiums & PUDs)	New or Existing Homes (including VA approved Condominiums & PUDs) Construction Loans Rehabilitation Loans Mobile Homes on Land Mobile Homes in Parks[1]	New or Existing Homes (including VA approved Condominiums & PUDs) Construction Loans Rehabilitation Loans Mobile Homes on Land Mobile Homes in Parks[1]
Down payment	0%	3%	20%
Funding Fee	1.25% - 3.2%[2] (may be financed)	1.25 – 2% (must be paid in escrow)[3]	None
Loan Origination Fee	1%	1%	1%
Other Requirements	VA Certificate of Eligibility for full entitlement		

[1] Mobile Homes in Parks must be funded with QVMB funds. The maximum loan is $125,000 and the interest rate is 1% higher (5.95%)

[2] The funding fee for CalVet/VA loans is waived for veterans with disability ratings of 10% or higher. The fee is not waived on CalVet97 loans

[3] The funding fee for CalVet 97 loans may be financed when the down payment is 5% or greater.

Loan Terms (6/1/2004)

Cal-Vet Loans (California Example)

CALIFORNIA DEPARTMENT OF VETERANS AFFAIRS
Farm and Home Purchases Division
CALVET LOAN APPLICATION INSTRUCTION SHEET

Thank you for your interest in the CalVet Loan Program. These instructions will assist you in completing your application. Staff in the local district office will be pleased to assist you further. Please feel free to contact us if you have questions. Please note that whenever original documents are requested we will make certified copies and return your originals.

Check when submitted:

1. **Fees**
   a) **Submit your non-refundable $50 APPLICATION FEE** in the form of a guaranteed or personal check made payable to the "Department of Veterans Affairs." ☐
   b) **Appraisal Fee** For existing properties including PUDs, $350; for condominiums, $375; for new houses, never occupied and less than 1-year-old, $400. Please be prepared to pay appraiser directly with certified funds when contacted. If your loan will be VA Guaranteed, we will advise you when to remit a personal check or guaranteed payment for the appropriate fee to CalVet.
   c) **A Loan Origination Fee of 1% of the basic loan, and a funding fee based on your down payment amount will be charged and collected at close of escrow. (See enclosed "Feenote" form)**

2. **Submit your completed UNIFORM RESIDENTIAL LOAN APPLICATION (Form 1003).** Note: PLEASE TYPE OR COMPLETE IN INK . Answer all questions completely Mark questions that are not applicable "N/A." IF YOU ARE MARRIED, YOUR SPOUSE MUST ALSO SIGN THE LOAN APPLICATION. ☐

3. **Submit verification of all income sources listed on your application.** ☐
   a) Submit your most recent pay stub(s) covering at least one full month **(originals)**, plus your W-2s for the past two years, **OR,** if self employed, submit current year-to-date financial statements including a profit and loss statement and balance sheet, and copies of your federal income tax returns (1040 and Schedule C) for the past two years.
   b) Submit verification of other types of income; for example: a *current* copy of your Award Letter for retirement, VA compensation or Social Security, or *current* verification of alimony, child support, interest, or dividends.

4. **Submit original statements for the past two consecutive months** for all accounts holding funds for the down payment or closing costs. ☐

5. **Submit a legible copy of your NOTICE OF SEPARATION FROM ARMED FORCES (form "DD214")**. If this form does not verify your CalVet eligibility, we will request additional military documentation. Original documents will be returned to you after copies have been made. If you are still on active duty and have never received a "DD214," submit a Statement of Service signed by your commanding officer. ☐

6. **If you are applying for a VA Guaranteed loan with CalVet submit your original VA Certificate of Eligibility (Form 26-8320).** If you do not have a Certificate of Eligibility issued by the United States Department of Veterans Affairs please complete the REQUEST FOR DETERMINATION OF ELIGIBILITY (VA Form 26-1880) included in this application package and submit it with your application. Note: Some veterans are not eligible for both CalVet Loans and VA Loan Guaranties. In order to obtain a CalVet Loan you must meet California veteran eligibility requirements. If you are eligible for CalVet and not for a VA Loan Guaranty, CalVet can still fund your loan. ☐

7. **Property Requirements**
   a) **Submit copies of the signed ESCROW INSTRUCTIONS AND SALES AGREEMENT,AND ALL AMENDMENTS, together with the REAL ESTATE TRANSFER DISCLOSURE STATEMENT** covering the proposed transaction, executed by all parties. Include any addendums or counter offers. ☐
   b) Submit two legible copies of a PRELIMINARY REPORT OF TITLE *not more than three months old*, with a plat map covering the property.

8. **DESIGNATION OF AGENT AND GENERAL RELEASE (Form A-3)**. This form is OPTIONAL. Submit it when you wish to have an agent act on your behalf and receive all loan correspondence during the processing of your loan. ☐

9. **Sign and return one copy of the FAIR LENDING NOTICE and WORD OF CAUTION (Form L-9), the BORROWER'S AUTHORIZATION and VERIFICATION OF BORROWER'S NAME Forms**. ☐

10. Read the enclosed brochure on the Life & Disability Insurance Program. All veteran applicants under the age of 62 **must complete the Application for Life & Disability Insurance**. Your spouse *may* apply for optional life insurance by requesting and completing the **Application for Spouse Life Insurance**. ☐
    (Instructions continue on reverse side)

A-1T (5/2004)

☞ **THE FOLLOWING ITEMS MAY BE REQUESTED AFTER LOAN APPROVAL:**

11. **TERMITE REPORT**. If the dwelling you are purchasing is more than *one year old or has ever been occupied*, the department will require a termite report and clearance. The report must not be over *four months old.*

12. **ROOF INSPECTION REPORT**. If the roof on the dwelling you are purchasing is more than *five years old*, a roof inspection completed by a licensed roofer, may be required.

13. **WELL/SEPTIC SYSTEM**. If the dwelling you are purchasing has private water and/or sewage disposal, you may be required to obtain an inspection verifying the adequacy of the systems.

14. **PERMITS/BUILDING CODE COMPLIANCE INSPECTION**. If the dwelling you are purchasing has had additions or substantial remodeling, the department may require copies of building permits or, in some cases, a code compliance inspection and clearance.

15. **SECONDARY FINANCING DOCUMENTS**. If the maximum CalVet loan is not adequate to purchase the property submitted, we may permit secondary financing to assist in the purchase of the property. The combined CalVet loan and secondary financing must not exceed 98% of the appraised value of the property (as determined by the department). If secondary financing is used, you will be required to submit the original signed Deed of Trust, a certified copy of the signed Note, and CalVet's Subordination Agreement, signed by the secondary lender.

    NOTE: CalVet will participate with most Community Housing down payment assistance programs. The 98% financing limit noted above is waived when these programs are used.

16. **CONDOMINIUM/PLANNED UNIT DEVELOPMENT**. If you are purchasing this type of property and the Homeowners' Association of the condominium or planned unit development has not been previously approved by CalVet, you will be required to submit documents governing the development.

17. **MOBILE HOME ON YOUR LAND**. If you are purchasing this type of property, you may be required to place the mobile home on a permanent foundation and furnish a copy of the recorded HCD Form 433 as evidence that this requirement has been completed. You must also obtain your own fire insurance coverage. You will be advised of the required amount of coverage after completion of the appraisal.

18. **MOBILE HOME IN A RENTAL PARK**. *Maximum Loan Amount is $70,000.00. The interest rate will be 1% above the current CalVet rate.* If you are purchasing this type of property, you will also be asked to:

    a) Submit, in writing, the name of the rental park, and the name and phone number of park manager.
    b) Submit a copy of the proposed rental agreement, space number/address, amount of monthly space rental, and map of the park.
    c) Advise whether the mobile home is used and whether the mobile home is already in place on the space. If the mobile home is new, advise when mobile home will be installed on the space.
    d) Submit a copy of the Sales Agreement (if a used mobile home), or a copy of the Purchase Order (if new).
    e) If a used mobile home, submit a Formal Title Search from the Department of Housing and Community Development (HCD).
    f) When the appraisal has been completed, submit a Certificate of Coverage verifying that the mobile home will be insured for the required amount. Also submit verification that a Loss Payable Endorsement, which names the Department of Veterans Affairs as the insured, will be provided in escrow when the loan is funded.
    g) If the mobile home you wish to purchase is more than *ten years old* or has structural modifications, you may be required to obtain a mobile home health and safety inspection from HCD (request HCD form 415).
    h) Provide the name, address, and escrow number of the company handling your escrow. If the escrow company you have chosen is not approved to handle CalVet transactions, your local CalVet district office will advise you.

APPEALS

Persons who disagree or are dissatisfied with actions taken or decisions made regarding their application may appeal to the Division Chief, Farm and Home Purchases Division, P. O. Box 942895, Sacramento, 94295-0001. If the problem is not resolved satisfactorily at that level, it may qualify for an appeal to the California Veterans Board. Further information regarding the appeal procedure is available upon request. Allegations of wrongdoing concerning state-supported veterans benefits programs should be reported to the Inspector General for Veterans Affairs at (877) 533-8772 (toll free).

Loan Processing Cycle

Step 1 Loan application (URLA Form 1003) is received in CalVet office and is reviewed for completeness. (See Loan Application Instruction Sheet for required documents)

Step 2 After an initial review of your eligibility, credit, and income a letter will be sent to you confirming receipt of your application. You will be advised at that time of any additional items or documentation needed, and the appraisal of your property selection will be ordered.

Step 3 Upon receipt of the appraisal it will be reviewed and a loan approval letter will be sent to you or your mortgage broker. This document will list any requirements that must be completed before your loan can be funded. In some cases requirements must be submitted before loan documents can be issued to your escrow holder. Whenever possible, requirements will be collected through the escrow.

Step 4 Your loan package will be forwarded to the Department's Escrow Unit where loan documents and instructions will be forwarded to your local escrow holder. You will be contacted by your escrow holder to sign the CalVet Contract and complete any final purchase requirements.

Step 5 The escrow holder will return the completed loan documents to CalVet and funds will be issued to close the loan.

Step 6 Your first CalVet Loan payment will be due on the first of the month occurring 30 days after closing (for example, if you loan closes on May 15, your first payment would be due on July 1).

A-2 (5/2004)

HOME LOANS

IMPORTANT NOTICE

Loan Guaranty: In order to protect the program from losses should any loan go into default, and to insure that the CalVet loan continues to offer the best possible value to the veterans of our state, the California Department of Veterans Affairs obtains mortgage protection coverage on all loans when the down payment is less than 20% of the purchase price. When the applicant and property are eligible and have their full entitlement remaining, the loan guaranty provided by the United States Department of Veterans Affairs (USDVA) is obtained. In all other cases the Department obtains private mortgage protection. Adding this protection to the CalVet Loan made it possible for us to reduce the cost of the funds that we use, and thereby reduce the interest rate that we charge.

The cost of the guaranty, 1¼ to 3% of the amount of the loan, may be paid by the seller or the veteran applicant at close of escrow, or in the case of the VA loan guaranty, may be financed as part of the loan.

Interest Rate: It is important for applicants to realize that the CalVet loan is <u>not</u> technically a fixed interest rate loan. You will be advised of the rate on your loan shortly after your application is received. The CalVet contract you sign will indicate that the rate may be increased during the loan term by a maximum of one-half of one percent (0.5%). This feature of the loan has been retained in order to enhance the rating received on the bonds sold to fund CalVet loans and thereby make lower interest rates possible. Please inquire further if you are not clear on this important point.

C-4 (5/2004)

FUNDING SOURCES

CalVet Home Loans are funded through the sales of tax-exempt bonds. From the program's beginning in 1921 until 1980, only general obligation bonds were sold to support the program. General obligation bonds are backed by the full faith and credit of the State of California and must be authorized by a vote of the people at a general, statewide election. All general obligation bonds sold to support the CalVet loan program are repaid by CalVet loan holders through the payment of principal and interest on their loans.

Even though the CalVet Home Loan program has been totally self-supporting and no taxpayer funds have been used to repay its bonds, there are state and federal limitations on the amounts of general obligation bonds which may be sold for the program. Because demand for CalVet loans was exceeding the ability to fund with general obligation bonds, legislation was passed which enabled CalVet to sell revenue bonds to supplement general obligation bonds. The first CalVet revenue bonds were sold in 1980. These bonds are also repaid by CalVet loan holders.

Federal laws and regulations resulting from the Mortgage Subsidy Bond Tax Act of 1980, the Deficit Reduction Act of 1984, the Tax Reform Act of 1986, and subsequent amendments, have affected the ways in which all CalVet bond funds may be used. The following paragraphs explain how general obligation bond funds and revenue bond funds may be used to make CalVet loans.

QUALIFIED VETERANS MORTGAGE BOND PROGRAM (GENERAL OBLIGATION BONDS)   ▶ **Veterans with wartime service**

Under federal law, general obligation veterans bonds may be used to fund loans only to veterans who served on active duty prior to January 1, 1977, and who apply within thirty years from their release from active duty. Under state law, set forth in the California Military and Veterans Code, the veteran must have served during a qualifying war period or received an armed forces expeditionary medal or campaign medal awarded by the federal government for the period served. Although unremarried spouses of veterans may qualify for CalVet loans under state laws, federal laws prohibit them from being funded with general obligation bond proceeds.

General obligation bond funds may be used to purchase homes (which include condominiums and planned unit developments), farms, mobile homes on land owned by the applicant and mobile homes in mobile home parks. There are no purchase price restrictions on the properties which can be purchased with general obligation bond funds, nor are there income limitations on the veteran borrower.

QUALIFIED MORTGAGE BOND PROGRAM (REVENUE BONDS)   ▶ **All veterans subject to income and purchase price limits**

If an applicant is an eligible veteran or unremarried spouse of a veteran under provisions of the California Military and Veterans Code, he or she may qualify to receive a loan from revenue bond funds if qualified under one of the following two categories:

1. "First-time home buyer." A first-time home buyer is defined by the federal government as one who has not owned an interest of record in his/her principal place of residence during the three years prior to closing escrow on the revenue bond funded loan. Both the applicant and spouse, if applicable, must qualify as first-time homebuyers.

2. "Targeted area" purchaser. A targeted area is defined by the federal government as an area of low income or chronic economic distress. Each CalVet district office maintains a list and/or map of targeted areas within its service area. Note: When a county has been declared a disaster area by the Federal Emergency Management Administration (FEMA) the entire county may be considered a "targeted area" and the targeted area restrictions apply (first time homebuyer requirement is waived) for a two year period following the date of the declaration.

Properties purchased with revenue bond funds must qualify under purchase price limitations established under guidelines provided by the Internal Revenue Service. The purchase price for non-target areas cannot exceed 90% of the average area purchase price for the statistical area or county in which the property is located. If an applicant is purchasing in a targeted area, the purchase price cannot exceed 120% of the average area purchase price for the statistical area or county in which the property is located. The applicant must also qualify under income limitations which are issued annually by the U. S. Department of Housing and Urban Development. **PURCHASE PRICE AND INCOME LIMTS FOR TARGET AND NON-TARGET AREAS ARE ON THE BACK OF THIS PAGE.**

Revenue bond loans are available only on single-family residences and mobile homes on land owned by the applicant. Single-family residences includes individual units in condominium and planned unit developments.

Purchasers whose loans are funded with revenue bonds <u>may</u> be liable for a federally imposed Recapture Tax if the property being purchased is disposed of (sold) within the first full 9 years following the funding date. This tax is intended to repay the federal government for the benefit of using tax-exempt bonds. There is no Recapture Tax due if the disposition of the property is by reason of the death of the veteran.

The foregoing provisions governing the uses of revenue bonds are dictated by federal laws contained in the Internal Revenue Code.

UNRESTRICTED (PRE-ULLMAN) BOND PROGRAM   ▶ **Veterans with wartime service**

CalVet has a <u>limited amount</u> of funds available for veterans who do not qualify for either General Obligation or Revenue Bonds. Check with your nearest CalVet office for availability of these funds before you commit to the purchase of a property.

L-10 (Rev 5/2004)   Page 1

This chart sets forth the current purchase price limitations and the current income limitations in various areas of the state. **Only loans made with QMB (Revenue Bond) proceeds are subject to these limitations** which are set according to guidelines provided by the federal government. Those administering the CalVet loan program have no discretion regarding these limitations.

AVERAGE AREA PURCHASE PRICE LIMITATIONS – QMB Funded Loans Only (Effective 4/1/2004)

STATISTICAL AREA or COUNTY	NON-TARGETED AREAS New	NON-TARGETED AREAS Existing	TARGETED AREAS New	TARGETED AREAS Existing
Amador County	$196,875	$196,875	$ NA	$ NA
Chico MSA (Butte Co.)	208,687	208,687	255,062	255,062
Fresno MSA (Fresno Co.)	193,068	193,068	235,973	235,973
Humbolt County	191,250	191,250	233,750	233,750
Inyo County	318,375	318,375	NA	NA
Los Angeles-Long Beach-Santa Ana MSA (Los Angeles & Orange Cos.)	448,259	370,152	547,872	452,409
* Los Angeles County	**547,872**	**452,409**	**547,872**	**452,409**
Madera MSA	193,068	193,068	235,973	235,973
Mendocino County	281,250	281,250	343,750	343,750
Merced MSA	208,125	208,125	254,375	254,375
Modesto MSA (Stanislaus Co.)	261,427	261,427	319,522	319,522
Mono County	309,799	309,799	NA	NA
Napa MSA	483,846	420,836	NA	NA
Nevada County	289,332	322,991	NA	NA
* Oxnard-Thousand Oaks-Ventura MSA (Ventura Co.)	**618,700**	**444,167**	**618,700**	**444,167**
Redding MSA (Shasta Co.)	205,282	205,282	250,901	250,901
* Riverside-San Bernardino-Ontario MSA (Riverside & San Bernardino Cos.)	**353,375**	**353,375**	**353,375**	**353,375**
Sacramento-Arden-Arcade-Roseville MSA				
(Sacramento, El Dorado, Placer, & Yolo Cos.)	332,466	332,466	406,347	406,347
Salinas MSA (Monterey Co.)	467,771	431,859	571,720	527,827
* San Diego-Carlsbad-San Marcos MSA (San Diego Co.)	**534,805**	**467,217**	**534,805**	**467,217**
San Francisco-Oakland-Fremont MSA				
(Alameda, Contra Costa, Marin, San Francisco & San Mateo Cos.)	488,614	454,271	597,195	555,220
San Jose-Sunnyvale-Santa Clara MSA (Santa Clara & San Benito Cos.)	561,195	458,190	685,906	560,010
* San Luis Obispo- Paso Robles MSA (San Luis Obispo Co.)	**474,089**	**461,195**	**474,089**	**461,195**
Santa Barbara-Santa Maria-Goleta MSA (Santa Barbara Co.)	343,799	343,799	420,198	420,198
Santa Cruz-Watsonville MSA (Santa Cruz Co.)	399,959	474,656	NA	NA
Santa Rosa-Petaluma MSA (Sonoma Co.)	408,566	365,135	NA	NA
Stockton MSA (San Joaquin Co.)	309,799	309,799	378,644	378,644
Tuolumne County	219,375	219,375	NA	NA
Vallejo-Fairfield MSA (Solano Cos.)	343,799	343,799	NA	NA
Yuba City-Marysville MSA (Sutter & Yuba Cos.)	247,500	247,500	302,500	302,500
ALL OTHER AREAS				
(*Alpine, Calaveras, Colusa, Del Norte, Glenn,* Imperial, Kern, Kings, Lake, *Lassen, Mariposa, Modoc, Plumas, Sierra, Siskiyou, Tehama,* Trinity, & Tulare Cos.)	$189,682	$189,682	$231,833	$231,833

* Counties in bold are subject to disaster area declarations which allow target area limits to be applied to all applications. NA indicates that there are no target areas in that MSA or County. Counties in *Italics* in All Other Areas also do not have target areas.

FAMILY INCOME LIMITATIONS
(For counties identified above as disaster areas use Targeted Area limits.)

County	NON-TARGETED 1 & 2 Person	NON-TARGETED 3+ Person	TARGETED 1 & 2 Person	TARGETED 3+ Person	County	NON-TARGETED 1 & 2 Person	NON-TARGETED 3+ Person	TARGETED 1 & 2 Person	TARGETED 3+ Person
Alameda	$82,800	$95,220	$99,360	115,920	San Francisco	$113,100	$130,065	$135,720	$158,340
Contra Costa	$82,800	$95,220	$99,360	115,920	San Mateo	$113,100	$130,065	$135,720	$158,340
El Dorado	$64,100	$73,715	$76,920	$89,740	Santa Barbara	$64,700	$74,405	$77,640	$90,580
Marin	$113,100	$130,065	$135,720	$158,340	Santa Clara	$106,100	$122,015	$127,320	$148,540
Napa	$73,900	$84,985	$88,680	103,460	Santa Cruz	$78,200	$89,930	$93,840	$109,480
Nevada	$63,600	$73,140	$76,320	$89,040	Solano	$73,900	$84,985	$88,680	$103,460
Orange	$75,600	$86,940	$90,720	105,840	Sonoma	$74,600	$85,790	$89,520	$104,440
Placer	$64,100	$73,715	$76,920	$89,740	Ventura	$77,400	$89,010	$92,880	$108,360
Sacramento	$64,100	$73,715	$76,920	$89,740	ALL OTHER COUNTIES	$62,500	$71,875	$75,000	$87,500
San Benito	$71,900	$82,685	$86,280	$100,660					
San Diego	$68,500	$78,775	$82,200	95,900					

CALIFORNIA DEPARTMENT OF VETERANS AFFAIRS
Farm and Home Purchases Division

SPECIAL NOTICE REGARDING YOUR CALVET LOAN APPLICATION

CalVet loans are funded with proceeds from the sales of both state and federal tax-exempt bonds, at no cost to California taxpayers. Since we finance the program with these bonds, both state and federal laws govern the CalVet loan program.

Except in certain limited circumstances, CalVet is <u>prohibited</u> from refinancing existing loans on real property. Internal Revenue Service regulations <u>prohibit</u> refinancing except for "construction period loans, bridge loans, or similar temporary initial financing." The regulations define temporary initial financing as "any financing which has a term of twenty-four months or less." The 24 months commences with the date stated on the note and deed of trust and ends with the date the loan is due and payable in full. There must be no provisions for extension or renewal. A construction loan should have as short a term as possible which is reasonably consistent with the anticipated construction period, and should not be converted to an interim loan with a term in excess of 24 months.

☞   YOU MUST FILE YOUR CALVET LOAN APPLICATION BEFORE OBTAINING AN INTEREST OF RECORD IN THE PROPERTY YOU WISH TO PURCHASE WITH CALVET FUNDS.

☞   IF YOU INTEND TO OBTAIN TEMPORARY FINANCING, SHOW THIS NOTICE TO YOUR LENDER TO ASSURE THAT YOUR LOAN COMPLIES WITH ALL STATE AND FEDERAL REGULATIONS.

CalVet cannot and will not refinance an existing loan which does not comply with these regulations.

INFORMATION

The California Information Practices Act of 1977 requires that all applicants be informed of the purposes and uses to be made of information solicited. The following is furnished to explain the reasons why information is requested and the general uses to which that information may be put.

AUTHORITY: The California Department of Veterans Affairs is authorized to request information under the authority of the Military and Veterans Code of the State of California, particularly Section 987.56.

PURPOSE: The information requested is considered relevant and necessary to determine entitlement to and qualification for the benefit for which you are applying.

USES: The information will be used in your best interest in determining eligibility for the maximum benefits allowable by law. There is no presently known or foreseeable interagency or intergovernmental transfer which may be made of the information. However, the information may be transferred to a governmental entity when required by state or federal law, and certain other disclosures or transfers may be made as permitted by Section 1798.24 of the California Civil Code.

EFFECTS OF NOT PROVIDING INFORMATION: Disclosure of the information is voluntary. No penalty will be imposed for failure to respond. However, your qualifications for the benefit requested must then be made on the basis of the available evidence of record. This may result in a delay in the processing of the application, receipt of less than the maximum benefit, or deferral or complete disallowance of your loan request. Failure to provide information in connection with the benefit currently being sought will have no detrimental effect on any other benefit to which you are entitled.

RIGHT OF REVIEW: Individuals have the right of access to records containing personal information on them at all times during regular office hours of the department.

DEPARTMENT OFFICIAL RESPONSIBLE FOR INFORMATION MAINTENANCE: District Office Manager

(District Office Address and Phone Number)

L-8 (5/2004)

HOME LOANS

The California Department of Veterans Affairs currently has offices in the following locations. It is suggested that you call the nearest office to confirm office hours before visiting. Any of our offices will be pleased to answer your questions and provide loan application materials. All numbers listed are <u>toll free</u>.

Fresno:	**866.653.2511**	**Bakersfield:**	**866-653-2507**
1752 E. Bullard Ave., Suite 101		5500 Ming Avenue, Suite 155	
93710	Fresno@cdva.ca.gov	93309	Bakersfield@cdva.ca.gov
Fairfield:	**866.653.2506**	**Santa Clara:**	**866.653.2506**
370 Chadbourne Road, 2d Floor		68 North Winchester Boulevard	
94534	Fairfield@cdva.ca.gov	95050	SantaClara@cdva.ca.gov
Sacramento:	**866-653-2510**	**Redding:**	**866-653-2508**
1227 O Street, 4th Floor		930 Executive Way, Suite 125,	
95814	Sacramento@cdva.ca.gov	96002	Redding@cdva.ca.gov
San Diego:	**866.653.2504**	**Riverside:**	**800.700.2127**
Camino del Rio South, Ste. 112		1770 Iowa Avenue, Suite 260	
92108	SanDiego@cdva.ca.gov	92507	Riverside@cdva.ca.gov
Ventura:	**866.653.2509**		
1000 South Hill Road, Suite 112			
93003	Ventura@cdva.ca.gov		

You may also reach the California Department of Veterans Affairs at:

California Department of Veterans Affairs
P.O. Box 942895
Sacramento, CA 94295-0001

Toll Free Information Number: 800.952.5626

Internet Web Site: www.cdva.ca.gov
General Information Email address: loanserv@.cdva.ca.gov

ADDRESS LIST (6/2004)

HOME LOANS

Interest Rate / Loan Origination Fee / Funding Fee

I understand that CalVet has multiple interest rates, and that the rate on my loan will be "locked in" at the interest rate in effect for the funding source that I qualify for as of the date my application is received. If the interest rate is reduced during processing and prior to funding of my loan, I will receive the benefit of the reduced rate. I also understand that the CalVet interest rate is a variable rate that can be increased by no more than one half of one percent (0.5%) over the term of the loan. I also understand that a 1% Loan Origination Fee will be charged, and that if my loan amount exceeds 80% of the sales price, I will be charged a funding fee. This funding fee will be charged regardless of whether or not the California Department of Veterans Affairs (CDVA) purchases a guaranty from USDVA or obtains mortgage protection from another source.

I intend to pay these fees as follows:

Application Fee - $50   Must be submitted with application.

Loan Origination Fee of 1% (of loan amount) to be:

❑ Paid in escrow by me

❑ Paid in escrow by seller*

CDVA/USDVA Funding Fee (see table) to be:

❑ Paid in escrow by me

❑ Paid in escrow by seller*

❑ Added to my loan (VA Loans only)

Down payment	Funding Fee ▶
20% or more	N/A
10% to 19%	1.25%
5% to 9%	1.5%
2% to 4%	2%

VA Loan guarantees are currently obtained only on CalVet loans on existing homes where the loan amount does not exceed $203,000 including the funding fee if financed. The applicant must be eligible for the full VA guaranty entitlement. The funding fee for VA loans is waived for veterans who have a service connected disability of 10% or greater. For veterans who have previously used their VA guaranty entitlement, the funding fee is increased to 3% for subsequent guaranties. Neither of these exceptions apply to CalVet loans using private mortgage protection.

This fee is a percentage of the <u>loan amount</u> and will be used by CDVA to purchase a loan guarantee from VA, or if the VA guarantee cannot be obtained, to secure mortgage protection for your loan from a private mortgage insurance provider. **This is a one time charge and does not affect your interest rate or monthly payment (unless you choose to finance the VA fee with your loan.)**

Veteran Applicant: _____   **Date:** _____

Seller: _____   **Date:** _____

*Seller must sign if you are indicating above that fees will be paid by the seller.

C-14 (5/2004)

HOME LOANS

Verification of Borrower(s) Name(s)

I understand and agree that I will take title as my name is shown below, regardless of the way my name is shown or signed on my loan application. I am aware that all legal documents will carry my name exactly as shown below and understand that I will be required to sign exactly as it is shown below.

_____   _____

Print Name (Veteran)   Signature

_____   _____

Print Name (Spouse)   Signature

V-11 (5/2004)

BORROWER'S AUTHORIZATION

We hereby give our consent to have CalVet Home Loans, or any credit reporting bureau which it may designate, obtain any and all credit information concerning our employment, checking and/or savings accounts, obligations, and all other credit matters which they may require in connection with our application for a loan and any quality control review of such loan. This form may be reproduced and photocopied and a copy shall be effective as the original which we have signed.

_____   _____
Signature of Veteran Applicant   Date   Signature of Spouse   Date

I hereby certify this to be a true and correct copy of the original.

_____
CalVet Home Loans   Date

Privacy Act Notice: This information is to be used by the agency collecting it or it's assignees in determining whether you qualify as a prospective mortgagor under its program. It will not be disclosed outside the agency except as required and permitted by law. You do not have to provide this information, but if you do not, you application for approval as a prospective borrower may be delayed or rejected. The information requested in this form is authorized by Title 38, USC, Chapter 37.

C-11-3 (5/2004)

HOME LOANS

THE HOUSING FINANCIAL DISCRIMINATION ACT OF 1977
(Pursuant to Title 21, California Code of Regulations, Section 7114)

FAIR LENDING NOTICE

It is illegal to discriminate in the provision of or in the availability of financial assistance because of the consideration of:

1. Trends, characteristics or conditions in the neighborhood or geographic area surrounding a housing accommodation, unless the financial institution can demonstrate in the particular case that such consideration is required to avoid an unsafe and unsound business practice; or

2. Race, color, religion, sex, marital status, national origin or ancestry.

It is illegal to consider the racial, ethnic, religious or national origin composition of a neighborhood or geographic area surrounding a housing accommodation or whether or not such composition is undergoing change, or is expected to undergo change, in appraising a housing accommodation or in determining whether or not, or under what terms and conditions, to provide financial assistance.

These provisions govern financial assistance for the purpose of the purchase, construction, rehabilitation or refinancing of one-to four-unit family residences occupied by the owner and for the purpose of the home improvement of any one-to four-unit family residence.

If you have questions about your rights, or if you wish to file a complaint, contact the management of this financial institution or the:

> Office of the Secretary
> Business, Transportation and Housing Agency
> 1120 N Street
> Sacramento, CA 95814

<u>Acknowledgment of receipt</u>

I (we) received a copy of this notice.

_____   _____
Signature of Veteran Applicant   Date   Signature of Spouse   Date

WORD OF CAUTION

The processing of your home loan is a detailed process and requires accurate information. Please keep in mind that this process may take longer than expected and requires final updating prior to the funding of your loan. Because of these last minute updates, it is imperative that the information you give us, and subsequently verified by our office, does not change appreciably. Therefore, please continue to make your mortgage payments and all other financial obligations as usual until the close of escrow.

Please notify us before you do any of the following, or please delay doing the following if at all possible:

1) Change employment or department.
2) Move any funds from one bank account to another or close an existing account.
3) Make any large purchases such as an automobile, furniture, or high cost items.

All of the above situations might be dealt with appropriately if we know about the changes prior to their occurance. Failure to notify us about any significant changes to your original loan file, or any material fact regarding your financial condition could seriously effect the outcome of your loan transaction. **YOUR LOAN FILE MAY BE UPDATED PRIOR TO THE CLOSE OF ESCROW!**

_____   _____
Signature of Veteran Applicant   Date   Signature of Spouse   Date

L-9 (5/2004)

Cal-Vet Loans (California Example)

BUYERS INFORMATION FORM
Please Complete

1. Veteran's birthday_____Spouse's birthday_____Date Married_____.

2. Have you had a CalVet loan before?   Yes_____ No_____.

   Have you had a VA loan before?   Yes_____ No_____.

   If yes to either of the above, please complete the following:
   Loan number_____.
   Date loan was paid off_____.
   Location of property_____.

3. Are you buying a new home that has never been previously occupied?   Yes_____ No_____.

   If not already completed, when is the estimated completion date? _____.

4. Is the property you are purchasing a Condominium or is it in a Planned Unit Development (PUD)?
   If YES, circle Condo or PUD   No_____.

   If yes, how much are the monthly dues and what is the name of the Association?
   Association Name_____ $ _____per mo.

   If yes, is the hazard insurance on the unit a master policy carried through the Association?
   Yes_____ No_____.

5. Is this loan to purchase a mobile home in a rental park?   Yes_____ No_____.

   If yes, what is the monthly space rental? $_____

6. Are you currently in receipt of or eligible to receive VA Compensation?
   Yes_____ No_____.   If yes, VA Case #_____.

7. In order to gain access to the home you are buying the appraiser should contact:

   _____ at phone # (___)_____.

BUYER'S INFORMATION (5/2004)

CALIFORNIA DEPARTMENT OF VETERANS AFFAIRS
Division of Farm and Home Purchases

DESIGNATION OF AGENT
AND
GENERAL RELEASE

I hereby appoint and designate _____ as my
agent for all purposes in connection with the processing of my application for a CalVet Loan to include, but not be limited to, working with
the district office, the division, and the department to provide and obtain any and all information necessary to complete the processing of my
loan and the purchase of my farm or home.

I understand that if the person or firm designated by me is licensed as a real estate agent or broker, they may be the agent or
broker for the seller of the property. I also understand that the department assumes no responsibility for and makes no recommendations as
to the acts, conduct, duties, qualifications, or status of the person or firm I have so designated. Nevertheless, I so designate said person or
firm freely and voluntarily, on my own accord, with full knowledge of all necessary facts.

I authorize the department to obtain from and disclose or release to my designated agent any and all information, whether
confidential, personal, or otherwise, which may be desirable or necessary in the processing and completion of my CalVet loan, and this
authorization and consent shalt be effective from the date hereof to the date my CalVet Loan is completed or made or is otherwise
terminated. I understand that all communications and contacts concerning my Cat-Vet Loan processing will be made through or with my
designated agent, and that it is the agent's responsibility to keep me informed and to provide me with copies of all correspondence and
documents.

This authorization and designation may be revoked only by another writing signed by me, and such revocation shalt be effective
only when received by the department.

IN CONSIDERATION of the department's acceptance of this designation and the terms thereof, the undersigned hereby release
the State of California, the Department of Veterans Affairs of the State of California, and their assigns, employees, officers, and successors,
from any and all actions, claims, demands, liability, or suits of any kind, arising out of or by reason of this designation, the department's
working with the designated agent pursuant hereto, and the obtaining or the disclosure or release of any and all information pursuant to this
designation.

The undersigned agree, in further consideration hereof, that this Release shalt apply to all unknown and unanticipated claims arising out of
said matters, as welt as to those now known, if any, and expressly waive the provisions of Section 1542 of the California Civil Code, which
reads as follows: "A general release does not extend to claims which the creditor does not know or suspect to exist in his favor at the time of
executing the release, which if known by him must have materially affected his settlement with the debtor."

The undersigned declare that the terms of this designation and release have been read comptetely by them, and that the terms are fully
understood and freely and voluntarily accepted by them.

IN WITNESS WHEREOF, the undersigned have executed this Designation of Agent and General Release

this _____ day of _____ , _____ .

_____   _____
Veteran Applicant   Applicant's Spouse

ACCEPTANCE BY AGENT

I hereby accept the above designation as agent, and assume all responsibilities incident thereto

Dated: _____ , _____ .

_____   _____
Signature of Agent   Name of Business

_____   _____
Name of Agent (Type or Print)   Business Address

_____   _____
Telephone Number   City   Zip

A-3 (Rev 5/2004)

Cal-Vet Loans (California Example)

CALIFORNIA DEPARTMENT OF VETERANS AFFAIRS
Division of Farm and Home Purchases

PURCHASER'S AFFIDAVIT
(CalVet Loan Contract)

*As an applicant(s) for a CalVet loan, you must read this affidavit carefully, **INCLUDING THE INSTRUCTIONS ON THE REVERSE SIDE**, and complete the affidavit (print in ink or type) and sign it under penalty of perjury. By doing so, you certify and declare that all statements in it are true. (See instructions on reverse)*

I (We) CERTIFY AND DECLARE THAT:

1. The home being purchased is intended for use as my (our) principal residence and will be occupied as such within 60 days after the CalVet loan is funded and will be maintained as my (our) principal residence for the duration of the CalVet contract. I (We) do not intend to and have not entered into any agreement to rent or sell the home.

2. I (We) will not allow the CalVet loan to be assumed by someone else without the prior written consent of the California Department of Veterans Affairs.

3. I (We) will not use the home in a business or trade or for any other commercial purpose, or as an investment property.

4. I (We) will not use the home as a recreational property, or as a vacation or "weekend" home.

5. I (We) do not have and have not had previous financing for the house, whether paid in full or not, except for a construction loan or other temporary interim financing with a term of 24 months or less.

6. I (We) have not made and will not make an agreement to purchase the department's bonds, directly or indirectly, in an amount related to the amount of the CalVet loan.

7. The land being purchased with the home is required to maintain the basic livability of the residence, and will not provide a source of income.

8. The home is ☐ is not ☐ permanently attached to the lot.

9. I (We) ☐ have ☐ have not had an ownership interest in a home used as my (our) principal residence during the three years immediately prior to the closing of the CalVet loan.

10. I (We) ☐ have filed ☐ have not filed and were not required to file federal income tax returns for the three years preceding the loan.

11. Borrower's name _____ Spouse's name _____

12. The number of full time members of the household who will reside in the property, including all children anticipated to reside in the residence at least 50% of the time, and including any live-in attendants is _____.

13. The home to be financed is located at _____

14. The "acquisition cost" of the home is $ _____

15. My (our) "annualized gross income" is $ _____

I (we) hereby certify and declare under penalty of perjury under the laws of the United States and the State of California that the foregoing is true and correct.

Executed this _____ day of _____, 20___, in the City of _____,
County of _____, State of California.

Signed: _____   Signed: _____
        Loan Applicant   Applicant's Spouse

AP-2 (Rev. 5/2004)

PURCHASER'S AFFIDAVIT
(CalVet Loan Contract)
Instructions

#9. The term "*present ownership interest*" includes, in addition to outright ownership, the following types of interests:
  a. A joint tenancy, tenancy in common, tenancy by the entirety, or community property interest.
  b. The interest of a tenant-shareholder in a stock cooperative or similar interest.
  c. A Life Estate
  d. An interest under an installment land contract granting current possession of the house with legal title to follow at a later date.
  e. Any of the above interests, including outright ownership, held in trust for you.

#10 *Present ownership interest*" **does not** include the following types of interest:
  a. A remainder interest (an interest you would have only upon termination of an interest granted by someone else to another person).
  b. A lease without and option to purchase
  c. A mere expectancy to inherit an interest.
  d. An interest created as the purchaser in a marketing contract (any interest you might acquire upon the signing of a real estate deposit receipt or similar contract, where you have not completed the purchase).
  e. An interest in any property not used as your personal residence during the previous three years.

#12 This information is necessary to determine if you qualify under the small family income limits or the higher large family income limits. For this purpose, the number of "*full time members of the household who will reside in the property*" is not the same as the number of dependents for income tax purposes, and may include individuals who will reside in the home and may have separate incomes that cannot be included as qualifying income, and do not have to be included in "*annualized gross income*". "*Full time members of the household*" includes the following:
  a. All adults who will reside in the home.
  b. Children, including children expected to be born to pregnant women, children in the process of being adopted, children whose custody is being obtained by an adult member of the household, children subject to a joint custody agreement who will live in the home at least 50% of the time, and children who are temporarily absent due to a custody order.
  c. Live-in attendants

  "*Full time members of the household*" does not include the following:
  a. Adult children on active military duty
  b. Permanently institutionalized family members
  c. Visitors

#14 "*Acquisition Cost*" includes the following costs:
  a. All amounts paid in cash or in any other way as the purchase price of the house.
  b. If the house is incomplete, the reasonable cost of completing the house.
  c. Any additional amounts paid for fixtures (items permanently affixed to the house), including light fixtures and wall to wall carpeting.

  "*Acquisition Cost*" does not include the following costs:
  a. Settlement costs such as title and transfer costs, title insurance premiums, and survey fees.
  b. Financing costs such as credit report fees, legal fees, appraisal expenses, and funding fees.
  c. The cost of the lot upon which you are building your home if you have owned the lot for at least two years prior to the start of construction.
  d. The amount of any lien or assessment to which the home is subject.

#15 "*Annualized gross income*" is the gross monthly income multiplied by 12, of those individuals who will both reside in the property <u>and</u> be liable on the loan. It includes:
  a. Gross pay, overtime pay, bonuses, military allowances and income from part-time employment.
  b. Pension checks and US Department of Veterans Affairs compensation.
  c. Dividends, interest, net rental income, and any additional income from business activities or investments.
  d. Other income such as alimony, child support, public assistance, sick pay, social security benefits, unemployment compensation, and income from trusts.

AP-2 (Rev. 5/2004)

Cal-Vet Loans (California Example)

CALIFORNIA DEPARTMENT OF VETERANS AFFAIRS
Division of Farm and Home Purchases

SELLER'S AFFIDAVIT
(Cal-Vet Loan Contract)

The purpose of this affidavit is to determine the acquisition cost of the house being purchased with Cal-Vet financing. Please read this affidavit carefully, including the INSTRUCTIONS FOR SELLER'S AFFIDAVIT printed on the reverse side. Fill in (print in ink or type) the appropriate section of this affidavit (1., 2., or 3.). Sign the affidavit under penalty of perjury. By doing so, you certify and declare that all the statements in it are true.

YOU CERTIFY AND DECLARE THAT:
(check appropriate box)

1. A. **You are the seller(s) of the house located at** _____,
which is being purchased with Cal-Vet financing.   Address

   B. You are selling the house to _____ and
                                                      Loan Applicant

   _____ .
                 Applicant's Spouse

   C. The total "acquisition cost" of the house is $_____. (See Instructions)

2. A. **You are the construction / interim lender for the house** located at _____
                                                                                                     Address
   _____, which is being purchased with Cal-Vet financing.
                        Address

   B. You have lent interim funds to purchase the above house to _____
                                                                                               Loan Applicant

   and _____ .
                 Applicant's Spouse

   C. The total "acquisition cost" of the house is $_____ (See Instructions)

3. A. **You are the Loan Applicant (and spouse).** I (We), _____
                                                                                       Loan Applicant
   and _____ , own the land located at _____
                 Applicant's Spouse   Address
   _____ . on which I (we) are building the house
                 Address
   which is to be purchased with Cal-Vet financing upon completion.

   B. The total 'acquisition cost" of the house is $ _____ (See Instructions)

I (we) hereby certify and declare under penalty of perjury under the laws of the United States and the State of California that the foregoing is true and correct.

Executed this _____ day of _____, _____, In the City of _____ ,

County of _____ , State of California.

Signed: _____
                         Seller's Name

_____
            Title (if applicable)

Signed: _____
                         Seller's Name

_____
            Title (if applicable)

_____
      Name of Company (if applicable)

AP-3 (Rev 5/2004)

473

INSTRUCTIONS FOR SELLER'S AFFIDAVIT

1. Decide which situation best describes our role in this transaction. Check the appropriate box (either 1, 2, or 3). Fill in the blanks for your situation only.

2. You need to calculate and state the "acquisition cost" of the house being sold to the loan applicant or being built by the loan applicant.

    "Acquisition cost" includes the following types of costs:

    a. All amounts paid, in cash or in any other way, as the purchase price of the house.

    b. If the house is incomplete, "acquisition cost" also includes the reasonable cost of completing the house.

    c. An additional amounts paid for fixtures, such as light fixtures, curtain rods, wall-to-wall carpeting and similar items.

    "Acquisition cost" does not include these types of costs:

    a. Settlement costs, such as title and transfer costs, title insurance premiums, and survey fees.

    b. Financing costs, such as credit reference fees, legal fees, appraisal expenses and 'points' which are paid by the loan applicant.

    c. The value of work done by the loan applicant and family in completing the house.

    d. The cost of the lot upon which the loan applicant is building your house, if the loan applicant and/or spouse owned the lot for at least two years before construction.

3. Sign the affidavit under penalty of perjury.

AP-3 (Rev 5/2004)

Prequalification Information

Veteran's Name: _____

Veteran's Age: _____

Soc. Sec.# _____

Active Duty Service Dates:

From: _____ To: _____

Spouse's Name: _____

Soc. Sec.# _____

No. of Children (dependents): _____

Address: _____

_____

Daytime Phone: _____

Evening Phone: _____

Previous Cal-Vet loan? ____ Yes ____ No

V.A. loan? ____ Yes ____ No ____ Paid
****

Veteran's Employment: _____

(Gross Monthly)
Income: _____ Years* _____

Spouse's Employment: _____

(Gross Monthly)
Income: _____ Years* _____

Other Income:
Source: _____ Amount: _____

Source: _____ Amount: _____

*If on the job less than 2 years, indicate previous employment: _____

VA Disability rating? ____ Yes ____ No
_____ %
****

Monthly Long-term Debts (don't include any which will pay off within 10 months. Exclude rent or house payments)

Type	Amount Owed	Monthly Pmt.

Do you pay child support? ____ Yes ____ No

Amount: $ _____

Totals:
(Include monthly payments on long-term debts and child support, if any)

Current rent/housecost: _____

Do you have a loan amount in mind?

$ _____ What area/county? _____

Source of funds for the down payment: _____

Any known credit problems? _____

****

Home type (house, condo, mobile)? _____

First-time home Buyer? ____ Yes ____ No

Veteran Signature: _____

Spouse Signature: _____

Date: _____
****

Are you currently working with a Real Estate Agent?

Name: _____

Company: _____

Phone Number: _____

Figure 17-2

CAL-VET LOAN APPLICATION FORMS PACKAGE

This package contains forms and instructions for obtaining a Cal-Vet loan to purchase a home. If you are planning on purchasing an existing home, you will need these forms, plus you will need to download the <u>Cal-Vet Basic Home Loan Package</u> and the <u>Cal-Vet Loan Life and Disability Coverage Package</u>. If you are planning to build a new home, you will *also* need to download the <u>Construction Loan Supplemental Package</u> of forms and instructions. This supplemental package also contains instructions on which forms from which package you will need.

Before you begin:

If you have not already done so, download and read the Cal-Vet Basic Home Loan Package. Carefully read the material on the Cal-Vet Home Loan Program on our web site. Choose the home you wish to purchase. If you have questions, feel free to send us e-mail or contact the nearest Cal-Vet District Office. A list of Cal-Vet District Offices and the areas they cover is available on CDVA's WWW site at www.ns.net/cadva/calvet/offices.htm.

<u>Optional, but highly recommended</u>: Download and fill out our Prequalification Form, a FREE service of Cal-Vet. This information will allow us to estimate whether you meet the eligibility qualifications for a loan. Send the completed form to the Cal-Vet District Office for the area where you plan to buy your home.

Please read all of the forms and instructions before submitting your application.

Contents of this package:

● VA Form 26-1880: Request for Determination of Eligibility

If you do not have a Certificate of Eligibility issued by the United States Department of Veterans Affairs (VA Form 26-8320) please complete this form and submit it with your application.

● Form 1003: Uniform Residential Loan Application

This is the actual loan application.

Cal-Vet Loan Application Forms Package Cover Sheet, page 1 of 1

Cal-Vet Loans (California Example)

OMB Approved No. 2900-0086
Respondent Burden: 15 minutes

VA Department of Veterans Affairs

REQUEST FOR A CERTIFICATE OF ELIGIBILITY

TO

Department of Veterans Affairs
Attn: Loan Guaranty Division

NOTE: Please read information on reverse before completing this form. If additional space is required, attach a separate sheet.

1. FIRST-MIDDLE-LAST NAME OF VETERAN	2. DATE OF BIRTH	3. VETERAN'S DAYTIME TELEPHONE NO. ( )

4. ADDRESS OF VETERAN (No., street or rural route, city or P.O., State and ZIP Code)	5. MAIL CERTIFICATE OF ELIGIBILITY TO: (Complete ONLY if the Certificate is to be mailed to an address different from the one listed in Item 4)

6. MILITARY SERVICE DATA (ATTACH PROOF OF SERVICE - SEE PARAGRAPH "D" ON REVERSE)

A. ITEM	B. PERIODS OF ACTIVE SERVICE DATE FROM	DATE TO	C. NAME (Show your name exactly as it appears on your separation papers or Statement of Service	D. SOCIAL SECURITY NUMBER	E. SERVICE NUMBER (If different from Social Security No.)	F. BRANCH OF SERVICE
1.						
2.						
3.						
4.						

7A. WERE YOU DISCHARGED, RETIRED OR SEPARATED FROM SERVICE BECAUSE OF DISABILITY OR DO YOU NOW HAVE ANY SERVICE-CONNECTED DISABILITIES?

☐ YES ☐ NO (If "Yes," complete Item 7B)

7B. VA CLAIM FILE NUMBER

C-

8. PREVIOUS VA LOANS (Must answer N/A if no previous VA home loan. DO NOT LEAVE BLANK)

A. ITEM	B. TYPE (Home, Refinance, Manufactured Home, or Direct)	C. ADDRESS OF PROPERTY	D. DATE OF LOAN	E. DO YOU STILL OWN THE PROPERTY? (YES/NO)	F. DATE PROPERTY WAS SOLD (Submit a copy of HUD-1, Settlement Statement, if available)	G. VA LOAN NUMBER (If known)
1.						
2.						
3.						
4.						
5.						
6.						

I CERTIFY THAT the statements herein are true to the best of my knowledge and belief.

9. SIGNATURE OF VETERAN (Do NOT print)	10. DATE SIGNED

FEDERAL STATUTES PROVIDE SEVERE PENALTIES FOR FRAUD, INTENTIONAL MISREPRESENTATION. CRIMINAL CONNIVANCE OR CONSPIRACY PURPOSED TO INFLUENCE THE ISSUANCE OF ANY GUARANTY OR INSURANCE BY THE SECRETARY OF VETERANS AFFAIRS.

FOR VA USE ONLY

11A. DATE CERTIFICATE ISSUED	11B. SIGNATURE OF VA AGENT

VA FORM
FEB 2000 **26-1880**

SUPERSEDES VA FORM 26-1880, MAR 1999,
WHICH WILL NOT BE USED.

477

INSTRUCTIONS FOR VA FORM 26-1880

PRIVACY ACT INFORMATION: No Certificate of Eligibility may be issued unless VA receives sufficient information to determine that you are eligible (38 U.S.C. 3702). You are not required to furnish the information, including the Social Security Number, but are urged to do so, since it is vital to proper action by VA in your case. Specifically, your Social Security Number is requested under authority of 38 U.S.C. 3702 and is requested only if the service department used your Social Security Number as a service number. Failure to provide a completed application will deprive VA of information needed in reaching decisions which could affect you. Responses may be disclosed outside VA only if the disclosure is authorized under the Privacy Act, including the routine uses identified in the VA system of records, 55VA26, Loan Guaranty Home, Condominium and Manufactured Home Loan Applicant Records, Specially Adapted Housing Applicant Records, and Vendee Loan Applicant Records - VA, published in the Federal Register.

RESPONDENT BURDEN: VA may not conduct or sponsor, and respondent is not required to respond to this collection of information unless it displays a valid OMB Control Number. Public reporting burden for this collection of information is estimated to average 15 minutes per response, including the time for reviewing instructions, searching existing data sources, gathering and maintaining the data needed, and completing and reviewing the collection of information. If you have comments regarding this burden estimate or any other aspect of this collection of information, call 1-800-827-1000 for mailing information on where to send your comments.

A. Mail this completed form, along with proof of service, to the Eligibility Center at P.O. Box 20729, Winston-Salem, NC 27120 (for veterans located in the eastern half of the country) or P.O. Box 240097, Los Angeles, CA 90024 (for veterans located in the western half of the country). Veterans stationed overseas may use either address.

B. Military Service Requirements for VA Loan Eligibility: (NOTE: Cases involving other than honorable discharges will usually require further development by VA. This is necessary to determine if the service was under other than dishonorable conditions.)

1. Wartime Service. If you served anytime during World War II (September 16, 1940 to July 25, 1947), Korean Conflict (June 27, 1950 to January 31, 1955), or Vietnam Era (August 5, 1964 to May 7, 1975) you must have served at least 90 days on active duty and have been discharged or released under other than dishonorable conditions. If you served less than 90 days, you may be eligible if discharged because of service-connected disability.

2. Peacetime Service. If your service fell entirely within one of the following periods: July 26, 1947 to June 26, 1950, or February 1, 1955 to August 4, 1964, you must have served at least 181 days of continuous active duty and have been discharged or released under conditions other than dishonorable. If you entered service after May 7, 1975 but prior to September 8, 1980 (enlisted) or October 17, 1981 (officer) and completed your service before August 2, 1990, 181 days service is also required. If you served less than 181 days, you may be eligible if discharged for a service-connected disability.

3. Service after September 7, 1980 (enlisted) or October 16, 1981 (officer) and prior to August 2, 1990. If you were separated from service which began after these dates, you must have: (a) Completed 24 months of continuous active duty for the full period (at least 181 days) for which you were called or ordered to active duty, and been discharged or released under conditions other than dishonorable; or (b) Completed at least 181 days of active duty and been discharged under the specific authority of 10 U.S.C. 1173 (hardship discharge) or 10 U.S.C. 1171 (early out discharge), or have been determined to have a compensable service-connected disability; or (c) Been discharged with less than 181 days of service for a service-connected disability. Individuals may also be eligible if they were released from active duty due to an involuntary reduction in force, certain medical conditions, or, in some instances, for the convenience of the Government.

4. Gulf War. If you served on active duty during the Gulf War (August 2, 1990 to a date yet to be determined), you must have: (a) Completed 24 months of continuous active duty or the full period (at least 90 days) for which you were called or ordered to active duty, and been discharged or released under conditions other than dishonorable; or (b) Completed at least 90 days of active duty and been discharged under the specific authority of 10 U.S.C. 1173 (hardship discharge), or 10 U.S.C. 1171 (early out discharge), or have been determined to have a compensable service-connected disability; or (c) Been discharged with less than 90 days of service for a service-connected disability. Individuals may also be eligible if they were released from active duty due to an involuntary reduction in force, certain medical conditions, or, in some instances, for the convenience of the Government.

5. Active Duty Service Personnel. If you are now on active duty, you are eligible after having served on continuous active duty for at least 181 days (90 days during the Persian Gulf War) unless discharged or separated from a previous qualifying period of active duty service.

6. Selected Reserve Requirements for VA Loan Eligibility. If you are not otherwise eligible and you have completed a total of 6 years in the Selected Reserves or National Guard (member of an active unit, attended required weekend drills and 2-week active duty training) and (a) Were discharged with an honorable discharge; or (b) Were placed on the retired list or (c) Were transferred to the Standby Reserve or an element of the Ready Reserve other than the Selected Reserve after Service characterized as honorable service; or (d) Continue to serve in the Selected Reserve. Individuals who completed less than 6 years may be eligible if discharged for a service-connected disability. Eligibility for Selected Reservists expires September 30, 2007.

C. Unmarried surviving spouses of eligible veterans seeking determination of basic eligibility for VA Loan Guaranty benefits are NOT required to complete this form, but are required to complete VA Form 26-1817, Request for Determination of Loan Guaranty Eligibility-Unmarried Surviving Spouse.

D. Proof of Military Service

1. "Regular" Veterans. Attach to this request your most recent discharge or separation papers from active military duty since September 16, 1940, which show active duty dates and type of discharge. If you were separated after January 1, 1950, DD Form 214 must be submitted. If you were separated after October 1, 1979, and you received DD Form 214, Certificate of Release or Discharge From Active Duty, 1 July edition, VA must be furnished Copy 4 of the form. You may submit either original papers or legible copies. In addition, if you are now on active duty submit a statement of service signed by, or by direction of, the adjutant, personnel officer, or commander of your unit or higher headquarters showing date of entry on your current active duty period and the duration of any time lost. Any Veterans Services Representative in the nearest Department of Veterans Affairs office or center will assist you in securing necessary proof of military service.

2. Selected Reserves/National Guard. If you are a discharged member of the Army or Air Force National Guard you may submit a NGB Form 22, Report of Separation and Record of Service, or NGB Form 23, Retirement Points Accounting, or it's equivalent (this is similar to a retirement points summary). If you are a discharged member of the Selected Reserve you may submit a copy of your latest annual point statement and evidence of honorable service. You may submit either your original papers or legible copies. Since there is no single form used by the Reserves or National Guard similar to the DD Form 214, it is your responsibility to furnish adequate documentation of at least 6 years of honorable service. In addition, if you are currently serving in the Selected Reserve you must submit a statement of service signed by, or by the direction of, the adjutant, personnel officer or commander of your unit or higher headquarters showing the length of time that you have been a member of the unit.

Uniform Residential Loan Application

This application is designed to be completed by the applicant(s) with the lender's assistance. Applicants should complete this form as "Borrower" or "Co-Borrower", as applicable. Co-Borrower information must also be provided (and the appropriate box checked) when ☐ the income or assets of a person other than the "Borrower" (including the Borrower's spouse) will be used as a basis for loan qualification or ☐ the income or assets of the Borrower's spouse will not be used as a basis for loan qualification, but his or her liabilities must be considered because the Borrower resides in a community property state, the security property is located in a community property state, or the Borrower is relying on other property located in a community property state as a basis for repayment of the loan.

I. TYPE OF MORTGAGE AND TERMS OF LOAN

Mortgage Applied for:	☐ V.A. ☐ Conventional ☐ Other: ☐ F.H.A ☐ FmHA	Agency Case Number	Lender Case Number

Amount $	Interest Rate %	No. of Months	Amortization Type: ☐ Fixed Rate ☐ GPM	☐ Other (explain): ☐ ARM (type):

II. PROPERTY INFORMATION AND PURPOSE OF LOAN

Subject Property Address (street, city, state, ZIP)	No. of Units

Legal Description of Subject Property (attach description if necessary)	Year Built

Purpose of Loan ☐ Purchase ☐ Construction ☐ Other (explain): ☐ Refinance ☐ Construction-Permanent	Property will be: ☐ Primary Residence ☐ Secondary Residence ☐ Investment

Complete this line if construction or construction-permanent loan

Year Lot Acquired	Original Cost $	Amount Existing Liens $	(a) Present Value of Lot $	(b) Cost of Improvements $	Total (a+b) $

Complete this line if this is a refinance loan.

Year Acquired	Original Cost $	Amount Existing Liens $	Purpose of Refinance	Describe Improvements ☐ made ☐ to be made Cost $

Title will be held in what Name(s)	Manner in which Title will be held	Estate will be held in: ☐ Fee Simple ☐ Leasehold (show expiration date)

Source of Down Payment, Settlement Charges and/or Subordinate Financing (explain)	

III. BORROWER INFORMATION

Borrower	Co-Borrower
Borrower's Name (include Jr. or Sr. if applicable)	

Social Security Number	Home Phone (incl. area code)	Age	Yrs. School			

☐ Married ☐ Unmarried (include single, divorced, widowed) ☐ Separated	Dependents (not list by Co-Borrower) no. ages	☐ Married ☐ Unmarried (include single, divorced, widowed) ☐ Separated	Dependents (not list by Co-Borrower) no. ages

Present Address (street, city, state, ZIP) ☐ Own ☐ Rent ___No. Yrs.	Present Address (street, city, state, ZIP) ☐ Own ☐ Rent ___No. Yrs.

If residing at present address for less than two years, complete the following:

Former Address (street, city, state, ZIP) ☐ Own ☐ Rent ___No. Yrs.	Former Address (street, city, state, ZIP) ☐ Own ☐ Rent ___No. Yrs.
Former Address (street, city, state, ZIP) ☐ Own ☐ Rent ___No. Yrs.	Former Address (street, city, state, ZIP) ☐ Own ☐ Rent ___No. Yrs.
Former Address (street, city, state, ZIP) ☐ Own ☐ Rent ___No. Yrs.	Former Address (street, city, state, ZIP) ☐ Own ☐ Rent ___No. Yrs.

California Department of Veterans Affairs Cal-Vet Loan Application   Page 1 of 6   Borrower _____   Co-Borrower _____

Chapter 17

IV. EMPLOYMENT INFORMATION						
Name and Address of Employer	☐ Self-Employed	Yrs. on this job	Name and Address of Employer	☐ Self-Employed	Yrs. on this job	
		Yrs. employed in this line of work/profession			Yrs. employed in this line of work/profession	
Position/Title/Type of Business		Business Phone (incl. area code)	Position/Title/Type of Business		Business Phone (incl. area code)	

If employed in current position for less than two years or if currently employed in more than one position, complete the following:

Name and Address of Employer	☐ Self-Employed	Dates (from-to)	Name and Address of Employer	☐ Self-Employed	Dates (from-to)	
		Monthly Income $			Monthly Income $	
Position/Title/Type of Business		Business Phone (incl. area code)	Position/Title/Type of Business		Business Phone (incl. area code)	
Name and Address of Employer	Self-Employed	Dates (from-to)	Name and Address of Employer	Self-Employed	Dates (from-to)	
		Monthly Income $			Monthly Income $	
Position/Title/Type of Business		Business Phone (incl. area code)	Position/Title/Type of Business		Business Phone (incl. area code)	

V. MONTHLY INCOME AND COMBINED HOUSING EXPENSE INFORMATION						
Gross Monthly Income	Borrower	Co-Borrower	Total	Combined Monthly Housing Expense	Present	Proposed
Base Empl. Income*	$	$	$	Rent	$	$
Overtime				First Mortgage (P&I)		
Bonuses				Other Financing (P&I)		
Commissions				Hazard Insurance		
Dividends/Interest				Real Estate Taxes		
Net Rental Income				Mortgage Insurance		
Other (before completing see the notice in "describe other income." below				Homeowner Assn. Dues		
				Other		
Total				Total	$	$

*Self Employed Borrower(s) may be required to provide additional documentation such as tax returns and financial statements

Describe Other Income Notice: Alimony, child support, or separate maintenace income need not be revealed if the Borrower (B) or Co-Borrower (C) does not choose to have it considered for repaying this loan.

B/C		Monthly Amount
		$

California Department of Veterans Affairs Cal-Vet Loan Application   Page 2 of 6   Borrower _____
Co-Borrower _____

Cal-Vet Loans (California Example)

VI. ASSETS AND LIABILITIES		

This statement and any applicable supporting schedules may be completed jointly by both married and unmarried Co-borrowers if their assets and liabilities are sufficiently joined so that the Statement can be meaningfully and fairly presented on a combined basis; otherwise separate Statements and Schedules are required. If the Co-Borrower section was completed about a spouse, this Statement and supporting schedules must be completed about that spouse also.

Completed ☐ Jointly ☐ Not Jointly

ASSETS Description	Cash or Market Value	Liabilities and Pledged Assets. List the creditor's name, address and account number for all outstanding debts, including automobile loans, revolving charge accounts, real estate loans, alimony, child support, stock pledges, etc. Use continuation sheet, if necessary. Indicate by (*) those liabilities which will be satisfied upon real estate owned or upon refinancing of the subject property.	Monthly Payt. & Mos. Left to Pay	Unpaid Balance
		Liabilities		
Cash deposit toward purchase held by	$	Name and address of Company	$ Payt./Mos.	$
List checking and saving accounts below				
Name and address of Bank, S&L, or Credit Union				
		Acct. no.		
		Name and address of Company	$ Payt./Mos.	$
Acct. no.	$			
Name and address of Bank, S&L, or Credit Union				
		Acct. no.		
		Name and address of Company	$ Payt./Mos.	$
Acct. no.	$			
Name and address of Bank, S&L, or Credit Union				
		Acct. no.		
		Name and address of Company	$ Payt./Mos.	$
Acct. no.	$			
Name and address of Bank, S&L, or Credit Union				
		Acct. no.		
		Name and address of Company	$ Payt./Mos.	$
Acct. no.	$			
Stocks & Bonds (Company name/ number & description)				
		Acct. no.		
		Name and address of Company	$ Payt./Mos.	$
Life insurance net cash value				
Face amount: $	$			
Subtotal Liquid Assets	$			
Real estate owned (enter market value from schedule of real estate owned)	$	Acct. no.		
Vested interest in retirement fund	$	Name and address of Company	$ Payt./Mos.	$
Net worth of business(es) owned (attach financial statement)	$			
Automobiles owned (make and year)	$			
		Acct. no.		
		Alimony/Child Support/Separate Maintenance Payments Owed to:		
Other Assets (itemize)	$		$	
		Job Related Expense (child care, union dues, etc.)	$	
		Total Monthly Payments	$	
Total Assets a.	$	Net Worth (a-b)	$	Total Liabilities b.	$

California Department of Veterans Affairs Cal-Vet Loan Application   Page 3 of 6   Borrower _____

Co-Borrower _____

481

VI. ASSETS AND LIABILITIES (cont.)

Schedule of Real Estate Owned (if additional properties are owned, use continuation sheet.)

Property Address (enter S if sold, PS if pending sale or R if rental being held for income)	Type of Property	Present Market Value	Amount of Mortgages and Liens	Gross Rental Income	Mortgage Payments	Insurance Maintenance Taxes & Misc.	Net Rental Income
		$	$	$	$	$	$
	Totals	$	$	$	$	$	$

List any additional names under which credit has previously been received and indicate appropriate creditor name(s) and account number(s):

Alternate Name	Creditor Name	Account Number

VII. DETAILS OF TRANSACTION

a. Purchase price	$
b. Alterations, improvements, repairs	
c. Land (if acquired separately)	
d. Refinance (incl. debts to be paid off)	
e. Estimated prepaid items	
f. Estimated closing costs	
g. PMI, MIP, Funding Fee	
h. Discount (if Borrower will pay)	
i. Total costs (add items a through h)	
j. Subordinate financing	
k. Borrower's closing costs paid by Seller	
l. Other Credits (explain)	
m. Loan amount (exclude PMI, MIP, Funding Fee financed)	
n. PMI, MIP, Funding Fee financed	
o. Loan amount (add m & n)	
p. Cash from/to Borrower	

VII. DECLARATIONS

If you answer "yes" to any questions a through i, please use continuation sheet for explanation.

	Borrower Yes No	Co-Borrower Yes No
a. Are there any outstanding judgements against you?	☐ ☐	☐ ☐
b. Have you been declared bankrupt within the last 7 years?	☐ ☐	☐ ☐
c. Have you had property foreclosed upon or given title or deed in lieu thereof in the last 7 years?	☐ ☐	☐ ☐
d. Are you a party to a lawsuit?	☐ ☐	☐ ☐
e. Have you directly or indirectly been obligated on any loan which resulted in foreclosure, transfer of title in lieu of forclosure, or judgement? (This would include such loans as home mortgage loans, SBA loans, home improvement loans, educational loans, manufactured (mobile) home loans, any mortgage financial obligation, bond, or loan guarantee. If "Yes," provide details, including date, name and address or Lender, FHA or VA case number, if any, and reasons for the action.	☐ ☐	☐ ☐
f. Are you presently delinquent or in default on any Federal debt or any other loan, mortgage, financial obligation bond, or loan guarantee? If "Yes," give details as described in the preceding question.	☐ ☐	☐ ☐
g. Are you obligated to pay alimony, child support, or separate maintenance?	☐ ☐	☐ ☐
h. Is any part of the down payment borrowed?	☐ ☐	☐ ☐
i. Are you a co-maker or endorser on a note?	☐ ☐	☐ ☐
j. Are you a U. S. citizen?	☐ ☐	☐ ☐
k. Are you a permanent resident alien?	☐ ☐	☐ ☐
l. Do you intend to occupy the property as your primary residence? If "Yes," complete question m below.	☐ ☐	☐ ☐
m. Have you had an ownership interest in a property in the last three years?	☐ ☐	☐ ☐

(1) What type of property did you own — principal residence (PR), second home (SH), or investment property (IP)? _____ _____

(2) How did you hold the title to the home — solely by yourself (S), jointly with your spouse (SP), or jointly with another person (O)? _____ _____

IX. ACKNOWLEDGEMENT AND AGREEMENT

The undersigned specifically acknowledge(s) and agree(s) that: (1) the loan requested by this application will be secured by a first mortgage or deed of trust on the property described herein; (2) the property will not be used for any illegal or prohibited purpose or use; (3) all statements made in this application are made for the purpose of obtaining the loan indicated herein; (4) occupation of the property will be as indicated above; (5) verification or reverification of any information contained in the application may be made at any time by the Lender, its agents, successors or assigns, either directly or through a credit reporting agency, from any source named in this application, and the original copy of this application will be retained by the Lender, even if the loan is not approved; (6) the Lender, its agents, successors or assigns will rely on the information contained in the application and I/we have a continuing obligation to amend or supplement the information provided in this application if any of the material facts which I/we have represented herein should change prior to closing; (7) in the event my/our payments on the loan indicated in this application become delinquent, the Lender, its agents, successors or assigns, may, in addition to all their other rights and remedies, report my/our name(s) and account information to a credit reporting agency; (8) ownership of the loan may be transferred to successor or assign of the Lender without notice to me and/or the administration of the loan account may be transferred to an agent, successor or assign of the Lender with prior notice to me; (9) the Lender, its agents, successors or assigns make no representations or warranties, express or implied, to the Borrower(s) regarding the property, the condition of the property, or the value of the property.

Certification: I/We certify that the information provided in this application is true and correct as of the date set forth opposite my/our signature(s) on this application and acknowledge my/our understanding that any intentional or negligent misrepresentation(s) of the information contained in this application may result in civil liability and/or criminal penalties including, but not limited to, fine or imprisonment or both under the provisions of Title 18, United States Code, Section 1001, et seq. and liability for monetary damages to the Lender, its agents, successors or assigns, insurers and any other person who may suffer any loss due to reliance upon any misrepresentation which I/we have made on this application.

Borrower's Signature	Date	Co-Borrower's Signature	Date
X		X	

California Department of Veterans Affairs Cal-Vet Loan Application   Page 4 of 6   Borrower _____ Co-Borrower _____

Cal-Vet Loans (California Example)

X. INFORMATION FOR GOVERNMENT MONITORING PURPOSES

The following information is requested by the Federal Government for certain types of loans related to a dwelling, in order to monitor the Lender's compliance with equal credit opportunity, fair housing and home mortgage disclosure laws. You are not required to furnish this information, but are encouraged to do so. The law provides that a Lender may neither discriminate on the basis of this information, nor on whether you choose to furnish it. However, if you choose not to furnish it, under Federal regulations this Lender is required to note race and sex on the basis of visual observation or surname. If you do not wish to furnish the above information, please check the box below. (Lender must review the above material to assure that the disclosure satisfy all requirements to which the Lender is subject under applicable state law for the particular type of loan applied for.)

BORROWER ☐ I do not wish to furnish this information

BORROWER ☐ I do not wish to furnish this information

Race/National Origin:
☐ American Indian or Alaskan Native
☐ Black, not of Hispanic origin
☐ Hispanic
☐ Asian or Pacific Islander
☐ White, not of Hispanic origin
☐ Other (specify) _____

Race/National Origin:
☐ American Indian or Alaskan Native
☐ Black, not of Hispanic origin
☐ Hispanic
☐ Asian or Pacific Islander
☐ White, not of Hispanic origin
☐ Other (specify) _____

Sex: ☐ Female ☐ Male

Sex: ☐ Female ☐ Male

To be Completed by Interviewer	Interviewer's Name (print or type)	Name and Address Interviewer's Employer
This application was taken by: ☐ face-to-face interview ☐ by mail ☐ by telephone	Interviewer's Signature Date Interviewer's Phone Number (incl. area code)	

California Department of Veterans Affairs Cal-Vet Loan Application   Page 5 of 6   Borrower _____
                                                                                          Co-Borrower _____

483

CONTINUATION SHEET/RESIDENTIAL LOAN APPLICATION		
Use this continuation sheet if you need more space to complete the Residential Loan Application. Mark B for Borrower or C for Co-Borrower.	Borrower:	Agency Case Number:
	Co-Borrower:	Lender Case Number:

I/We fully understand that it is a Federal crime punishable by fine or imprisonment, or both, to knowingly make any false statements concerning any of the above facts as applicable under the provisions of Title 18, United States Code, Section 1001, et seq.

Borrower's Signature	Date	Co-Borrower's Signature	Date
X		X	

California Department of Veterans Affairs Cal-Vet Loan Application   Page 6 of 6

Cal-Vet Loans (California Example)

Figure 17-3

Standard Insurance Company
Cal-Vet Team, 920 SW Sixth Avenue   Portland OR 97204

Medical History Statement for Life and Disability Coverage

DIRECTIONS FOR APPLYING FOR COVERAGE

This form must be completed when Evidence Of Insurability is required. To apply for coverage (as a Contractholder or Spouse), read the Information Practices Notice(s). Then complete all items, date, and sign as instructed. Send the original to Standard Insurance Company, at the address above. Please keep a copy for your records.

CONTRACTHOLDER INFORMATION

Name of Group **Department of Veterans Affairs, State of California**	Group Number 642177	Loan Number	Loan Amount	Are You a Veteran? ☐ Yes ☐ No
Contractholder			Birthdate (Mo/Day/Year)	Date Hired (Mo/Day/Year)
No. of Hours Scheduled to Work per Week	Salary	Social Security Number	Check who is Applying (One per form) ☐ Contractholder ☐ Spouse	

APPLICANT INFORMATION

Applicant's Name (Person to be insured)		
Current Address:	Future Address:	
Sex ☐M ☐F	Birthdate (Mo/Day/Year) Birthplace	Social Security Number	Work Phone ( ) Home Phone ( )

APPLICATION INFORMATION

Type of Application (check one)   ☐ Initial application   ☐ Change in coverage

Check the insurance coverage you are requesting.

☐ Regular Life   ☐ Optional Regular Life   ☐ Spouse Life   Disability – ☐ Option 1   ☐ Option 1a   ☐ Option 2

Are you now receiving or eligible for Veterans Compensation for a military service-connected disability?   ☐ Yes   ☐ No

If yes, what percent? _____ Specify disability/condition: _____

If yes, please provide the USDVA document which verifies the service-connected disability. You may contact USDVA at 1-800-827-1000 to obtain a copy of this information.

Veterans Compensation Claim No. _____ and/or Military Services No. _____

MEDICAL HISTORY STATEMENT QUESTIONS

Check yes or no for each of these questions, and give details for any "yes" answers. Attach a separate sheet if necessary.

1. Have you had any physical, mental or emotional condition, injury, sickness, or surgery in the past 5 years? . . . . . . ☐Yes ☐ No
2. Have you consulted or been attended by a physician or practitioner for any cause in the past 5 years? . . . . ☐Yes ☐ No
3. Are you now unable to work full time because of any physical, mental or emotional condition, injury, or sickness? . ☐Yes ☐ No
4. Has a medical professional ever treated you for, diagnosed you as having, or prescribed medication for you for any of the following:
   - A. High blood pressure, cardiovascular disease, heart ailment, arteriosclerosis, or stroke? . . . . ☐Yes ☐ No
   - B. Mental condition, depression, epilepsy, or nervous system disorder? . . . . ☐Yes ☐ No
   - C. Cancer, diabetes, or nephritis? . . . . ☐Yes ☐ No
   - D. Arthritis, strained or injured back, slipped disc, or any bone, joint, or muscle disorder? . . . . ☐Yes ☐ No
   - E. Lung, kidney, stomach, genital, urinary, liver, pancreas, or intestinal ailment? . . . . ☐Yes ☐ No
   - F. Blindness or deafness? . . . . ☐Yes ☐ No
   - G. An immune system disorder not related to Human Immunodeficiency Virus (HIV)? . . . . ☐Yes ☐ No
5. Has a medical professional ever diagnosed you as having or prescribed medication to you for Acquired Immune Deficiency Syndrome (AIDS), AIDS-Related Complex (ARC), or HIV infection? . . . . ☐Yes ☐ No
6. Have you sought or received advice or treatment for the use of alcohol or drugs in the past 10 years? . . . . ☐Yes ☐ No
7. In the past 10 years have you had a persistent cough, unintentional weight loss of 10 pounds or more, persistent fatigue, persistent lymph node enlargement, prolonged night sweats, pneumonia, lesions, or growths? . . . . ☐Yes ☐ No
8. Do you take medication for any physical, mental or emotional condition, injury, or sickness? . . . . ☐Yes ☐ No
9. Do you plan any operation or visit to a doctor or practitioner for an existing physical, mental or emotional condition, injury, or sickness? . . . . ☐Yes ☐ No
10. Are you now pregnant? . . . . ☐Yes ☐ No

Height	Weight	Physician or Medical Facility with Applicant's Complete Medical Records
		Name and Full Mailing Address

Applicant Name	Social Security Number

Describe below any "yes" answers. (Please provide the entire question number.)

Question Number	Description of Injuries, Disorders and Operations	Month/Year	Duration	Final Result	Physicians Consulted, City & State

ACKNOWLEDGMENT AND AUTHORIZATION FOR RELEASE OF INFORMATION *(Please read carefully)*

- I represent that the statements contained herein, including those made in response to the Medical History Statement questions and any attachments, are true and complete, to the best of my knowledge and belief, and I understand that they form the basis of any coverage under the Group Policy(ies). I understand that any misstatements or failure to report information which is material to the issuance of coverage may be used as a basis for rescission of my insurance and/or denial of payment of a claim. I agree to notify Standard Insurance Company of any change in my medical condition while my enrollment application is pending. I agree that if my application is approved by Standard Insurance Company, the effective date of any coverage will be determined in accordance with the terms of the Group Policy(ies), including any applicable Active Work requirement. I agree that if my application is declined, Standard Insurance Company's liability is limited to the return of any premium which may have been paid.

- To any physician, health care provider, hospital, insurance or reinsurance company, the Medical Information Bureau, Inc. (MIB), or any employer: I authorize you to release to Standard Insurance Company or its reinsurers all medical information you have about me including medical history, diagnosis, prognosis and treatment of any physical, mental or emotional condition. I understand that Standard Insurance Company will use the information obtained by this authorization to determine my eligibility for group insurance coverage. I further authorize Standard Insurance Company to release this information to its reinsurers, MIB, and to other insurance companies to which I have applied for insurance coverage or benefits.

- I understand that if my application is approved, premiums shall be paid in accordance with the provisions of the Group Policy(ies), and my coverage will be subject to all terms and conditions of the Group Policy(ies) and state limitations.

- For the Contractholder: Regular Life Insurance, Optional Regular Life Insurance, and Disability Insurance benefits will be paid to the Policyholder.

- Benefits paid to the Policyholder will be applied against the loan contract which is subject to insurance under the Group Policy.

- I understand that Spouse Life Insurance if any, is payable to the Policyholder.

- I acknowledge that I have read and received the Information Practices Notice and I have kept a copy of this Medical History Statement.

- I understand a copy of this authorization will be provided to me, or my authorized representative, upon request. This authorization will remain valid one year from the date below. A photocopy of this authorization shall be as valid as the original.

- I understand that I have the right to revoke this authorization at any time by sending a written statement to Standard Insurance Company. I further understand that the revocation of the authorization, or the failure to sign the authorization, may impair Standard Insurance Company's ability to evaluate or process my application and may be a basis for denying my application for insurance coverage.

- I understand that I will not be rated uninsurable for life insurance coverages other than Spouse Life solely on the basis of a military service-connected disability, and that I must be actively working at least 30 hours per week in order to be eligible for disability coverage.

Signature of Applicant	Dated

Note: Declinations do not affect either Guarantee Issue Amounts not subject to Evidence Of Insurability or other coverages already inforce with Standard Insurance Company.

CI 0040 642177

2 of 3

(6/03)

Applicant Name	Social Security Number

INFORMATION PRACTICES NOTICE

- To help us determine your eligibility for group insurance, we may request information about you from other persons and organizations. For example, we may request information from your doctor or hospital, other insurance companies, or MIB, Inc. (Medical Information Bureau). We will use the authorization you signed on this form when we seek this information.

- MIB (MEDICAL INFORMATION BUREAU) – Information we collect about you is confidential. However, Standard Insurance Company or its reinsurers may make a brief report to the MIB. MIB is a nonprofit corporation. It exchanges information among its member life insurance companies. If you later apply to another MIB member company for life or health insurance coverage, or if you submit a claim for benefits to such member company, MIB will supply the member company with any information it has about you in its files. This will be done only upon the member company's request. Standard Insurance Company or its reinsurers may also release information about you to Standard Insurance Company's reinsurers or to other insurance companies to whom you have applied for life or health insurance or made claim for benefits.

- MIB will disclose any information it has about you at your request. If you believe that the information MIB has about you is incorrect, you may contact MIB and request a correction. Your request for correction will be handled by MIB in accordance with the procedures outlined in the federal Fair Credit Reporting Act. The address of the MIB information office is: P.O. Box 105, Essex Station, Boston, Massachusetts 02112. MIB's telephone number is (617) 426-3660.

- DISCLOSURE TO OTHERS – The information collected about you is confidential. We will not release any information about you without your authorization, except to the extent necessary to conduct our business or as required or permitted by law.

- YOUR RIGHTS – You have a right to know what information we have about you in our underwriting file. You also have a right to ask us to correct any information you think is incorrect. We will carefully review your request and make changes when justified. If you would like more information about this right or our information practices please write to us, at Cal-Vet Team, Standard Insurance Company, 920 SW Sixth Avenue, Portland, Oregon 97204 or call 1-800-378-1613.

Cal-Vet Office Locations

Sacramento Office

1227 O Street, 4th floor
Sacramento, CA 95814
Robert Washington, Manager
(866) 653-2510 - Toll Free
(916) 503-8359 - PHONE
(916) 651-9085 - FAX
E-Mail: Sacramento@cdva.ca.gov
Office Hours: 8:00 AM to 5:00 PM Monday through Friday

Counties:

Alameda	Placer
Alpine	Sacramento San Francisco
Amador	San Joaquin
Calaveras	San Mateo
Colusa	Santa Clara
Contra Costa El Dorado	Santa Cruz
Marin	Solano Sonoma
Napa	Sutter
Nevada	Yolo
	Yuba

Redding Office

930 Executive Way, Suite 125
Redding, CA 96002
(866) 653-2508 - Toll Free
(530) 224-4955 - PHONE
(530) 224-4959 - FAX
E-Mail: Redding@cdva.ca.gov
Office Hours: 8:00 AM to 5:00 PM Monday through Friday

Counties:

Butte	Modoc
Del Norte	Plumas
Glenn	Shasta Sierra
Humboldt	Siskiyou
Lake Lassen	Tehama
Mendocino	Trinity

Cal-Vet Loans (California Example)

Fresno Office

1752 East Bullard Avenue, Suite 101
Fresno, CA 93710
(866) 653-2511 - Toll Free
(559) 440-5132 - PHONE
(559) 440-5172 - FAX
E-Mail: Fresno@cdva.ca.gov
Office Hours: 8:00 AM to 5:00 PM Monday through Friday

Counties: Merced Monterey
Fresno   San Benito
Kings   San Luis Obispo
Madera   Stanislaus
Mariposa   Tuolumne

San Diego Office

3160 Camino Del Rio South, Room 112
San Diego, CA 92108
(866) 653-2504 - Toll Free
(619) 641-5840 - PHONE
(619) 641-5851 - FAX
E-Mail: SanDiego@cdva.ca.gov
Office Hours: 8:00 AM to 5:00 PM Monday through Friday

Counties:
Imperial
Orange
San Diego

Bakersfield Office

5500 Ming Avenue, Suite 155
Bakersfield, CA 93309
(866) 653-2507 - Toll Free
(661) 833-4720 - PHONE
(661) 833-4732 - FAX
E-Mail: Bakersfield@cdva.ca.gov
Office Hours: 8:00 AM to 5:00 PM Monday through Friday

Counties:
Inyo
Kern
Mono Santa Barbara

North and West Los Angeles
County
Tulare
Ventura

Riverside Office

1770 Iowa Ave., Suite 260
Riverside, CA 92507
(800) 700-2127 - Toll Free
(951) 774-0102 - PHONE
(951) 774-0111 - FAX
E-Mail: Riverside@cdva.ca.gov
Office Hours: 8:00 AM to 5:00 PM Monday through Friday

Counties:
Riverside
San Bernardino
South and East Los Angeles County

CHAPTER 18

ESCROW PROCEDURES

The last step in the loan process is *CLOSING, when the loan proceeds are distributed and a deed to the property is transferred and recorded.* These steps are usually carried out by an escrow agent. The escrow agent makes sure that all necessary documents are prepared and properly signed, calculates any necessary prorations, makes sure that all necessary funds have been deposited, and provides a settlement statement. Once everything is in order, the loan funds are disbursed, the deed and other documents are recorded, and the transaction is completed.

An *ESCROW is where a neutral third party holds the items deposited by the parties to a transaction and disburses them after the conditions of the transaction have been met.* Attorneys, title companies, and independent escrow companies all perform this function. Many lending institutions have their own escrow departments for the transactions that they finance.

Every state has laws governing the operation of escrow agents.

The typical escrow involves many people. In addition to the buyer/borrower, seller, broker, lender, and escrow agent, important functions are performed by title companies, notaries public, local county officials (recording office and inspectors), and structural pest inspectors.

One of the key functions of the escrow process is the recordation of documents.

Any document relating to real estate ownership should be recorded.

While agents and loan officers do not act as escrow agents, they need to be very aware of the steps in the process. All real estate escrows involve the following essential steps:

1. Gathering information necessary to prepare escrow instructions.

2. Obtaining a preliminary title report from the title company.

3. Satisfying existing loans secured by the property.

4. Preparing documents such as escrow instructions, loan documents, deeds, etc.

5. Depositing funds from a buyer or a seller.

6. Prorating expenses and allocating closing costs.

7. Preparing a Uniform Settlement Statement.

8. Issuing policies of title insurance for the buyer and the lender.

9. Disbursing funds and delivering documents.

I. Opening Escrow

It is a good idea for agents and loan brokers to use an escrow progress chart. (**See Figure 18-1**.) By utilizing such a chart, the progress of the escrow can be monitored and the parties can be reminded of items that still need to be completed to close the transaction.

The first step in the process is to open the escrow. This is done by providing the escrow agent with the preliminary escrow instructions. Once the instructions are prepared and signed, the escrow agent will order a preliminary title report. This preliminary report will then be forwarded to the buyer/borrower's lender along with the escrow instructions. Note that the escrow instructions must correspond to the lender's terms. Any discrepancy will require amended escrow instructions since the lender will not disburse funds into the escrow account until the instructions correspond to their loan terms.

Early in the process, the escrow agent will send a "demand for payoff" to the previous lender, if necessary. A structural pest inspection will also be immediately ordered so as to complete any needed repairs and not unduly delay the close of escrow. The results of the pest control inspection will then be forwarded to the borrower's lender.

Once the lender has carried out its underwriting functions and obtained an appraisal (if necessary), it will then issue loan approval and forward the loan documents (note, deed of trust, and Truth in Lending Statement) to the escrow agent.

Once all contingent conditions have been met (such as purchase of a new hazard insurance policy), the escrow agent will have the borrower sign the loan documents and record them. Copies of the documents will be provided to the lender. The borrower will then have a statutory rescission period before final closing. At the end of the rescission period, the lender will disburse funds into the account.

At final closing, the prior lender will be paid off, the final closing statements will be prepared, and all other parties to the escrow will receive their funds. The policy of title insurance will be issued at this time and the borrower will receive his or her copies of all the loan documents and inspection reports.

Figure 18-1   ESCROW PROGRESS CHART

	Sch. Date	Actual Date	Escrow Operations
1			Notice of Sale to multiple listing service
2			Buyer's deposit increased to $
3			Escrow opened with
4			Preliminary title searched
5			Clouds on title eliminated
6			Credit report ordered from
7			Credit report received
8			Report of residential record ordered
9			Report of residential record received
10			Pest control inspection ordered
11			Pest control report received; work —
12			Pest control report accepted by seller
13			Pest control work ordered
14			Pest control work completed
15			Other inspections ordered
16			Report received; work —
17			Report accepted by
18			Special contingencies eliminated
19			Payoff or beneficiary statement ordered
20			Payoff or beneficiary statement received
21			Payoff or beneficiary statement ordered
22			Payoff or beneficiary statement received
23			1st loan commitment ordered from
24			Received: @ % Fee Pts.
25			2nd loan commitment ordered from
26			Received: @ % Fee Pts.
27			Loan application submitted to
28			Loan application approved
29			Loan/assumption papers received by escrow
30			Hazard insurance placed with
31			Escrow closing instructions requested
32			Client called for closing appointment
33			Closing papers signed
34			Closing papers to escrow holder
35			Funds ordered
36			Deed recorded

After Close of Escrow

Received	Delivered	
		Final adjusted closing statement
		Check of seller's proceeds
		Check of buyer's refund
		Commission check
		Seller's "Loss Payee" insurance policy
		Recorded deed
		Title insurance policy

Notations

_____
_____
_____

II. Settlement Statement and Closing Costs

A *SETTLEMENT STATEMENT is a listing of all the amounts involved in a transaction.* In sales of residential property financed by institutional investors, the Uniform Settlement Statement is used. (**See Figure 18-2**.)

Items on the statement are listed as either debits or credits. A *DEBIT is any charge payable* **by** *any party.* For instance, the purchase price is a debit to the buyer and the sales commission is a debit to the seller. A *CREDIT is any item that's payable* **to** *any party.* The buyer would be credited with the new loan and the seller would be credited with the sales price. The easy way to think of the statement is to compare it to a check register. Debits are checks written against the account or payouts. Credits are similar to deposits to the account or pay-ins. When the transaction closes, the balances for both the buyer and the seller should equal zero. Loan officers and agents are often asked to calculate an estimate of the buyer's cash requirements for closing and the seller's net proceeds. This can be done by utilizing a worksheet similar to that shown in **Figure 18-3**.

A. BUYER'S COSTS

The main cost to the buyer is the purchase price.

In most transactions, the purchase price cost is offset by some form of financing. The difference between the sales price and the loan amount is partially accounted for by a down payment. However, this is only one of the many costs the borrower will incur. There is generally a loan origination fee to cover the lender's administrative costs. The lender may also charge points to make the loan. There is an appraisal fee, a credit report fee, attorney fees, notary fees, a fee for the lenders title insurance policy, and possibly impound fees for taxes and insurance. Depending on the escrow agreement, the borrower may share costs with the seller for escrow and recording fees and possibly the title insurance policy as well as any inspections and repairs. In addition, the borrower/buyer is responsible for any special costs that he or she incurs.

B. SELLER FEES

The seller will have to pay off any existing loans, including any pre-payment penalties, at the close of escrow. The seller will also pay the

Figure 18-2

A. Settlement Statement

U.S. Department of Housing
and Urban Development

OMB Approval No. 2502-0265

B. Type of Loan

1. ☐ FHA 2. ☐ FmHA 3. ☐ Conv. Unins.   6. File Number   7. Loan Number   8. Mortgage Insurance Case Number

4. ☐ VA 5. ☐ Conv. Ins.

C. Note: This form is furnished to give you a statement of actual settlement costs. Amounts paid to and by the settlement agent are shown. Items marked "(p.o.c.)" were paid outside the closing; they are shown here for informational purposes and are not included in the totals.

D. Name and Address of Borrower	E. Name and Address of Seller	F. Name and Address of Lender

G. Property Location	H. Settlement Agent	
	Place of Settlement	I. Settlement Date

J. Summary of Borrower's Transaction		K. Summary of Seller's Transaction	
100. Gross Amount Due From Borrower		**400. Gross Amount Due To Seller**	
101. Contract sales price		401. Contract sales price	
102. Personal property		402. Personal property	
103. Settlement charges to borrower (line 1400)		403.	
104.		404.	
105.		405.	
Adjustments for items paid by seller in advance		*Adjustments for items paid by seller in advance*	
106. City/town taxes to		406. City/town taxes to	
107. County taxes to		407. County taxes to	
108. Assessments to		408. Assessments to	
109.		409.	
110.		410.	
111.		411.	
112.		412.	
120. Gross Amount Due From Borrower		**420. Gross Amount Due To Seller**	
200. Amounts Paid By Or in Behalf Of Borrower		**500. Reductions In Amount Due To Seller**	
201. Deposit or earnest money		501. Excess deposit (see instructions)	
202. Principal amount of new loan(s)		502. Settlement charges to seller (line 1400)	
203. Existing loan(s) taken subject to		503. Existing loan(s) taken subject to	
204.		504. Payoff of first mortgage loan	
205.		505. Payoff of second mortgage loan	
206.		506.	
207.		507.	
208.		508.	
209.		509.	
Adjustments for items unpaid by seller		*Adjustments for items unpaid by seller*	
210. City/town taxes to		510. City/town taxes to	
211. County taxes to		511. County taxes to	
212. Assessments to		512. Assessments to	
213.		513.	
214.		514.	
215.		515.	
216.		516.	
217.		517.	
218.		518.	
219.		519.	
220. Total Paid By/For Borrower		**520. Total Reduction Amount Due Seller**	
300. Cash At Settlement From/To Borrower		**600. Cash At Settlement To/From Seller**	
301. Gross Amount due from borrower (line 120)		601. Gross amount due to seller (line 420)	
302. Less amounts paid by/for borrower (line 220)	( )	602. Less reductions in amt. due seller (line 520)	( )
303. Cash ☐ From ☐ To Borrower		603. Cash ☐ To ☐ From Seller	

Previous Edition Is Obsolete

HUD-1 (3-86)
RESPA, HB 4305.2

L. Settlement Charges

	Paid From Borrowers Funds at Settlement	Paid From Seller's Funds at Settlement
700. Total Sales/Broker's Commission based on price $ @ % =		
Division of Commission (line 700) as follows:		
701. $ to		
702. $ to		
703. Commission paid at Settlement		
704.		
800. Items Payable In Connection With Loan		
801. Loan Origination Fee %		
802. Loan Discount %		
803. Appraisal Fee to		
804. Credit Report to		
805. Lender's Inspection Fee		
806. Mortgage Insurance Application Fee to		
807. Assumption Fee		
808.		
809.		
810.		
811.		
900. Items Required By Lender To Be Paid In Advance		
901. Interest from to @$ /day		
902. Mortgage Insurance Premium for months to		
903. Hazard Insurance Premium for years to		
904. years to		
905.		
1000. Reserves Deposited With Lender		
1001. Hazard insurance months@$ per month		
1002. Mortgage insurance months@$ per month		
1003. City property taxes months@$ per month		
1004. County property taxes months@$ per month		
1005. Annual assessments months@$ per month		
1006. months@$ per month		
1007. months@$ per month		
1008. months@$ per month		
1100. Title Charges		
1101. Settlement or closing fee to		
1102. Abstract or title search to		
1103. Title examination to		
1104. Title insurance binder to		
1105. Document preparation to		
1106. Notary fees to		
1107. Attorney's fees to		
(includes above items numbers:)		
1108. Title insurance to		
(includes above items numbers.)		
1109. Lender's coverage $		
1110. Owner's coverage $		
1111.		
1112.		
1113.		
1200. Government Recording and Transfer Charges		
1201. Recording fees: Deed $; Mortgage $; Releases $		
1202. City/county tax/stamps: Deed $; Mortgage $		
1203. State tax/stamps: Deed $; Mortgage $		
1204.		
1205.		
1300. Additional Settlement Charges		
1301. Survey to		
1302. Pest inspection to		
1303.		
1304.		
1305.		
1400. Total Settlement Charges (enter on lines 103, Section J and 502, Section K)		

Figure 18-3

SETTLEMENT STATEMENT

	BUYER'S STATEMENT		SELLER'S STATEMENT	
	Debit	Credit	Debit	Credit
Sales Price	52,000.00			52,000.00
Deposit		1,500.00		
Commission — 7%			3,640.00	
Mortgage Balance			35,822.24	
Prepaid Interest	261.00		156.70	
New Loan		45,000.00		
Taxes — Prorated		327.10	327.10	
Loan Origination Fee - 1%	450.00			
Fire Insurance	192.00			
Title Insurance — standard			238.10	
Title Insurance - extended	135.00			
Tax Reserve — 2 months	183.00			
Appraisal Fee	75.00			
Credit Report	50.00			
Survey Fee	255.00			
Discount Points			2,850.00	
Documentary Stamps			57.20	
Balance Due From Buyer		6,773.90		
Balance Due To Seller			8,908.66	
TOTALS	$53,601.00	$53,601.00	$52,000.00	$52,000.00

Settlement statements are written interpretations of the financial elements of the contract.

sales commission and his or her portion of the attorney fees, escrow fees, notary fees, and recording fees. Depending on local custom, the seller may also pay none, all, or a portion of the title insurance premium, the structural pest control inspection/repairs, the buyer/borrower's loan discount, and a home warranty contract.

C. BUYER CREDITS

The buyer will normally be credited with any payments initially made out of pocket for an earnest money deposit, appraisal fee, credit report, and prorated taxes or rents due.

D. SELLER CREDITS

In addition to receiving funds from the purchase price, the seller may be due credits for items such as prorated taxes, insurance premiums, and the balance in any existing impound account that was required for the seller's prior loan. If the property is income property, there might be a credit for prorated rents.

III. Real Estate Settlement Procedures Act (RESPA)

The *REAL ESTATE SETTLEMENT PROCEDURES ACT (RESPA) applies to the sale of one-to-four unit properties that involve financing from institutional lenders where the purchase loan is secured by a first trust mortgage.*

RESPA does not apply to purchases of vacant land, properties of 25 or more acres, or transactions where the borrower assumes an existing first mortgage loan.

In transactions subject to RESPA, the lender must give the borrower a **good faith estimate** of the closing costs at the time of the loan application. (**See Figure 18-4**.) The lender is also required to give the borrower a booklet published by HUD which describes closing costs, settlement procedures, and the borrower's rights. The entity handling the closing must prepare the settlement statement on the Uniform Settlement Statement.

RESPA prohibits all kickbacks and unearned fees.

If the lender requires a particular closing agent, any business relationship between the escrow agent and the lender must be disclosed, and an estimate of the agent's charges for the services to be provided must be given. Also, a sale may not be conditioned upon the use of a particular title insurer or escrow company chosen by the seller.

IV. Additional Disclosures

Many states require additional documentation to transfer property or to obtain a loan. In many cases, this consists of disclosures to the prospective borrower or purchaser. The following are a list of the disclosures required by the state of California.

Figure 18-4

GOOD FAITH ESTIMATE

Applicants: Prepared By:

Property Address:

App No/Loan Prog: Date Prepared:

The information provided below reflects estimates of the charges which you are likely to incur at the settlement of your loan. The fees listed are estimates - actual charges may be more or less. Your transaction may not involve a fee for every item listed.

The numbers listed beside the estimates generally correspond to the numbered lines contained in the HUD-1 settlement statement which you will be receiving at settlement. The HUD-1 settlement statement will show you the actual cost for items paid at settlement.

Total Loan Amount $ _____ Interest Rate: _____ % Term: _____ mths   MIP/FF Financed $ ____

800	**ITEMS PAYABLE IN CONNECTION WITH LOAN:**	
801	Loan Origination Fee	$
802	Loan Discount	
803	Appraisal Fee	
804	Credit Report	
805	Lender's Inspection Fee	
808	Mortgage Broker Fee	
809	Tax Related Service Fee	
810	Processing Fee	
811	Underwriting Fee	
812	Wire Transfer Fee	

900	**ITEMS REQUIRED BY LENDER TO BE PAID IN ADVANCE:**		
901	Interest for _____ days @ $ ____	per day	$
902	Mortgage Insurance Premium		
903	Hazard Insurance Premium		
904	Tax and Assessment		
905	VA Funding Fee		

1000	**RESERVES DEPOSITED WITH LENDER:**		
1001	Hazard Insurance Premiums ____ months @ $	per month	$
1002	Mortgage Ins. Premium Reserves ____ months @ $	per month	
1004	Taxes and Assessment Reserves ____ months @ $	per month	

1100	**TITLE CHARGES:**	
1101	Closing or Escrow Fee:	$
1105	Document Preparation Fee	
1106	Notary Fees	
1107	Attorney Fees	
1108	Title Insurance:	

1200	**GOVERNMENT RECORDING & TRANSFER CHARGES:**	
1201	Recording Fees:	$
1202	City/County Tax/Stamps:	
1203	State Tax/Stamps:	

1300	**ADDITIONAL SETTLEMENT CHARGES:**	
1302	Pest Inspection	$

TOTAL ESTIMATED SETTLEMENT CHARGES

COMPENSATION TO BROKER (Not Paid Out of Loan Proceeds):

                                                             $

TOTAL ESTIMATED FUNDS NEEDED TO CLOSE:		**TOTAL ESTIMATED MONTHLY PAYMENT:**	
Purchase Price/Payoff	$	Principal & Interest	$
Loan Amount	0.00	Other Financing (P & I)	
Est. Closing Costs		Hazard Insurance	
Est. Prepaid Items/Reserv		Real Estate Taxes	
Amount Paid by Seller		Mortgage Insurance	
		Homeowner Assn. Dues	
Total Est. Funds needed to close	0.00	**Total Monthly Payment**	

☐ This Good Faith Estimate is being provided by _____, a mortgage broker, and no lender has been obtained. A lender will provide you with an additional Good Faith Estimate within three business days of the receipt of your loan application.

These estimates are provided pursuant to the Real Estate Settlement Procedures Act of 1974, as amended (RESPA). Additional information can be found in the HUD Special Information Booklet, which is to be provided to you by your mortgage broker or lender. The undersigned acknowledges receipt of the booklet "Settlement Costs," and if applicable the Consumer Handbook on ARM Mortgages.

_____   _____   _____   _____
Applicant   Date   Applicant   Date

1. **Real Estate Transfer Disclosure.** This disclosure divulges the material facts about a property that could affect its value. It lists the age, structural components, the presence or absence of easements, fences, and driveways. The disclosure statement also lists alterations or additions without building permits, zoning violations, deed restrictions, lawsuits involving the property, environmental contamination, adverse soil conditions, and flooding hazards.

2. **Pest Control Inspection Report.** While the law does not require a pest control report, virtually all lenders do.

3. **Disclosure of Geologic Hazards.** By law, disclosure of possible landslide activity, erosion, expansive soil, and proximity to a fault line is required.

4. **Disclosure of Hazardous Waste Deposits.** The owner of any property that was utilized for the disposal of hazardous waste, or within 2,000 feet of such a property, must disclose this information to a buyer.

5. **Thermal Insulation Disclosure.** Sellers of new homes must disclose the type of material used, and the thickness or R-value to prospective buyers.

6. **Special Flood Area Disclosure.** The seller must disclose to a potential buyer if the property is included in a special flood hazard area, as shown on a flood hazard map.

7. **City and County Ordinances.** Sellers must inform buyers of any special ordinances that affect the property being sold, including occupancy standards, zoning and use, building code compliance, and fire, health, and safety requirements.

8. **Condominium Documents Disclosure.** The seller must provide the buyer a copy of the governing documents of the project (CCRs), a copy of the subdivision restrictions, including any limitation on occupancy due to age, a copy of the most recent financial statement of the homeowner's association, and a written statement from the association as to the amount of any unpaid assessments.

9. **Disclosure for Real Property Loans.** This is a written statement on a form approved by the Commissioner of the California Department of

Real Estate. It details the expected maximum overall costs to be paid by a borrower for a loan. It includes all taxes, fees, commissions, points, bonuses, and charges. If the loan is an ARM, the *Consumer Handbook on Adjustable Rate Mortgages*, published by the Federal Reserve Board, must be provided to the borrower. All information required by Regulation Z, RESPA, and ECOA must be provided. Finally, the lender must comply with the Housing Financial Discrimination Act (Holden Act). This is a state act that forbids discrimination based on race, religion, color, sex, marital status, national origin or ancestry. The act also prohibits the practice of redlining.

In effect, these state disclosures and laws extend protection to purchasers and borrowers who might be outside of the federal umbrella. In many cases, they extend additional protections that are somewhat localized in nature and might not apply to other areas or be a necessary part of federal legislation.

Acceleration—The process of calling an entire loan balance immediately due and payable, usually because of default or sale of the secured property.

Accrued Depreciation—The loss in value to a property due to physical, functional, and economic detrimental conditions.

Appraisal—An opinion of value stated by a professional appraiser.

APR—The annual percentage rate. The rate of interest on a loan on an annual basis.

Alienation—The transfer of title to real estate by any means.

All-inclusive Trust Deed—A trust deed that is the equivalent of a wrap-around mortgage.

Amortize—To structure loan payments so that a series of level payments, including principal and interest, will retire the debt in full at the end of the loan term.

ARM—Adjustable rate mortgage; a loan in which the interest rate is tied to an index and periodically changed to reflect market trends as indicated by the index.

Arm's Length Transaction—A sale where neither the buyer nor the seller is acting under unusual pressure; the property is offered in the marketplace for a reasonable time, and both buyer and seller are aware of the property's merits and defects.

Assumption—The substitution of a buyer for the seller as the person primarily responsible for the continued repayment of an existing loan.

Balance—Economic principle which states that maximum value is achieved when the four agents of production (land, labor, capital, and coordination) are in balance.

Balloon Payment—The payment due at the end of the term of a partially amortized loan.

Bank Insurance Fund (BIF)—A fund under the control of the Deposit Insurance Corporation, which insures commercial bank and savings bank deposits.

Beneficiary—The person entitled to payment on a loan secured by a deed of trust.

Bearer Note—A banknote that is payable to the bearer on demand, rather than a specific individual.

Block Busting—The illegal practice of persuading people to sell their property by creating and spreading fear that people of other races and religions moving into a neighborhood will lower property values.

Bonds—Instruments of debt issued by a corporation or government agency.

Bond Type Securities—Debt instruments issued by the secondary market that are backed by mortgages.

Buy-down—When points are paid to a lender to buy down the interest rate on a loan so the borrower will be able to afford the payments.

Buyer's Market—A market in which there are more sellers than buyers. Prices tend to decrease at these times.

Cash Flow Analysis—A method of qualifying borrowers by analyzing the amount of income left over after all monthly obligations have been met.

CAP—The maximum amount of interest for an adjustable rate mortgage.

Call Provision—The right of a lender to accelerate payment of a loan if a property is sold or transferred.

Census Tracts—Demographic areas that have similar economic characteristics as determined by the Bureau of the Census.

Central Bank—A bank of last resort. In the United States, this is the Federal Reserve System.

Certified Appraiser—An appraiser that holds a state certification level license. Certified Appraisers may appraise any property without limitation.

Certificate of Eligibility—A VA document that certifies that a veteran is eligible for a VA loan.

Chattel—Personal property as opposed to real property (real estate and the bundle of rights).

Civil Rights Act of 1866—A federal law that makes it illegal to discriminate by race in the sale of real estate.

Civil Rights Act of 1968—An extension of the 1866 act that outlaws discrimination on the basis of sex, religion, or ethnicity, as well as race.

Commercial Bank—A financial institution whose main function is to facilitate commercial transactions. Commercial banks hold most of their assets in the form of demand deposits (checking accounts).

Community Reinvestment Act—A federal law that prohibits "redlining."

Community Support Statement—Federally required documentation from lenders that shows the amount of loans and to whom they are made in the local area.

Co-mortgager—A co-signer on a loan.

Compound Interest—Interest calculated as a percentage of both principal and accumulated unpaid interest.

Conforming Loans—Loans that may be readily sold into the secondary market.

Contingent Interest—A lender's share of the appreciation on a SAM loan.

Conventional Loan—Any loan that is not directly guaranteed by the federal government.

Convertible ARM—An ARM that gives the borrower the option of converting to a fixed rate loan within the first few years of the loan term.

Cost Approach—An appraisal methodology that determines value by finding the cost to build a new residence, subtracting accrued depreciation, and adding the result to the value of the land.

Cost of Funds Index—An average of the rates paid by savings institutions on deposits. The index is often used as a basis for mortgage interest rates.

Credit Report—A listing of a borrower's credit history, including amount of debt and record of repayment.

CRV—A certificate of reasonable value; an appraisal form used by the VA.

Deed—A written legal document that conveys title to a property.

Deed of Reconveyance—A document to release and convey title to a property to the borrower when the mortgage debt on it is paid in full.

Deed of Trust—An instrument that makes real property the security for a loan; unlike a mortgage, it may be foreclosed non-judicially.

Default—The failure to fulfill a legal obligation. The non-repayment of a legal debt.

Deferred Interest—Interest that is accumulated over the course of one or more payment periods, but not payable until some future time. This is a common element of adjustable rate and graduated payment plans.

Deficiency Judgment—A court judgment ordering a debtor to pay the difference between the amount of a debt and the proceeds raised by foreclosure and sale of the secured property.

Demand—The economic principle that states that the quantity desired for a good or service is dependent on the price level.

Demand Deposit—A deposit that may be withdrawn at any time, such as a checking account.

Demographics—The study of economic trends in a geographic area.

Deposit Insurance Fund—The federal fund that controls the Bank Insurance Fund (BIF) and the Savings Association Insurance Fund (SAIF), which insure customer deposits in banks and savings banks.

Deposit Receipt—A simple real estate contract that lists the price of the property and acknowledges any down payment made by the buyer.

Direct Endorsement Lender—A lender that has been approved to make loans that are insured/guaranteed directly by the federal government.

Disclosure—A written statement that details for a buyer/borrower all the information involved in the transaction. Real estate agents, lenders, and appraisers are all required to provide disclosure statements.

Discount—The charging of points on a loan for the purpose of increasing the yield of the loan.

Discount Rate—The interest rate charged by the Federal Reserve to member banks who borrow funds on a short term basis.

Disintermediation—The process by which savings institutions lose deposits to higher paying investments.

Due-on-Sale Clause—A clause in a mortgage allowing the lender to accelerate the loan if the property is sold; also called an alienation clause.

Economic Obsolescence—A loss in property value due to outside forces over which the owner has no control.

Effective Interest Rate—The actual rate of interest after all discounting, fees, and points have been paid.

Entitlement—The loan amount that the VA will provide for a veteran based on their military service.

Equal Credit Opportunity Act—A 1974 Act of Congress to further eliminate discrimination (Chapter 5).

Equitable Interest—The real property interest of the vendee in a land contract; it includes the right to possession of the property and the right to acquire title by paying the contract according to its terms.

Equitable Right of Redemption—A borrower's right to redeem a property during the foreclosure process.

Equity—The difference between the value of a property and the outstanding indebtedness secured by the property.

Escrow—The use of a disinterested third party to hold documents and funds when a property is being transferred.

Estate—An interest in a property or in the property rights.

Estoppel—A legal doctrine that requires lenders and others to abide by prior agreements.

Federal Reserve System—The government body that regulates the activities of the nation's commercial banks.

FDIC—The Federal Deposit Insurance Corporation provides insurance for depositors. This program provides stability to the banking system, as well as security for depositors.

Federal Funds Rate—The rate the Federal Reserve charges its member banks for unsecured loans.

Federal Housing Finance Board (FHHB)—A board created by FIRREA to take over the duties of the Federal Home Loan Bank board.

Federal Open Market Committee—The committee in charge of selling government securities. Open Market Operations control the nation's money supply.

Federally Related Transaction—Any transaction that involves an institution that is federally regulated.

Fee Simple Absolute—The highest form of property ownership. It includes all property rights.

FHA—A government agency that provides federal insurance for mortgage loans.

FHLMC—The Federal Home Loan Mortgage Corporation (Freddie Mac).

Fiat Money—Literally, money by decree. Money that has no backing other than a government's decree that it is money.

Fiduciary—A person in a position of financial trust.

Financial Statement—A summarized statement showing an individual's financial condition. It lists assets and liabilities and is used to determine net worth.

FIRREA—The Financial Institutions Reform, Recovery and Enforcement Act was enacted in 1989 in response to a crisis in the S&L industry. The legislation governs lending activity for all federally related transactions.

Fixed Rate Mortgage—A mortgage wherein the interest rate remains constant throughout the life of the loan.

FNMA—The Federal National Mortgage Association. A private corporation supervised by HUD. FNMA is a major secondary market entity.

Functional Obsolescence—An appraisal term to describe a property that has faulty or outmoded design features.

GEM—A growth equity mortgage is characterized by gradually increasing payments over the term of the loan. The interest rate is constant.

General Warranty Deed—A type of deed used to convey the highest form of ownership in a property. Used in the eastern states.

G.I. Bill—The federal legislation that provided for VA loan insurance.

Good Faith Estimate—A document required by RESPA. In it the lender must state all of the costs of the loan to the borrower before closing the loan.

GNMA—The Government National Mortgage Association or "Ginnie Mae" is a government agency supervised by HUD. It promotes investment by guaranteeing payment on FHA, FMHA, and VA loans.

GPM—A graduated payment mortgage is a loan in which the payments are increased periodically during the early years of the loan.

Graduated Payment Term—The number of years during which payments may be adjusted in a GPM.

Grant Deed—A bare or "naked" transfer of real property. Used in the western states.

Grantee—A person who receives a transfer of real property.

Grantor—A person who transfers real property to the grantee.

Gross Income—Income from all sources before deductions for expenditures and taxes.

Gross Rent Multiplier—A GRM is developed by dividing the monthly rental payment into the sales price of an income property. This method is often used by brokers and appraisers to help develop an estimate of an income property's value.

Homebuyer's Summary—An FHA document that must be presented to the borrower by the lender. It list all property defects found by the FHA appraiser.

Income Approach—An appraisal methodology used to value properties based on their income.

Indemnity Obligation—An obligation by a VA borrower to pay back the loan, even in the case of a default by a subsequent purchaser.

Index—A measure of the cost of money used as the basis of rate adjustments for an ARM.

Interest—The charge for renting or borrowing money. Usually expressed as a percentage of the outstanding loan amount.

Interest Rate Cap—The maximum rate of interest that may be charged on an ARM.

Interest Shortfall—The failure to collect accumulated interest due to the graduated payment or adjustable rate feature of a loan.

Intermediary—A person or institution who originates loans on behalf of another.

Investment Quality Loan—A loan that meets the guidelines of the secondary market.

Judicial Foreclosure—A court supervised foreclosure proceeding.

Jumbo Loan—A non-conforming loan. A loan that exceeds the maximum limits of the secondary market.

Law of Supply and Demand—The basic law of economics which states that prices rise when supply decreases or demand increases; and that prices fall when supply increases or demand decreases.

Legal Tender—Lawful money. U.S. banknotes are a legal tender for payment of any debt.

Lease/Option—A combination of a lease on real property and an option to purchase the real property during the term of the lease.

Leased Fee Estate—A landlord's property interest.

Leasehold Estate—A tenant's property interest.

Level Payment Loan—A loan that is repaid in equal periodic payments over its entire term.

Licensed Appraiser—An appraiser whose practice is limited to conforming loans and SFRs valued at under $1,000,000.00.

Life Estate—An estate that is held by an individual for their own lifetime and that will revert to the original owner(s) upon their death.

Line of Credit—An amount of money held by the lender against which a borrower may draw funds. The account is secured by the borrower's equity in his/her real estate.

Liquidity—A term that describes the relative ability to convert property quickly to cash. A liquid investment is easily convertible to cash.

Loan Application—A document filled out by a borrower that details the amount to be borrowed and information regarding the borrower's credit and employment history.

Loan Fee—A one-time fee charged by the lender for origination of a loan; often a percentage of the loan amount; also called a loan service fee or loan origination fee.

Loan Underwriting—The process of determining if a loan may be made that will provide minimum risk for the investor.

LTV—The loan-to-value ratio is the percentage of a property's market value that a lender is willing to loan, with the property offered as collateral.

Maker—A person who signs a promissory note.

Margin—The difference between the index rate and the interest charged on an ARM.

Market Approach—An appraisal technique that utilizes sales of comparable properties to determine value.

Market Value—The highest price a property would bring if sold in a competitive market, where all conditions for a fair sale are met. The conditions for a fair sale are: reasonable exposure to the market; arms-length transaction; knowledgeable buyer and seller; no coercion to either buy or sell; and terms in cash or the equivalent.

MIP—Mortgage insurance premium; especially the one time premium charged by FHA.

Mixed Use Property—A property that has two or more uses such as a combination of residential and commercial use.

MMI—Mutual mortgage insurance; the FHA's loan insurance program.

Money—From the Latin word moneta. Money is a medium of exchange. It is portable, in the form of currency or coins; and is accepted by the public due to its legal tender status. The U.S. Dollar is the world's most acceptable form of money.

Money Market Funds—Non-insured, private market investment funds.

Mortgage—An instrument wherein property is pledged as a security for a debt, creating a lien on the secured property. A mortgage must be foreclosed judicially.

Mortgage-Backed Securities—Instruments issued by various agencies such as GNMA FHLMC to raise investment funds.

Mortgage Banker—An individual or company that makes mortgage loans.

Mortgage Broker—An individual who acts as a go-between for lending institutions and borrowers. The mortgage broker handles the paperwork involved in transaction. The mortgage broker does not make loans.

Mortgage Company—An institution designed to originate and service real estate loans on behalf of large institutional investors.

Mortgagee—The one who receives a mortgage (the lender).

Mortgagor—The person who gives a mortgage (the borrower).

Mutual Savings Bank—A type of financial institution designed for small savers; often found in the Northeast.

Negative Amortization—An increase in an outstanding loan balance brought about by deferred interest.

Negative Amortization Cap—A limit on the amount of negative amortization allowable in an ARM or GPM.

Negotiable Instrument—An instrument, such as a promissory note, that is freely transferable.

Net Income—A person's after-tax income.

Net Worth—The worth of an individual after personal liabilities are subtracted from personal assets.

Nominal Rate—The interest rate specified in a promissory note.

Non-Judicial Foreclosure—Foreclosure of a trust deed without judicial proceedings by means of a trustee's sale.

Open Market Operations—The purchase or sale of treasury bonds by the Federal Reserve. This process helps control the money supply.

Optionee—A person who receives an option.

Optionor—A person who gives an option.

Option Money—An amount paid by the optionee to have the optionor grant an option.

Origination—The process of making a new loan.

Participation Loan—A loan made in exchange for a portion of a borrower's equity in the secured property. Also known as a shared appreciation mortgage.

Pass-Through Securities—A GNMA program wherein the principal and interest payments on mortgages purchased by investors are passed through to them as they are collected.

Payee—The party to whom a mortgage is made payable.

Payment Adjustment Period—The minimum interval between successive adjustments of payments on an ARM or GPM.

Payment Cap—A limit on the size of payments on an ARM.

Physical Obsolescence—An appraisal term that describes the ordinary aging process of a building.

PMI—Private mortgage insurance; protects against loss from default on conventional loans.

Points—A point is 1% of a loan. Points are charged by lenders in order to increase yields on below market interest rate loans.

Portfolio—The collection of mortgages held by a primary lending institution and not sold into the secondary market.

Power of Issue—The legal right to issue or create money.

Predatory Lending—The usage of unethical and often criminal lending practices.

Primary Market—Local lending institutions.

Prime Rate—The lowest rate that a bank charges its best customers.

Principal—The amount of a loan balance representing the original funds advanced.

Private Mortgage Insurance—See PMI.

Promissory Note—Written evidence of debt.

Proration—The apportionment between buyer and seller of previously paid expenses, such as the refund of the unused portion of a seller's prepaid property tax for the year.

Purchase Money Loan—A loan made by a lender or a seller of a property which is used to finance the purchase of the property.

Qualifying—The process of checking to make sure that the borrower is not likely to default, and that the property has sufficient value to satisfy the loan in the event of a default.

Quiet Title—A court action to settle any dispute to a title, such as liens or other encumbrances. The court will issue a new title to the property.

Rate Adjustment Period—The minimum interval between successive adjustments of the interest rate on an ARM.

Real Estate—The physical land and buildings of a property.

Real Estate Contract—An installment sales contract for the purchase of real estate.

Real Estate Cycle—The upward and downward movements of real estate prices created by the forces of supply and demand.

Real Property—The rights enjoyed by an owner of real estate.

Re-Amortization—The recalculation of level payments for a loan, necessitated by either a change in the loan term or an increase in the loan balance due to negative amortization.

Recast—to re-amortize.

Recording Acts—State laws requiring that information regarding property transfers become part of the public record by being recorded by public authorities.

Redemption—The process of recovering foreclosed property after a sheriff's sale.

Redlining—The illegal practice of not making loans in certain neighborhoods due to religious, racial, ethnic, or other social reasons.

Reduction-Option Mortgage—A fixed rate mortgage with an option to reduce the interest rate once during the life of the loan.

Regulation Z—The Truth in Lending Law overseen by the Federal Reserve.

REIT—A Real Estate Investment Trust is an association that invests in real estate mortgages. If the trust is properly constituted, there are tax advantages.

REMIC—A Real Estate Mortgage Investment Trust is an entity that can avoid double taxation when issuing collateralized mortgage obligations.

Reserve Requirement—The percentage of a bank's deposits that may not be loaned out.

RESPA—The Real Estate Settlement Procedures Act of 1974 seeks to prevent fraud by requiring full disclosures to consumers before loan closings.

Reversion—The return of real estate and real property rights to an owner at the end of a lease term.

Right of Rescission—The right of a borrower to refuse a loan.

RTC—The Resolution Trust Corporation was an agency formed to manage the disposition of the assets of failed S&Ls.

SAM—A shared appreciation mortgage. See participation mortgage.

Savings Banks (Formerly called S&Ls)—Savings banks hold long-term deposits and invest them in long-term loans such as real estate markets. Savings banks are primary lenders.

Secondary Financing—Money borrowed from any source to pay a portion of the required down payment or settlement costs of a loan.

Secondary Liability—Liability that arises only in the event that the person primarily liable cannot satisfy the debt.

Secondary Market—Institutions such as FNMA, FHLMC, and others who purchase mortgages from the primary market.

Securities—Instruments, such as mortgages and trust deeds, that pledge assets as security for debt.

Seller's Market—A time period of high demand for real estate and a low supply being offered for sale.

Senior Pass-Through—The principal amount of a pass-through.

Servicing—The process of collecting loan payments, keeping records, and handling defaults.

Shared Equity Loan—See participation mortgage.

Simple Interest—Interest calculated as a percentage of the principle only.

Special Warranty Deed—While similar to a Warranty Deed, defects in title are only covered as far back as the time when the grantor acquired title.

Spread—The difference between the note rate and the payment rate on a GPM.

Stable Monthly Income—A borrower's base income plus earnings from reliable secondary sources.

Steering—The illegal practice of directing clients only into neighborhoods that are similar in racial or ethnic background to the client.

Step Rate Loan—A loan using a temporary buy-down which decreases over the buy-down period. See buy-down.

Stock—An ownership interest in a corporation.

Subordinate Pass-Through—The over-collateralized portion of a pass-through.

Supply—The available amount of a good or service that is in demand.

Teaser Rate—A below market rate of interest. It often applies only under very specific conditions.

Title—A legal document that shows evidence of property ownership.

Total Debt Service Ratio—The ratio between the total of housing expense plus long term obligations and the borrower's stable monthly income.

Trigger Words—Language in advertisement that triggers the federal disclosure laws.

Trustee—A person or entity that holds property in trust for another. This is a fiduciary relationship.

Trustor—The person or entity that creates the trust.

Truth in Lending Law—See Regulation Z.

Underwriting—The process of evaluating a borrower's willingness and ability to pay, along with the collateral offered as security. The person who does this is called an underwriter.

USPAP—The Uniform Standards of Professional Appraisal Practice require appraisers to follow certain ethical and professional requirements for all appraisal assignments involving federally related loan transactions.

U.S. Treasury—An executive department of the U.S. Government that serves as the nation's fiscal manager.

Usury—Charging more interest than is legally allowed.

VA Entitlement—See Entitlement.

VA Guaranty—The dollar amount of a loan that the VA will pay in the event of a default.

Valuation Conditions Form—An FHA document that requires the appraiser to report all property deficiencies.

Vendee—The purchaser/borrower under a real estate sales contract.

Vendor—The seller/lender under a real estate contract.

Verification of Deposit—A form sent by a lender to a borrower's bank requesting verification of a borrower's funds.

VRM—A variable rate mortgage. Any loan in which the interest rate may change, whether the rate is tied to an index or not. Such loans have been replaced by ARMs and AMLs.

Wrap-Around Mortgage—A type of mortgage where part of the payments are used to retire an existing loan.

Yield—The lender's overall rate of return on a loan, taking into account interest, points, and fees.

Order Department

SOMETIMES OUR TEXTBOOKS ARE HARD TO FIND!

If your bookstore does not carry our textbooks, send us a check or money order and we'll mail them to you with our 30-day money back guarantee.

Other Great Books From Educational Textbook Company:

California Real Estate Principles, 10th ed., by Huber...................... $65.00 _____
How To Pass The Real Estate Exam (850 Exam Questions), by Huber.. $50.00 _____
California Real Estate Law, by Huber & Tyler............................... $50.00 _____
Real Estate Finance, by Huber & Messick................................... $50.00 _____
Real Estate Economics, by Huber, Messick, & Pivar....................... $50.00 _____
Real Estate Appraisal, by Huber, Messick, & Pivar........................ $50.00 _____
Mortgage Loan Brokering, by Huber & Pivar................................ $50.00 _____
Property Management, by Huber & Pivar..................................... $50.00 _____
Escrow I: An Introduction, 3rd. ed., by Huber & Newton.................. $50.00 _____
California Real Estate Practice, 4th ed., by Huber & Lyons.............. $50.00 _____
Real Estate Computer Applications, by Grogan & Huber.................. $50.00 _____
Homeowner's Association Management, by Huber & Tyler................ $50.00 _____
California Business Law, by Huber, Owens, & Tyler........................ $65.00 _____
Hubie's Power Prep CD - 100 Questions - Vol. 1, by Huber.............. $50.00 _____

Subtotal _____
Add shipping and handling @ $5.00 per book _____
Add California sales tax @ 8.25% _____
TOTAL _____

Allow 2-3 weeks for delivery

Name: _____
Address: _____
City, State, Zip: _____
Phone: _____

Check or money order:
Educational Textbook Company, P.O. Box 3597, Covina, CA 91722

For cheaper prices and faster results, order by credit card direct from Glendale Community College:
1-818-240-1000 ext. 3024
1-818-242-1561 (Direct)
Check us out at: www.etcbooks.com